PHENOMENOLOGY
AND NATURAL EXISTENCE

MARVIN FARBER

Phenomenology and Natural Existence

Essays in Honor of Marvin Farber

Edited by Dale Riepe

STATE UNIVERSITY OF NEW YORK PRESS
ALBANY, NEW YORK, 1973

First Edition

Published by State University of New York Press,
99 Washington Avenue, Albany, New York 12210

Printed in the United States of America

Library of Congress Cataloging in Publication Data

Main entry under title:
Phenomenology and natural existence.

Includes bibliographical references.

CONTENTS: The career of Marvin Farber: Reflections on the career of Marvin Farber, by R.W. Sellars. Marvin Farber and the program of naturalistic phenomenology, by D.C. Mathur, Marvin Farber as teacher, by J.E. Hansen. Marvin Farber bibliography to 1971, by L.W. Farber. [etc.]

1. Phenomenology – Addresses, essays, lectures. 2. Naturalism – Addresses, essays, lectures. 3. Farber, Marvin, 1901. 4. Husserl, Edmund, 1859-1938. I. Farber, Marvin, 1901. II. Riepe, Dale Maurice, 1918, ed.
B829.5. P445 142.7 71-171185
ISBN 0-87395-099-2

CONTENTS

ACKNOWLEDGEMENTS

I wish to thank the contributors and translators among whom Kah Kyung Cho, Shia Moser and William T. Parry should receive special commendation. Mrs. Donna Iversen was indispensable in preparing the manuscript and handling the details of correspondence. My daughters Kathrine and Dorothy helped prepare the index, without which a book is never complete. Many others assisted in various ways. Their gracious help made preparing the book a most pleasant task.

Dale Riepe
Buffalo, New York
25 August 1970

INTRODUCTION

THE students and colleagues of Marvin Farber pay him honor in this volume for a long and rich career of philosophical teaching, writing, and editing. The book is divided into three major parts : First, original essays and materials relating to Farber's career as outstanding teacher and productive scholar; second, original essays explicating difficult and fascinating problems of phenomenology and its interpretation under the influence of Farber's approach; and third, original essays on the philosophy of naturalism with references to the role played by Farber in its development and maturation.

Marvin Farber, The Man.

Marvin Farber is one of the few living American philosophers with an established international reputation. He is known throughout the world as a leading interpreter and reformer of phenomenology and a defender of critical naturalism or materialism (terms used interchangeably by him). He has served as President of the American Philosophical Association, Editor of *Philosophy and Phenomenological Research* for thirty years, Editor of the American Lecture Series and Modern Concepts of Philosophy, President of the International Phenomenological Society, Dean of the Graduate School at the University of Buffalo, Chairman of the Department of Philosophy at the University of Pennsylvania, and is now Distinguished Professor of Philosophy at the State University of New York at Buffalo. As chairman of the philosophy department and later as its distinguished senior professor, Farber has led scores of students into the career of philosophy while at the same time publishing numerous books in the sphere of phenomenology and naturalism. Among Farber's characteristic qualities are intellectual vigor, scholarly rigor, critical acumen, radiant health, forbearance of ignorance, and a telling and forceful wit. He is impatient of sloth, rigidity, conservatism, mystical flights, and academic pompousness. To the student who is searching for the truth he is kind, helpful, gentle, forgiving, and concerned.

Nowhere is Farber's handiwork more visible than in his editorship of *Philosophy and Phenomenological Research* which he founded during the second World War. As its chief editor for more than thirty years he has won a world-wide respect as a philosopher open to all fairly rational winds of doctrine. Many times he has published articles with which his agreement could scarcely be called more than minimal. This openness has often astonished his colleagues as well as other contributors. His journal is held in the highest esteem throughout the philosophical world from New York to New Delhi, and from Belgrade to Rio. While many philosophical journals have published little but idealism, materialism, or linguistic analysis, for example, he has not only regularly published articles on phenomenology, but also on naturalism, linguistic analysis, existentialism, personalism, Thomism, Zen, and Hinduism. He numbers among his admirers and correspondents, thinkers of many faiths as well as various social and political persuasions. Few philosophers have kept up with current developments in both Europe and Latin America as has Farber. In addition he has kept on top of the currents of thought in American philosophy. Yet, despite his ecumenical good will and catholicity he has had direction and focus. He is, not surprisingly, somewhat partial to those sharing his own predilections in philosophy, particularly the naturalists and critical materialists.

There was never any doubt where his sympathy lay in each social and cultural crisis in the United States and abroad. He was active in helping those attacked by fascism and repression or any other forces of intolerance and irrationalism. This keen and deeply felt awareness may be inferred from his work on phenomenology where he constantly warns us that the philosopher cannot be for long removed from the existent, from historical movements, or from the social life of his own times.

Marvin Farber on Phenomenology and Natural Existence

In each of his works on phenomenology from the 1920's onwards, he has shown constant development. His first work is a summation of his earliest study and was written while Farber was still strongly under the personal influence of Edmund Husserl. The later works reveal a growing impatience of the idealistic strains in Husserl's work, until in his latest book, *Phenomenology and Existence,* Farber reveals his own philosophy and demonstrates how it has developed to correct the excesses of Husserl. There are still important points of agreement between Farber and Husserl in this most recent work, but the differences are seldom subtle.

At first Farber is deferential about the supposed and imputed values of phenomenology, while at the same time opposed to the idealistic and fideist direction in which it was propelled by Husserl as well as a number of his disciples. Later Farber reveals the dangers of pursuing such a path while still crediting the method of phenomenology with certain unique values. Yet he looks upon these values as contingent and hypothetical, for they depend upon naturalistic interpretation and coherence with the confirmed findings of scientific inquiry in the broadest sense. Farber believes that it is dangerous to pursue the path of phenomenology when it parts company with reason and science. For all his talk and thought about presuppositions and predispositions, Husserl is not very critical of his own. Farber does not systematically show what all this baggage is, but that it is not negligible becomes obvious as he analyses Husserl's propensity to puristic illusions and other idealistic trends.

In *The Aims of Phenomenology,* a work which epitomizes much of his thinking about phenomenology and the impact of Husserl, Farber leaves his own philosophy in the background. But in *Phenomenology and Existence* he conveys his most recent view concerning Husserl's position shown within the clear context of Farberian philosophy. The first book is largely a work of exposition and to some extent discipleship, although critical discipleship, while the second is an independent work with phenomenological airs and melodies. But there is no doubt in the last work that the master theme is Farber's own philosophy largely emancipated from Husserl. Nevertheless, even in the earlier work which is based on his thinking beginning in the 1920's until he decided that the debt to his master had been sufficiently paid and he had freed himself from the idealistic constraints of the phenomenological method, Farber cannot completely hide his dissatisfaction with the formalism and highly attenuated irrationalism of the idealism and antinaturalistic subjectivism of Husserl and his antinaturalistic followers. Farber is perhaps kinder to Husserl in his last and most emancipated volume, but it is clear that he is guided ultimately only by naturalistic reason.

Certain basic commitments or principles or temper of mind in Farber must be understood if one is to comprehend his ultimate response to phenomenology. In discussing these I shall interweave with them Farber's stated reaction to phenomenology. First of all Farber is an empiricist, and although a rationalist "in the scientific sense" of that term he is allergic to formalism that tries to set itself up as an arbiter of existence, of reality, of what is out there, or of what is independently existing. This does not imply any antilogical or antimathematical stance. Rather it is an impatience with a view that places formal systems outside nature and pretends that they are full-blown philosophies with ontologies and value-theories. Although some students of Farber may complain about his insistence on the independent existence of external objects, I think he is justified in holding the rudder straight in this course. The swamps of idealism are filled with philosophers who have shipped much water in their dugouts. They might have been rescued if they had only decided whether external objects were independent of consciousness. Many of Dewey's ambiguities arise from this source. Indeed, the idealist must find it odd to be made breathless, not by water, but by his consciousness of water, as he sinks slowly into the marshes. Man, for Farber, is root and branch a part of nature. Even when man "brackets himself or his thought" he is still bound to the earth, is standing on it – this with the help of biological parents. To him, the question : "Who is my mother? " is sophistry.

Second, Farber is a realist. His attachment to the notion that the world is independent of any consciousness is powerful and elemental. His scorn for philosophers who search in their consciousness for ultimate reality when they are living in biological nature is consistent and continuous. Idealists who have left their senses to dwell in the land of "purity" are for him objects of pity as well as alarm for they might infect the younger philosophers. As Farber wryly observes: "one does not pitch horseshoes or woo his future wife in pure consciousness; there is no danger of nuclear warfare in the realm of nontemporal essences." Farber consequently engages in a never ending polemic against the unrealists, the antiempiricists, the antinaturalists, and the fideists posing as bona fide methodologists.

Third, Farber also believes that the philosophical enterprise is valuable, although at times he seems a little dismayed by its limitations among the seemingly more alert if not more industrious sciences. Perhaps he sees it as a ponderous, swaying elephant among the swiftly advancing gazelles, the running zebras, and the chattering baboons, all so busy in the bush of data and entangled correlations. Like the elephant, the philosopher may quietly go about uprooting undergrowth as well as established but dogmatic trees and calmly clearing the ground of their desiccated if microscopic leaves and twigs. As Farber says, "Husserl showed great skill in finding complexity where others see only simplicity, and in this respect he did indeed extend the vision of philosophy."[1] If some critics should complain that complexity is not intrinsically valuable, Farber replies that "there is merit in carrying through the 'radical' suspension of all beliefs,"[2] while one is engaged in the analysis of consciousness. Phenomenology may also contribute to scientific thought Farber maintains, "if it is successful" in carrying out its own "well-defined dimension of problems."[3] The doctrine of the fundamental discipline of order, or ontology, as Hans Driesch characterized Husserl's primary investigations, could be turned into a science according to Farber.[4]

Fourth, Farber is a critical naturalist or a critical materialist. To say that he is a realist is not specific enough. What kind of a realist is he? He is an evolutionist, but in addition to this, he is a historical naturalist. In short he is a realist who believes in the pervasive conditioning factors of nature-in-evolution and society-in-evolution as well. The emphasis is biological, anthropological, and sociological. Farber sees man as a potentially rational animal within society which is itself within nature. A philosophy which leaves out these salient facts will not do justice to the nature of man. Salient history provides a description of man as he has developed his societies (hence himself) within nature. It is impossible sensibly to go behind these basic qualifying conditions of human and natural existence. Farber believes that they are not simply beliefs. Rather they are the substratum of events upon which all human science and rational speculation must rest. It is in this last point that Farber stands out among the phenomenologists. Unlike many of them who are idealists, he does not believe for an instant that much of history or any of nature are dependent either upon mind or upon our subjective perspective, although he makes necessary allowances for man's subjectivity. Most philosophers who do not express this clearly have fideist, subjectivist, antirational, mystical, or puristic tendencies.

We have now set down Farber's own basic commitments. Consequently we have a good notion of his point of view which is perhaps as unambiguously stated as that of any other philosopher of our time. We now turn, therefore, to Farber's critique of phenomenology. I shall treat this critique in terms of : (1) what Farber finds praiseworthy in phenomenology; (2) what he considers to be worthy of condemnation; and (3) his final assessment of phenomenology and its possible future.

As a foremost critic of the weaknesses of phenomenology, Farber does recognize its potential for scientific analysis and philosophical analysis when revised and reinterpreted in a manner not inconsistent with naturalistic or materialistic principles. Since we have noted what these are there should be no mystery about his critique. Indeed it is a model of unequivocal scrutiny, which may make it suspect in the eye of the idealist who craves ambiguity and mystery. Some idealists would rather speculate about what is in the birthday present than open it to see what is inside. Husserl, whom Farber eloquently defends from charges of complete idealism or total irrelevance, "showed great skill in finding complexity where others see only simplicity, and in this respect he did indeed extend the vision of philosophy," Farber says. We have quoted this passage earlier and now quote it again in preparation for its significance in a different sense.

Beyond Descartes' fondest dream, Husserl carried through the radical suspension of belief. For this he deserves the highest praise according to Farber.[5] Within the domain it has chosen, "phenomenology has its own well-defined dimension of problems; and if it is successful, it should prove to be of value to all scientific thought."[6] Most of this has been quoted before, but I now expand this quotation for our new context. If a carping critic were to comment, "yes, but what has phenomenology contributed up to now?" Farber would caution him about closing inquiry before the method can be properly (naturalistically) assessed. Furthermore, Husserl's work on time-consciousness is a definite and important contribution to science according to Farber. Phenomenology may well contribute to science because it itself "is admittedly a rigorous science."[7] Husserl has also been an outstanding proponent of a method that, while bringing back the information and insights once sought by introspective psychology, undertakes to probe more deeply into the nature of experience. We cannot predict what will be discovered, although time-consciousness analysis would be one example of what is possible. Finally, Husserl has recognized the provisionalism of much philosophic thought, in opposition to the view that systems emerge from the head of some Zeus.[8] Husserl along with Brentano may be seen as a master of descriptive philosophy of experience, Farber maintains. This he says has been one of the four important developments in European philosophy since Hegel. The remaining three are neo-Hegelianism of the naturalistic bent, evolutionism, and the development of modern logic.

Up to now we have been mostly discussing Farber's favorable reactions to Husserl's phenomenology before Farber had published his *Phenomenology and Existence*.[9] Now I should like to share with the reader Farber's estimate of Husserl's phenomenology in his most recent published thinking, *Phenomenology and Existence* which had developed over the past forty years.

Farber begins by stating that "Edmund Husserl must be considered. . . as the most elaborate and the most nearly perfect expression of pure subjectivism."[10] That was not intended to state that his thought was free from inconsistencies or that he never departed from his program. He did indeed try to avoid the errors incurred by previous idealists. Thus Berkeley fell into such objectivist traps as positing an independently existing deity to underwrite what appeared in consciousness and disappeared from it as well. But if the special descriptive discipline envisaged by Husserl for the analysis of experience is overextended to yield a universal idealistic philosophy, one might be tempted to translate Farber's description of Husserl here into something like William James' alleged comment on Santayana's doctoral dissertation that it was "the perfection of rottenness." However, if the descriptive program of phenomenology is adhered to with all the indicated changes, including fundamental revisions of such concepts as "transcendental," "a priori," "eidetic," "constitutive," etc., Husserl's findings, Farber says, "may well be of permanent value."[11] I think that one can see in Farber's own work an aspect of its permanent value, This consists in the critique of subjectivism it has elicited from Farber, which has wide repercussions throughout critical philosophy. It is a constant warning, a philosophical radar system, that enables the unsophisticated to become aware of the subjectivist missiles almost noiselessly threatening natural existence. "Nevertheless," Farber states, "when closely defined and strictly controlled [away from idealistic smothering] the methodological technique will be recognized as continuing and extending already recongized procedures."[12] This is a long step towards the scientific assessment of the subjective (reflective) examination of experience. Insofar as methodology is examined, says Farber, Husserl "was the first philosopher to succeed in defining explicitly what is involved in that kind of [subjectivist] approach. His contribution to methodology was in itself one of the major elements in the philosophical scholarship of the last century."[13] That Husserl is sufficiently clear in this catacomb of psychology follows from "the possibility of presenting [his] own attempt at a scientific construction of philosophy coherently."[14]

The chief merit of pure subjectivism, Farber maintains, "like phenomenology in general. . . is to be found in its descriptive program of experience."[15] And despite his strictures against the idealism of phenomenology as developed by Husserl and his idealistic followers, Farber maintains that "something is indeed achieved by phenomenological idealism. Its great merit lies in its descriptive findings, in its value for the understanding of experience in all forms, and its full recognition of the dynamic and creative aspects of thought processes. But it cannot yield a metaphysics."[16] This discovery of merit in idealistic phenomenology reminds us perhaps of Plekhanov's praise of the German idealism that led to Marx. The reason that idealistic phenomenology cannot have a metaphysics is that without an ontology one cannot have a metaphysics. Husserl has no ontology because he refuses to go outside of pure experience to the world of nature. He falls into the ontology of nothingness. In my opinion Husserl here is close to the Hindu doctrine of *māyā.* Māyā muffles consciousness within the wrappings of perishable production. The ego is entrapped in a cocoon from which it cannot escape. *Māyā-shakti* is the Eternal Feminine and perhaps Husserl finds it through *das Ewig-Weibliche,* the preeminent enigma that appears in earlier German idealism. Yet Husserl's desire is contradictory. On the one hand he wishes to explain the mystery and on the other to keep it forever secret. Hegel tried to *unveil* the direction of man's self-consciousness. Freud tried to uncover his unconscious and dreams; and Marx revealed much of his social development. Husserl claimed to wish to uncover man's innermost consciousness but cannot do so because he has no ontology. His insatiable purity kept him from the one ingredient he needed to be successful. Farber has of course said all this in his own technical way.

In summary, Farber finds phenomenology to be one of the four important streams of post-Hegelian European philosophy. Its importance lies in its method which makes possible descriptions of experience not found elsewhere. Farber's cautionary remarks, however, suggest that these descriptions must be viewed with extreme prudence to see if they are consistent with a natural world and scientific description.

Farber's criticisms of phenomenology are of special interest in his last work because through them he reveals his own philosophy, the four bases of which we have already mentioned to be empiricism, realism, historical naturalism, and belief in the value of philosophical inquiry. Perhaps a fifth should be mentioned since it does not follow strictly from empiricism. And that is his enthusiasm for scientific method in the broad sense which permits all logically organized knowledge to be regarded as scientific, and for the critically viewed findings of science. In constructing his critique of phenomenology Farber also shows himself to be one of America's foremost psychologists of abnormal philosophy especially when he examines the motives that create such concerns as making experience, methodology, and thought "pure." His skill and solidity as a teacher are seen when he anticipates, one by one, the arguments that will be used to advance idealistic theses.

Wherever Husserl violates Farber's own basic principles, he will be found wanting. And I believe that Farber is justified in this. What kind of world would we live in where subjectivism and idealism played a more prominent role than empiricism and realism? Certainly one that reverted back to one of the less palatable stages of mankind under Hindu, Hebrew, Buddhist, Christian, or Moslem domination. Without the leavening influence of empirical and realistic considerations the results were not only the death of critical philosophy but of the philosophers themselves. Farber is socially and historically justified in this concern. His perspective is wider and longer than his teacher's.

Other criticisms Farber makes of phenomenology, particularly that of Husserl, but occasionally some of his idealistic followers, include (1) that phenomenology cannot restore the external, independent world to a position of stability after the kind of pure analysis it carries out; (2) that phenomenology gains its world of subjectivism at the price of detachment from natural existence and hence "The world as appearance carries within itself the true world,"[17] instead of the true world carrying within itself the world of appearance. This again is the problem of *māyā*. When Chuangtze the Taoist asks: Am I a man dreaming I am a butterfly or a butterfly dreaming I am a man ? he is engaged in the same ingenious, but ontologically unsound enterprise as Husserl. That the reduction in consciousness "is not temporary, but permanent, deliberate abstention from belief in the affairs of the world,"[18] demonstrates the dangers into which Husserl stepped. The special, pristine world of phenomenology implied retirement into a private problem in which a special [almost sacred] terminology was invented : an analogue to what occurred is linguistic analysis when it was decided to reduce philosophy to talk about talking; (3) and finally, that phenomenology misleads us with its questions. Such a question as "how is a world of existence possible? " is, according to Farber, at best misleading and at worst foolish. When Husserl speaks of the "nullification" or "annihilation" of the world he is speaking of the realm of pure consciousness achieved through bracketing. But the point is that one is led by such expressions actually to believe that the external world is nonexistent. Such thought and talk is misleading and particularly dangerous for softer heads attempting to replace one form of idealism for another.

In *Phenomenology and Existence* Farber pulls out most of the stops that had been silent in the earlier, more moderate expression of these views. The emphatic language of this important work shows that Farber has moved away from Husserl.

Husserl's formalistic as opposed to empirical approach is considered by Farber to be a slight gain in one sense and in another a loss to the scientific analysis of consciousness.[19] Husserl also made it difficult to separate the idealistic trends in his thought from the methodological phenomenology.[20] Farber's version of phenomenology is intended to be distinctive, and to help to make a rigorous descriptive philosophy of experience possible, by extruding dogmatic elements and opening the descriptive field to include all the conditions of experience. He has repeatedly called attention to a "strong" and a "weak" version of Husserlian phenomenology, both of which one can find selectively in Husserl's writings. The "weak" version injects idealism into the method; the "strong" version does not. Hence one cannot defend Husserl on the ground of consistency, at this point. Farber claims, in this connection, that Husserl frequently resorted to the traditional idealistic arguments under a cloud of technical apparatus that was likely to stun the unsophisticated.[21] The obfuscation of Wittgenstein was easier to understand and also easier to reject. Farber states that Americans will not gladly tolerate such obfuscation unless they are already punting in the idealistic swamps.

According to Farber, Husserl had misgivings about the irrationality of the transcendental factum. The use of the word "irrationality," is itself a sign of Husserl's uncertainty and his feeling of inadequacy in his ideal of sheer description. Instead of a frank acceptance of the transitory world as the true reality, Husserl chose the model of eternalism. Thus the existence of "facts" suggests "irrationality." The Advaita Vedantists and the Mādhyamika Buddhists developed the same kind of notion in their lust to be rid of material entanglements. They finally ended up maintaining that the cognitive organs produced intrinsic falsity. In the *Brhadaranyaka Upanisad* III. 9.6; IV. 2.24, it is finally decided that only the Self is real and that it can be known only negatively. "That Self is not this, it is not that *(neti, neti).*" Farber believes that considering the previous history of this concept in such writers as Schopenhauer and [Eduard] Von Hartmann, its results can hardly be felicitous.[22] And Husserl's emphasis upon "purity" looks like an attempt to outflank naturalism, a naturalism which cannot partake of this idealistic manna except perhaps in universal biological sterilization.

Farber takes Husserl further to task for maintaining that reality presupposes a transcendental subject. "Neither is it plausible when there is no existent reality 'there,'"[23] Whether much can be saved of this manner of thought and expression will depend upon what present and future phenomenologists can do about making rational such notions as the "unreal," "presupposition," and "reality." There is some hope if "all sense of mystery [is] expunged."[24] The Upaniṣadic notion of the buried treasure of the really real comes to mind. Let us not forget, Farber warns, that "there can also be a 'transcendental naïveté,' parallel to the 'natural naïveté.'"[25]

The problem of existence was manufactured by Husserl employing the phenomenological method idealistically. "This problem has never been solved phenomenologically," according to Farber because "no *real* problem [as opposed to a formalistic one] is to be solved solely in terms of 'pure' experience. "Whatever one may establish," he continues, "by means of purely reflective analysis belongs to a subjective-ideal order. Such knowledge may prove useful; but it is not prescriptive so far as natural events are concerned. Natural events are not to be imprisoned 'eidetically,' nor by any subjective-ideal means."[26] Many of Husserl's difficulties would never have arisen had he not preferred "the rarified atmosphere of the eidetic realm for it impeded his vision for the purposes of ordinary facts of experience, as illustrated by existing human beings and social relations."[27] The line of the American popular song "Did you ever see a dream walking? " gives some notion of the difficulty Husserl forged for himself out of eidetic foam. Although Farber has advised caution in ascribing religious motives to Husserl, in view of his strong commitment to rational science and the paucity of his references to this theme, the contribution of Roman Ingarden to this volume suggests that Husserl's idea of double teleology may have been partly responsible for his idea of double transcendence both concepts having their ground in divine being.

Concomitant is the Husserlian "life-world." According to Farber, no life-world ever existed, "for if it had . . . it would have a time, a place, and a concrete embodiment; and it could have a historical name."[28] Yet the life-world was posited as an ideal analogue of the real world. This is a major prop of idealism from the days of the theosophists in India. First, one denies the naive world. Second, he posits an ideal world. Third he is faced with the question of peopling the ideal world. All that any idealist knows just like any simple-minded materialist or naturalist is the naive world and the sophisticated world based on it. So he peoples the ideal world with creatures and events [but usually more implausible and horrible] similar to those in the naive world. All philosophies, Farber correctly points out, are historically conditioned despite the contention of Husserl himself that he was "unmotivated" in any naturalistic [hence for Farber, historical] sense. The most pure and transcendental suspension of belief can hardly lift even Husserl out of History, out of nature, and indeed out of existence, Farber believes.[29]

If phenomenology is to be a viable part of scientific methodology, according to Farber, it must be naturalized. It cannot wander forever between ideal continents in galactic purity. With proper caution it can critically examine not only the data of consciousness and attempt to strip away layer upon layer of presuppositions, but do so in a manner that makes it meaningful for rational existence. That is the outcome of Marvin Farber's critical analysis of Husserl's phenomenology and his realistic and naturalistic improvements on it.

Original Essays on Phenomenology and Natural Existence by Marvin Farber's Students and Colleagues.

The original essays on Phenomenology and Natural Existence are in the context of Farber's philosophy. This requires showing its relation to Husserlian phenomenology and natural existence. To facilitate finding which essays are most germane to the reader's immediate concern, we have arranged them in the same order in which they appear in this book. The author, title, and short abstract is then presented.

In part I, D.C. Mathur's "Marvin Farber and the Program of Naturalistic Phenomenology" shows the direction of Farber as he parts company with Husserl. Husserl is accused of ivory-towerism, verbal jugglery, subjectivity, idealism and a morbid search for certainty. Nevertheless, Farber sees in Husserl's method in mathematical and temporal analysis insightfulness and value. According to Mathur, Farber has given us a robust, well-informed, healthy-minded philosophy within which naturalistic phenomenology can find a comfortable home. Roy Wood Sellars in "Reflections on the Career of Marvin Farber," speaks out of a friendship and collaboration of fifty years. Farber's originality on the American scene and his international soundness and perspective are emphasized. James E. Hansen, in "Marvin Farber as a Teacher" states that Farber sees philosophy as a concrete activity within historical context. The emphasis is always upon criticism and self-criticism to make sure that we are not caught in a snarl of delusions and illusions. "Bibliography of the Writings of Marvin Farber," prepared by his wife Lorraine, reveals that Farber has published twelve books, five of them with coauthors and coeditors, contributed twenty-one chapters to volumes edited by others, edited one journal and two philosophical series: American Lectures in Philosophy and Modern Concepts of Philosophy, published thirty-six articles, translations and discussions, and twenty-four reviews by 1971 when it was compiled. No mention is here made of the committee and dissertation work or very little else. We graphically picture a scholar and teacher of great gifts, application, energy, and dedication. He has served as a model in teaching and scholarly activity for three generations of Buffalo students.

Part II is a discussion of various problems of phenomenology in reference to the naturalistic approach. This section is of special interest because it is the most voluminous criticism of phenomenology to appear in any language. Kah Kyung Cho in "Mediation and Immediacy" points out that Husserl has been unable to grasp the concrete meaning of experience because he has insisted on the super-transcendence over nature. Nature is thus beyond all human experience; in effect it simply does not exist or subsist.

Looking at phenomenology from an aesthetic point of view, Mikel Dufrenne tries to penetrate the depths of the origin of appearing, or "the primordial moment at which subject and object have not yet become separate."

Husserl's motives, according to Roman Ingarden, in "The Motives of Husserl's transcendental Idealism," are as follows :

(1) Husserl's desire for formal rigor and clarity which he carried over from his mathematical training, (2) his proclivity towards idealism seen first of all in his contention that real objects (thing, events) form no part of the perceptual experience, (3) his belief in a contingency and "wonderful" teleology that transcends the absolute being of consciousness and regulates it – contingency and being that may be equated to God, and (4) Husserl's profoundly negative attitude towards the real world, the human world of man, which made him appear to want to get rid of this existential burden by whatever "rigorous" means could be found. Ingarden does not mention that this outlook of Husserl's is not greatly alien to Schopenhauer's. Farber is of course certainly aware of it.

Shia Moser claims in "The Illusion of Presuppositionlessness," that not only Husserl but also Descartes has been taken in by the illusion of presuppositionlessness. Instead of this, however, we would be doing ourselves a philosophical favor by admitting the important, indeed indispensable, function of learning what the presuppositions of such areas as ethics really are. Enzo Paci in "From Naturalism to the Phenomenological Encyclopaedia" claims that Husserl's phenomenology is tremendously fecund because it impels one to go beyond Husserlian analysis. In particular we must advance from psychic to economic analysis. This appears to be congruent with Farber's assessment also even though he puts less emphasis upon the economic factor alone.

Against the gloomy view of Heideggerian existentialism that death is the most important activity of the human being, Augusto Pescador (Sarget) replies that the most important activity is living since only in living do I have possibilities where I can choose "since dying is not a possibility but a necessity," in his "Temporal Description of Human Life." Nathan Rotenstreich lists the ambiguities of Husserl's concept of *konstituieren* in "Ambiguities of Constitution in Husserl." They are (1) the referring to a whole being composed of simpler elements, (2) the referring to the reduction of a sphere to an elementary stratum, (3) establishing an order of things, (4) the creating and fixing of things, (5) the ordering of images, (6) the establishing of meanings, (7) the inquiry into the sources of primitive concepts, (8) the discovery of the relation existing between a thing and its nexus, (9) the finding of the essence of a thing. Husserl uses *konstituieren* in relation to the acts by which we grasp that which subsists in itself. To sum up : "Husserl's theory of constitution attempts to discern and articulate the primordial synthetic character of consciousness."

Part III is a series of articles focused on problems of explicating philosophical issues from the naturalistic point of view. According to John P. Anton in "The Natural Right to Aesthetic Satisfaction," technology should be considered as a means rather than as an end. At fault is the disequilibrium in our institutional values which have short-changed the democratic right to aesthetic satisfaction. Arnold Berleant in "Aesthetic Function" finds that the functions of aesthetics include disinterestedness, mechanical excellence, organicity, and sensuous usefulness. Beyond all is the humanistic function which allows man his widest range, intensity, and purity of existence. According to Tad Clements, it is highly likely that it is possible to expose presupposed elements and guiding principles of many metaphysical systems in "Metaphysics as a Metascience." Metaphysics "should seek plausible conceptual syntheses limited to what can reasonably be inferred or extrapolated from tested (logically and scientifically controlled) inquiry." In "Naturalism and the Sense and Nonsense of Free Will." C.J. Ducasse points out that we talk sense when free will means that "there are some things. . . one is free to do or to abstain from doing." If we maintain, however, that human volitions have no cause we are talking nonsense.

Rollo Handy finds that naturalistic ethics has neatly survived the nonnaturalistic onslaughts, diversions, and traps laid for it in "The Rejection of Naturalistic Ethics." Paul Kurtz finds that in naturalistic humanism value judgments are not wholly logically deducible from factual premises in "Ethical Naturalism and the Evidential-Valuational Base." They are, he thinks, connected to facts by practical decision. In "The Contributions of Charles S. Pierce to Linear Algebra," V.F. Lenzen remarks that after Boole, C.S. Peirce contributed most to the algebra of logic. Peirce was able to add to our knowledge of linear algebra and matrix theory through his work on relatives. Examples of the dual relative are ' teacher of" or "pupil of."
"Teacher" is a dual relative because it relates one individual from the body of teachers to one individual from the body of pupils. How Peirce came to this notion is described in some

detail. Franco Lombardi in "The Fear of Freedom" states that we must have the courage to be free. To have this courage requires the knowledge of what is true and the desire to do what is moral. Edward Madden and William Parry in a joint article entitled "The Ontology of Causality" emphasize the resolution of terminological difficulties involved in talking about cause. They show how some writers have created what Farber calls "methodogenic problems" by their approach to causality. Norman Melchert in "Persons, Determinism and Evidence," maintains that a naturalistic view of the determinism – free will problem can lead one to the belief that determinism is both compatible and incompatible with determinism, depending upon the contextual approach.

V.J. McGill in "Self-Evidence and Perceptual Theories" examines the views of D.M. Armstrong and R.M. Chisholm. Armstrong tries to bypass sense-perception and Chisholm ends in circularity. Perhaps, McGill says, a behaviorist theory of perception still affords the best answer : "If discrimination is the basic process in perception. . . we can say that what is reported is discrimination of stimulus values in relation to learning and prospective responses."

Raising the question as to when the moral judgment constitutes a real commitment on the part of the person making it, E.P. Papanoutsos in "The Moral Weight of Deontic Statements" lays down two conditions for such commitment. It requires first, that the person must be autonomous, and second, that he be fully aware of the consequences of his judgment.

In "A Naturalistic Interpretation of Authority, Ideology, and Violence," Chaim Perelman maintains that to "keep social and political life from being pure pitting of force against force, we must recognize the existence of a legitimate power... based on a recognized ideology." Ideologies provide the spiritual life of the modern world. Wilfrid Sellars maintains in "Reason and the Art of Living in Plato" that for Plato the Realm of Forms is a complex system of recipes. These recipes are for building an intelligible world, the intelligibility of which is practical rather than merely theoretical. The totality of recipes is for the purpose of satisfying either divine or human life. "Is Art Language? " asks Wladyslaw Tatarkiewicz. He answers that although art is not a natural or ethnic language its expressiveness recommends it as some kind of language. All such discussions, however, are a waste of time. As Michelangelo recommended in 1546, "lasciar tante dispute."

Following the last article, we find the list of contributors, translators, and bibliographers identifying each by position and publication.

DALE RIEPE

NOTES

1. *The Aims of Phenomenology* (New York : Harper Torchbooks, 1966), p. 87.
2. Ibid., p. 90
3. Ibid., p. 122.
4. Ibid., p. 134.
5. Ibid., p. 90.
6. Ibid., p. 122.
7. Ibid., p. 134.
8. Ibid., p. 150.
9. (New York : Harper Torchbooks, 1967).
10. Ibid., p. 1.
11. Ibid., p. 2.
12. Ibid., p. 31.
13. Ibid., p. 7.
14. Ibid., p. 22.
15. Ibid., p. 112.
16. Ibid.
17. *Aims.* p. 111.
18. Ibid., p. 127.
19. *Phenomenology and Existence,* p. 10.
20. Ibid., p. 11.
21. Ibid., p. 23.
22. Ibid., p. 89.
23. Ibid., p. 109.
24. Ibid.
25. Ibid., p. 111.
26. Ibid., pp. 113-114.
27. Ibid., p. 118.
28. Ibid., p. 119.
29. Ibid., p. 155.

1

THE CAREER OF MARVIN FARBER

REFLECTIONS ON THE CAREER OF MARVIN FARBER

Roy Wood Sellars, University of Michigan, Emeritus

AS I understand it, a *Festschrift* is a cooperative recognition of the standing and achievements of a colleague in his field of endeavor. Professor Farber has given steady and persistent support to international contacts in philosophy, Franco-American and German-American and Latin-American. These are still much needed, as I shall show. In so doing, Farber has also brought out his own realistic and naturalistic outlook which I take to be somewhat of an American note. He has also produced many publications developing his own personal views. These show, as we would expect, a wide horizon.

I shall begin with a remark on what has seemed to me an outstanding feature of Professor Farber's career. This I call his *constantia,* a union of balance and perseverance. He has, however, avoided *gravitas,* a virtue the Romans somewhat overdid.

It has seemed to me that *constantia* has been somewhat lacking in many contemporary thinkers who have set fashions. There are so many winds of doctrine blowing hither and thither. For instance, mathematical logic was regarded by many to be a *magic wand.* The thing to do was to show technical competence by translating any statement or argument into symbols. Then one was supposed to have something equivalent to Holy Writ. But we know now that Russell did not escape from his Humean presuppositions by this technique. But he did uncover certain unclarities by stressing the importance of words. We hear now of ordinary language as a reaction. But it has never seemed to me that either device threw much light on the question of the reach and nature of perceiving, which was to me a pet problem. And then there were the enthusiastic logical positivists, who emerged from Vienna with a magic formula about meaning to offer. I have the impression that it had the promise of undercutting German speculative philosophy which irked them as devoted to science. There was, surely, some provincialism in this move. Moore and Wittgenstein came to the front with their stress on analysis. All this enriched philosophy, no doubt, but tended to narrow emphasis.

To show that it was still effervescent and not stodgy like America, Europe finally produced *existentialism* and exported it chiefly in Sartrean, Heideggerian, and Tillichian forms.

All this kept young philosophers busy. It was well to have an older man, like Farber, in the background. There was need of his *constantia,* his unwillingness to be stampeded. He had a broad base. I think he devoted himself at first to exploring Husserl's methodology. He did this so thoroughly that some thought he was an outright Husserlian. But he reacted strongly against Husserl's lapse into idealism. Sartre seems to have thought that Husserl overemphasized the Self. But it seems clear that Farber was fundamentally naturalistic in his outlook. He has spoken out strongly against the subjectivistic and antinaturalistic trend in German philosophy. He collaborated with McGill and me in our joint work on modern materialism in the book entitled *Philosophy for the Future.* This book came out during the McCarthy period and was not too hospitably received. It was an attempt to integrate science and philosophy.

I first met Farber when, as a young man fresh from his years at Harvard and in Germany, he was beginning his teaching career. Soon after he went to the University of Buffalo, since become the State University of New York at Buffalo. Under his tutelage, it has become one of the centers for philosophy in the United States with what seems to an oldtimer like me an enormous staff. There were only five at the University of Michigan when I began teaching there in 1905.

I shall not concern myself with the details of his career for they will be handled elsewhere. I can quite understand his interest in Husserl who was, on all accounts, an intellectually vigorous man with a strong belief in his adopted procedure. I recall that my colleague, Charles Bruce Vibbert, visited Husserl in 1908 and asked him about a point in William James' *Principles of Psychology.* I think it concerned the famous last chapter. According to Vibbert's account, Husserl made the classic reply, "Ich habe meine Arbeit." And it is clear that he had. His production was astonishing. Just to keep in touch with it was no mean job. Farber did so to an amazing degree. He was also the editorial continuer of the German *Jahrbuch* which henceforth became the journal *Philosophy and Phenomenological Research.* It secured from the first international standing. Farber was judicious in his editing. All shades of opinion were welcomed so long as they came up to scholarly standards.

I come now for a moment to the question of Ideas as essences. This always seemed to me to smack of Platonism. I had come to stress the informative reach of concepts. I thought of myself as a realistic empiricist. Hence I was very interested in noting Farber's view of the status of *Noemata.* I quote from his remarkable essay in *Diogenes*: "The so-called 'eidetic reduction' of phenomenology involves the concept of essence, of essential structures and relations. This concept was never clarified satisfactorily . . . The contingency of the natural world was emphasized repeatedly, in contradistinction to the necessity attached to essences . . . In the *Ideas* Husserl gave some attention to the concept of essence. In his view, to say that a given thing could be essentially different would be to admit that it has an essence. Of course, if by essence is meant 'that without which a thing would not be what it is,' there is nothing to insure the continued reality of an essence . . . Essences would then be affairs of knowledge . . ."

Now this raises the question whether essences are not affairs of knowledge, or a kind of idealization. If not, one might have something like Leibniz's position. What Caesar is to become lies in his essence. As I see it, Farber takes the naturalistic, contingency line. He also stresses the cultural base. This is longitudinal. But he still regards phenomenology as an important discipline for technical explication. I can understand this position though I have not used it in my own thinking. Perhaps, I have used something analogous to it and linguistic analysis. One must stress the content of thought as well as what it is about.

I want next to say a few words about national differences in philosophy. These I take it to be not racial but expressions of historical involvements. In England, Cambridge talked to Oxford and Oxford replied. I was, for instance, always intrigued by the neglect of the ethical thought of Hobhouse, which seemed to me broadly based on anthropology and sociology. I was rather irked by the dominance of the dialectical moves of G. E. Moore with its nonnaturalistic view of the good. This did not seem to me to fit in with an axiological approach. John Passmore, a remarkable polymath, points out that the Germans moved into Neo-Kantianism and an interest in epistemology even as the British turned away from it in Anglo-American idealism. I have always thought that John Dewey inherited this lack of interest. He made some tirades against epistemology. Everything was to be an affair of experience.

But, in Germany, as I understand it, Neo-Kantianism got into a dead end. I am not surprised that Husserl turned away from it and sought a new lead, finding it, to some degree, in Brentano's emphasis on intention.

But, to continue this glance at national differences in philosophy, I think that there was a freshness in classic American thought when idealism, pragmatism and realism contended. There was also an openness to science and a trend to naturalism.

Now I may be wrong. But I had the feeling that Husserl's methodological emphasis expressed, to some degree, a turning away from epistemology. Was this not reflected in his bracketing? I am going to use Merleau-Ponty as an illustration. I understand that Farber has criticized him also. He was influenced in his psychology by the *Gestalt* movement. He called his outlook that of a philosophical psychology rather than an epistemology. But Merleau-Ponty was very interested in sense-perception. And here came the question of Husserl's bracketing. Did it not tend to make consciousness an affair of immanence? Merleau-Ponty spoke of a perceptual relationship to the outside world. But he seems to have been rather puzzled by it. How do we get to an external world?

Now Farber is a naturalist and I am going to question him about the kind of transcendence involved in perceiving. It has been my thesis that perceiving involves a from-and-to operation resulting in reference to things and the use of sensations as informational about them. It is in this fashion that the percipient surveys the world around him and science builds on this framework. Now I have the feeling that Husserl's technique turned him away from this problem. In examining Sartre, Heidegger and Jaspers, I seemed to find a corresponding opaqueness here. Sartre simply postulates two kinds of being and lands in a kind of phenomenalism. Heidegger wants to get an ontology but does not see any clear way to it. Jaspers seeks to squirm through the Kantian subject-object frame to some kind of transcendence. I suggest that these able men did not find a lead in Husserl. Now I know that Farber is an evolutionary materialist and merely wish to question him on this point. In what sense do we perceive external things? Here, as elsewhere, our thinking has run along parallel lines. I think an explicit statement on this point might influence German philosophers.

Since Professor Farber has – and I think rightly – criticized German thought for its tendency to subjectivism and anti-naturalism, I shall want to take up the way in which he includes human experience in nature. I quite agree with him. This is a topic which a critical materialism, such as his, must be clear about. Here, again, our thoughts seem to me to run in parallel channels. I take up, first, the topic which he calls the assimilation of subjectivism.

While granting the value of reflection under suspension, Farber raises the question of its completeness. May it not ignore too much certain features of human experience, the social, for instance? From the naturalistic point of view there exists a world antecedent to all reflection. Farber's social interests come out here. He mentions miners and other workers. And, incidentally, he suggests that the existentialists put too much stress on the abstract.

Farber displays a comprehensive knowledge of the thought of Marx and Engels. While they rejected idealism as connected with the supremacy of the spirit, they equally turned away from narrow mechanical notions. They stressed history and social problems. But, perhaps they overstressed the practical. There has been a renewed interest in a critical form of materialism. This is a challenge to thought. Science has passed from concentration on the inorganic world to biology and the social scene. As he sees it, materialism is strictly connected with the level of scientific knowledge. As I see it, Farber qualifies the materialistic theory of history to give weight to all relevant factors, much as Engels tried to do.

What Farber envisages is an integral materialism able to satisfy both scientific and logical demands. He formulates five principles essential to this approach. The first is that all existence is immanent in nature. The fifth is that all research is situated in the bosom of nature. He is very skeptical of the arguments on which idealism has been historically based.

The realistic note comes out clearly in Farber's declaration that metaphysics ought not to let itself be shut into the concept of experience nor should experience become a sort of garment imposed on existence. Experience is, therefore, a type of existence.

Needless to say that I have sympathy with this comprehensive outlook. Inevitably we approached some of the questions from different angles. I moved from critical realism to the mind-body problem and thence to an evolutionary materialism. Farber, on the other hand, wrestled with the phenomenological approach. But we seem to have reached much the same conclusions. That is to me heartening. And I welcome this opportunity to stress it.

As supernaturalism and dogmatism retreat in the cultural age of science and technology, I hope Professor Farber will join me in the furtherance of a naturalistic humanism with its stress on human values. I take religion to express man's effort to understand his situation in the world. I am ninety-two years old, near the end of my tether, but he has many years of constructive endeavor before him.

MARVIN FARBER AND THE PROGRAM OF NATURALISTIC PHENOMENOLOGY

D.C. Mathur, University of Rajasthan and State University College, Brockport

REACTING to ideas and prespectives derived early in his career from Marx and the Evolutionists, Marvin Farber belongs to that distinguished tradition in American philosophy to the shaping of which Dewey devoted a lifetime in the not too distant past. Notwithstanding his legitimate criticism of some aspects of Dewey's philosophy he, like Dewey, has seen the philosophic enterprise in the total context and perspective of social and historical factors against the backdrop of Nature.[1] Having studied with Edmund Husserl, the founder of "pure" phenomenology, in the latter's Freiburg period Farber has performed an important historical function of not only interpreting Husserl's philosophy in its developing phases and bringing it to the American shores, but also pointing out with clarity, vigor and characteristic boldness the limitations of phenomenology when viewed in the light of the comprehensive aims of general philosophy. *The Foundation of Phenomenology* first published in 1943 and now in its third edition (State University of New York Press, 1967), remains a source book, and is one of Farber's major contributions to a critical understanding of Husserl's *Logische Untersuchungen.* During his philosophical career, spanning over a period of four decades, commencing in an important sense with his *Phenomenology as a Method and as a Philosophical Discipline* (University of Buffalo Publications in Philosophy, 1928) he has maintained a continuity of outlook in viewing phenomenology as one of the important methods of philosophizing but at the same time pointing out that when adopted as an exclusive method it has led to perverse subjectivism. He has regarded phenomenology as the last stronghold of antinaturalistic philosophy of subjectivism and idealism. Instead of throwing out the baby with the bathwater and repudiating phenomenology altogether, he has been developing throughout these years the theme of a "naturalistic phenomenology" based on the concepts of "ontological monism, and logical and methodological pluralism". His *Naturalism and Subjectivism,* and the recent Harper and Row Torchbooks publications[2] have continuously pointed towards that goal. And in one of his most recent papers[3] he has used the phrase "the program of a naturalistic phenomenology," and explored and developed the outline of such an enterprise. It will be our aim to explicate and evaluate Farber's concept of "naturalistic phenomenology."

Could there be such a thing as "naturalistic phenomenology"? Orthodox followers of Husserl as well as those who have taken the various forms of "existentialism" seriously might react strongly against the very possibility of such a program, and even regard it as preposterous. Is it not the case that a thoroughgoing naturalist like Farber, in conceiving of an alliance between phenomenology and naturalism, is evincing a strong continuing influence – subterranean – of "one of the honored masters of his youth"? Scholars outside the phenomenological tendency might wonder as to the reasons why Farber has not been able to throw off the "uncanny spell" cast by Husserl on his mind and thought. Professor B.E. Bykovsky – a Russian scholar – has gone to the extent of saying that though Farber is "trying to avoid the reactionary consequences of phenomenology", yet his thought represents an attempt to "cultivate phenomenology without raising its fruits."[4] A careful reading of Farber's works will show that unlike many uncritical admirers of phenomenology he has endeavored to bring out both the importance as well as the limitations of phenomenology. He has reacted strongly against the subjectivistic program of Husserl's later "transcendental and constitutive phenomenology." He has been unsparing in his criticism of "existentialism" in its diverse forms by branding them as "irrational off-shoots" of classical Husserlian phenomenology. They have been seen as having inherited the subjectivistic thesis of the primacy of the human experience combined with a nonrationalistic concept of experience. Husserl had at least maintained throughout a thoroughgoing *rationalistic* conception of philosophy as a "rigorous science." "Philosophical anthropology" as envisaged by Max Scheler and the "existentialisms" of Heidegger and Sartre have, in Farber's view, opened the floodgates of irrationalism. Their attempt to understand the world through the so-called "primary structures" or universal human *existentialia* of care (*Sorge*), anxiety (*Angst*), being-unto-death (*Sein-zum-Tode*), estrangement (*Entfremdung*), guilt (*Schuld*) and resolve (*Entschlossenheit*) in the case of Heidegger, and those of "naughting" *(néantisation),* "radical freedom" and "nausea" in the case of Sartre, have proved abortive in their pretended presumptuousness. These dramatically selected emotional moods and traits of human experience have been isolated, mystified and absolutized for effect, and declared, *ex cathedra,* as significant ontological categories. Farber has pricked the pomposity of such self-styled profundities.[5] Nor does Farber see eye to eye with some uncritical attempts at "phenomenologizing" at certain American universities because of their failure to see the subjectivistic implications of such a procedure.

In order to assess Farber's concept and program of naturalistic phenomenology it will be advisable to begin with the aims and functions of philosophy as viewed by Husserl through the various phases of his phenomenology. What are, after all the aims of philosophy? What is philosophy about? Where do we begin? What is the "given" for philosophical reflection? It is easier to raise such questions than to answer them. There is such a bewildering disagreement among practicing philosophers today about the *meaning,* aim and function of the philosophical enterprise that it will be hazardous to give any simple dogmatic answer to these questions. Is it advisable to limit the scope of philosophizing to a "perpetual sharpening of tools" in the form of mere linguistic or conceptual analysis after the fashion of ordinary-language philosophers? Or again, should philosophy be identified with a phenomenological "clarification" of all concepts in terms of the consciousness of an individual knower? However useful these attempts may be in their limited perspective both these approaches share a common weakness of "detaching" the philosopher from his social and historical context. They are philosophies of "withdrawal" and "resignation" trying to justify their standpoint on the dubious separation of the philosopher *qua* philosopher from the philosopher *as* man. Probably they reflect the troubled and uncertain times in which we live and are a sign of the philosopher's unwillingness to "rub his shoulders and hurt his elbows" in the rough-and-tumble of difficult and often distressing social and political problems of the contemporary world. It is heartening to find that Farber, and there he is in agreement with the tradition of Dewey, is highly critical of such an "ivory-tower" concept of philosophy, and the narrow and limited role of philosophers as solving or "dissolving" philosophical puzzles which they themselves have helped to create. In other words, as Dewey would say, contemporary philosophers have developed a rigid "in-group" attitude and, as such, they address their papers of technical analysis to the alleged solving of one another's problems rather than to the substantive issues and "problems of men." No wonder the world of concrete social and historical realities passes them by. Farber warns us against such an artificially created atmosphere of aloofness and academic irresponsibility when he says:

"If philosophy is to bring wisdom to others, it must not be misled by narrow and unclarified motives, or warped by irrationalism and verbal jugglery, which at times seems indistinguishable from downright lunacy."[6] He reminds the philosophers "of the time-honored functions of philosophy : clarification of basic ideas, periodical synthesis of the chief results of the sciences, methodology, and the continued elaboration of a theory of values."[7]

Equipped with such a comprehensive and imaginative concept of the role of philosophy, Farber has reacted critically to the aims and functions of Husserl's phenomenology. Husserl was motivated by the quest for *certainty* and *absoluteness* of knowledge. His search was directed toward an absolutely *presuppositionless* beginning. He did not find such "givenness" either in the natural-inductive sciences or in the deductive mathematical sciences because, according to him, all of these disciplines *assumed* some *concepts* which were left unclarified. He was inspired by the grandiose rationalistic program of founding philosophical knowledge in an absolutely certain and indubitable *insight.* His *Ideas* and his *Cartesian Meditations* were attempts to radicalize Descartes' dream of an absolute beginning. He hit upon the concept of phenomenological "seeing" or "insight" into the essential structures of experience. Conceiving philosophy as a rigorous science, Husserl performed the now famous *epoché* – putting the whole of natural knowledge in "brackets" and making no assumptions about anything whatsoever. With his call "Back to the things themselves" he sought the ultimate foundations of all our rational knowledge in an immediate vision – the original data of our consciousness. His guiding rule was that whatever manifests itself "originarily" in its "primordial self-givenness" or "bodily presence" to our consciousness is apodictically evident, true and certain. It needs no other foundation. With the master stroke of a genius Husserl put forward the phenomenological method of suspending all judgments, shedding all bias and prejudice, putting in abeyance our habitual modes of perceiving things, and thus learning to "see" things in an original and radical way. Phenomenological reflection was thus a call for a radical change of attitude (it should not be confused with psychological introspection) – a methodic procedure to penetrate deeper and deeper into things and unravel "layers" beneath what we habitually saw or thought. To arrive at such a rock-bottom foundation of our knowledge he made use of the eidetic reduction and the various phases of the "phenomenological reduction." Eidetic reduction was meant to "reduce" the world of facts to the world of general a priori *essences,* because facts were contingent, and therefore could not be used as an absolute foundation. This reduction opened for him the entire field of noetic-noematic structures of experience for analysis, such as perceiving, remembering, imagining, judging, believing, etc., etc. With the help of memory, modifications in perception and "free-variation" in phantasy, he sought to arrive at those immutable and invariant *essences* of things which could not be changed without changing the *nature* of the things under study. These identical "pre-constituted" essences were, however, to be seized in an active grasp of intuition. Apart from the eidetic reduction there was to be the strictly phenomenological reduction by which the whole "world of being" was put within "brackets" together with our cultural-scientific world which was reduced to the *Lebenswelt* or the world of our immediate experience. Farber has rightly recognized Husserl's originality and genius in not only conceiving such a rationalistic descriptive method of phenomenological analysis in a programmatic manner, but also in the many fruitful and illuminating analyses he offered in the field of logic and mathematics – which he presented in his famous trilogy of *Logische Untersuchungen, Formale and Transzendentale Logik,* and *Erfahrung und Urteil.*[8] Such an appreciation has, however, not prevented Farber from strongly criticizing Husserl's shift to subjectivism and idealism via the latter's concept of *intentionality* of consciousness and the *transcendental reduction* which leads us from the phenomenologically reduced world of objects and the worldly "I" to the transcendental Ego or Subjectivity. In his later "constitutive phenomenology" Husserl almost forgot that his phenomenological reduction was merely a methodological procedure for radical reflection, and that his definition of consciousness in terms of its *intentionality* or directedness to a "meant" object was suited only for a descriptive analysis of the noetic-noematic structures of experience. No doubt for such descriptive purposes "real" historical objects could be "suspended" but no illicit use of such a definition of intentionality could be made for denying the ontological independence of those objects. As conceived by Husserl the "object" appears as essentially determined by the structure of consciousness, and his treatment of the 'transcendence' deals not with the reality of the historical object but with the essential meaning of the object. Consequently intentional analyses become "constitutive analyses" meant to describe and explain how the meaning of things is primordialy constituted in and through consciousness.

Recognizing the merits of some of Husserl's admirable analyses of, say, time-consciousness, the act of perception in which the perceived object is given *perspectively* with its "internal" horizon and "external" horizon, and of the origin of logical forms and concepts in experience, Farber has, however, pointed out practically in all his major works that no metaphysical use could legitimately be made of such analyses. But as a matter of fact, in his transcendental phenomenology, Husserl not only "bracketed the world" but almost "nullified" it, and conceived its program as that of "constituting" not only the *meaning* but also the *existence* of the world. The fatal idealistic slip was made and existence was declared to be dependent on the knowing mind. Even the *Lebenswelt* of immediate experience was to be "constituted" in and by transcendental subjectivity. It is evident that Husserl's alleged "radical" beginning was not so radical after all. The actual historical world of existence and the existence of other Egos became a *problem* for Husserl's "constitutive phenomenology." He failed to see that these were purely, in Farber's words, "methodogenic" problems. In his excessive preoccupation with essences and absoluteness Husserl ignored the *basic* fact that the knowing subject is not a "bloodless" transcendental spectatorial Ego but a living, historical person conditioned by nature, evolution and cultural traditions. Farber writes :

"The phenomenologist proposes to reflect with the greatest possible thoroughness, and to question his experience about the evidence for other persons, so that he feels compelled to begin as an individual. Unless he is careful to acknowledge clearly the factual and *real* priority of nature and society to the individual, he is apt to become involved in archaic nonsense, no different from the speculative excesses so prominent in the tradition of philosophy."[9]

Again,

"The process of reflection must be extended to include a view of the thinker in his historical conditions. There must not only be an *epoché* with regard to concepts and principles; the thinker must be viewed in his position in society and in cultural history. What are his interests? He may indeed, and with right, be led by his interests. So long as he does so explicitly and announces that fact, he is not guilty of the usually covert error of being influenced by his interests while claiming personal detachment and social 'neutrality'. It is necessary to reduce all normative statements, all preferences, to theoretical propositions, so that they can be tested. The philosopher who has no preferences, no interests of any kind, is a fiction."[10]

Farber, in the interests of truth does not shrink from almost a "frontal" attack on Husserl when he says that

"Husserl never freed himself from all antecedent, philosophical commitments, despite his claims of neutrality and evidence."[11]

Again,

"While radical in his way, Husserl was himself naive with respect to human society and history. He knew very little about the positive findings of social scientists and objectivistic philosophers, and he was really not very much interested in socioeconomic problems. He was interested in a nontemporal ("supertemporal") order which he extolled as being above the lowly mundane order of problems. Even his treatment of intellectual history in one of his most mature writings was detached from the realities of history."[12]

After all, can one really *begin* in philosophizing with an absolutely clean slate without any presuppositions? One can, of course, become aware of one's assumptions and avoid getting involved in ordinary fallacies and alleged "insoluble" entanglements. Husserl himself was a very sophisticated thinker – rooted in his times and reacting to what he conceived to be the dogmatic naturalism and psychologistic tendencies of the period. It is another matter that his understanding of naturalism turned out to be a bit naive. It requires a very sophisticated outlook – a trained reflective mind – to make a "presuppositionless" beginning. In strictness, for Farber as for Dewey before him, all beginnings in philosophizing are *contextual,* and as such are rooted in specific problems, whether they are epistemological, logical, scientific, moral or social. Sheer description is merely an ideal. Farber does not deny the importance and legitimate place for what he correctly calls "cross sectional" phenomenological analysis, especially in the field of formal logic and mathematics. But that does not mean that any ontological conclusions in favor of idealism and subjectivism can be drawn from such an analysis. Of course, the concept of being or existence too can be "clarified" through phenomenological analysis in terms of direct experience of an individual thinker. But as Farber points out, "if one is not to incur the use of a dogma that may be called 'determination by initial clarification', declaring the clarified being to be the only possible being, one must return to actual facts. That is to say, to our knowledge of being, of existence, of the world, and of man and his activities, as provided by our common experience, direct and culturally inherited, and by the sciences."[13]

Moreover, is not this pursuit of *certainty* in knowledge a bit too morbid? May it not masquerade a desire to "safeguard one's vested interests? " In most practical problems of empirical nature one has to be satisfied with adequate practical verification. In formal disciplines one may not violate the law of contradiction. But the attempt to found all knowledge whether formal-mathematical or natural-empirical in an indubitable intuition of essences "constituted" in pure consciousness is too ambitious and presumptuous. One does commit errors in the description of these so-called essential structures as in the case of naturalistic descriptions. All these descriptions are subject to the demands of intersubjective comparison and verification, and no one, including Husserl, can be credited with the *final* authority in such matters. If one insists on such an indubitable certainty one will be condemned to what Farber calls a "solipsism of the immediate moment" and that too at the moment of its occurence. Often, as in the analysis of the occurrence of a thing in terms of "perspectival shadings," what is declared to be on the basis of a priori "eidetic insight" can be equally arrived at on the basis of *factual* knowledge. What is gained by all this talk about "eidetic insight" except a dubious claim to self-styled "seeing" with certainty and absoluteness.[14] Commenting upon such analyses of the perceptual situation Farber says,

> "the formulation of this fact in terms of essences is merely a way of borrowing empirical facts and outfitting them as 'essential necessities,' expressing' rules,' "[15]

Farber raises the very pertinent issue of the value and usefulness of "intentional analyses" and phenomenological "clarification" of concepts, especially in the field of social and moral inquiry. Do we gain in "clarification" (if so, of what sort?) when we say with Husserl that the valuing consciousness constitutes a new kind of "axiological" objectivity giving rise to a new regional ontology? Is it not a bit too trifling to say that we become aware of value in valuing consciousness? Do not our actual social and moral problems merit a better treatment of value than is offered in "intentional analysis? " Much has been made of the "tremendously" important discovery that consciousness is essentially intentional in the sense of being directed to a *meant* object. Without totally disparaging a phenomenological description of values Farber, however points out that,

> "the major value problems of our time may be stated, understood, and possibly solved, without waiting for the phenomenological clarifications. It will be sufficient at this time to mention such problems as capital and labor, war and peace, and the individual and society. It would be a sad thing, if agreement among philosophers on "timeless" fundamentals were prerequisite to the solution of the great problems of mankind. The world might well go to ruin before even an appreciable minority got to the second underpass in the 'reduction.'"[16]

It will be apparent from what has been said above that Farber is highly critical of Husserl's transcendental phenomenology because of its idealistic and subjectivistic implications. He is prepared to give due place to conceptual clarifications at a reflective level. And here descriptive phenomenology is welcome as *one* of the methods for dealings with specific types of problems. But no metaphysical or ontological conclusions can be allowed to be drawn from such a descriptive procedure. "Clarified" concepts and meanings are always fruitful in all inquiries – both natural and phenomenological. Farber will go along with such "clarifications" provided they are recognized to have their place in the context of nature. No talk of "transcending" nature is to be brooked if philosophers are to avoid making a laughing-stock of themselves. To say that all objects are experienced and therefore their *existence* depends on our experiencing is to repeat a childish argument. Subjectivism cannot toy with the statement that one never gets beyond experience. Farber says,

> "It is unavoidably true, but trivial, that experience indicates and presupposes the presence of experience. There are no ontological consequences of that statement. On the other hand, it can be said that as a matter of fact one never gets beyond nature. But one can think "beyond" nature, in the sense that ideal entities and possibilities can be entertained or utilized. That does not mean transcending nature. Even the capacity to entertain ideal entities in thought, and the occasion for devising them, may be traced out to real social-historical conditions."[17]

Farber's pervasive naturalism is meant to restore healthy-mindedness and bring in "fresh air" to the stuffy atmosphere of the highly strung and the "tremendously serious" posture of transcendental phenomenology. It is time to have a look at what he means by "nature" and the way he conceives man's place in it. Though Farber sometimes uses "naturalism" and "materialism" interchangeably to describe his position it will be a mistake to interpret him to mean by these terms any narrow mechanistic view of nature. He places man and his experience within nature and relies on the cumulative and the progressively correctible methods and findings of the natural and social sciences. His concept of nature is a comprehensive, imaginative and open-textured picture which emerges as a generalized result of the findings of the special sciences. It may be proper to regard him as a "critical" naturalist or materialist without incurring any of the opprobrium attached to the latter designation.[18] Because of recent interest in existence and especially in human existence in the writings of those who are grouped under "philosophical anthropology" and various types of "existentialism," Farber has devoted a good deal of attention to the general problem of existence and a critical evaluation of the "pompous" philosophies of Heidegger, Sartre, Oskar Becker and Jaspers. Farber's treatment of human existence and its place in natural existence is also immensely useful in evaluating the recent proliferation of what is called "philosophical psychology" within the movement of ordinary-language philosophers. The assumption common to both "philosophical anthropology" (including "existentialism") and "philosophical psychology" is to treat mind and human existence as completely *sui generis* – to the understanding of which causal-genetic analysis is declared to be totally irrelevant. A sharp distinction is made between reasons and causes, values and facts, normative commitments and causal conditions. An impression is sought to be created according to which man is conceived to belong altogether to an independent and autonomous realm of being – which can be disclosed through either an esoteric "existential" analysis of *Dasein* or through a verbal report of reasons which a particular man gives for his behavior. No critical student of philosophy will disagree with the following evaluation of the existentialistic mode of philosophizing made by Farber after careful study :

> "The subjectivistic limitations of phenomenology brought on efforts to correct them within the fold of the idealistic and fideistic traditions. Existence had to be dealt with, or at least the word existence had to be brought to the forefront of interest. The extravagant claim has been made that the problems of existence and of being were at least lost sight of until recent existentialists called attention to them. Heidegger has been given credit for deepening the understanding of these problems, despite the unusual amount of plodding necessary to extract meanings from a frequently opaque text. The results are largely disappointing and unsatisfactory. Banal platitudes are dressed up to serve as profundities; sweeping generalizations (such as care as a fundamental feature of existence, and the role of the idea of death) are foisted upon the reader as absolute verities, with no attempt at critical justification, and linguistic turns, whether subtle or outrageous, are trumpeted as philosophical advances. The persistent fog and the awkward difficulty of the text seem to have the function of protecting, the small amount of thought and magnifying its importance."[19]

There is therefore no sense in speaking of a general problem of "human existence." There are concrete, specific and particular problems, such as social, political, personal, economic and moral – which man faces in the ongoing course of transaction with natural and cultural events. There is no evidence to believe that the human mind is "above" or "beyond" nature. There is no shortcut to the understanding of the human mind and existence through "mystical" and "profound" pronouncements or through verbal reports of "transparent reasons" given by individuals for their behavior. The whole mode of such an approach is too deceptive and simplistic. Farber rightly points out that the "understanding of the human mind depends upon physical, physiological and psychological facts; but also upon social and cultural facts. It is added to by the structural findings of 'pure' phenomenological inquiry."[20] Thus Farber is not assimilating the human mind and behavior to a single mechanistic type of explanation. Though human behavior is conditioned by physiological and physical factors, it also reveals "emergent" qualities due to the complex organization of the human brain and the social-historical nature of the cultural environment with which man is in continuing and cumulative transaction. Farber contends cogently that a sound and reliable ontology can be constituted on the basis of the principle of "ontological monism" combined with "methodological and logical pluralism." Such a position can take care of the diversity of the facts involved without giving up the basic unity of "natural and physical events." He says,

> "The nature and organization of the basic physical units account for the different types of properties and behavior in the inorganic, organic, and cultural realms. This view leaves out nothing that can be descriptively established. Even the most abstract activities of the "pure" reflective (or "transcendental-subjectivistic") investigator may be fully allowed for on this monistic basis. Man is not debased thereby. On the contrary, he feels a greater sense of dignity, earned by the understanding that progress through science in all its forms – natural and formal, empirical and abstract – may eventually enable him to solve all important problems. Therein lies the optimistic outlook of this balanced and logically weighted naturalism."[21]

"Methodological pluralism" implies that no single method is suitable for solving all kinds of problems. Methods are to be judged on the basis of their suitability and relevance for solving specific types of problems. Thus a place is found for "cross-sectional" subjectivistic method of descriptive analysis (conceptual and formal) as well as for "longitudinal" (historical and evolutionary) method depending upon the type of problem encountered. Farber scouts all attempts at "phenomenologizing" – seeking to give a "phenomenological foundation" to our natural and social sciences as misguided and overly ambitious. Such a "rationalistic ideal of a simple tree of knowledge, with all the sciences branching out from the one trunk, underlying which are a few "root ideas,"[22] is a utopian pomposity. Of course, concrete problems encountered in the natural sciences between "experienced qualitative objects" and "scientific objects" (electrons, genes, ions, etc.) can be handled through the scientific determination of evidence and competent inquiry without falling into a subjectivistic trap. Once it is recognized that inquiry itself is a complex event and "all inquiry is within nature, with multiple conditioning factors"[23] within a social and cultural tradition, no subjectivistic conclusions need follow. Moreover, one should never forget that the "causal conditions of experience are physical, organic and cultural,"[24] and as such its locus is in nature. Farber's principle of "logical pluralism" recognizes that different systems of knowledge can be validly constructed in the natural, social and formal sciences on the basis of the principle of "cooperation of methods." In the social and the human sciences a descriptive analysis of the concepts of freedom, purpose, vision and normative value-commitments can be given, which is not inconsistent with factual-empirical inquiry into the cultural and historical conditions in which these realities emerge. To assume a complete dichotomy between the empirical-factual and the normative-valuational analyses is to perpetuate obscurantism. There is no inherent logical incompatibility between the concept of "empirical anthropology" and a reasonable descriptive "philosophical anthropology." Any possibility of "radical freedom" as the defining property of human existence is ruled out as romantic moonshine.

The above account shows that Farber has successfully conceived and suggested a fruitful alliance between phenomenology and naturalism through a critique of Husserl's philosophical writings in the various stages of their development. His close acquaintance with Husserl's works and a knowledge of the methodology of the natural and social sciences have qualified him to develop, in the course of his long philosophical career, the illuminating concept and program of "naturalistic phenomenology" on the principle of "cooperation of methods." To any dogmatic critics of such a program he has to say that a

> "truly descriptive view of attitudes and of interpretations of existence is not opposed to causal analysis. It is misleading to have what purports to be a descriptive view function as something superior to causal anal-

ysis. The methods for determining causes are themselves descriptive. Hence it is simply pretentious to speak of rising above or digging beneath the methods of causal analysis and of scientific description."[25]

Such a naturalistic philosophy of robust and well-informed common sense is bound to have a "freeing" influence on the rigidity of many competing varieties of philosophical postures reared on exclusive methods. Farber's naturalistic phenomenology is not committed to put an exclusive reliance on the descriptive-phenomenological method and thus make the well-nigh impossible yet unnecessary effort to penetrate the depths of nature through the narrow and thin aperture of the "experience" of an individual knower. No loss of prestige is involved for even the most original and outstanding philosopher to make use of the descriptive method in cooperation with the well-tested methods of scientific inquiry with their standards of evidence, supplemented by a judicious and reasonable use of the "dialectic" method according to which experience and inquiry are to be understood as complex natural events occurring within and interacting with specifiable social, cultural, and organic conditions. The "dialectic" method too is not to be narrowly conceived as implying a one-sided dependence of the "superstructure" of our social, cultural, moral systems on the "substructure" of our economic systems. Farber has made a lasting contribution to sound and healthy-minded philosophy based on the explicit recognition and judicious use of the principle of the "cooperation and interaction of methods" functioning within a broad and pervasive naturalism.

NOTES

1. Cf. Marvin Farber, *Naturalism and Subjectivism,* Albany : State University of New York Press, 1968, pages 24-31, *passim.*

2. Cf. *The Aims of Phenomenology,* 1966; *Phenomenology and Existence,* 1967; *Basic Issues of Philosophy,* 1968.

3. Cf. "Toward a Naturalistic Philosophy of Experience," *Diogenes,* No. 60, Paris, 1967, pp. 103-129.

4. B. E. Bykovsky,"The Deobjectification of Philosophy," *Voprosy Filosofii,* 1956, No. 2. pp. 142-151, quoted from M. Farber, *Naturalism and Subjectivism,* p. 381.

5. Cf. *Naturalism and Subjectivism,* pp. 297-377.

6. *Naturalism and Subjectivism,* p. 386.

7. *Op. cit.,* p. 386.

8. For Farber's appreciative comments on the last part of the trilogy, cf. Marvin Farber, *The Aims of Phenomenology,* New York : Harper and Row, 1966, pp. 229-232.

9. *Naturalism and Subjectivism,* p. 37.

10. *Op. cit.,* p. 51-52.

11. *Basic Issues of Philosophy,* New York : Harper and Row, 1968, p. 212.

12. *Op. cit.,* p. 232.

13. Marvin Farber, "Toward a Naturalistic Philosophy of Experience," *Diogenes,* No. 60, Winter 1967, p. 116.

14. *Cf. Naturalism and Subjectivism,* pp. 92-93.

15. *Op. cit.,* p. 168.

16. *Op. cit.,* pp. 159-160.

17. "Toward a Naturalistic Philosophy of Experience," *Op. cit.,* p. 119.

18. For a comprehensive exposition of Farber's philosophical position see (1) *Naturalism and Subjectivism,* pp. 337-386; (ii) *Basic Issues of Philosophy,* pp. 184-235; (iii) "Toward a Naturalistic Philosophy of Experience," *Op. cit.,* pp. 126-129; (iv) *Phenomenology and Existence,* pp. 38-112.

19. *Basic Issues of Philosophy,* p. 232.

20. "Toward a Naturalistic Philosophy of Experience," *Op. cit.,* p. 122.

21. *Naturalism and Subjectivism,* pp. 384-385.

22. *Op. cit.,* p. 384.

23. "Toward a Naturalistic Philosophy of Experience," *Op. cit.,* p. 126.

24. *Naturalism and Subjectivism,* p. 385.

25. *Basic Issues of Philosophy,* p. 230.

MARVIN FARBER AS TEACHER

James E. Hansen, Brock University

WHAT FOLLOWS is a brief paper which deals with what it is like to study with Professor Farber, and how such a process of studying relates to his philosophical perspective. There will no doubt be many students of Professor Farber, both past and present, who will disagree with much of what I have to say here, but this, I think, only testifies to the range of possibilities which are opened to Professor Farber's students. If students pursue different philosophical paths it is obvious that there will be great differences in the ways in which they view the man with whom they have studied. In any case, what is said here is not only my view, but is also that of a goodly number of students with whom I have discussed this paper.

One of the very first themes presented to a student of Professor Farber concerns philosophy as a concrete activity. Philosophy ought not to be considered as some sort of bloodless abstraction, ahistorical in character and devoid of social content and impact. Rather, as is said in *Naturalism and Subjectivism* and elsewhere, philosophy ought to be considered as an intellectual activity which is rooted in given social frameworks and which is comprehensible in historical terms. There is a good deal more historicity to one's philosophical activity than is nowadays widely believed. Philosophy has had, and has today, an historical structure and an historical function. Professor Farber seeks to remind his students of this fact throughout the course of their study, and this necessarily involves his students in what today might be termed "extraphilosophical" issues, as if there were to be found problems which are exclusively "philosophical."

The theme that philosophy is historical in character becomes doubly important in the modern period, given what is occuring in the academies. The prevalence of what Professor Farber terms the "methodogenic error, the methodological reification of problems which generates a kind of philosophical bed of Procrustes, points to the very necessity of understanding philosophy in its historical character. (Indeed, the appearance and presence of the "methodogenic error" must itself be understood historically. We might fruitfully investigate this phenomenon in terms of the contemporary bifurcation of theory and practice.) This fundamental error has led to the stultification of philosophical activity to the point where philosophy is now relegated to the function of merely springing the fly from the fly-bottle. Professor Farber asks his students to inquire of the origins and historical function of the fly-bottle itself. In this respect, philosophy plays a decidedly negative or critical role, and insofar as we are led to this path, we necessarily move beyond the given historical situation in which we find ourselves to begin with. If, on the other hand, we commit the "methodogenic error" and blind ourselves to the historicity of the philosophy, we obviate the possibility of resolving those very issues to which we direct our attention.

In the "Contribution to the Critique of Hegel's Philosophy of Right" Marx points out that Hegel's critique of the given historical situation of Germany, although the "most logical, profound and complete expression" of the philosophical view of the time, is itself a function of those very conditions which it seeks to criticize. In this way, because the philosopher fails to comprehend the historical function of philosophy, the alleged critique turns out to be a most sophisticated apology, albeit an unself-conscious one; we assume philosophically what we seek to overcome concretely. Perhaps it would not be unjust to say that this is one of the lessons one learns from studying with Professor Farber : philosophy must be self-critical, viz., we must be concerned with its historical function, and not merely with its own peculiar philosophical (i.e., abstract) suppositions. As Feuerbach has said : we ought to avoid becoming like "those philosophers who pluck out their eyes that they may think better." Failure to observe this dialectical rule leads to circularity of argument or a procrustean philosophy.

Another element in this thesis which ought to be mentioned concerns what obviously follows from considering philosophy historically. Once philosophy is so considered, we immediately find ourselves with a demystified panorama of philosophers. Professor Farber continually demystifies and concretizes both the history of philosophy and the men who constitute its development. It is not the case that there is a (or *the*) history of philosophy, as Sartre has recently pointed out, and object-men who contribute to *its* development. Once philosophy is understood historically, then we immediately can understand philosophy as a concrete activity carried on by human beings in structured socioeconomic conditions. Here, Professor Farber repersonalizes philosophy and philosophers. Plato did not think it philosophically unimportant that Socrates the man willingly drank the hemlock, and Marx similarly understood philosophy and philosophers concretely, in terms of social praxis. Professor Farber has also shown that once we leap into the abstract realm of pure thought, we end with reified philosophy and abstract philosophers. It cannot be overemphasized that this concrete approach is sorely needed in our time, for perhaps none are more mystified by their own discipline than the modern academic philosophers themselves. Socrates asked : What is the question? Professor Farber asks : Why is the question? The modern academician asks : What is the answer? The differences in these approaches can be understood only as the differences between certain historical consciousnesses. Professor Farber has shown that it is a particular kind of historical consciousness – perhaps "historical unconsciousness" is a more appropriate expression – that allows itself to get entangled in its self-generated web of confusion. It is this phenomenon which Professor Farber points to and overcomes in the very way in which he teaches.

As a result of the primary thesis discussed above, it behooves the philosopher to be prepared to embrace what Professor Farber has called "methodological pluralism." This pluralism includes a plurality of logics as well. This pluralism, however, is one of *method,* and not one of content – which in any case is always the historical-natural lives of human beings. We may require a variety of methods to understand this content. Once it is recognized that philosophy is historical in character it is no longer possible to maintain that any one method in philosophy is *the* method of philosophy. Indeed, if we remain attentive to this structural historicity, we thereby avoid ontologizing that which is merely historically contingent, and avoid dogmatism. It is an open question as to whether or not there is an underlying thread of coherence to all the possible methods, e.g., a dialectical one, but in any case Professor Farber continually reminds his students that they must begin to do philosophy with their feet on the ground in order not to close questions off before they are even raised. If we restrict ourselves to one particular method, we may create difficulties which on other grounds would be absent, and ignore difficulties which on other grounds would be manifestly important.

The effect of this approach to philosophy on the students is as interesting as it is varied. There is invariably a good deal of discussion regarding the presuppositions lying behind the various views offered both by the students in discussion and the philosophers under discussion. Frequently, much time is spent in opening up arguments so as to reveal their philosophical and historical foundations, the effect being both embarrassing and illuminating – the former perhaps being a precondition of the latter. Professor Farber has a superbly trained ability to penetrate to the heart of a thesis by asking what at first glance appear to be innocent questions, but which more often than not turn out to be the fundamental questions to be answered if any progress at all is to be made. I recall that time after time Professor Farber would suggest to a student that he or she was overlooking certain questions, or was assuming unjustified positions, or was committing what he calls "the fallacy of illicit ignorance." i.e., ignoring what, for the *telos* of the thesis under consideration, ought obviously not to be ignored. This had the unusual result that we ended up thinking about what we had never considered before.

As the other side of this same philosophical coin, to complement the penetrating analysis confronting the student, Professor Farber invariably opened up numerous possibilities of investigation by introducing his vast knowledge of history and the history of philosophy. Time and again, just as we students thought we had virtually exhausted the possibilities of a position, we found ourselves propelled still further by Professor Farber's suggestions. His knowledge of social and economic history and its causal relations to philosophy often made discussions in his seminar some of the most illuminating I have engaged in. Because of the so-called "extra-philosophical" elements Professor Farber introduces into discussion, philosophy once again becomes a function of social beings in pursuit of concrete historical goals. Again, this had a twofold effect : frustration and stimulation. Here it seems appropriate to mention that because of Professor Farber's continual critical perspective, no students was ever *led* to a particular philosophical position; rather, the student was himself forced to think out these matters for himself.

It would seem that the elements mentioned above melt into a coherent philosophical perspective with which the student of Professor Farber is confronted, through which he learns, and which he hopefully will retain. This perspective does not at all take the form of a doctrine or a so-called "system." Perhaps the most terse way of expressing this approach is expressed by Professor Farber himself : "Idealization occurs in the actual process of experience and every case of idealization is an event in the order of natural existence that comes into being and passes out of existence." All such philosophical "idealizations" are rooted in, and comprehensible in terms of, the concrete natural-historical conditions in which they occur. We students learned that the acknowledgement of this is the precondition to doing meaningful philosophy. A superb example of this perspective is again provided by Professor Farber when, in writing of Scheler, he tells us that "the concept of a 'work-world,' presented in his early work on *The Transcendental and the Psychological Method,* should also be examined in the context of historical materialism." What this means is familiar to all of Professor Farber's students : if we are to avoid various kinds of mystification and reification, we must necessarily be critical of philosophical views in terms of the natural-historical conditions in which they are discovered. Thus, to repeat, philosophy is critical and historical and this lesson I consider to be the most valuable one attained while studying with Professor Farber.

There are many who have the opinion that this approach to philosophy is "one-sided" and perhaps even uniquely derived from 19th century philosophy. Nothing could be further from the truth. If we just glance at Plato's *Meno* or *Euthyphro,* for example, we see that this view finds its roots in Socrates. Perhaps it takes a Hegel to see this and to embark again, if only for a brief time in his early Jena period, on this path to a concrete understanding of the historical function of philosophy. In our time, a man of Professor Farber's bent once again reminds us of the basic truth of philosophy. The prevalence of "pure thought" and "pure subjectivism" points not to the growth of concrete philosophy, philosophy with a structured historical *telos,* but instead is a new attempt to lead us back into Plato's cave. Professor Farber's concrete approach to philosophy, and phenomenology in particular, is embodied in the way he continues to conduct seminars with students. He seeks to escape the contemporary opaque *Ideenkleid,* and those of his students who have themselves seen, will follow along the historically necessary path.

MARVIN FARBER BIBLIOGRAPHY TO 1970

Compiled by Lorraine W. Farber

Books :

Phenomenology as a Method and as a Philosophical Discipline. Buffalo : University of Buffalo Publications in Philosophy, 1928.

The Foundation of Phenomenology : Edmund Husserl and the Quest for a Rigorous Science of Philosophy. Cambridge: Harvard University Press, 1943. 2d ed., New York: Paine-Whitman, 1962. 3d ed., Albany: State University of New York Press, 1967.

Husserl. Spanish trans. by J. M. Coco Ferraris. Buenos Aires : Ediciones Losange, *Colección Filosofos y Sistemas,* 1956.

Naturalism and Subjectivism. Springfield, I11. : C. C. Thomas, 1959. 2d ed., Albany: State University of New York Press, 1968.

The Aims of Phenomenology : The Motives, Methods, and Impact of Husserl's Thought. New York : Harper & Row, 1966. Italian trans. by Stefano Poggi, *Prospettive della Fenomenologia : Bilancio del Pensiero di Husserl.* Firenze : G. C. Sansoni, 1969. Greek trans. by Leonidas Bargeliotes. Athens : Library of Philosophy, Psychology, and Education, 1970.

Phenomenology and Existence : Toward a Philosophy within Nature. New York : Harper & Row, 1967.

Basic Issues of Philosophy : Experience, Reality, and Human Values. New York : Harper & Row, 1967. Italian trans. by Silvia Federici and Paul Piccone, *I Problemi Fondamentali della Filosofia.* Milano : U. Mursia & C., 1970.

Contributions to Cooperative Volumes :

"Phenomenology." *Twentieth Century Philosophy,* ed. by D. Runes. New York: Philosophical Library, 1943. 2d ed.,

Living Schools of Philosophy (Twentieth Century Philosophy). Ames, Iowa : Littlefield, Adams & Co., 1956.
"Aspects of Phenomenology and Existentialism." *Philosophie : Chronique des Années de Guerre 1939-1945,* ed. by R. Bayer. Paris : Hermann & Cie, No. 1088, 1950.
"Aspects of Phenomenology and Existentialism from 1945-1948." *Philosophie : Chroniques des Années d'après Guerre* 1945-1948, ed. by R. Bayer. Paris : Hermann & Cie, No. 1110, 1950.
"Reflections on the Nature and Method of Philosophy." *Structure, Method and Meaning : Essays in Honor of Henry M. Sheffer,* ed. by P. Henle, H. M. Kallen, and S. K. Langer. New York : Liberal Arts Press, 1951.
"Freedom and the Concept of Equality." *Enquête sur la Liberté, Publié avec le concours de l'UNESCO.* Paris : Hermann & Cie, 1953.
"On the Meaning of Radical Reflection." *Edmund Husserl: 1859-1959,* ed. by H. L. Van Breda. The Hague : Martinus Nijhoff, 1959.
"Phenomenology." *The Concise Encyclopedia of Western Philosophy and Philosophers,* ed. by J. O. Urmson. New York : Hawthorn Books, Inc., 1960.
"Max Scheler." *Encyclopedia Americana, International Edition.* Vol. 24, 1965.
"Edmund Husserl." *Collier's Encyclopedia.* Vol. 12, 1965.
"Phenomenology." *Collier's Encyclopedia.* Vol. 18, 1965.
"Standpoint Commitments and the Function of Philosophy." *Current Philosophical Issues : Essays in Honor of Curt John Ducasse,* ed. by F. C. Dommeyer. Springfield : C. C. Thomas, 1966.
"Existence and the Life-World." *Philosophy, Religion, and the Coming World Civilization : Essays in Honor of William Ernest Hocking,* ed. by L. R. Rouner. The Hague : Martinus Nijhoff, 1966.
"Phenomenology and Problems of Subjectivism." *Contemporary Philosophy : 1956-1966,* ed. by R. Klibansky. Firenze : La Nuova Italia Editrice, 1969.
"Humanistic Ethics and the Conflict of Interests." *Moral Problems in Contemporary Society : Essays in Humanistic Ethics,* ed. by P. Kurtz. Englewood Cliffs, N.J.: Prentice Hall, Inc., 1969.

"The Aims of Education in a Changing World." *Contemporary Philosophic Thought,* Vol. III : *Perspectives in Education, Religion, and the Arts,* ed. by H. E. Kiefer. Albany : State University of New York Press, 1969.

"On 'Who We Are' as a Philosophical Question : Comments on Derrida," to appear in *Language and Human Nature : A French-American Philosophers' Dialogue,* ed. by P. Kurtz. St. Louis : Warren H. Green, Inc., 1971.

"Value and Existence," to appear in *Philomathès : Studies and Essays in the Humanities in Memory of Philip Merlan,* ed. by R. B. Palmer and R. G. Hamerton-Kelly. The Hague : Martinus Nijhoff, 1971.

"Values and the Scope of Scientific Inquiry," to appear in *Phenomenology and Social Reality : Essays in Memory of Alfred Schutz,* ed. by M. Natanson. The Hague : Martinus Nijhoff, 1970.

"Theses on the Existence of the World as a Philosophical Problem," to appear in a Roman Ingarden memorial issue of *Studia Filosoficzne,* Warsaw, 1972.

"The Goal of a Complete Philosophy of Experience," to appear in *Essays in Honor of Ludwig Landgrebe,* ed. by W. Biemel. The Hague : Martinus Nijhoff.

"The Philosophic Impact of the Facts Themselves," to appear in *Essays in Honor of Dorion Cairns,* ed. by Richard Zaner and Fred Kersten. The Hague: Martinus Nijhoff. 1973.

"Recent American Philosophy," to appear in the forthcoming edition of Ueberweg's *Geschichte der Philosophie.* Basel : Benno Schwabe & Co.

Editor and Coauthor :

Philosophical Essays in Memory of Edmund Husserl. Cambridge: Harvard University Press, 1940, 2d ed., New York: Greenwood Press, 1968.

Philosophic Thought in France and the United States : Essays Representing Major Trends in Contemporary French and American Philosophy. Buffalo : University of Buffalo Publications in Philosophy, 1950. 2d ed., revised, Albany : State University of New York Press, 1968.

L'Activité Philosophique Contemporaine en France et aux États-Unis. Paris : Presses Universitaires de France, 1950.

Coeditor (with R. W. Sellars and V. J. McGill) and Coauthor :

Philosophy for the Future : the Quest of Modern Materialism. New York : Macmillan Co., 1949.

Filosofia del Futuro. Exploración en el Campo del Materialismo Moderno. Trans. by Manuel Pumarego. Mexico : Compañia General de Ediciones, S. A., 1951.

Coeditor (with E. H. Madden and R. L. Handy) :

Philosophical Perspectives on Punishment. Springfield : C. C. Thomas, 1968.

The Idea of God : Philosophical Perspectives. Springfield : C. C. Thomas, 1969.

Founder and Editor :

Philosophy and Phenomenological Research : an International Quarterly Journal. Buffalo : State University of New York at Buffalo, since 1940.

Editor :

American Lectures in Philosophy. Springfield : C. C. Thomas, since 1951.

Modern Concepts of Philosophy. St. Louis : W. H. Green, Inc., since 1968.

Articles, Discussions, and Translations :

Trans. of "Contemporary German Philosophy" by Arthur Liebert, *Philosophical Review,* Nov., 1928.

"Theses Concerning the Foundations of Logic," *Philosophical Review,* May, 1929.

"Recent Phenomenological Literature," *Journal of Philosophy,* June 19, 1930.

"The Method of Deduction and Its Limitations," *Journal of Philosophy,* Sept. 11, 1930.

"Professor Driesch on Philosophical Methods of Procedure," *Journal of Philosophy,* Nov. 24, 1932.

"Relational Categories and the Quest for Unity," *Philosophical Review,* July, 1934.

"Husserl's *Méditations Cartésiennes,*" *Philosophical Review,* July, 1935.

"Edmund Husserl and the Background of his Philosophy,"

Philosophy and Phenomenological Research, Sept. 1940.
"The Function of Phenomenological Analysis," *Philosophy and Phenomenological Research,* June, 1941.
"Logical Systems and the Principles of Logic," *Philosophy of Science,* Jan., 1942.
"Types of Unity and the Problem of Monism," *Philosophy and Phenomenological Research,* Sept., 1943.
"The Significance of Phenomenology for the Americas," *Philosophy and Phenomenological Research,* Dec., 1943.
Comments on the Function of Philosophy in "From the Commission's Mailbag," ed. by B. Blanshard, *Philosophical Review,* May, 1945.
"Remarks about the Phenomenological Program," *Philosophy and Phenomenological Research,* Sept., 1945.
"On Unity and Diversity," *Philosophy and Phenomenological Research,* June, 1946.
"Aspects de la Philosophie Américaine de 1940 à 1946," *Les Études Philosophiques,* Dec., 1946.
"Comments Concerning Freedom from Presuppositions," *Philosophy and Phenomenological Research,* Mar., 1947.
"Aspekte der Philosophie in USA von 1940 bis 1946," *Zeitschrift für Philosophische Forschung,* Band II, Heft 2-3, 1948.
"Modes of Reflection," *Philosophy and Phenomenological Research,* June, 1948.
"Sobre la Reflexión Natural y la Reflexión Pura," *Filosofía y Letras,* Apr.-June, 1948.
"La Liberté et les Valeurs Humaines," *Les Études Philosophiques,* Apr.-June, 1948.
"Sobre la Democracia," *Las Españas,* Vol. X, Nos. 15-18, Mexico, 1950.
"Experience and Transcendence: A Chapter in Recent Phenomenology and Existentialism," *Philosophy and Phenomenological Research,* Sept., 1951.
"False Abstractionism and the Problem of Objective Ethical Knowledge," Actes du XIème Congrès International de Philosophie, Vol. X, Bruxelles, Aug., 1953.
"Max Scheler on the Place of Man in the Cosmos," *Philosophy and Phenomenological Research,* Mar., 1954.
"La Existencia, el Valor y la Filosofía de la Existencia,"

trans. by Mario H., Otero, Montevideo, 1956.
"Heidegger on the Essence of Truth," *Philosophy and Phenomenological Research,* June, 1958.
"What is Philosophy? ," *Philosophy and Phenomenological Research,* Dec., 1960.
"The Phenomenological Tendency," *Journal of Philosophy,* Aug. 2, 1962.
"First Philosophy and the Problem of the World," *Philosophy and Phenomenological Research,* Mar., 1963.
"Le Monde-de-la-Vie et la Tradition de la Philosophie Américaine," *Les Études Philosophiques,* Apr.-June, 1964.
"The Phenomenological View of Values," *Philosophy and Phenomenological Research,* June, 1964.
"The Philosophical Interest in Existence," *Proceedings of the American Philosophical Association,* Oct., 1964.
"Pervasive Subjectivism," *Philosophy and Phenomenological Research,* June, 1965.
"Toward a Naturalistic Philosophy of Experience," *Diogenes,* Winter, 1967-68.
"Pour une Philosophie Naturaliste de l'Expérience," *Diogène,* Oct.-Dec., 1967.
"The Idea of a Naturalistic Logic," *Philosophy and Phenomenological Research,* June, 1969.
"Remarks about Pluralism," *Revue de Métaphysique et de Morale,* 1970.

Book Reviews :

Symbolism : Its Meaning and Effect, by A. N. Whitehead, *The Christian Leader,* Apr. 21, 1928.
Begriff und Beziehung, by W. Burkamp, *Philosophical Review,* July, 1929.
Von Husserl zu Heidegger, by J. Kraft, *Philosophical Review,* May, 1933.
Lebensphilosophie und Phänomenologie, by G. Misch, *Philosophical Review,* Sept., 1934.
Philosophie der Symbolischen Formen, Vol. III : *Phänomenologie der Erkenntnis,* by E. Cassirer, *Philosophical Review,* Jan., 1935.
Philosophia Perennis, ed. by F. J. von Rintelen, *Philosophical Review,* May, 1935.

Scientologie, by A. Nordenholz, *Philosophical Review,* Sept., 1936.

Philosophy of Edmund Husserl, by A. D. Osborn, *Philosophical Review,* Sept., 1936.

Der Erkenntnistrieb als Lebens- und Todesprinzip, by J. Klatzkin, *Philosophical Review,* Jan., 1937.

Language, Truth, and Logic, by A. J. Ayer, *Philosophical Review,* Jan., 1938.

Symbol and Existenz der Wissenschaft, by H. Noack, *Philosophical Review,* Mar., 1938.

Le Transformisme et les Lois de la Biologie, by G. Mercier, *Philosophical Review,* May, 1938.

Das Problem der reinen Anschauung, by W. Cramer, *Philosophical Review,* Nov., 1938.

Sein und Denken, by J. König, *Philosophical Review,* Jan., 1939.

Die Einheit des Erkenntnisproblems, by K. Boldt, *Philosophical Review,* Mar., 1939.

Erfahrung und Urteil, by E. Husserl, *Journal of Philosophy,* Apr. 27, 1939.

Untersuchung über die Metaphysischen Grundlagen der Leibnizschen Zeichenkunst, by H. L. Matzat, *Philosophical Review,* July, 1940.

Die Psychische Kausalität und ihre Bedeutung für das Leibnizsche System, by K. Kanthack-Heufelder, *Philosophical Review,* May, 1941.

Amor y Mundo, by J. Xirau, *Philosophic Abstracts,* 1945-46.

Soviet Philosophy, by J. Somerville, *Philosophy and Phenomenological Research,* Dec., 1947.

Existence and Being, by M. Heidegger, *Philosophy and Phenomenological Research,* June, 1952.

Realms of Value, by R. B. Perry, *Philosophy and Phenomenological Research,* June, 1955.

Die Philosophie Westeuropas im Zwanzigsten Jahrhundert, by H. Noack, *Archiv für Geschichte der Philosophie,* Band 48, Heft 3, 1966.

Reflections on American Philosophy from Within, by Roy Wood Sellars, *Philosophy and Phenomenological Research,* Dec., 1970.

2

PHENOMENOLOGY

MEDIATION AND IMMEDIACY FOR HUSSERL

Kah Kyung Cho, Seoul National University 1957-1970
State University of New York at Buffalo 1971

HUSSERL expanded the concept of "experience" to include the "prepredicative" mode of conscious life and thereby brought the curricula of philosophical analysis down to the level of what is "immediately perceived." Both experience and immediate perception are terms that must be weighed with care to put his ambitious program in its proper setting. Experience, for one thing, is not in the least concerned with apprehension of "eternal forms" or intellectual intuition of some transcendent reality. "Evidence of individual objects constitutes the concept of experience in the widest sense. Thus experience in the primary and most significant sense is defined as direct reference to the particular."[1] Its object is what is factually given and as such contingent. Each object of experience must be there for the consciousness "bodily" and "originally," in contrast to a mere representation or an empty, simply indicative idea of it.

In line with this avowedly earthbound view of experience, the whole undertaking of phenomenology is now declared to be "a function and method of this life." Its interest lies in the "factual." In a style reminiscent of Kant's, who rendered the connotations of "transcendental idealism" and "empirical realism" interchangeable,[2] Husserl goes on to say that phenomenology is conceived in the service of the facts, as a "tool or method for the transcendental science of facts."[3] Similarly, the talk of perceptual immediacy is meant to anchor the experience squarely in what can be made evident, i.e., immediately seen or "intuited." Neither the Cartesian quest for certainty à la *deus ex machina,* nor the Kantian regression, to be sure, from the *fact* of "I think" to the "conditions" under which experience is possible – conditions that can never themselves become objects of experience – would stand a model for Husserl. For he has ostensibly cut off the eventual passage into metaphysical argumentations by raising to a philosophical principle the primacy of the factual over against the logical or whatever is mediated by thought.

So far as the defence of the status of the "given" and, along with it, the rejection of metaphysics may be said to make up the common ground for all varieties of positivism, Husserl let it be known clearly that he was siding with the same cause. Not only did he stress verbally the need to restore the positivistic standpoint of givenness which the high style of speculative tradition has done so much to discredit, but he spelled out a practical program to "found all sciences absolutely and without prejudice on the 'positive,' i.e., that which can be grasped originally," and claimed the title of "genuine positivist" for himself.[4]

What assumptive and sheerly impractical goal has been staked off by this assertion can be only guessed at the outset. But the occasion to be skeptical about the feasibility of grounding the science, strictly speaking, in facts is not very far to seek. Husserl was well acquainted with the historical precedent of Hume. To him the empiricist Hume was a pathfinder of "immanence,"a transcendental region that would have guaranteed the apodictic truth of the science of facts, and the first modern philosopher who started out with pure data of senses as the sole pregivenness of consciousness and thus gained the distinction of having attempted, though deviously and still trapped in a "prephilosophical naiveté," to fathom the origin of objective knowledge. Had Hume been more consistent, he should have been led, argues Husserl, to a "solipsism," or a new science of pure subjectivity. But of course he could not draw the "enormous consequence" to reduce the world into a "construct of consciousness." Whatever the result of this adventure within the purview of Hume's own inquiry, Husserl saw in it a "value of immeasurable significance," marking an epoch of the "teleological process of history" in the development of empiricism.[5]

A renewed attack on the problem of reconciliation between the originally given fact and the immanent sphere of consciousness had now to be launched in full awareness of the burdening consequences of Humean skepticism and, in addition to it, Kant's critical philosophy. Although phenomenology is "critically determined more directly from the side of Descartes and

British empiricism, especially Hume, than through Kant," Husserl considers it necessary to orient himself to Kant, in order to gain a clarity over the "real problem of transcendental philosophy and a method of final justification." Kant, however, was not radical enough to question the very premise on which he stood. The "meaning of being *(Seinssinn)* of the everyday world as well as the meaning of being of the world which is pretended to be scientifically true reality, – this puzzle was never solved."[6] Thus there was more than a mere rhetorical purpose in his queries when he questioned the justice of falling back upon the realm of "passive pregivenness": What good is it to refer back to the domain of *doxa* with its "vague experience" and "deceptive appearance"? Should not the predicative judgment remain the sole seat of knowledge, of genuine and authentic evidence? How can the essence of something superior be clarified by a reference to something inferior?[7]

The oddity with the notion that the apodictic truth of science can be founded on the factually and contingently given is brought home all the more clearly when we are told, as we shall presently examine, that a new "science" of contingent facts is not only possible, but it should have a higher dignity than the existing objective sciences. Those who are wary of such promissory notes may settle for a softened interpretation by saying that Husserl in actual practice must have shifted his interest from the guiding idea of philosophy as "rigorous science" to the exploration of nonscientific facts which are forced upon us by the pressure of evidence. Indeed, when it became known that Husserl's program of the science of what he termed the "life-world" seemed to overshadow the hitherto reigning principle of the transcendental ego, it was not uncommon to oppose the one to the other and see in his later phenomenology an irreconciled problem. Jean Wahl, for instance, spoke of two tendencies which stood in a state, even though fruitful of tension.[8] Earlier, it was the issue of idealism versus realism among the Neo-Kantians and the Humean empiricists that awakened the impression that the phenomenological trend was to fall into line with the "turning toward the object" *(Wendung zum Objekt).*

The real meaning of the precept "Back to the things themselves" *(Zu den Sachen selbst),* which was sometimes confused with the above catchphrase that epitomized the realistic tendency of the older phenomenological school, including also Nicolai Hartmann,[9] was an appeal to "intuitive giveness." That Husserl employed and could employ a whole set of terms varying freely their commonly accepted meaning, is due partly to a strongly honorific intent, sometimes at the cost of precise import. But undoubtedly it was due more to the peculiar nature of phenomenological procedure itself. To institute a radically empirical philosophy implied a certain amount of concession, if merely verbal, to its historically preceding forms. The terms positivism, empirical science, facts, givenness, perception, direct seeing and the like recur in his writings and a great stress was laid on the "normative" competence of the factual. But in all cases their use is to be critically differentiated from the "naive" usage of prephenomenological thinking. The general characteristic of the procedure which gives them an added nuance should be brought out at once.

"Going back to the things themselves" needs not be taken contrary to what it promises at its face value from the beginning. It is meant strictly as a procedure of an exclusive thematization of an object as object. Anything and everything that does not belong to it must be excluded. If we may call this procedure of grasping the given object purely as it is "reduction," in the simple sense that it is restored to itself by way of eliminating whatever factors accreted to it extraneously, then we may believe we have performed the necessary reduction. That, according to Husserl, is not at all the case. While we intend to validate a particular object in its particularity through sense perception, we realize the impossibility of performing a reduction that concerns the particular object solely as such. For the object under observation is not simply abstractly there, but is within a *horizon,* or it is given together with a horizon. To say the bare minimum, it has its various aspects to be revealed in perspective, its sides that must be perceived one at a time, and the "prospect" of further possibilities to be revealed "if" – and this is all-important – additional "subjective" conditions are met, such as change in location and distance, shift of angle, lapse of more time to watch and so on. "It is paradoxical and yet beyond any doubt that there is no experience in the serious and straight sense of a thing-experience which, in grasping the thing and knowing it at first, does not know already more than what is given to knowledge."[10] Thus the primary meaning of experience as an evidence of individual objects or as direct reference to the particular turns out to be "primary" indeed, – it is only *provisional.*

If it is true that Husserl saw in the positivist an ally who adheres to the principle of describing what is immediately given, it is also true that he at once parts company with him to dwell at greater length on those ideal and subjective conditions of experience in which, above everything else, the capacity of the knower is presupposed. True, the reference to the "subjectivity" is restricted in turn by the normative force of the factual. No free play of speculative reasoning is tolerated. But the perceived sense object and sense data lose their meaning outside the referential frame of this subjectivity. On this point, Husserl is more outspoken, The capacity of subject or ego to uncover, to explicate and to obtain the wealth of determinations of an object is *the* condition of experience in such a way that this object would not *be* what it is without ego. Against this apparently strategically intended assertion of Husserl that his interest lies in the factual, we may now thus qualify: The fact and factual has never been, and will never become, a problem for phenomenology when disengaged from the contributive, meaning-bestowing function of the subjectivity. We are at least warned in advance that in the horizon of phenomenological problematic, there is no single focal point. Even while Husserl pretends to direct our look straight to a given, positive object, our *mind's eye* is reflected back to the act of looking, so to speak. And to the extent that a greater nay, almost exclusive stress is laid on the role of the subject in analyzing the structure of experience, to that extent phenomenology assumes, Husserl's alleged alliance with positivism notwithstanding, the character of an idealism. Apart from its metaphysical implications which may be as grave as with any idealism that purports to give a final account of the nature of knowledge in terms of mind's constitutive function, Husserl's self-styled interest in the facts of life-world needs a further elucidation. For he spoke of his genuinely positivistic standpoint not only with a view to criticizing so-called positivism for failing to take into account the constitutive role of consciousness, but also in a gesture of acknowledgement to the empiricist tradition in which he saw definitely the historical precedent of phenomenology.

His concept of life-world contains the measure of determining the meaning, from a phenomenological point of view, of the positivistic science and empirical philosophy in general. That is to say, he finds the philosophical justification of empiricism in its orientation toward the "inductive" style of everyday life. There is in empiricism the "tendency to scientifically discover the life-world with which we are familiar in our daily life but which is unknown to the sciences themselves."[11] The apparent ignorance of science of its relation to the life-world does not mean that it exists without any positive function to fulfill for the prescientific world. On the contrary, the very meaning of science is seen as an extension of prescientific need of life, in making possible an infinitely extended "prescience" or "forecast" *(Voraussicht)* about life. "On forecast, or we may say on *induction* instead, rests all our life." All praxis, including "perception" as well as "scientific praxis", so far as it perceives or knows already *more* than what is immediately given, implies inductions.[12] Thus phenomenology may also claim the title of an "empirical science," insofar as it works out explicitly the tendency toward induction which is inherent in all the praxis of life. But it does so consciously and systematically, or more fittingly, radically reflectively. Reflection is carried to its "root," i.e., to the consciousness, from which all conceivable meaning is supposed to spring out. Nothing is to be left unvalidated within the context of natural and spontaneous life. Everything must be summoned before the bar of consciousness for the final test of its meaning, Our belief in the naturally given world must be suspended (reduction), in order for this world to be critically and significantly reconstructed (constitution).

But even so, was Husserl justified in stretching the concept of evidence beyond the competence of predicative judgment? Did he not already *presuppose* the validity of the life-world without any constitutive exhibition when he criticized the scientific objectivism? How could he legitimize his claim that "perhaps the scientificity, which this life-world as such and in its universality calls for, is a peculiar, if not exactly objective-logical one, and that as the finally founding scientificity it is in point of value not a lesser, but higher one?"[13] Is it not a circular argument to say that "a novel problem requires a new method," but that "the clarification of the meaning is already an evidence of those aims as aims, to which the evidence of possible means must essentially belong"? The mere presence of evidence in the sense of a factually given problem, without the warranty of methods to handle or solve it, is a far cry from a secure knowledge. Facing such a difficulty, Husserl after all did not hide his perplexity as to just in what way the life-world should become "an independent, thoroughly self-contained theme" of inquiry. At times the grandeur of the task to be done seems to be matched only by an equally great but irrational faith, a persistent hope to find because one seeks, to be given because one asks. And as if to seal his own fate, Husserl scornfully called an "oracular faith" the evidences that take recourse to the authority of common sense and objective sciences, including even "formal logic and mathematics"![14]

It is perhaps due more to the circumstances in which the concept of life-world has been introduced to our contemporary discussion than to its substance and even to Husserl's own attitude toward the problem that recent studies in phenomenology appear to thrive on this "one of the best confirmed discoveries"[15] of his later period. Husserl undoubtedly has done his share in dramatizing the significance of the concept. It may be said in all fairness that his enforced silence in his native country could little affect the voice of phenomenology that had already an international hearing. Names such as Roman Ingarden, Marvin Farber, Aron Gurwitsch (who gave impetus to Merleau-Ponty's work), Van Breda and others will be immediately recalled. But it was with the posthumous publication of the provocative *Crisis of European Sciences and the Transcendental Phenomenology*[16] that the life-world issue, though bred in his mind more than a generation ago,[17] was to make its full impact.

The life-world was, strictly speaking, no new discovery. Husserl envisaged it as a correlate of the so-called "natural attitude" and gave his early attention to it in carrying out the program of reduction. What interested him about the world-knowledge of this natural attitude was of course neither the bare facts with which one is familiar, nor the factual execution through which those facts are perceived. It was solely the "phenomenon" in its essential relations and structures and corresponding essential acts of consciousness that stood in the center of his life-world problematic. But its reception on the international scene – the stage is now much widened with a flood of publications and frequent conferences – shows that his philosophy has become something of a vogue, something of a catch phrase. Being a catch phrase, people took it not by literal meaning but rather by its resonance, much amplified by and attuned to the prevailing temperament of the age.

The ideal of a rigorous science has now become strangely equivocal. On the one hand, there is still the perceptible echo in the generally analytic vigor of the practicing phenomenologists to the call of philosophical scientificity which signaled a refreshing change for those who have become weary of the existentialists' verbal fare. On the other, a part of some phenomenologists' avowed claim in seeking "objective truth higher than the scientific objectivity" blends readily with an unscientific motive which is often the negative virtue for those who may take to philosophy because their innocence is spoiled for religion. A promise, therefore, to be a science with a yet greater dignity than conventional science, with a far richer catalogue of revealing experiences, culled, however, from within the sphere of pristine life as immediately lived, must attract not a few restless souls. The paradoxical fight against science in the name of science transcendentally purified gives the book *Crisis* an air of novelty which, upon closer look, turns out to be an old problem taken up again. It is, as already pointed out, the problem of reconciliation between the datum of senses and the immanent region of consciousness. The way Husserl formulated the problem by opposing the evidence of judgment against the evidence of immediate seeing or intuition is new. Similarly he opposed the predicative mode of experience against the prepredicative mode of experience; objective science against the science of life-world. The same issue recurred since the days of Descartes to mark the major epochs of modern philosophy. Descartes' attempt to prove the interaction between *res extensa* and *res cogitans* was just as futile as his ontological distinction of the two realms of being was definitive. With British empiricism, the basic Cartesian division of sensation and reflection remained unchallenged, although the Humean account of the nature of human knowledge as restricted to a series of disconnected events had in a way restored the concreteness of our sensuous experience. Kant, however, who felt that the consequences thus drawn from Hume's epistemology were a grave enough threat to undermine science, turned the scale in favor of the understanding, whose active, contributive function in providing essentially synthetic predicative experience had the corollary of defining the sensibility as a merely receptive, data-giving faculty.

Later, in spite of Feuerbach's hearty defence of the senses against the tyranny of reason in what is so well remembered as an "anthropological" reaction to the excesses of speculative idealism, the status of senses and sense perception still suffered from the lack of a thoroughgoing, cohesive account which would put it back into its place in the element of lived experience. From the Husserlian perspective, the subsequent positivism of Mach and Avenarius did little to amend the situation. For the positivistic notion of the sense datum as the immediately given in experience rests on the untenable assumption that there exists between this datum *as lived* by a subject and the objectively measurable physical stimulus an exact correlation. Presupposed thereby was also the objective condition of human body standing among other physically definable and determinable bodies and susceptible of exact observation and description.

According to Ludwig Landgrebe, it is the "historical significance of Husserl's phenomenology" to have resumed "the necessary process of the confrontation of thinking reason with itself by way of its relation to what is immediate in experience."[18] The move to return to prepredicative evidence or to the evidence of "intuition" (i.e., not merely the sensuous intuition) meant the first of such decisive steps. Concerning the extent to which Husserl himself was aware of his own historical role, we are not left to fumble in the dark. The *Crisis* is an eloquent documentation of it. The crisis, it should be noted, is that of science, or that posed by science. To descend, as it were, to the primary and immediate in experience signifies to pass by the world of science. Husserl's methodical radicalism makes our "disengagement" from the world of science a prerequisite for "discovering" the life-world intact, unbiased by science and purely as it exists before any scientific interpretations. It is not that he denies the constant factual interwovenness of the life-world with some amount of scientific interpretations. These are there, but already in a *modified* form, as the changes brought about by science can be now immediately perceived in the products and processes that have become self-evident or intuitive aspect of the life-world. The "return" to this life-world, left in abeyance while transcendental reduction was performed, was thus triggered by the unmistakable motive to produce the evidence of senses against the evidence of logic and objective, scientific thinking. But the retrieval of this vast "universe of anonymous evidences", determining the *eidos* of the life-world itself and the breadth of its variation, is not conceived in the spirit of defending the irrational, even mystical element at the source of our life. With the thematization of life-world occurs no basic deviation from the original intent, but it is steered according to its main course. For the technique of essential description as implied in Husserl's original program of phenomenology must necessarily extend itself to everything that *is*, really or ideally, and life-word could not possibly be an exception.

Already his "thoroughgoing rationalism and faith in the boundlessness of objective reason" and his contention "that everything that is, is knowable *in itself*" were noted before the publication of the *Crisis.*[19] But he now unrolls in it a far-flung historical *coulisse* and restates his confidence in the reason of history in passages whose *hauteurs* at once revive the image of Hegel. Through its movement in history, in the medium of philosophy and science, the *telos* of rational humanity is to come to a final self-revelation. Phenomenology knows itself to be at the crossroads, because the current "crisis in the European way of life" can be either precipitated or overcome by its attempt to institute "rationalism" once again. Philosophy as "science" in this case is not a particular species of science within the genus science. On the contrary, the very crisis of European sciences was brought about as the result of this confusion, namely that the true spirit of philosophy or rationalism is eclipsed by their one-sided engrossment in "naturalism" and "objectivism." Hence the present "estrangement of the sense of rationality of life." The alternative to the final downfall of Europe is the "regeneration of Europe out of the spirit of philosophy through a heroism of reason which is to overcome the naturalism once for all."[20] Thus for Husserl philosophy must assume a restraining responsibility over the objective sciences which indeed "secure the objectivity" but fail to "understand the objectivity." "No science, however exact and objective, seriously explains or can explain anything." "The only real explanation is to make transcendentally understandable,"[21] i.e., by taking into account the constitutive role of subjectivity.

Despite this strongly antiscientific emanation, it should be noted that Husserl was evoking the power of "reason" and "sense of rationality" to curb the one-sided sway of objective sciences. In contradistinction to "naive" or "naturalistic" objectivity and scientificity, the transcendental phenomenology reserves for itself an allegedly higher objectivity and scientificity. It is called at the same time "radically empirical", "truly positivistic" and "thoroughly rationalistic." Such a verbal fastidiousness may convey only an impression of barrenness to those who already hold little of the reflective procedure peculiar to phenomenology. But by its detachment it gives us an enriched theory of knowledge – a pure descriptive psychology. Anyone who tries to comprehend the meaning of the special and specialized enterprise called science in its relation to the phenomenon of life in general would do so best by assuming an attitude that is committed, at least directly, to the interest of neither side. If a spatial metaphor is allowed, he would have to place himself outside of the two worlds, one that of objective science, and the other of the prescientific experience. The sphere of transcendental subjectivity is thought of as such an artificial position contrary to the natural attitude. The real question, however, is whether Husserl was sufficiently aware of the paradox that the transcendental subjectivity was itself a dependent term of what he called life-world and that the latter still had to be constituted first in the former. Has he not assumed the validity of life-world even before its origin and construction were accounted for in the constitutive realm of consciousness? In having accepted the *primacy* of life-world evidence, the primacy to wit of subjective-relative intuition over against the evidence of objective science prior to the constitutive validation of the experience of life-world, Husserl seems stranded in a sheerly inextricable predicament. As if to forestall this difficulty, he raises the expected question : How can a partial being of the world, the human subjectivity as a part of this world, constitute the whole world as its "intentional construct"? "The subject as partial being of the world devours so to speak the entire world and, together with it, himself. What a paradox." But the course of its solution is as quickly suggested as the doubt is raised. For the paradox is now declared to be more apparent than real, arising as it does from the "persistent tension between the power of self-evidence of the natural objective attitude (the power of common sense) and the attitude of 'disinterested observer' as opposed to the former."[22] The tension will be resolved when, and only when, the self-evidence of the givenness of the world is persuaded of its own questionability – existence of the world is "the greatest of all the riddles" – and transformed into a phenomenologically validated "understandability."

Self-evident givenness as a philosophical problem, perhaps as the virtual key issue of phenomenology which in effect has prepared the concepts of intentionality, of the constitution of the stream of consciousness and of the horizon, has in the Husserlian scheme of investigations two planes on which it can be separately articulated. The one is the givenness of the world as objective science sees it. For the objective science, the existence of the world in its unquestionable self-evidence is the "primary fact." The reaction of phenomenology to this objectivism is that it has left its ground unexamined, taking what is inseparable (subject-object correlation) as separated, with the immediacy of experience consigned to the realm of fiction and poetry. The other level is that of prescientific experience which has not yet objectified itself and hence ranks lower in terms of the unconditionally generalized possibility of understanding. But the givenness in this life-world layer of experience has, according to Husserl, the advantage of structurally predelineating the subject-object correlation as the authentic pattern of our world-knowledge. Viewed through this prism of correlation, the world is shown to be "for us," to be "our world in its essence and existence, deriving its meaning altogether from our intentional life."[23] It is not true that the scientific objectivism can wholly dispense with such correlative schema. Its very drawback is seen in its naive and unquestioned assumption to do without it, or in its blindness to the "wonder of all wonders," the achievement of transcendental subjectivity as the concealed source of all our objective knowledge.

Husserl's strenuous effort to rewrite the geneology of our conscious experience is considered by many an exemplary exhibition of descriptive rigor. "His skill in finding great complexity where others see only simplicity" has done its service to "extend the vision of philosophy."[24] For that matter, his painstaking inquiry into the area of prepredicative experience appears to signify an important addition to the scope, if not the rigor already noted, of such philosophical vision. The first section of his *Experience and Judgment* deals minutely and extensively with the modes of prepredicative or receptive experience. Since meaningful statements in science must either affirm or deny something apprehended, predicative judgment has become the formal distinction of scientific thinking as such, whereas the prepredicative experience, lacking as it does such formal-logical structures, tends to be branded ipso facto prescientific or unscientific, however lively and convincing it may be in its personally lived immediacy. But what is the true status of givenness in this vivid and yet vague, personal and yet anonymous, subjective-relative life prior to science if it is to have a greater dignity than established sciences? That it cannot be of the same quality as the sense datum of which positivism speaks needs not be reemphasized. Nor is it anything like the disorderly, complex material of intuition, to which, according to Kant, our sensibility is passively related through affection. The given in the lowest and most immediate encounter of intentional subject with the passively preexisting world is now revealed as a microcosm in its own right, for the sensuously given data are "already product of a constitutive synthesis, which, as the lowest products, presuppose the achievement of synthesis in the internal time-consciousness."[25] By implication, there is no such thing as a simple apprehension that cannot be shown to contain an infinity of determinations in terms of "being bodily there relatively more clearly or opaquely" for the consciousness. Hence, every perception, however pure and simple, is a composite, a synthesis, already predicated by the "objectifying acts of ego" even before the judgment in the sense of conventional logic is passed upon it.

Thus Husserl takes the liberty, though not surprisingly, of extending the meaning of judgment. The return to the prepredicative experience does not free him from applying to it the basic structure of predication. The analysis of the perceptual consciousness runs parallel to that of the spontaneous act of predicating judgment (thinking), although the receptive experience as a mere preliminary stage to the active "will to knowledge" must be duly noted for its restricted character, e.g., it has not yet become our "property" which is at our disposal and which we may impart to others.[26] Beside this characteristically pervasive idealism that seems to leave nothing, even the passively pregiven, outside the reaches of the all-powerful constitutive ability of consciousness, Husserl's theory of perception shows how firmly he is convinced that *seeing,* more than any other act, predominates in all the founding hierarchy of our intentional relationship. Herein he sharply differed from Heidegger, who also carried the concept of understanding *(Verstehen)* beyond the limits of its conventional meaning as "intellect" in order to embrace the subjective, prescientific modes of experience.

On a broader basis, both Husserl and Heidegger left the epistemological subject-object schema behind and replaced it by the act-character of the intentionality of consciousness or the existential category of "being-in-the-world." But, while Heidegger places the "presence ready-to-hand" in man's every-day dealings with utensils in the foreground to account for the primary mode in which the world is encountered,[27] Husserl considers the "simply subjective-relative" seeing as the "really first"[28] and comes in *Experience and Judgment* to comment on the issue. He distinguishes between simple, straightforward experiences and those that are "founded" on the former. Straight experience is sensuous, having as its existent substratum material body. The unity of all material bodies, insofar as the sensuous experience can be universalized to apply to all bodies, is called "nature." "Thus in the world of our experience, nature is the lowest stratum on which all other strata are founded." Our evaluations and actions, including the "interest" in the usefulness of the objects for certain purposes, all presuppose the existence of nature with its straightly experienced sensuous properties as the invariable foundation. Opposed to this straight perception is the perception of that which can be perceived solely through "understanding the expression," such as the "understanding of an equipment or tool in its referential 'remembrance' of men who made it for a certain purpose or for whom it is designed." Such a reference may seem ever so self-evident, the association of the one with the other ever so natural and inextricable, but all the same, this mode of perception is derivative and obtained as an "augmentation" *(aufgestuft)* and "in diversion from the straightforward direction."[29]

Heidegger, on the other hand, holds the reverse to be true. Not the sensuous properties of a corporeal being in a pure perception are what is primarily discovered. Rather, it is the "assignment or reference of something to something." or the *pragmatic* structure of being-ready-to-hand in which our immediate encounter with worldly things is revealed. "These things (i.e., inkstand, ink, paper, blotting pad, table, lamp, furniture, windows, doors, room, etc.) never show themselves proximally as they are for themselves." They all refer to their uses and users. Before any "individual item" of equipment shows itself, a totality of equipment has already been discovered. "No matter how sharply we just *look* at the 'outward appearance' of things in whatever form this takes, we cannot discover anything ready-to hand". Thus, throwing upside down the founding order of intentional relationship as Husserl sees it, Heidegger claims that nature itself can be uncovered and defined simply in its presence-at-hand only "if its kind of being as ready-to-hand is disregarded." Nor does he believe that the equipment-structure is known as such even in the using. "The hammering." for instance, "does not simply have knowledge about the hammer's character as equipment, but it has appropriated this equipment in a way which could not be more suitable." Since the use of a visual metaphor seems inevitable in describing even the prepredicative and preconceptual mode of experience when we are appropriating an object pragmatically, Heidegger takes advantage of the word "circumspection" *(Umsicht)* which serves him in good stead in more than one respect. It means to look around to tell the assignment character as well as to have in sight the readiness of the use of the instrument, underscoring the practical attitude to which the dealings accommodate themselves. But his use of this visual metaphor is a pure coincidence, because, unlike Husserl who begins with the experience of sense perception in which the sight does play a material role, and who makes a systematic attempt to expand the visual approach by categorically equating "genuine seeing" *(echte Erschauung)* with the final justification of truth,[30] the actual look at outward appearance is already discredited by Heidegger as being prejudicial and diversionary. It hides rather than shows the immediacy of largely instrumentally oriented dealings of man with his environment.

In a sense, Heidegger has made a more telling point of starting from man's immediately lived, life-world experience, though the promising concreteness was soon to give way to a saga of

"Being" not to be comprehended by any "rational" thinking. The fact that Husserl recurred to the predicative structure even in describing the expressly prepredicative experience would seem to vitiate his position, as it arouses the suspicion that his straightforward perception remains undistinguished from one that is mediated by logical reflections. There is a danger that what is constituted in consciousness or retraced in thinking may not do, after all, full justice to the subjective-relative aspect of our life-wordly encounter with things in first person. In our fleeting moment to moment "ecstatic" experience, it would appear that we more often *overlook* than simply directly look at the perceptual qualities of those objects around us, especially when they have the familiar equipment character. But the function of phenomenology is to demonstrate the meaning of being in constitutive analysis instead of giving a factual account, though it may be factual in existential-analytic terms only. Even when man's life-world experience is under consideration, it is the *eidos* of his being in that type of world-horizon that finally matters. The perception in the sense of perceived properties and the act of perceiving in its essential structures must be presupposed as the substratum at all times regardless of whether man's actual interest is directed to such properties or to some other pragmatic relations. Both the ostensibly primary dealings with the tools and the "deficient mode" of consciousness which "disregards" such dealings are possible on the basis of what Husserl calls the passively preconstituted unity of all perceived bodies, namely, nature. It is the invariable foundation whose perceived meaning subsists in all varicties of interested or disinterested, practical or theoretical attitude which may be brought to bear upon it.

The primary givenness for Heidegger was answered in terms of what is nearest *for* us. It is the cultural object, a tool or an equipment, and its use and usefulness to which he thinks man is primarily and proximally oriented. Husserl, however, by placing sensuously perceived qualities of natural objects at the basis of our intentional structure, offers us a welcome opportunity critically to examine the meaning of the constitution of the world in the transcendental subjectivity and, together with it, the measure of critical self-appraisal of phenomenology as idealism. Of course, under no circumstances should he be taken to indicate that what is first is, in contrast to Heidegger's position for instance, what is there simply in itself. The naive supposition of a preexisting world is ruled out, even though he seems to admit the priority of natural objects as against the cultural objects. It is always *within* the hierarchical order or the founding relationship of our intentional structure itself that the "primacy" of sense perception must be examined as to its true significance. Husserl never sharply clarified whether the perceptually given is already the product of synthetic achievement of consciousness whereby the unity is so to speak fitted on by the constitutive a priori, or whether the possibility of such synthetic achievement presupposes in turn the "organization" in the sensuously given elements themselves. It is a question which A. Gurwitsch has pointedly raised in his own way. He has answered the question to the effect that the unity of the given in the consciousness must be referred back to the condition of order which belongs to the immediate phenomenal givenness itself.[31] That this meant a revision of Husserl's own standpoint and involved a justification on the basis of a renewed examination of his therory of passive synthesis and beyond that the theory of "free variation" will be generally acknowledged. Husserl himself knew that there are limits to the range of free imaginative variation and that the essential structures obtained therewith had to lead to the highest regional concepts through which the being of one particular region is thought of as distinguishable from the being of another region. But that was perhaps as far as he went. The doubt remains unresolved whether the absolute subjectivity should be interpreted in the sense of an absolute idealism which has already *posited* what is otherwise naively held to be given, or it should mean a critical, transcendental idealism which retraces and describes in reflection the essential relations and structures of what is unequivocally pregiven.

The scale appears to tip in favor of the first view when we are reminded by Husserl that "a real and ideal being which lies beyond the total transcendental subjectivity is nonsense and must be understood absolutely as nonsense."[32] Or, more explicitly, that "the total spatio-temporal world.... is according to its own meaning mere intentional being" and it is "a being which the consciousness posits in its experience. . . . Over and beyond this, it is just nothing."[33] Or again, he compares the act of constituting the world to the act of production or even "creation of the world."[34] But Husserl's absolute idealism that at times so closely verges on the Fichtean subjectivism is not without a poised reappraisal of the veracity of the view of nature existing *in itself*. He speaks of a tension between two concepts of nature; one that "stood in the beginning" and the other that "emerged for us in the connection of community."[35] It goes without saying that in both cases nature is thought of as a correlate of consciousness, but the question is now what is the meaning of nature being "in itself" as related to what function of subjectivity. Nature in the first sense is given through "original sensibility" *(Ursinnlichkeit)*, prior to all achievement of subjectivity that predicates, knows or produces. By original sensibility is meant the passivity of sensuous perception in which no residues of earlier active positing achievement are contained. It is only by virtue of this passively given nature that a community of subjects in mutual communication comes to life. For, the experience of other psyches is impossible without its being "appresented" in the body, a material thing to be perceived by the senses. But the nature of this passivity of pure givenness is yet without any positive determinations. It is given simply as an "empty, identical something," or as a "rule," according to which our consciousness becomes aware of the identity of the object in spite of the changing series of its appearances, perspectives and adumbrations. By being in itself is meant just as much, and no more, in the first case.

In the second case, nature appears as the "construct," as the product of the active achievement of subjectivity in intersubjectivity. Here nature is no longer an empty, identical something, but is the idea of all things to which objective, scientific determinations are attributed. If we speak of an independent existence with regard to nature in the present context, it is in the sense that the given series of appearances can be determined through purely conceptual means independently of the function of any class of sense perceptions. Because this methodically secured scientific determination enables any number of repetitive attempts by any number of subjects to understand the series of appearances of the object, such common achievement in understanding can be regarded to assure "objectivity" in direct proportion to its intersubjective validity and vice versa. In other words, the meaning of scientific objectivity and of the givenness of an "independently" existing order of the physical universe is shown to consist in the possibility of describing the world in logically valid formulations for as many intelligent subjects as there may be who share the common rational language. The idea of *truth in itself* is no exception. It is valid only in correlation to the subjectivity which can experience truth, and experience it reflectively as founded originally in its own sphere of transcendental "ego-universe" *(Ichall).*

This pendular swing back to the transcendental ego invariably seems to leave life, life-world, prepredicative experience and nature – everything that there is – dependent on the "mercy" of consciousness for their being.[36] Both the constituting ego and the constituted world as its correlate are "undeclinable," we are told by Landgrebe, because they are unique in being the a priori conditions under which one may have a world under the changing circumstances of history. This subjectivity transcends even the opposition of the "universal and particular" and lies "beyond the dialectic of the one and the many." Such a dialectical mediation is not needed because, following Landgrebe, the transcendental subjectivity "in its uniqueness implies in itself the *one* world common to all and, therefore, humanity." Subjectivity is as it were an "immediacy which mediates itself,"[37] i.e., it is the immediate being as the final source of constitutive achievement, and it mediates itself at the same time in the sense that the meaning of the constitutive achievement can and must become evident to all because each member of the community of subjects partakes in, and is mediated by, this one world of intersubjectivity or rational humanity. However, the transcendental subjectivity as the "absolute being" should not be confused with each particular subjectivity which is "discovered in the phenomenological reflection." The former can never be exhausted in the latter, nor in its particular world-constituting achievements, since it is, as absolute being, the "universe of transcendental subjects, the transcendental ego-universe."[38] The invariant structures of the life-world which the transcendental subjectivity has discovered are never, it will be reminded further, a priori conditions in a static and conclusive sense. The concepts of variant structures are but an "idealization" or "project," which allows no closure, but must be "transcended while being acquired."[39] To grasp the invariant essence of our flowing life, to arrest the "Heraclitean flux" as it were in its flux without bringing it to a standstill, that is what Husserl had in vision when the reconciliation of the irreconciliable, the a priori of the immanence of consciousness in its relation to the a posteriori of the positive givenness of the senses, was brought up as the fundamental philosophical problem underlying the "crisis of European sciences." The concept of the dynamic process of *self-transcendence* of ego and that of the "functioning intentionality"[40] were to provide an effective leverage to cope with the itself ever flowing, dynamic process of our world-life *(Weltleben).*

That the consciousness constantly transcends its own horizon is readily granted, without any commitment to specific phenomenological procedures, to be sure. But what if with the self-transcendence is implied the metaphysical thesis that the ego, the absolute consciousness, in transcending its horizon, performs the material transition toward the world? It is precisely at this point that the essential correlation of the transcendental ego with the totality of being must become, once again, problematic. For, had not the correlation been possible only because the *existing* world in its entirety had been bracketed? Was not the absolute subjectivity that was left after the world had been "anihilated," in reality an empty horizon, purged of any rest of spatiotemporal ties and severed from the existing, finite and mundane subjectivity itself? How else could the ego claim the *totality* of the world as its intentional correlate, if the world still contained the ego as a *part* in itself? Quite logically, then, must not the ego have its place beyond and outside of the world? So that its transcendence has as its *terminus a quo* and *terminus ad quem* the emptiness of its own horizon? Even if the transcendental ego is an "ego" only by "equivocation" and must refer more properly to the "inseparable unity of world experience and its intentional correlate" rather than to the correlated term of such unity,[41] the very question of transforming the "empty consciousness" *(Leerbewusstsein)* into a "comprehensive total consciousness" *(umfassendes Gesamtbewusstsein)* conjures at once the ghost of Schelling who attacked the impossible transition from the "absolute idea" to "nature" in Hegel's philosophy. The pure thought as "subject," conceived also in this case as the higher unity in which the separated aspects of so-called subject and object or "inner" and "outer" spheres of existence are overcome and preserved in a dialectical synthesis, would, according to Schelling, never be able to bring itself to a true movement or to a living understanding of the reality, because it was, in its assumed presuppositionlessness of its movement, wholly devoid of any empirical élement. Only a being that exists positively is able to step out of itself and come back to itself on its own.[42] There will be left only an existentialist solution to the problem by retaining the subjectivity but at the same time restricting its freedom of pure reflection and its constitutive omnipotence. It is a solution that among others Merleau-Ponty has adopted. The human body reveals to him the prehistory of ego over which it has no control, and through sense perception it is possible to derive a meaning from nature quite independently of any constitutive achievement.[43] The dialectic of freedom and necessity, of transcendental project and the pregiven situation never at any moment absolves man of his inner-worldy facticity. But the basically subjectivist approach, with the consciousness still as the hub of the universe, though the topography of the conscious experience may now be subjected to a far more detailed psychophysical and perceptional description, is retained. It is doubtful that Husserl would have sanctioned the total or even partial delivery of the transcendental subject to a mundane, individual subject. In all likelihood he would have surrendered anything, small or great, that is part of this world in order to save the transcendental subjectivity, since the final aim of his philosophy was to lay hold of the attitude of pure seeing, of being a disinterested spectator[44] dissociated from an interested life of praxis and engagement.

If, however, a disinterested attitude is what emerges as a practical lesson from the study of phenomenology, then a radically disinterested view which even dissociates itself from the basic presuppositions of phenomenology will hardly be considered a disservice to its own critical spirit.

A rare combination of such detached attitude and an insider's experienced insight is the background of Marvin Farber's criticism which centers on two major points : the limits of the subjectivist approach of phenomenology and the plea for a methodological pluralism.[45] The most fundamental, and itself reflectively unexamined, presupposition of phenomenology is seen by Farber in the correlation of the "class of knowing" with "being," or of the sum of real and possible experience as constituted meaning on the one hand with the totality of existence on the other. This "self-imposed limitation of one's analysis", i.e., the positing of consciousness as the absolute being, must sooner or later face the problem of its own "deliverance." Existence of the world or transcendence toward it necessarily becomes a problem once the knowing subject has bracketed it, though for purely methodical considerations it may have been in the beginning. But in having raised the claim of total reflection and of handling the totality of being through this *one* reflective procedure, phenomenology carries, throughout its involuted stages of searching self-reflection, the stigma of an "initial excess of the subjectivity," which in the words of Whitehead it is the task of philosophy to "correct."[46] Transcendence to the existing world remains an unresolved "methodogenic problem," as Farber points out, because of the nonacceptance of the "basic fact" of the givenness of the "external world." "To be sure," he reminds us further, "every factual statement that supports this non-dependence principle (i.e. non-dependence of existence on human knowers) *could* be stated in phenomenological terms. . . . But there are also facts about experience that enable us to view the entire process of experience and 'possible' experience in its actual place in existence. It is a fact that existence is bigger and more complex than actual knowledge can ascertain, and *more so than all accretions in an assumed endless process of experience.*"[47]

By forcing upon distinctive systems of knowledge a general unity, phenomenology tended to obscure the totality of things. Its lack of the reflective awareness of the very selective character of its own procedure is conspicuous. Though Farber readily acknowledges that the "merit of phenomenology is its full recognition of the dynamic and creative aspects of thought process," he is equally quick to add that the phenomenological "frame" should always be thought of as a specialized supplement to the primary "frame" of natural knowledge and its established facts about the world and man, or existence and experience.[48] Since all scientific pursuit is a "response to a purpose" and there are purposes in our life other than the one envisaged by phenomenology, such purposes, natural or social, may call for distinctive methods – inductive, deductive, explanatory and other – different from the transcendental. Hence the unity which our philosophical reason strives after is more likely to be an unity in diversity, taking into account the relative plurality of purposes and interests of human life, including, of course, also the disinterested attitude of seeing for the sake of seeing, which is but one way to define the purpose of philosophy. Pointing to the basic fact that the realm of existence is disclosed to us to a very small extent through experience, the author of the celebrated commentary on Husserl's phenomenology urges "cooperative spirit and due modesty" on the part of phenomenologists and nonphenomenologists alike. If the great diversity of questions and problems is to be dealt with on all levels of their challenges, he makes it plain that philosophers should accommodate themselves to the conception of a methodological pluralism. Thus he not only sees the need of our day, but also the hope of its fulfillment : "The time may not be far when the antagonism between two fundamental approaches (objectivist and subjectivist) will be no more serious than the difference between inductive and deductive methods in logic."[49] Those who are aware of the recent rise of the interest – in the birthplace of phenomenology and among active phenomenologists at that – in the diversity of approaches and the concomitant discussions of methodologies with a view to transforming the "coexistence with mutual non-respect" among groups of philosophers and scientists into a cooperative togetherness,[50] will find both Farber's long standing plea and his optimism amply justified.

Along with the unresolved problem of the transition from the transcendental ego to the existence of the world, another methodogenic legacy of Husserl is the irreconciled relation of the former to the mundane, individual subjectivity. Within the phenomenological perspective, the tension may be explained away simply because it has its origin in the inability of our natural and objective attitude to assume a disinterested, i.e., transcendental view of the world. It is easily said that they are just two different attitudes of which one and the same human being is capable. But this is in effect to belittle the problem and significance of the transcendental subjectivity itself, since the empirical, psychophysical ego must depend on the former for the constitution of its own being, and hence cannot possess equal validity with its transcendental namesake. Ingarden has already pointed out the mutually exclusive properties of the two egos and the resultant problem of identifying the one with the other.[51] The identity has to remain unestablished, as long as the phenomenological concept of the primary given is riveted to the pure consciousness divested of any inner-wordly residue of natural and cultural ties. What Husserl promisingly held out under the name of the transcendental science of facts has done indeed much groundwork by clearing the "fringes" and "horizons" of facts and factual givenness. But by making the most basic of all given facts, the existence of nature which "transcends on its part all human transcendence,"[52] dependent on the "in itself primary" (fact) of subjectivity, his search for the concrete meaning of experience through the prepredicative and life-world layers of consciousness has paradoxically ended in merely marking time. In the barren emptiness of the horizon, the parallax of two images, the transcendentally primary and the naturally primary, remain unadjusted. The absolute ego may mediate itself within ever so extended a horizon of total consciousness, but it remains unmediated with the truly immediate in itself, the total plenitude of being. And nothing less than the universe itself that transcends the transcendental ego will be worthy of the name of the horizon of philosophical inquiry.

NOTES

Quotations from German source materials, if not otherwise specified, are in the present writer's own translations.

1. *Erfahrung und Urteil* (to be quoted as *Experience and Judgment* hereafter), Hamburg 1949, p. 21. Cf. also *Formale und transzendentale Logik,* § 84.

2. *Critique of Pure Reason,* First original edition of 1781, pp. 370-371.

3. *Erste Philosophie I,* (1923-24), *Husserliana VII,* The Hague 1956, p. 258.

4. Cf. *Ideen zu einer reinen Phänomenologie und phänomenologischen Philosophie, I,* (to be quoted *"Ideen I"*), *Husserliana III,* The Hague 1950, p. 46.

5. Cf. *Krisis der europäischen Wissenschaften und die transzendentale Phänomenologie* (to be quoted *Crisis*), *Husserliana VI,* The Hague 1954, Beilage XI, XII, pp. 432ff. What compelled Hume to stay within the critical confines of factual experience was a prudence equally far removed from naive objectivism and dogmatic subjectivism. Husserl's imputation of "prephilosophical naiveté" to him because of his failure to reduce the world into a "construct of consciousness" is arguable, to say the least, in point of naiveté, as the usual distinguishing mark of this negative virtue is the lack of deliberation rather than an excessive possession of it, while nobody would admit Hume possessed less than an average person's share of it.

On the other hand, it may be recalled that Whitehead coincided with

Husserl in evaluating Hume's historical significance. He not only associated Hume with Kant in advancing the doctrine of "the objective world as a construct from subjective experience," but contrasted Hume's relatively "vague and inadequate" conception of the "act of experience as a constructive functioning" with that of Kant who had "the full sweep of the notion." Cf. A. N. Whitehead, *Process and Reality*, New York 1929, p. 236.

6. *Crisis*, Beilage XV, p. 455.

7. *Experience and Judgment*, p. 22.

8. Cf. *Husserl. Cahiers de Royaumont. Philosophie* Nr. III. Paris 1959, p. 429.

9. Hence Hartmann's criticism of the phenomenologists' concept of "phenomenon." He charged them for failing to distinguish between what appears (to us) and what is in itself. The "determinations of a real being," he argued, cannot be exhausted by the "determinations of a phenomenon." See *Der Aufbau der realen Welt*, 2nd ed., Meisenheim 1949, pp. 210 f.

10,. Husserl's *Unpublished Manuscript A VII 8*, p. 2. Cf. also Gerd Brand, *Welt, Ich und Zeit*, The Hague 1955, p. 9.

11. *Crisis*, Beilage XIV, p. 449.

12. Cf. Ibid., p. 51.

13. Ibid., p. 127. Cf. Ibid., p. 177.

14. Ibid., p. 192.

15. John Wild, *Existence and the World of Freedom*, Englewood Cliffs 1963, p. 46.

16. Published by Walter Biemel in 1954. See above Note 5. for the original title.

17. Cf. *Ideen II*, Husserliana IV, p. 375.

18. Ludwig Landgrebe, "Von der Unmittelbarkeit der Erfahrung" in *Edmund Husserl 1859-1959, Recueil commémoratif*, The Hague 1959, p. 251.

19. Marvin Farber, *The Foundation of Phenomenology*, New York 1943, pp. 491 f.

20. *Crisis*, pp. 347 f.

21. Ibid., p. 193.

22. Ibid., p. 183.

23. Ibid., p. 184.

24. Farber, op. cit., p. 517.

25. *Experience and Judgment*, p. 75. A fuller consideration of this topic is now available in English, *The Phenomenology of Internal Time-Consciousness*, translated by J. S. Churchill, Indiana 1966.

26. On the structural difference between the receptive "interest of perception" and the active "interest of knowledge", see Section II of *Experience and Judgment*, especially pp. 232 ff.

27. Martin Heidegger, *Being and Time*, English translation by J. Macquarrie and E. Robinson, New York 1962, pp. 98 ff.

28. *Crisis*, p. 127.

29. *Experience and Judgment*, p. 55.

30. "Without genuine seeing (*echte Erschauung*). . . . all striving after

knowledge is meaningless, ... all talk about truth which is valid in itself loses its meaning." "Absolute justification presupposes absolute seeing." Cf. *Erste Philosophie II, Husserliana VIII,* Beilagen, pp. 365-367. Of course Husserl was not talking about "sensuous seeing" in the present case. By "empirical intuition" is meant the originary perception in which an individual object is given. But such "empirical or individual seeing can be transformed into 'essential insight' (*Wesensschauung*)," in which case the universal essence or *eidos* can be just as clearly seen as an individual object. Cf. *Ideas* (translated by B. Gibson), Chapter I, 3, "Essential insight and individual intuition," pp. 48 f.,

31. Cf. Aron Gurwitsch, *Théorie du champs de la conscience. Textes et études anthropologiques.* Brügge 1957.

32. *Erste Philosophie II, Husserliana VIII,* p. 482.

33. *Ideen I,* p. 93. Cf. *Ideas,* p. 139.

34. Eugen Fink, "Die Phänomenologie Edmund Husserls in der gegenwärtigen Kritik," in *Kantstudien XXXVIII,* 1933, pp. 319-383.

35. *Ideen II* p. 208.

36. "Every being which is not itself consciousness assumes therefore the character of what is 'merely' constituted, as opposed to the absolute consciousness which constitutes. . . . everything is what it is for this consciousness in such a way that it has its being 'due to the mercy' of the latter." See Landgrebe, "Seinsregionen und regionale Ontologien in Husserls Phänomenologie, in *Der Weg der Phänomenologie,* Gerd Mohn 1963, p. 147.

37. Landgrebe, Das Problem der transzendentalen Wissenschaft vom lebensweltlichen Apriori," in *Phänomenologie und Geschichte,"* Gerd Mohn 1968, p. 164.

38. Landgrebe, "Husserls Abschied vom Cartesianismus," in *Der Weg der Phänomenologie,* p. 191.

39, Landgrebe, see *op. cit.,* in above Note 37, pp. 164-165.

40, Fink, "Das Problem der Phänomenologie Edmund Husserls" in *"Revue Internationale de Philosophie,"* Brussels, 1ère annés, No. 2, janvier 1939, p. 266.

41. Landgrebe, see op. cit., in Note 36, p. 190.

42. Cf. Karl Löwith, *From Hegel to Nietzsche,* New York 1967, pp. 114f.

43. Cf. Maurice Merleau-Ponty, *Phénoménologie de la Perception,* Paris, 1945.

44. Landgrebe, "Merleau-Pontys Auseinandersetzung mit Husserls Phänomenologie," in *Phänomenologie und Geschichte,* p. 181. Against this existentialist interpretation of Merleau-Ponty, Landgrebe points to the fact that Husserl insisted on keeping the transcendental subjectivity as "freedom *from* the world" apart from the being-*in*-the-world or engagement and indicates that Husserl's separation of the two attitudes must have a "deeper right."

45. Farber, *Phenomenology and Existence, Toward a Philosophy within Nature,* New York 1967. Cf. especially the Chapters I, "The Role of Reflection in Phenomenology" (p. 6), II "Descriptive Nature of Philosophy and the Nature of Human Existence" (pp. 34 f.), IV "On the

Existence of the World" (pp. 81 f.) and VI "The Life-World" (p. 148) for passages quoted.

46. Whitehead, *Process and Reality,* New York 1929, p. 22

47. Farber op. cit., pp. 73-74. The emphasis in italics is by the present writer.

48. Cf. Ibid., p. 161.

49. Ibid., p. 148.

50. The Ninth Congress of German Philosophers 1969, for instance, chose as its general theme "Philosophy and Science," with the presidential address by Ludwig Landgrebe on "The Philosophy and the Responsibility of the Sciences." The detailed program worked out by A. Diemer, another noted phenomenologist and executive secretary of the congress, shows preeminent interest in methodological and epistemological issues. The existing state of incommunicado among different disciplines or schools is registered with regret and the timeworn attempt of philosophy to cope with the problem "from above" and by way of "general reflections" is rejected. Cf. *Vorankündigung, Thema des Kongresses 1969,* published by L. Landgrebe and A. Diemer.

51. *Cartesianische Meditationen und die Pariser Vorträge, Husserliana I,* Beilage, p. 213.

52. What Farber calls the "principle of non-dependence" is sustained indirectly by Gerhard Krüger, who criticizes the modern subjectivism and its "emancipation from the innerwordly ties of 'ontic truth'" and who pays tribute to the insight of ancient Greek philosophy into the self-sufficient order of the universe. Cf. *Grundfragen der Philosophie,* Frankfurt am Main, 1958. Similarly, Karl Löwith attacks the subjectivist tendency in existentialism and phenomenology and advances the metaphysical thesis that nature "transcends all human transcending" and emphasizes the significance of the "eccentric vision" of the world. By this is meant the restitution of a "natural" world outlook in which man is no longer at the hub of the "constituted" or "projected" world as "cosmological idea" (Kant), "total horizon" (Husserl), etc. Cf. *"Natur und Humanität des Menschen"* in *Wesen und Wirklichkeit des Menschen,* Göttingen 1957, especially p. 84; *Gott, Mensch und Welt in der Metaphysik von Descartes bi zu Nietzsche,* Göttingen 1967, pp. 43ff.

ON THE PHENOMENOLOGY AND SEMIOLOGY OF ART[1]

Mikel Dufrenne, University of Paris at Nanterre

AT PRESENT in Europe phenomenology does not always enjoy the highest esteem among those who investigate the nature of art. Neopositivist thought, derived from Anglo-American logical positivism, sees in phenomenological aesthetics a speculative enterprise which obstructs the strictly scientific study of art; this situation echoes the earlier dispute in Germany between *Aesthetik* and *Kunstwissenschaft.* Semiology is the current form assumed by the "science of art." In what follows, I should like to show that phenomenology need not be ashamed of preserving the rights of philosophical reflection. Moreover, instead of condemning the scientific approach to art as practised by semiology, phenomenology has perhaps inspired it in the first place. In any case, phenomenology commends this approach; and in showing its limits, it does not seek to do it an injustice.

Semiology is the study of systems of signification. Language is one of these systems. When Ferdinand de Saussure instituted a new linguistics, he envisaged it as a mere province within the semiological kingdom. He did not foresee that because of the special status he gave to this province it was destined to play the determining role in the kingdom. For semiology now deliberately borrows its conceptual apparatus from linguistics.

How is it then that art is accessible to semiological description? The basis for this lies in the fact that art offers us images, which can in turn be inscribed in signifying systems and thus constitute visual languages. Of course, images in a strict sense are found only in the plastic arts, in architecture or in urban design, that is, in the arts which let us *see;* the image is first of all conceived as a visual image. But semiology can also be applied to music – not so much because psychologists speak of "sound images" as because musical discourse can be considered to possess meaning and especially because it lends itself (perhaps more than any other aesthetic object) to structural analysis. For what finally matters is that a certain method of analysis can be applied to the work and to a body of works. However, the signifying character does appear most propitiously in the visual arts : Erwin Panofsky's semiology was established as an investigation into iconology in painting and the graphic arts. Thus we shall accord a certain priority to plastic images.

These images do not necessarily belong to what is usually considered art. As W.J. Bowman writes in his *Graphic Communication,* "The difference between words and pictures is the difference between telling and showing, and this book is for the person who is concerned with showing."[2] Bowman goes on to treat the vocabulary and syntax of graphic language, that is, the language inherent in diagrams, networks, and maps – and in no way related to the plastic arts. The learned work of J. Bertin, *La sémiologie graphique* (Mouton, 1967), is concerned with the same kind of meaningful units *(ensembles signifiants).* It is clear that such units lend themselves especially well to semiology, since they have been constructed to transmit information which is as neat and precise as possible. With little redundance and no polysemy, these signs are not affected by the instability, complexity, or ambiguity of linguistic signs (though these very traits are also responsible for the richness and suppleness of language). Graphic communication is analyzable into meaningful units because its elements are always catalogued and defined in a rigorous code. Moreover, the level of comprehension required of the interpreter is strictly determined : quite simply, he must know the code in order to decipher the message. We would also observe that the correct use of such communicative signs may give rise to a specific form of thought – a "graphic thought" – whose powers of understanding and of invention are not yet known. It is incontestable that graphic communication shows what is conceived and can be said; the image is the substitute for, and illustration of, the concept; but it does not always remain in this subordinate function : it can lead to new concepts or to a new kind of thinking. In this connection, it is noteworthy that Pierre Francastel projects a "figurative thought" creative of a "visual order" at work in the arts.[3] This suggests that graphic thought and figurative thought might be brought together in semiological research. Such a rapprochement is all the more tempting when we consider that artists like Michaux, Noël, and Mathieu interpret their own works as forms of graphic communication.

Thus a semiology of art begins to look feasible. We need only consider that works of art are meaningful objects whose signification can be deciphered through an act of decoding; hence we must also presuppose that a certain code dictates the composition of the work in terms of discriminable elements organized by fixed procedures. Immediately, however, a series of questions arises. Where does the signification reside? Is the act of meaning *(le signifier)* exhausted in the act of showing? What precisely is shown in nonrepresentational painting, in a monument, or in music? What is the relation [in representational arts] between what is represented and the mode of representation? But let us bracket these questions for a moment and indicate what seems most important in the semiological approach : namely, that it prescribes the immanent analysis of works of art. We may call this kind of analysis structural or not; but it *is* structural in a broad sense insofar as it discerns determinate relations between the elements of a work. Thus the possibility of a combinatory logic of relations emerges; the choice of certain combinations within this logic defines a style or at least the degeneration of a style into a stereotype. Long before the rise of structuralism – even before Saussurian linguistics – this type of analysis was attempted by the *Sichtbarkeit* school, the Moscow circle of linguists and critics, the Warburg group, and by Suzanne Langer and the American semanticists.

Phenomenology itself has practiced "structural" analysis : witness Ingarden's *The Literary Work of Art.* What in fact is the method of phenomenology? Its proper method is intentional analysis – the analysis of the manifold ties between the intentional aiming of the subject and the object aimed at. If the object is given with sensory or rational evidence, how and to what kind of attention is it given? One might say that the major enterprise of phenomenology is an analysis of seeing. This is the case even when it is a question of essences, since they still give themselves to a vision, that of the *Wesensschau.* As is well known, Husserl follows Descartes in this respect : to understand is always to intuit; and the method of imaginative variations also calls for vision. What vision? This is the question we must eventually answer, and phenomenology will aid us in this inquiry. But we should observe beforehand that a reference to vision or view introduces the scheme (proper to all transcendental philosophy) of the subject-object distinction. Where Aristotle invoked a somewhat mysterious act common to feeling and what is felt, a philosophy of seeing describes a relation between, and thus separates, seeing and the seen. The analysis of this relation is "intentional" because it is the analysis of an intention which is fulfilled in an intuition. Husserl subdivides it into noetic and noematic analysis. Noematic analysis is immanent analysis, and it tends to orient itself in the same general direction as semiology to the extent that the noema offered to the noesis is considered meaningful. In this sense, phenomenology is capable of contributing to the semiological study of the aesthetic object.

It is not a question here of contesting the originality of semiology. In briefest terms, this originality consists in the relation maintened by semiology with linguistics of Saussurian extraction. This relation is extremely close, even when it is supported by polemics. Although linguists of the stature of Jakobson or Greimas do not themselves embrace semiology, there are many others, barely initiated to linguistics, who only too willingly borrow its nomenclature and conceptual apparatus. This constant reference to linguistics is explained by the epistemological prestige of linguistics. But such reference also poses problems, the principal one of which for our purposes is the following : to what extent can categories derived from verbal discourse be applied to images? In other words, how extensively may we identify seeing and understanding? We shall return to this problem, but we snould note now that a few semiologists are fully aware of this difficulty, especially those familiar with phenomenology : e.g., Christian Metz in his essav "Le cinéma : langue *ou* langage? "[4] We should also point out Susanne Langer's attempt to distinguish the presentative, unconsummated symbols of art from linguistic signs; some of our own phenomenological observations will agree in all essentials with her results.

Phenomenology can be called upon to show the limits of semiology. It should be stressed that to indicate the limits of an enterprise is in no way to disavow it; on the contrary, showing limits may even justify the enterprise and help it escape the fatal temptation of dogmatism : a temptation always menacing an objectifying thought that is self-assured, from determining its object rigorously. The first difficulty semiology encounters has to do with the solidarity of subject and object : of noetic and noematic in phenomenological language, of interpreter and interpretation *(lecture)* in semiological terms. The distinct merit of semiology lies in teaching us to interpret, that is, to decipher a coded object in order to discover its meaning. In the case of language, our education has made us so familiar with the codes of speech and writing that we are unconscious of the decoding process we effect when we listen or read. As a result, the verbal sign seems to disappear behind the representation, and in dialogue we have the impression of exchanging ideas rather than words. But we cannot forget that speech has meaning only for someone who knows what speaking means : for a receiver who knows the code and can decode the message or emit one himself. There is interpretation only for an interpreter within a culture. When the sign is an image, the above proposition is still true, but the decoding requirement is easier to satisfy : witness the images in Gothic cathedrals which served as signs for men who could decipher them though they could not read. While the written sign is arbitrary and thus must be learned, the figurative image is the natural analogue of the object it represents and can be comprehended by the crudest perception. And yet primitive people, shown a photograph of a man, do not recognize the image as that of a man; similarly, to recognize Saint Peter in a cathedral requires knowing that he is identifiable by the key he holds in his hand. Here again interpreting an image presupposes the mediation of a culture, along with the noetic activity of an interpreter formed by this culture. This is why we are such poor interpreters of primitive objects in a museum: interpretation is never simple or immediate.

Perhaps interpretation would be transparent if the code were truly natural; but, though it is not as arbitrary as the code constituting the structure of language, it is still never totally natural. Yet what is natural? Langevin[5] said that the concrete is often the abstract made familiar through use; we might say as well that the natural is often the artificial rendered familiar in use. Musicologists have for a long time thought they could justify harmony by founding it on nature; but the mathematization of intervals refers to an *intelligible* nature. Only a cultivated ear appreciates consonance and dissonance, experiencing the need for a certain resolution of chords. Alberti and his contemporaries termed "artificial" a perspectival code founded on the geometrization of space, but the so-called "natural" perspective which they opposed was just as artificial. As Panofsky shows, the *Agregatraum* – a discontinuous and heterogeneous space which surrounds objects, belonging to them and subordinating itself to them rather than ordering them – implies a systematic conception of space, even if it is not a *Systemraum.* Just as artificial is the color code invented by impressionists to express depth in a different way from drawing : Monet's water-lilies are no less complicated and no less meant for trained perception than the flowers in Van Eyck's celestial meadows.

We should mention parenthetically the difference between verbal and artistic language – a difference which semiology must take into account. Verbal language as a system is a code confined to the "speaking mass"; like the global culture which structures this mass, such a language evolves only slowly : imperceptibly for the individual. By contrast, artistic codes such as those just cited are offered by a more sensitive historicity because they are more directly related to what is arbitrary in invention (not in convention). While daily speech submits mechanically to common usage, artistic creation in its most authentic gestures constantly surpasses pre-existing codes, inventing new procedures and even new ground-rules. Styles vary, and each great work introduces a new poetics *(art poétique)* by calling for a new vision. Thus artistic codes are more supple and elastic than linguistic or graphic codes; they are also less exacting in their demands upon the interpreter.

For the deciphering of a given work cannot be said always to imply knowledge of its singular poetics or even (more simply) general codes governing collective styles. If one had to be a musician to enjoy music, a large musical audience would not exist; the same holds in painting (as if one had to know how to paint) or in architecture (as if it were necessary to know the principles and techniques of construction). This observation leads us to the notion that there are different levels of interpretation in the aesthetic object corresponding to different interpreters. Semiological analysis must itself be inscribed in the hierarchy which it institutes : semiology itself constitutes an interpretation at the highest level because it is the interpretation of an expert who not only knows how to interpret more intelligently than others but also knows that other interpretations are possible. At the other extreme is found the interpretation of those who are profane or ignorant – which we all are to a certain degree, including the expert. At this level, the only operative code is the perceptual code inculcated in us by all our experience. This code, which is in fact already cultural, enables us to see and hear, to embrace music with our body, to discern colors, appreciate distances, find ourselves in the world and recognize things by their images. But is this not just what art expects of us? It provides us with objects to perceive, and it calls for perception before all else : a felicitous perception, as it also aims at pleasing us (even when it harms or scandalizes us; but we are not treating the problem of beauty and the criterion of pleasure here). Art may also solicit an *intelligent* perception, called forth in varying degrees.

Thus the representational work proposes a task other than merely recognizing what is represents in terms of the natural Relation between image and thing. It may ask us to see *better,* that is, to grasp the 'how' of the representing : in this case, it is calling for formal analysis, consequently for a knowledge of the poetics or code which regulates its composition. The eye that feeds on the painting, as Klee said, is in search of those points of articulation, lines of force, and accents which perhaps already control it but which consciousness would like to ascertain so as to appropriate the work more fully. These elements are already meaningful, not so much in themselves but rather to the extent that their rhythmic or harmonic combinations confer on the sensuousness of the work a sort of internal necessity underlying its equilibrium and its movement : its plastic sense. Therefore, formal analysis can be readily incorporated into semiology. Moreover, an intelligible meaning is always linked to this plastic sense : in representational painting, a beach which accords or contrasts with another beach always possesses a color which falls within a certain range of color-tones, a diagonal is always punctuated by identifiable objects, an arabesque is always linked to the representation of a movement.

The representational work also invites us to comprehend

more profoundly the intelligible meaning contained in what is represented. But what does "meaning" mean here? First of all, it may mean a more detailed identification of the represented object : thus we need to learn that a certain Biblical personage with a key is St. Peter or that a mandorla is a means of glorification. In the same vein, we need to know that a given procession is the image of a royal festival at Florence, that a *veduta* reproduces a theater decor, or that certain records of Delaunay are dedicated to Blériot. Our intelligence must gain a historical dimension in order to interpret the meaning in its cultural context; this process clearly demands special, and always incomplete, information on the part of the interpreter. The interpretation does not uncover here a hidden meaning; instead, it finds a connoted meaning. In saying itself, the work indicates for us the historical modes or circumstances of its expression; the "signified" is always the object designated by the image. What matters is to know how the various signifieds of an art-work relate to a culture – how they manifest this culture with a clarity dimmed only by the passage of time.

Yet the meaning may be of another sort; clarity – verisimilitude in classical terms – may conceal a meaning hidden from primary visibility. This invisible element which is present and yet dissimulated in the visible is the *expressed.* An expression may of course be specifically intended by the artist. In an unpublished work, Louis Marin finds this intentional factor operative in Jansenist painting at a time when the values of representation seemed to reign supreme. For instance, the painting of Philippe de Champaigne cannot be considered "vain" because in it a mundane object becomes a sign; running water signifies the redemption, and a broken column symbolizes the precariousness of worldly goods – just as, in Sartre's example, a tumultuous sky expresses anguish. In these cases we have symbols which are no longer emblems, such as St. Peter's key or halo. The meaning they express is no longer assigned by an easily knowable convention; in fact, it is no longer assignable at all, since it is always at a distance and always ambiguous in the open region created by metaphor. Gauguin's idols do not demand a prayer from us; rather, they present us with a question which haunts them : what are we? In the very act of furnishing us with means to see, painters like Gauguin turn us toward a truth which is no longer visible.

Is this the truth of the wholly other, the hidden God? Doubtless it is for those who think that painting is an act of charity to be compared with, but surpassing, the giving of alms. In this event, the interpretation of the work is established at a mystical level, and semiology must follow it even there. For such an interpretation, the meaning proffered by the symbol is inexhaustible. The work does not provide us with a message which we can definitely decipher; it opens up a world we can endlessly explore. Our relative impotence does not derive from the limited character of our information, for it is no longer a question of an historical world to which the work refers us as its context; it is rather a world borne by the work as the inaccessible totality of its meaning. Speaking in Heideggerian language, we might say that Being does not reveal itself dissimulatingly in one of its epochs; instead, it offers itself, in the very act of disappearing, in a singular experience. This also explains why semiology can enlist psychoanalysis in its ranks. The profound character of the meaning in question is accessible to depth psychology in a form that is shaped by desire : such as the enigmatic countenance of the Florentine beauty passionately caressed by the brush of Leonardo, or the turbid wisdom of the immemorial myths which haunt our imagination. The work transports us like a dream, and the world it opens up *per speculum et in enigmate* is the world of the unavowable.

Nevertheless, the ambiguity and inexhaustibility of the depth meaning is due not so much to the element of desire as to its "figured" nature – i.e., to its radical immanence in the sensuous. It is for this reason that semiological research must always return to the formal analysis of the sensuous. The miracle (to use the seventeenth century term) is that the sensuous is transfigured in "figuring" a meaning beyond any possible represensation. But then we must ask what this transfiguration means : what is this invisible with which the visible is pregnant? The ungraspable character of the meaning may mean that there is nothing to grasp, nothing other than the force and density of the sensuous in an expressivity expressive only of itself. Perhaps we may be allowed to convert mystical into metaphysical language by saying that what the sensuous offers is the truth of appearance, not the appearance of a truth which is to be glossed by religion. Nature can produce the eye in which the truth of appearance is mirrored, as well as the consciousness in which it is reflected. Of course, what the work expresses anguish, serenity, violence, or sublimity, or that a landscape is cheerful or majestic. Singular expressions, identified by feeling even if discourse cannot define them, individualize works. But these expressions are made possible only because we exist in an accord with the world as part of it.° Perhaps the final message of art is not merely that something appears to someone, but that there is first of all *appearing* – that a light surges forth in the opacity of the real. *Fiat Lux :* but it is Nature which makes itself light. This is a light which proceeds neither from the eye nor from the thing seen; on the contrary, it arouses *them,* so that the look is no longer our privileged possession : the work looks at us as much as we stare at it. It is one and the same flesh, capable of transforming itself into a look, that renders man and world consubstantial. This, of course, is a constant theme of Merleau-Ponty; but what phenomenology strives to think, art gives the feeling. The apothesis of the sensuous invites us to reforge the experience of an original vision.

For this reason, semiology should perhaps become phenomenological – to describe, so far as possible, this last mode of interpretation solicited by the work. An ultimate, but also initial, mode, since the eye is returning here to its beginning. The levels of the work referred to above articulate the organization of the signified as distinct from the signifying (though designated and represented by the latter). These levels call for an interpretation capable of distinguishing and grasping the signified in itself, an interpretation compelled at the same time to substitute an intellectual experience for aesthetic experience. But this activity of the spectator and of the semiologist tends to transcend, if not to renounce, itself as soon as it uncovers the immanence of meaning in the sensuous : the immanence of the totalizing meaning that I have called "world" in the totality of the sensuous marshaled by the look. The upsurge of this meaning is the truth of appearance, that is, of being as appearing : an untamed and savage being which is the real itself insofar as it is hallowed out or duplicated to become visible and complete in vision. As Merleau-Ponty said, this savage being is revealed only to a savage vision. Such a vision does not aim at representation; it operates within presence, within the fullness of being where the for-itself has not yet truly separated from the in-itself, the eye is still a thing, and desire is not yet frustrated.

The everyday vision implicitly invoked by semiology is a vision which operates in terms of measured distances. As Bergson showed, such a vision is regulated by practical and cognitive aims in trying to master the world. It is the vision of an automobile driver constantly deciphering the artificial and natural signs emitted by traffic signals, brute things, and his own body; these sings help him to know, foresee, and act. Language is integral to this intelligent vision, not only because the latter learns from language (or is interpreted by it) but also because our vision of the world is modeled on language : we see things as we understand words in the discrete succession of the sentence, or as we read words within the abstract spatiality of a page of linear series. Those things which signify and are perceived only for their signification – which always refer to something else – possess at the limit no more *presence* than linquistic signs in their ordinary usage. Speech makes us intelligent (and intellectualistic), but sight can revolt against it. As can art. What the aesthetic object demands of us is not the sovereign, reassuring vision which interprets, identifies, and judges but a naive and unarmed vision which accords to the sensuous all its rights : the right to surprise, shock, seduce, or fascinate the eye (or ear), the right to awaken desire or stir the imagination, the right to furnish an invisible sense at the limits of non-sense. All of this testifies that we are in the world and *of* it – that we can join in the game of being. Contemporary art, especially in its nonrepresentational forms, invites us to share this adventure; it discourages any interpretation that merely identifies objects, and it shows nothing explicitly except the fact of showing *that* it shows. But the adventure can also be experienced in classical art, which ignored savage and brute elements : such art can also enchant us, reminding us of the ontological enigma of a pure appearing.

Semiology can lead us to the threshold of this enigma of the origin of appearing but it is up to phenomenology to penetrate its depths. Phenomenology reflects on the meaning of the hyphen in the definition of intentional analysis as noetic-noematic : a hyphen that indicates the primordial moment at which subject and object have not yet become separate.

NOTES

1. Translated by Edward S. Casey, Yale University. All footnotes are those of the translator.

2. W. J. Bowman, *Graphic Communication* (Wiley, 1968), p. vii.

3. Cf. P. Francastel, *La figure et le lieu* (Gallimard, 1967) and *Peinture et société* (Audin, 1952).

4. In *Communications,* No. 4 (1965).

5. Paul Langevin (1872-1946), eminent French physicist.

6. For the concept of accord, see the author's *The Notion of the A Priori,* trans. Edward S. Casey (Northwestern, 1966), ch. 10-12.

ABOUT THE MOTIVES WHICH LED HUSSERL TO TRANSCENDENTAL IDEALISM[1]

Roman Ingarden, Kraków, Poland

I HAVE often asked myself what exactly the reason was that Husserl, whose standpoint was that of realism at the time of the *Logische Untersuchungen,* showed a distinct inclination towards transcendental idealism since the *Ideen I,* and finally arrived at a decision, concerning which it was no longer possible for him to have any doubt. As it seems to me, various groups of motives are here involved, and among them certain arguments can also be found which Husserl drew from his philosophy. As far as I can see, there are here the following groups of motives which, in spite of Husserl's originally realistic standpoint, became in the course of time more and more significant for him :

1. Arguments which result from Husserl's conception of philosophy as a rigorous science.
2. Postulates of a correct method of epistemology.
3. Positive results of Husserl's analysis of outer perception as well as of the so-called constitutive reflection.
4. Formal-ontological grounds of the decision in favor of idealism.
5. Religious-philosophical tendencies, and finally
6. A purely human attitude of Husserl towards the real world.

It is, of course, necessary to become aware of the particular motives which belong to these various groups. But first of all it is necessary to answer the question, in what Husserl's "realistic" standpoint originally consisted, and what the evidence is that he really held this position. There are indeed scholars who doubt whether Husserl held such a position at all. The basis for this doubt is the fact that Husserl actually never *explicitly* declared himself publicly for "realism" in one or another sense, either at the time of the *Philosophie der Arithmetik* or at the time of the *Logische Untersuchungen.* The realistic standpoint can only be inferred indirectly from certain pronouncements of Husserl. There is here, in the first place, the Husserlian conception of "truth in itself" found in volume I, p. 228, of the *Logische Untersuchungen.* Husserl contrasts here (1) the "connection between things" – in a very wide sense of "thing" – and (2) the "connection between truths" which form the necessary correlate of "being in itself." It is not said here that this "being in itself" is the real being of the world, or of the objectivities belonging to the world. And it is certain that at the time of the *Logische Untersuchungen* Husserl understood by "being" not only real, but also "ideal" being, without any further qualifications, and did not hesitate to assume "ideal objects", although he declared himself against the so-called Platonic "realism" in the conception of the "ideas."[2] Husserl namely explicitly regarded logical structures, like concepts, propositions, theories, as ideal objectivities. And there is no doubt that he sharply distinguished the mode of being of these structures from the mode of being of real things and events, and that he did not at that time doubt the existence of the real world. Of decisive importance is here the use of the concept of "being in itself" with regard to the "connection between things" as well as the "truths in themselves." And it is also noteworthy that in the last years of his life, in the defense of his transcendental idealism, Husserl vehemently fights against precisely this doctrine of being in itself. Being in itself is just that being which exists independently of the "truths in themselves," as well as of our experiences [*Erlebnissen*] and especially of our cognitive experiences, the being which one must find in experience if it is to be recognized as existing, the "in itself" of the things to which precisely one has to go "back" – according to the slogan, at that time, proclaimed by Husserl and the phenomenologists – in order to achieve truthful results, the "in itself" later so radically rejected by Husserl, although the existence of the world is not denied at all.

That the earlier position of Husserl, at the time of the *Logische Untersuchungen,* and his later position, radically differ from each other in the conception of logical structures and of the real world, is evidenced not only by Husserl's clearly pronounced view in the *Cartesianische Meditationen,* in the

Formale und Transzendentale Logik, and in the *Krisis,* but is already testified to in a letter of Husserl to me of April 5, 1918, in which he clearly writes about the rejection of his view regarding truths "in themselves" and logical structures.[3] But an oral pronouncement of Husserl also confirms this without any doubt. In the fall of 1927 Husserl once asked me what I read with my students in the seminar. I mentioned, among other things, volume I of the *Logische Untersuchungen,* especially the last chapter, in which the conception of truths in themselves and of theory is presented. Husserl then said, it was a pity I did it, as this conception is not tenable. "There I went very much astray," he said. At that time he was already firmly convinced that transcendental idealism is right. It is difficult to tell when this change of standpoint occurred. In the *Ideen I* there are already distinct traces of the decision in favor of idealism, but only with regard to the real world, and besides there are various passages which are not to be understood in this sense at all. Ideal objects are still treated in the same manner as before. It is also disputable when Husserl conceived the idea of phenomenological reduction. According to the second volume of the *Husserliana (Idee der Philosophie)* it seems that it occurred several years before the *Ideen I,* but one must not overlook that the formulations found in this volume are entirely provisional and not quite strict, so that only the later formulation in the *Ideen I* accurately corresponds to Husserl's intentions. But on the other hand, the *Vorlesungen zur Phänomenologie des inneren Zeitbewusstseins* show that the problems of constitution were well known to Husserl many years before the *Ideen I.* Nevertheless only problems concerning the constitution of objectivities that have their being in time are included. No wonder then that the "essence," the *species,* and thus ideal objects in general, are treated in the first section of the *Ideen I* in quite the same manner as in the *Logische Untersuchungen.* [4] But at any rate, when one considers the books published by Husserl himself, the transcendental-idealistic conception of logical objectivities and of ideas appears for the first time in the *Formale und Transzendentale Logik.* But again, one may conjecture that the change in the conception of the mode of being of logical objectivities occurred much earlier, but was perhaps presented in an explicit form only in the early twenties. However, that this change of view did occur, that Husserl thus was not a transcendental idealist from the beginning, and that he worked out for himself this new standpoint only in the course of laborious studies of many years, this can no longer be doubted. What was it that brought him to it?

ad 1. The conception of philosophy as a rigorous science (cf. the *Logos*-article of 1911) was at first related to Husserl's sharply critical attitude towards the then existing European philosophy. Husserl came to philosophy from mathematics and was, so to speak, brought up in the mathematical rigor of concepts and proofs. Thus he condemned not only the multiplicity of the existing philosophical viewpoints and the never ending "quarrel" – as he often expressed himself – between them, but above all he condemned the manner of philosophizing of that time; such as operating with unclarified concepts, setting up of groundless affirmations, striving after formation of systems, etc. – everything that made impossible a reconciliation between different philosophies and, above all, the achievement of a "firm ground" in philosophy. Husserl fought all his life for this "firm ground," for clarity not only of concepts, but also of intuitive apprehension, for keeping apart all that is often easily confused, and above all for responsibility of philosophical research, and he devoted many years to the working out of a method which – in his opinion – could secure the "scientific character" (*"Wissenschaftlichkeit")* of philosophy. But remarkably he – the mathematician – did not look for the salvation of philosophy in the mathematical method. And also mathematical logic – which to many of those who were distrustful of philosophy in the end actually blocked the way to it – could not satisfy him at all. Because precisely where he demanded clarity, understanding, and insight, there had been contentment with conventionalistic solutions and with a rather false skepticism, which subsequently assumed the shape of radical formalism and physicalism. An insight into the ultimate, not further definable, structures of the logical formations, an apprehension of the ultimate ground of the validity of axioms, all this had become something which in the whole controversy concerning the foundations of mathematics at the beginning of the century – and later – was programmatically given up. And these were exactly the points which according to Husserl – who just at that time defended in the *Logische Untersuchungen* the existence of one truth ultimately justified – were to be brought to clarity through insight. Thus for Husserl the rigor of mathematics served perhaps as an ideal to be striven after in philosophy, but not as the model of a method to be applied in philosophy. After all, he was also a disciple of Franz Brentano, who believed in evidence, and thought about realizing it in "descriptive psychology" as the fundamental science in philosophy, an evidence to be achieved in the "inner consciousness." Thus it is not surprising that, instead of the "mathematical" method (and of the skeptical-conventionalistic theory of mathematical cognition followed at that time on the margin of mathematics), Husserl posited the method of phenomenological analysis. To be sure, he had handled this method for years, but – even after the *Logische Untersuchungen* – he was not quite clear about its meaning and about what it possibly could accomplish. After all, in the first edition of this work phenomenology was equated by him with "descriptive psychology." Before he worked out its idea, what was important for the whole later shaping of phenomenology as a "transcendental" philosophy, was the emphasis he put, in his search for a "rigorous science" in philosophy, on the gaining of a "firm ground", i.e., a ground which is no longer shaky. Epistemologically speaking, this means a cognition no longer susceptible to doubt, thus "absolute" in its validity. To discover a cognition of this sort, and to invent at the same time a method that would guarantee its handling – this was the ideal and also the goal, which resulted from the postulate of philosophy as a rigorous science. The optimum of cognition at the disposal of Husserl on the ground of the *Logische Untersuchungen,* was ideation. With this, however, one could only – as once maliciously said by somebody – engage in "a hunt after the *species,*" and thus create a basis for a priori sciences, but what about philosophy in general? Could it be obtained in this way?

As we know, in the first decade after the *Logische Untersuchungen* Husserl in an essential way enlarged the scope of his problems, specifically on the one hand towards epistemological problems until then not cultivated, primarily the analysis of outer perception, on the other hand towards questions referring to the objective real world or its forms – time and space. And here it necessarily became apparent that outer perception cannot provide indubitable cognition, and why this is so. The question thus suggested itself, whether it might not be possible to achieve this in "inner" perception – more strictly speaking – in immanent perception. For Husserl as a disciple of Brentano this was a thought that easily suggested itself because, according to Brentano, the so-called "inner consciousness' was supposed to provide indubitable knowledge. It remained only to analyze more accurately the so-called "immanent perception" in its essential structure, and to show the ground of its indubitability, and this Husserl found in the "unmediated unity between the perceived experience [*Erlebnis*] and the immanent perceiving." This was the decisive step to "ultimate subjectivity." By adding to this the "intuition of essences" [*"Wesenserschauung"*] it was already easy to arrive at the idea of "pure" transcendental phenomenology, which was not only supposed to find the ultimate source of all knowledge about the world, by going back to the ultimate subjectivity of pure consciousness, but was also intended – in a shift of the problems for which there are several historical precedents – to derive the real world itself from the original sources of pure consciousness. In this way the purely methodological ideal of philosophy as a rigorous science prepared the transition to the basically metaphysical decision in favor of transcendental idealism. At the same time a methodological way of considering the objects given in outer perception was shown, consisting not in a direct attitude towards these objects, but in a peculiar roundabout way through an analysis of the corresponding state of consciousness. At that time, when Husserl outlined this way in his lectures after 1910 as well as in the *Ideen I,* it evoked a protest of his Göttingen disciples who were used to the slogan "Back to the things."

ad 2. It so happened, that just in the years in which Husserl decisively entered the field of the theory of knowledge in his research, a sharp attack on this theory was led by Leonard Nelson. As is well known, Nelson tried to prove the impossibility of epistemology by pointing out in it an alleged necessity of a petitio principii. As far as I know, Husserl never expressed an opinion about Nelson's theory. But he could not overlook the existence of his book. Be it as it may, Husserl, in his lectures and seminars, and also in his writings, from the *Ideen I* up to the *Krisis,* often pointed out the "absurdity" [*"Windersinn"*]committed when, for the purpose of solving an epistemological problem – let us say regarding the validity of outer perception – one appeals to the existence and the characteristics of the objects given in the mode of cognition which is in question. This happens, e.g., when in the events which have their starting point in physical things, one sees the so-called "physical stimuli" which affect our senses and force a determinate course of outer sensuous perception, when one thus seeks to prove in this physicophysiological way the so-called "subjectivity" of the secondary qualities. The phenomenological reduction – a new discovery of Husserl in the *Ideen I* – eliminates just this danger of committing such an absurdity, no matter how much Husserl emphasizes that the "reduction" is not meant to serve this purpose. But once this reduction is accomplished, one already finds oneself on the ground of pure transcendental consciousness, from which not only every epistemological reflection – and especially the so-called "questions of right" of reason – have to be carried out, but also every existence different from consciousness has to be derived, insofar as it may be accepted at all. Thus the priority of pure consciousness with regard to validity and cognition must be demanded in order to make any theory of knowledge possible, and this priority is shown by Husserl through a consideration of immanent perception and of the ultimately constituting conscious experiences [*der letzt konstituierenden Bewusstseinserlebnisse*]. But at the same time this priority begins to have metaphysical import, by transforming itself into an existential priority of pure consciousness, and transforming all transcendent being – especially of the real world – into being derivative from and dependent on pure consciousness. The danger of a petitio principii in epistemology is eliminated through the phenomenological reduction, but, instead, one gets in Husserl an interpretation of the meaning of the existence [*eine Ausdeutung des Seinssinnes*] of the world which, in spite of all the differences, always emphasized by Husserl, from, e.g., Berkeley's view, yet comes dangerously close to this view as well as, e.g., to neo-Kantian idealism.

ad 3. If one is not inclined to accept these consequences of the phenomenological reduction, then one must ask whether Husserl has not, nevertheless, discovered in his positive analyses states of affairs which lead to his transcendental-idealistic decision. After all he analyzed outer experience so carefully, that he achieved results of which no empiricist or positivistic philosophy can boast. At the same time he investigated so all-sidedly the various general structures of consciousness, and explored so deeply its relation to the real, that one might expect from him a decision with regard to the problem of idealism and realism.

And one can indeed find in Husserl's writings, beginning with the *Ideen I,* a series of assertions which may be regarded as arguments *for* idealism,[5] and which were used by Husserl for this purpose. I will here indicate some of them :

a) The real objects (things, events,. . .) given in outer sensuous perception, are "transcendent" in relation to that perception, i.e., they form no "real part" of the perceptual experiences. [*des Wahrnehmungserlebnisse*]. Therefore the given thing could cease to be there, or not be there at all, while the perceptual experience would continue in its existence.[6] On the other hand, an immanently perceived experience [*Erlebnis*] forms an "unmediated unity"[7] with the immanent perception which is based on this experience and is directed towards it, and consequently the being of this experience cannot be nullified. At the same time Husserl decisively rejects a causal connection between the thing which is perceived and which, according to the psychophysiological theory, sends out physical stimuli to our senses and evokes the perceptual experience, and that experience, maintaining that pure consciousness forms a sphere of being altogether closed in itself, which cannot remain in a casual connection with any other being.

b) Every outer sensuous perception is essentially [*ihrem Wesen nach*] partial and inadequate in relation to the thing given in it. It is an one-sided partial apprehension of the thing, where the "other" sides and the interior are only "meant with" what is apprehended [*nur mitvermeint sind*], and can be brought to direct givenness only in the further course of the perception, i.e., in other perceptions of the same thing. These later perceptions of the thing may confirm the results of the accomplished perception with regard to the aspects of the thing which are merely meant [*vermeinten*], but this is not necessary at all; because what was merely "meant with" could be meant falsely. It is always possible for the thing to be different in this respect, and the prospect of further experience cannot, on principle, exclude such a possibility. This would be excluded only if there would be an inner necessary connection between the determinations of the (material) thing. But the things given in sense perception do not seem to possess such an inner closed structure. The thing could also change in the time between two acts of perceiving. Therefore it is not possible to prove with certainty by an appeal to other later perceptions of the same thing, that it really had the qualities on the "other" side as they were perceived from "this" side. Thus the cognition of things by means of outer perception is not only one-sided and inadequate, but also essentially [*wesensmässig*] infected with an element of uncertainty. That which is apprehended, also in a multiplicity of sense perceptions, is always at least to a great extent something merely "supposed" [*"Vermeintes"*], and never an all-sidedly, evidently given being in itself.

c) Contrary to what the English empiricists used to maintain, in outer perception there is not only given *how* the thing is qualified, but also *what* it is. Of course, this does not hold for cases in which the perception is so devoid of sharpness and is so unclear, that for this very reason one is not clear as to what it is that is given. But these are exceptional or transitional cases, which have to be converted into a clear givenness of the object in its whatness [*in seinem Was*]. Between the whatness of a thing and its qualitative determination [*Wiebestimmheit*] there obtain strict relations of dependence. The whatness of a thing being given, its qualitative determination [*Wiebeschaffensein*] is not freely variable, but always only within certain determinable limits. As soon as these limits are transgressed, this leads to the destruction of the whatness of the thing and thus of the thing itself, it "explodes." in Husserl's terminology. Phenomenologically speaking : depending on the qualitative determinations of the given which enter into a certain perception, this given presents itself in the perception under the aspect of a determinate *what* [*eines bestimmten* Was] (of a nature, in my terminology). However, if the limit of permissible variability is transgressed in the course of further perceptions, the what of the given leaps over into another what. The thing earlier given in a sense disappears, and another thing appears in its place, or it turns out that the earlier perceptions brought the thing to appearance under a false aspect of a what which does not belong to it at all, and that "in reality" it is quite another thing. But is it certain that the newly given what is really the proper what of the given thing? Cannot an analogous situation always, on principle, repeat itself? Thus it always remains questionable on principle whether the "until now" given really exists at all, and whether in its place something entirely different exists, or nothing at all. It begins to become dubious in general whether there is at all an "in itself" of the what and of the qualitative determinations of the given thing. The thing is perhaps merely a what-phenomenon or a phenomenon of qualitative determinations, which is synthetically formed by the prevailing course of the perceptions, which is relative to the given multiplicity of perceptions, a mere correlate of this multiplicity of perceptions and of other determining acts, not a being "for itself" or "in itself" that is found in a receptive way. Thus one arrives again very close to the gates of transcendental idealism.

d) To every objectivity there belongs a multiplicity, at least in principle infinite, of possible perceptions, in which the objectivity is itself given, and indeed *"in persona."* This multiplicity can never, as a matter of principle, be *realiter* exhausted. But only after really exhausting it would one gain a conclusive and secure determination of the essence, the whatness and the character, and finally also of the existence, of that which is given in the perceptions (e.g., of a thing). Every unconditional attribution (absolutely categorical assertion) of a certain whatness and of a qualitative determination to the perceptually given is basically unjustified, is in reality a transgression of the validity of finite experience. But only if it were justified to be beyond finite experience, could one speak of the "being in itself" of the real which, after all, is originally accessible only in the way of perception. If one remains within the framework of finite experience, and strictly keeps within the limits of its validity, then it is permissible to speak of a thing only as of a correlate of the multiplicity of perceptions. To remain thus within the limits of validity is made imperative by the demand of a strict adaptation to what the given manner of cognition can accomplish. Therefore one is permitted to regard the things given in outer perception merely as intentional correlates, as "phenomena."

e) If one considers that the meaning of the objective what and of the qualitative determination, which is gained in the perceptual multiplicity of the moment, is a synthetic result of the multiplicity of perceptions belonging to each other through which one has already passed, and that, according to the above, it is not permitted to speak of a "being in itself" of that which was perceived, it is easy – as Husserl actually did – to regard this result as a "formation" [*"Gebilde"*] of this multiplicity and to say that it is "constituted," "instituted" (as Husserl said) in the course of experience. Thus considered, the perceived things (more strictly, the thing-meanings) become not only the intentional correlates of the perceptual multiplicities, but also their formations, "products." In this way one already gets the main thesis of transcendental idealism, according to which realities are nothing but "constituted", noematic meaning-unities of a special kind, which result in their being and nature [*Sein und Sosein*] from experiential multiplicities of a certain kind, without which they would not be possible at all. They exist *only for* the pure transcendental ego, which runs through such perceptual multiplicities. The "being" of the perceived is not an "in itself," but only a "for somebody", for an experienced ego. "If we cross out the pure consciousness, we cross out the world" – reads then the thesis of transcendental idealism, often repeated by Husserl in his lectures.

f) Still other assertions can be found in Husserl, which – in his opinion – lead to the same result. This is especially the case in the "constitutive reflection." Husserl has undoubtedly discovered here an extraordinarily rich area of problems, and has shown the existence of states of affairs which other investigators have only surmised.[8] Here only the general schema of the constitutive investigation can be sketched, to the extent to which this has significance for the idealistic decision.

In an unfolding multiplicity of perceptions of "the same" thing, many "constitutional layers" have to be distinguished. After the phenomenological reduction has been performed, it is always *"noemata"* or – as Husserl also says – "noematic meanings" which are in a sense super – or subordinated to each other. To each noematic meaning which belongs to an "upper" layer, belongs a multiplicity, ordered in a determinate way, of the respective "lower," in the constitutional sense "deeper," or more original, noematic meaning unities. This coordination means : if a multiplicity of "deeper" noematic meanings, which are merely experienced [*erlebten*] by the ego, but not meant as objects, is run through, there "constitutes" itself in this multiplicity the corresponding "higher" noematic meaning, which confronts the ego as something given. For example : to every thing (or thing-noema) perceptually given belongs a multiplicity of "views" (Husserl at first also said "aspects", later, from the time of the *Ideen I*, "perspective shadings" [*Abschattungen*] in which the thing is brought to appearance, is itself directly given. And, in particular, to every objective determination of the perceived corresponds an ordered, firmly regulated multiplicity of "perspective shadings," which are experienced by the percipient. The squareness of the top of a table appears in a multiplicity of experienced perspectival foreshortenings, e.g., rhombi, trapezes, etc., of different magnitudes and different distinctness and sharpness, depending on the viewpoint of the percipient, and on his more or less active manner of experiencing. These are all "views" of one and the same thing-shape, no matter how much they differ from one another in their content. What is more remarkable and yet cannot be denied is, that their sensuous content is different from the sensuous content of the corresponding, constitutively higher objective determination – is thus different from that square shape – to be sure in different degrees, depending on the manner of the perspectival foreshortening, and that yet, through the multiplicity of such experienced views running its course, one and the same square comes to givenness. This schema of coordination repeats itself : to every experienced view of something thinglike there belongs again a multiplicity of noematic meaning-unities of a still deeper layer, in which one and the same identical view of something constitutes itself. Thus, e.g., the sharpness of the outlines of the objective shape may change, the so-called "attentional transformations" may take place, which obviously is of importance for the particular "deeper" concrete noematic meanings, while the noematic meaning of a certain perspectival foreshortening (of a certain view) remains quite unchanged. At the lowest lie the multiplicities of original flowing "sense data." in the time-constituting consciousness which are only passively experienced [*erlebt*] by the ego. They lie in the ultimately original layer, which forms the ground for the constituting of experienced [*erlebten*], "fulfilled" time. These flowing sense data undergo, so to speak, during their "being sensed," a remarkable transformation from the potentiality of protention, when they announced themselves to the experiencing ego, through the actuality of the original impression, to the echo of retention, before they entirely disappear from the field of experience. The manner of actuality and presentation undergoes a continuous transformation, but there is retained within the framework of a living presence the *quale* of a sense datum (it is the same colored patch, with approximately the same original spread of the patch), so that here again one must contrast the continuity of the original sense data which change in our experience, with the sense datum which in a certain phase retains its constancy. The same holds everywhere : in spite of all the permissible changeability of the noematic meanings of the respective lower constitutive layer, a certain strictly defined limit of variability must not be transgressed, because in case of such a transgression the corresponding noematic meaning of the respective higher layer "explodes," i.e., cannot be experienced, meant, or given as identically the same. Husserl here poses the same question again and again : What must be contained, as noematic meanings, in the multiplicity of the respective deeper constitutional layer, so that the corresponding higher, determinate noematic meaning-unity can constitute itself? In many different spheres of meaning Husserl sought to answer this question, namely through showing the existence of quite concrete states of affairs. But, according to Husserl, there is here more than a mere problem of coordination of the noematic meanings of different constitutional layers. In the course of time, Husserl more and more interprets the "constitution" of the higher noematic meaning during the experiencing of the deeper constitutive multiplicity, in the sense of a "creating," a "founding" of this higher meaning. Of course, this "creating" – also according to Husserl – is not arbitrary, not left to the free choice of the pure ego. There is here a rule of strict, a priori laws, which are to be discovered in a constitutive transcendental reflection that has an eidetic attitude. To the fulfillment of this task Husserl devoted decades of his life – certainly with great success. In this he did not ignore the transformation in the *noeses* on which depends the manner of constituting the noematic meanings of various degrees. The principle adopted by Husserl – that to every transformation in the *noeses* (in the intentional acts) there belong strictly regulated transformations in the corresponding *noemata* –seems to find here its clearest confirmation. The *noemata* are, so to speak, very "sensitive" to the meaning-content of the corresponding *noeses,* but also to the manner in which these *noeses* are carried out by the ego. There also are in Husserl numerous analyses in which these different manners of carrying out the acts are distinguished and clarified. Especially to be considered here are the so-called "thetic" acts, in the carrying out of which something is "posited," thus, e.g., simply recognized in its being, or anchored as existentially "real" in a certain sphere of being. To these acts, which are very different from each other in respect of their "thetic" character, there corresponds in the content of the accompanying noematic meaning a specific character of being, e.g., of being real, or of being possible, or of being ideal, and so forth. This character also has its origin in consciousness in the mode of carrying out the acts. It is likewise a phenomenon, whose meaning-content – if one may say so – is determined by the mode of carrying out the corresponding act. Thus one may speak of "existence" only, when one questions the pure constituting consciousness. Thus it is not permitted – still according to Husserl – to attach freely, so to speak, a meaning to *the noemata,* or to establish their existence, without paying attention to the meaning-content of the corresponding acts, and to the mode of carrying them out. Not only the possible fact of the being of something, but also its essential [*wessensmässiger*] meaning is "constituted" in pure consciousness.

If one takes into consideration that the perceived "real" (given or meant as "real") things are treated in the constitutive reflection as nothing but elements of a special layer of constituted noematic meanings, and if one admits that everything found in this layer has its ultimate origin in the respective lower constitutive layers and in the performed *noeses* on which it is essentially [*wesensmässig*] dependent, then the exploration of these states of affairs acquires the character of a revealing of the ultimate genesis of phenomenally given things,[9] and this amounts to an adoption of the main thesis of transcendental idealism which affirms that the being of the experientially given real world depends on the being and the course of the constituting pure consciousness, without which it would not exist at all. And secondly, it would then even be absurd to ask at all about the "being in itself of the world," because this offends against the genuine meaning of constitution, which forms the ultimate ground of all questioning. The whole phenomenally given real world (and especially the so-called *"Lebenswelt"* of the *Krisis*) is regarded as nothing but a certain layer in the process of the transcendental constitution, a phase of "objectification," whose other, further or higher phase of objectification

– let us say of the physically determined material world – is supposed to follow.

Whether the whole process of constitution is traced back to the ultimate subjectivity of a single pure ego ("my" ego in each case), or to an open multiplicity of pure egos which are in mutual agreement, whether the positive analysis really pushes on to the most secret depths of the passive, original time-constituting consciousness, or whether something still more original could be found there, – all this already is – as Kant might say – rather a matter of the "elegance" of the inquiry than of a necessary decision. Because basically there is nothing essential to be further changed, once it is admitted that every "higher" noematic meaning-unity is "instituted" by the pure ego, when certain deeper *noemata* are experienced and certain *noeses* carried out, and when at the same time one is not allowed to distinguish between object-meaning and object, between the phenomenon of something that has being, or the phenomenon of that being, on the one hand, and that something or its being themselves, on the other hand. And actually everything is already decided when it is not permitted to enter a path on which, after a thorough investigation of all the constitutive problems under the condition of transcendental reduction, one would again set aside this reduction, and then directly ask about the existence, and especially about the mode of existence, of the real world, with the view of obtaining an existential solution. In other words, everything is also decided, when it is not permitted to put an end to the whole of phenomenology and to strive for a metaphysical solution. But precisely this is definitely forbidden by Husserl. He believes that the constitutive reflection provides the ultimate decisive investigation of the real world and its existence.

ad 4. There are, as I indicated at the beginning, formal-ontological grounds for the transcendental idealistic decision with regard to the real world and its existence. There are, at the top of the whole argumentation, two basic assertions, of which only the first may be regarded as formal-ontological, while the second is apparently material-ontological. With these two assertions Husserl puts himself in opposition to the usual view in the natural sciences, and especially in psychophysiology. According to this view consciousness and the physical real world are connected with each other in a double way, namely a) consciousness is conditioned by events in the brain, and b) the perceptual experiences [*Wahrnehmungserlebnisse*], and especially the so-called "sensations" are causally conditioned by "physical stimuli." And in connection with this it is maintained that consciousness is an element of the real world, and forms with it one whole. As against this Husserl establishes that : 1. Physical things are "transcendent" in relation to the perceptual experiences in which they are given, i.e., the things and the experiences form two wholes which are external to each other, and 2. There is an essential difference between physical things and experiences : the former are spatial, the latter entirely nonspatial. And now Husserl appeals to a formal-ontological principle which affirms that the wholeness of an individual object is possible only when there is an essential kinship between the elements (parts or attributes) of that object. The essential difference between consciousness and physical things, established by Husserl, excludes the possibility that consciousness could be an element of the real physical world, or form one whole with it. This essential difference also excludes the possibility, according to Husserl, that the experiences (especially the perceptual experiences) could be causally conditioned by any physical thing or event – be it a "physical stimulus" or an event in the brain. In this situation one could either arrive at a radical dualism, a radical theory of two worlds – the world of physical things and events, and the world of consciousness entirely separated and isolated from it – or, if one would yet want to preserve the unity of the really existing – the world – the only way out would be somehow to bring closer the physical world, in its essence, to the pure consciousness. And this is precisely the transcendental-idealistic decision : the real world of physical things and events forms in its entirety the *cogitata* of the *cogitationes*. The *cogitata* – the purely intentional objects – are, as the intentional correlates of the acts of consciousness, inseparably connected with these acts. In this way all doubt concerning the existence of this physical world is eliminated. This is the condition of saving the wholeness of all individual being of the material world and of pure consciousness.

It remains only to emphasize that this is not a speculation engaged in by an outsider on the margin of Husserl's reflections, but that it is found *expressis verbis* in *Ideen I* (cf. §§ 38-46). Crucial in this argumentation is the formal-ontological principle

that the essential kinship of all the elements of an object is the *conditio sine qua non* of its wholeness, and, on the other hand, the adherence to the view of the radical essential difference between *res extensa* and *res cogitans.*
§ ad 5. Is it probable that Husserl, furthermore, arrived at his idealistic decision from certain religious-philosophical or religious convictions? It is true, he never wrote anything in the field of philosophy of religion, and at first sight one may maintain that he never dealt with a problem of this kind.[10] There are, however, certain statements in *Ideen I,* which may be instructive in this respect.
§ In § 51, in connection with establishing the "teleology" in the framework of pure consciousness, Husserl says:[11] "If the element of fact [*Faktizität*] in the given order of the course of consciousness, in its differentiation into individuals and the *teleology* immanent in them, gives legitimate occasion for the question about the ground of precisely this order, the *teleological* principle which might rationally be presupposed here, *cannot,* for essential reasons, be accepted as a transcendence in the sense of world-transcendence . . ." " . . .since a world-God is evidently impossible, and since, on the other hand, the immanence in the sense of Being as experience [*Erlebnis*] (which would be no less absurd), there must be in the absolute stream of consciousness and its infinities other ways of manifesting the transcendent than the constituting of thing-like realities as unities of appearances that agree with each other; and finally there must be intuitive manifestations to which theoretic thought could adjust itself, and by following it in a reasonable spirit we might come to understand the single rule of the assumed theological principle." *(l.c.,* p. 96f). And further : *(l.c.,* § 58, p. 110f) "As the *rationality* embodied in the fact is not such as is required by the essence, there is in all this a wonderful teleology." ". . . the transition to pure consciousness through the method of transcendental reduction leads necessarily to the question about the ground of what now presents itself as the intuitable actuality [*Faktizität*] of the corresponding constituting consciousness." "What concerns us here, after merely touching on the different groupings of such rational grounds for the existence of a "divine" Being beyond the world, is that this Being should not only transcend the world, but obviously also the "absolute" consciousness. It would thus be

an *"Absolute" in a totally different sense from the Absolute of Consciousness* as, on the other hand, it would be a *transcendent in a totally different sense* from the transcendent in the sense of the world."

These statements mainly draw attention to the fact that apparently not all events within the pure (factual) consciousness can be clarified in a pure a priori manner according to laws, and that, seen from this viewpoint, there is in the actual course of consciousness, and especially the constitution of the real world, an element [*Faktor*] of contingency, the explanation of which leads Husserl to the problem of God. Instead of looking for this element of contingency, which is independent of the essential structure of pure consciousness, in the autonomy of the real world, in turning away from the world, a transcendental factor is pointed to, which "transcends" also the absolute being of consciousness, while at the same time regulating it "teleologically." This lends to the whole problem of the constitution of the real world – and in general to the whole inquiry into essences in the field of pure consciousness – a character essentially different from what is expected when one carries out this constitutional reflection in the basic conviction that the problems of constitution lead to the ultimate source of all subjectivity, and that this source is really found in the pure time-constituting consciousness, in which the primordial ground of all objectivity is revealed. For, after ascertaining the "teleology," this seems to be unattainable at a crucial point, so that subsequently the whole investigation would have to be diverted to another track. According to the basic methodological principle which Husserl pronounces after introducing the transcendental reduction, the transcendental constitution of God would have to be exhibited before redirecting the investigation, because only from the essence of the constitutively shown divinity could the course of the constitution of the real world be ultimately clarified, and thus the ultimately justified existential meaning [*Seinssinn*] of this world shown. But, as is well known, this exhibition is missing in Husserl (at least in the works so far published). The transcendence of God was excluded – in accordance with the program of transcendental phenomenology in the *Ideen I* – although it is supposed to be of an essentially different kind from the transcendence of worldly things. And an attempt was made to carry out a constitutional reflection of the real world that would be independent of the problem of God. Nevertheless, the conjecture suggests itself that the religious-philosophical background, which was not developed, may not have been without influence on the positive analyses and on the general conception of the mode of being of the world. The emphasis on a double teleology must be considered here especially – if one may say so – on the teleology in the concrete course of the constitution of the real world in pure consicousness, and the teleology "which is to be found in the empirical world itself, e.g., the actual development of the series of organisms up to man, the growth of culture in its treasures in the development of man, etc. . . " *(l.c.,* p. 11). These two teleologies are traced back to the same ground of the divine Being which intervenes in both regions of being (the world and pure absolute consciousness) at least in this way that it, so to speak, on the one hand regulates the development of the world towards ever higher value systems, and on the other hand regulates the constitution of the world towards an increasingly more encompassing rationality. The two somehow run parallel to each other. Reminiscences of Leibniz are called forth – at least in the writer – and the question arises whether this interference of the divine Being operates, so to speak, directly in both spheres, or whether it makes itself only mediately felt and discernible in the world, through a teleology somehow effected by the divine Being in the actual course of the constitution of the world in pure consciousness. And the question also arises whether the intentional existential dependence [*Seinsabhängigkeit*] of the world on pure consciousness does not turn out to be just a derivative manifestation of this existential dependence on the divine Being (at least in the regulation of the course of constitution of pure consciousness).

Of course, these are only conjectures that could be confirmed or rejected only if in Husserl's manuscripts studies were found which deal with cognate topics. But one thing seems to be certain : if the theological background, which did not receive a thematic treatment, did not exist, then the fact, established by Husserl himself, of a "wonderful" teleology which is not such "as the essence requires,"[12] would necessarily induce him either to look for the ground of this teleology in a factor of world-reality itself, a factor in its existence independent of consciousness, or, alternatively, to submit to a revision the whole problem of the constitution of the real, in order to bring to light that factor which is responsible for the appearance of teleology.

The question also suggests itself whether certain statements of Husserl about the pure consciousness do not also have a religious-philosophical or even a religious background. Thus, e.g., Husserl's well-known statement that the stream of experience [*Erlebnisstrom*] of the pure consciousness is infinite in a double direction – towards the past and towards the future – seems to be related to the problem of immortality. This is a statement which makes every phenomenologist ponder what the phenomenological states of affairs are that warranted its affirmation by Husserl. Also the emphasis – in the *Ideen I* – on the existential relativity of the real world and the existential absoluteness of pure consciousness, and thus on the existential independence of consciousness in relation to the world, must suggest the thought that this solution may have a connection with the question concerning the freedom of the will and the responsibility of man, or of the pure ego, which is in the sense of the constitutive reflection exalted above nature. Certain Kantian trains of thought from the border-area of his theoretical and his practical philosophy begin to stir in the reader, and to cause him to ask the question whether these problems did not after all play a certain role for Husserl in his seemingly purely theoretical reflections concerning the essence of transcendental consciousness and its relation to reality.

I would not like to go here beyond these conjectures and questions. What was said is meant only to draw the attention of the reader to these connections between the problems, and to lead him to a possible further inquiry in this direction. Some of Husserl's pronouncements in private conversations with me show that he actually had great interest in certain religious and religious-philosophical questions, and that these questions yet remained on the margin of his philosophy. This strengthens me in the belief that I am not going astray in the conjectures expressed above.

ad 6. In regard, finally, to the last group of possible motives that could exert a certain influence on Husserl's idealistic decision, I would only like to point to them as to a possible source, which would have to be more closely investigated. At least in the years in which I had personal relations with Husserl, it struck me more than once that Husserl had a profoundly negative attitude towards the real world, and especially – if one may say so – to the human world, or – as Husserl himself later said – to the *Lebenswelt.* Husserl seemed to be convinced of the badness of this world, a badness which at various times greatly oppressed him and whose burden he felt, and for which he at the same time felt that he shared responsibility to some extent – although he also despised it in his inner being. It seemed as if he was looking to philosophy for salvation and a liberation from his burden. The question thus arises whether the existential devaluation [*Seinsentwertung*] of reality, which finds its expression in transcendental idealism, did not help him to diminish the burdensome pressure of reality, or to gain a detachment from it, and to find an oasis of independence and inner autonomy in a philosophy which, as a matter of principle, begins with the transcendental reduction. Husserl never seemed to be really gay, really happy, and never seemed to have in his innermost being confidence in himself, in the world, in fate. He struggled, as he often said, struggled hard and always on the brink of despair, he struggled for a firm ground of an unshakeable truth that could give him rest and salvation. Only the illuminating evidence of the *Wesensschau* on the one hand, and of the immanence of the beholding or revealing of the ultimate grounds of subjectivity, on the other hand, could give him this firm ground. Transcendental idealism was in a sense only the way to bring some light into the darkness of the prephilosophical intercourse with reality, and this light was to be gained with the help of the constitutive reflection and of revealing the processes of the "founding" of the world in the primordial ground of subjectivity.

Now, in order to confirm these conjectures about the purely human, personal motives of the theoretical decisions in Husserl's philosophy, it would be necessary to investigate thoroughly, from this viewpoint, Husserl's extensive literary remains, and also to gain much more ample information about Husserl's life and personality. For the present one must content oneself with conjectures. Moreover, I would not ascribe too great an importance to the purely personal motives which could have an influence on the concrete shape of the Husserlian phenomenology. If they actually played a role, this would only bear witness to the fact that even such a responsible philosopher, who untiringly strove after the highest clarity and certainty of his assertions, could nevertheless not be quite independent of his soul. However, what I am here mainly concerned with, is to indicate that Husserl's idealistic decision probably had as its background various groups of motives and arguments, which must be, one after another, submitted to a critical consideration and control. The failure to distinguish these various types of motives may have the result that the whole problem of idealism in Husserl will be treated too summarily, and that as a consequence one will not be in a position to judge with sufficient criticism the particular problems, interwoven with each other, and the solutions to them. With this I must content myself here. Elsewhere[13] I have attempted to consider more closely the particular motives and arguments, and to examine them critically.

NOTES

1. Translated by Professor Shia Moser of the State University of New York at Buffalo.
2. This "realism" is, by the way, not so much "Platonic" as an interpretation of certain "Platonists," but with this I cannot deal here.
3. Cf. E. Husserl, *Briefe an Roman Ingarden,* 1968, p. 7.
4. In connection with this it is maintained by some of the students of the Husserl-archives that this section originated at an earlier time (thus before the *Ideen I*) and was simply inserted into the *Ideen,* without the suitable changes being made.
5. In my lecture at the Second Phenomenological Colloquium in Krefeld, in 1956, I sought to determine the exact meaning of this "idealism" on the basis of Husserlian texts, to be secure against the opinion of several participants of that colloquium, who denied the existence of this idealism in Husserl.
6. In another passage of the *Ideen* Husserl admits that in such a case the perceptual experience would be essentially changed, but yet would have to cease to exist.
7. Cf. *l.c.* p. 68.
8. One can, e.g., compare Husserl's results of the constitutive reflection with the "transcendental deduction" of the pure concepts of reason in the first edition of the *Critique of Pure Reason* or, let us say, with Mach's *Analysis of Sensations,* in order to convince oneself of the enormous progress reached in Husserl's work. Also in comparison with B. Russell's *Our Knowledge of the External World,* or R. Carnap's *Der Logische Aufban der Welt or finally with the explanations of Austin's Sense and Sensibilia,* Husserl is far superior in his reflections.
9. Strictly speaking, one should only say "of the thing," but Husserl in a sense forgets the necessity of this correction in the phrasing, or, to put it

more accurately, rejects the necessity of such a manner of speaking, as if he identified the "thing" with the noematic "thing-meaning."

10. Husserl told me once that as a Privatdozent in Halle he lectured on the proofs for the existence of God. In answer to my question, how this happened, he said : "Of course, this is Brentano, don't you know? " It would be interesting to inquire whether there are in the Louvain archives notes to those lectures. One should also search in the lecture-lists of the Halle University, to find out when and for how long a period Husserl gave these lectures.

11. I have used here Gibson's translation of the *Ideen,* with some modifications.

12. This phrase of Husserl's quoted here refers in the next of the *Ideen I* not to teleology but to the "rationality" in the construction and the constitution of the world. But the talk of teleology in this context shows that it is also something not required by the essence.

13. Cf. my book *Z badań nad filosofią wspótezesną* (in Polish, 1963) *Inquiries into Contemporary Philosophy.* The text given here differs in various details from the text published in Polish several years ago.

THE ILLUSION OF PRESUPPOSITIONLESSNESS

Shia Moser, State University of New York at Buffalo

IT CANNOT be denied that our beliefs in everyday life, as well as various scientific and philosophical doctrines, are often based on unwarranted assumptions. No building is more solid than its foundation, and it is therefore easy to understand why, in their quest for certainty, philosophers should look for some fundamental beliefs that would be absolutely unassailable, and would thus provide a basis on which the edifice of human knowledge could be securely erected.

Plato, e.g., maintains that even in mathematics our knowledge cannot be perfect, because the mathematician reasons deductively from unquestioned assumptions. Perfect knowledge, *episteme,* is attainable only through the method of Dialectic, where the assumptions are examined, and an attempt is made to trace them back to the Form of the Good, which is the foundation of knowledge as well as of being.[1]

In modern times the quest for certainty found its greatest champion in Descartes. His doubts cannot be resolved, he says, unless he is "happy enough to discover one thing. . . which is certain and indubitable."[2] This he finds in the *Cogito ergo sum,* and the doubts he had are replaced by certainty, both with regard to the propositions of mathematics and the existence of external bodies.

If this method were successful, the ideal of freedom from presuppositions would be resolved. Knowledge of great significance could be obtained, all founded on something entirely indubitable, without any presuppositions, i.e., *without taking anything for granted* outside of that absolutely certain insight. However, without underestimating Descartes' great ingenuity, one must regard his attempt to find an unshakable foundation for the sciences in the certainty of his own existence as a failure. This failure seems to me mainly due to what may be called the illusion of presuppositionlessness.

In Descartes' scheme the proofs for the existence of God play a decisive role in the overcoming of skepticism. Nevertheless, a criticism of Descartes' rational theology, even if it should prove destructive of the validity of his chain of arguments, would still leave open the question whether it might not be possible to use, in some other way, the *Cogito* as a foundation for our knowledge. It might be argued that Descartes fails only because he pursues several aims, logically independent of each other, such as a defense of theism against atheists and of rationalism against empiricists. Let us then, without touching upon the other problems raised by Descartes, confine ourselves to a brief discussion of the *Cogito* as a foundation for human knowledge.

The question of the fundamental importance of the *Cogito* may be divided into two parts : a) Is all doubt concerning the *Cogito* itself inconceivable? and b) Does the certainty of the *Cogito* lead to other certainties?

The *Cogito* has been the subject of various interpretations of which perhaps none is entirely adequate, as Descartes seems to be not quite consistent as to the meaning of that proposition. [E.g., although he denies that the *"ergo sum"* expresses an inference, he seems at other times to conceive it as an inference.] One thing, however, is evident. When Descartes introduces the *Cogito,* he attributes to it an indubitability not possessed, in his opinion, even by the simplest proposition of mathematics. In other words, he thinks that with regard to these propositions, error, though extremely unlikely, is yet conceivable, whereas the *Cogito* is beyond all possibility of doubt.

But what is the claim that can legitimately be made in the *Cogito,* if this proposition is to be unassailable by any doubt ? Error is certainly conceivable with regard to our memory. Thus the meaning of the "I" in "I think" and in "I am" has to be such that we can be absolutely certain of the existence of the self even if our memory should be regarded as unreliable. It is not the existence of the mind as a *substance* that is at issue here. Even those who reject the concept of substance and reduce the mind to a bundle of perceptions, do not deny that *in some sense* there is personal identity. They would not maintain, e.g., that everyone who thinks of himself as being the same person he was yesterday, is as mistaken about himself as the mental patient whose body seems to be inhabited, as it were, by more than one person. But if we consider the possibility of our memory being completely deceptive, it becomes doubtful whether we endure at all, even in the sense that there are certain relationships peculiar to those mental phenomena which we call *ours.*

From this it would follow that even if one grants that mental phenomena have an I-quality, and that the use of "I" is legitimate to designate something that may be of extremely short duration, our claim is susceptible to doubt if it extends beyond the fact of *momentary awareness.*

A radical doubt concerning memory would also weaken our confidence in the validity of deductive reasonings, as Descartes himself clearly saw. However, Descartes seems to regard memory as essential only for the *passage* from premises to conclusions, and not for the *understanding* of the propositions involved. It is true, the kind of understanding he does not question at all is that of simple concepts. Thus he says : "And when I stated that the proposition *I think, therefore I am* is the first and most certain which presents itself to those who philosophize in orderly fashion, I did not for all that deny that we must first of all know *what is knowledge, what is existence,* and what is certainty, and that *in order to think we must be,* and such like; but because these are notions of the simplest kind, which of themselves give us no knowledge of anything that exists, I did not think them worthy of being put on record." [3] But what Descartes considers to be a simple notion may be a very complex one, and if we have no confidence at all in our memory, we cannot be absolutely certain what the concepts are that we seem to have clearly before our mind.

Can the *Cogito* become a basis for other knowledge? Can it help us to eliminate radical doubts that may be raised about the commonly accepted beliefs in everyday life and in the sciences? First, it should be pointed out that Descartes seems to be inconsistent in passing from the *Cogito* to other propositions, regardless of whether we limit its certainty to the fact of momentary awareness or not. On the basis of the *Cogito,* Descartes says, "it seems to me that already I can establish as a general rule that all things which I perceive very clearly and very distinctly are true."[4] However, Descartes did not previously deny that the simple propositions of mathematics are "clear and apparent," and yet he found it possible to doubt them, while thinking it impossible to doubt the truth of the *Cogito*. He thus assumed that the latter has a *special status*. In other words, he implied that clearness and distinctness are no sufficient guarantee of truth, and it is only the *peculiar* clearness and distinctness of the *Cogito* that provides such a guarantee. It is true, Descartes now maintains that he could not have doubted the propositions of mathematics for any other reason than the possibility of a God causing him to err. While justifying his radical doubt, however, he said that even if he should grant "that all that is here said of God is a fable; nevertheless in whatever way they suppose that I have arrived at the state of being that I have reached. . . the greater will be the probability of my being so imperfect as to deceive myself ever, as is the Author to whom they assign my origin the less powerful."[5] Descartes has also, in several places, given another reason for doubting the truth of mathematical propositions, namely the fact that others deceive themselves in such matters.[6]

Descartes' inconsistency cannot be regarded as accidental. It rather illustrates the predicament of all those who espouse what may be called a maximal conception of certainty, and yet hope to obtain some significant knowledge. Once we insist on identifying certainty with *inconceivability of error,* we entrap ourselves in a skepticism from which there is no way out.

Let us return to the question of the validity of memory. As we have seen, a radical doubt regarding memory reduces the certainty of the *Cogito* to the indubitability of our momentary awareness. Such a doubt would also challenge the validity of all scientific laws, and, what is even worse, all the beliefs of our everday life would become doubtful.

The objection might be raised that a philosophical doctrine cannot be refuted merely by arguing that it questions the generally accepted beliefs of common sense. Would we not, one might argue, by doing this make short shrift of most philosophers, from Parmenides to Bertrand Russell? It may be difficult to give a satisfactory answer to this objection, but it seems to me that there are two quite different ways of challenging the world-view of common sense. It may be only necessary to reinterpret the beliefs of common sense in order to satisfy the philosophical critic who calls them into question, or the challenge may be such that, *if taken seriously,* it is destructive of our very sanity. A few illustrations will perhaps elucidate this point. Both Parmenides and Plato deny that the world of sense perception is "really real," but it is not, on that account, put in the same category as what is in ordinary life regarded as an illusion. Thus we find in the *Republic* an *analogy* between the inhabitants of the Cave who mistake the shadows for reality, and all those who believe the world of appearances to be real in the full sense of the word. But Plato does not contend at all that the experience of a man who would, in the literal sense, be dragged out of such a cave, would be *as illusory* as the experience of his fellow prisoners who remained inside.

Similar considerations apply to Berkeleyan or Kantian idealism. The world may be made of "mental stuff," space and time may be subjective, and the things in themselves quite different from the phenomena. But all this does not deprive the world of common sense of the kind of reality, a belief in which is a *necessary condition* for sanity. This does not mean that no appeal to experience is relevant to an evaluation of such philosophical doctrines. On the contrary, subjective idealism, e.g., is made very implausible by our ordinary as well as our scientific knowledge. Nevertheless, our experience could be reinterpreted so as to accord with such a doctrine, without thereby shattering the basis of rational discourse. On the other hand, should we seriously consider the possibility that our memory may be *extremely deceptive,* we would be left without any valid reason for believing anything which transcends the solipsism of the moment.

That the widely accepted views in ordinary life and in the sciences would lose their foundation without the support of memory, is quite obvious. But could we trust our memory without presupposing the truth of various beliefs concerning the external world? Although, *logically speaking,* this might not be as absurd as completely distrusting one's memory and yet believing in things not immediately perceived, it would seem that once we seriously question the existence of various external facts commonly regarded as known, we also lose the basis for the confidence in our memory.

A prisoner kept in solitary confinement for many years, and unable to communicate with anybody at all, may not have any doubts about his past. But he is convinced that, should he be released, he could see the places he knew before his confinement, that his old acquaintances would remember him, and, by and large, also the experiences they shared together. The situation would be entirely different should a man, e.g., have a strong suspicion that he is the victim of a general conspiracy of deception, and thus feel unable to confirm, by the behavior of others, what he seems to remember.

To vary the example, let us assume that a person whose contacts are confined to a small group of people, really *is* the victim of such a conspiracy. E.g., prisoner Ralph Smith who has been in an Oklahoma institution for years, is now addressed by everybody as John Miller, is told that he arrived yesterday, and that the prison is located in New Jersey. Should this hoax go on for a long time, could Ralph Smith continue trusting his memory as he did before? Is he not rather likely to lose his sanity altogether?

The main reason why the necessity of various presuppositions for any rational discourse has not been sufficiently appreciated in epistemology, is perhaps the circumstance that it is almost impossible to define the class of those beliefs which have to be presupposed. The anecdotes about mental patients who carry on an intelligent discussion until they excuse themselves because being emperors, they have to attend to the affairs of their empire, are a partial illustration of the difficulty. But, apart from the fact that a person may be rational in one area, and completely irrational in another, there is, of course, no general rule as to which beliefs an individual or a society must accept in order to be considered sane. It is, e.g., certainly not the same for a member of a Nilotic tribe, or for the tribe as a whole, to doubt the existence of New York City, as it would be for a Buffalonian to entertain such a doubt.

However, for our purposes it is not necessary to give a precise description of the presuppositions under consideration. It would suffice, with regard to the existence of external facts, for instance, to list, by *way of illustration,* a number of beliefs which could not be *all rejected* without removing the ground from under any rational investigation. As Marvin Farber says in his criticism of subjectivism : "It is wise for anyone using the subjective procedure to remind himself at regular intervals that he is still a part of the natural world."[7] One cannot reach the world when beginning with nothing in fact, because *"ex nihilo nihil fit.* From pure consciousness only pure consciousness follows, not natural reality."[8]

The essential role of presuppositions is not confined to the pursuit of knowledge in the realm of facts. Presuppositions are not less necessary for rational discourse in the field of values, especially in ethics. To the problem of the importance of ethical presuppositions, and to a few related problems, the following pages will be devoted.

Beginners in the field of moral philosophy, e.g., students who take an introductory ethics course, often seem to think that one should approach ethical problems with a mind that is, as it were, a moral tabula rasa, and that it is the task of the philosophical moralist to "prove ethics" to them. It seems to me that, in general, we tend to underestimate in ethics the role played by presuppositions, which are taken in the main from common sense morality and which the philosopher expects his audience to share with him. By and large, philosophical moralists seem to address themselves, consciously or unconsciously, only to those who agree with them on some basic moral tenets. It is, to a great extent, more a matter of converting the faithful to a more articulate and perhaps modified faith, than of converting the infidels.

A few examples from the history of philosophy may serve as an illustration. When Plato expounds his moral doctrines in opposition to those of some of the sophists, only one of the interlocutors of Socrates, Thrasymachus, comes very close to moral nihilism. Although it would be an exaggeration to say that Thrasymachus does not share any values at all with Socrates (in that case the discussion could not have gotten off the ground), he has morally, little in common with him, and therefore, from the viewpoint of convincing Thrasymachus, the discussion is futile.

Plato pictures other encounters of Socrates with sophists as marked by less moral disagreement than the confrontation with Thrasymachus. In the *Protagoras,* Socrates' opponent, Protagoras, does not, I believe, advocate ethical relativism, or any other doctrine that would be seriously opposed to the way of life preached by Socrates. On the contrary, the protagonists seem to be in agreement with each other and with the ethics professed by their society with regard to basic moral values.

An interesting example of common moral assumptions

among representatives of doctrines more seriously opposed to each other, we find in the *Gorgias*. Plato seems here almost to emphasize the point that Socrates can win an argument only because the opponent is not willing to reject the Socratic premises. This is why Gorgias changes his position, and admits that it is the duty of the rhetorician to teach his pupil justice, if the latter does not possess it yet when studying rhetoric. Polus rejects this admission, but he himself loses in the debate when he concedes that doing injustice, though not the greater evil, is *the greater disgrace* than suffering injustice. The more radical Callicles, in his turn, rejects this concession of Polus and preaches the theory that by nature, might is right. However, he too is forced by Socrates to make various admissions and thus to weaken his position. When the view is imputed to him that he identifies superiority with physical strength, he becomes indignant and insists that he means by superior "wise politicians who understand the administration of the state, and who are. . . also valiant and able to carry out their designs."[9] It also turns out that Callicles is not insensitive to Socrates' moral passion, although the unworldly way of life preached here by Socrates cannot be quite acceptable to him. "Somehow or other," he says, "your words, Socrates, always appear to me to be good words, and yet, like the rest of the world, I am not quite convinced by them."[10]

Aristotle adheres more closely than Plato to common sense ethics and, perhaps with the exception of his identification of the highest happiness with contemplation, it was easier for "the rest of the world" to be convinced by his words than by those of Plato. According to Aristotle, the basic moral principle which defines what the good for man is, can be taught only to those in whose consciousness this principle is already contained in an implicit form. "Hence the necessity that he should have been well trained in habits, who is to study, with any tolerable chance of profit, the principle of nobleness and justice and moral philosophy generally."[11]

There are various elements in Kant's ethics which seem to create a gap between it and the ordinary moral consciousness. E.g., it does not sound plausible to most of us that an action done from inclination, even though in accordance with duty, has no real moral value. And it would probably be hard to find a person who would think it wrong to lie to a man in order to frustrate his plan to commit a murder. Neither is the formalism of Kant's ethics in accordance with common sense.

Three points should be made, however. With regard to the normative part of Kant's ethics, it differs only in a few details from the morality of common sense. Kant certainly does not recommend a way of life that would be essentially out of harmony with our ordinary moral consciousness. Secondly, Kant emphasizes that his doctrines are implicit in ordinary human reason. The concept of a will estimable in itself, he says, "is already present in a sound natural understanding and requires not so much to be taught as merely to be clarified. . . "[12] He also maintains that in its practical judgments ordinary reason always has the Categorical Imperative before its eyes, i.e., the principle that "I ought never to act except in such a way *that I can also will that my maxim should become a universal law* . . . "[13]

The third point I wish to make is the following. It has often been remarked that there would be no inconsistency in willing an *evil* universal law. Thus, according to Mill, Kant fails to show, on the basis of the Categorical Imperative, "that there would be any contradiction, any logical. . . impossibility, in the adoption by all rational beings of the most outrageously immoral rules of conduct."[14] I would venture the hypothesis that Kant would not have overlooked this possibility, had he not, perhaps unconsciously, *excluded villains* from the audience to which he addresses himself. On the other hand, if this hypothesis is wrong, and there are really no presuppositions behind the Categorical Imperative, Kant's ethics is seriously deficient.

That the arguments of a moral philosopher may seem to lack cogency because some basic assumptions he shares with common sense morality are not made explicit, can be seen, I believe, in Mill's proof for the Principle of Utility. The attacks on this proof are, to a great extent, based on a misconception of what Mill is trying to do. His aim is not to prove the validity of the doctrine of Utilitarianism to people who are morally indifferent. On the contrary, he has in mind those who share with him, and with society in general, at least those moral beliefs which are commonly accepted and regarded as important. Mill thinks that genuine reflection on what *is essential* in these beliefs, combined with the factual knowledge that men desire happiness and only happiness, should be sufficient for the acceptance of the Principle of Utility.

To throw some further light on the problem of presuppositions, let us compare their role in our pursuit of factual knowledge with their role in ethics. The most important analogy consists in their being *indispensable* in both areas. The problem of their indispensability for the sciences of fact has already been dealt with. It would seem that certain presuppositions are *equally necessary* for any rational discussion of values, especially of moral values, although a precise description of these presuppositions is no more feasible than of the factual ones. Whether we choose as example a relatively concrete political issue, like that of socialism vs. free enterprise or pacifism vs. militarism, or a more abstract doctrine like Kant's theory of good will or Utilitarianism, it is obvious that a discussion of these matters with a person who does not see anything intrinsically evil in killing or torture, in the destruction of society and in similar activities, would lack a rational basis.

It may be observed, that the presuppositions involved may be related in different ways to the doctrines which presuppose them. They may be the major premise in a practical syllogism in which the given doctrine is a conclusion. E.g., a pacifist may argue in this manner that wars are evil. In the case of more general ethical doctrines, the presuppositions are *not sufficient* to prove them, even with the help of the relevant factual judgments. Utilitarianism, for instance, does not follow from the various moral beliefs of common sense, but what is essential in these beliefs should rather follow from *it.* However, in such cases also, there is *no good reason* for a person to accept the doctrine if presuppositions like those mentioned above are rejected by him.

Presuppositions of this sort may be related in still another way to a moral view. Such a view may not be unreasonable in itself, and yet it may be *incongruous* to accept it while rejecting the presuppositions. It may, e.g., be plausibly argued that society has a moral obligation to encourage the fine arts, but it would be incongruous to hold this view while insisting that we have no obligation whatsoever to prevent mass starvation.

It is not contended here that presuppositions in ethics function in precisely the same way as in epistemology. I will here makely draw attention to one difference, related to the role of the ordinary moral consciousness in philosophical ethics.

Although both epistemological-factual and ethical presuppositions are indispensable in their respective areas, they may play different roles in the process of further inquiry. They are much less subject to *reinterpretation* in ethics than they are in epistemology and metaphysics. The epistemologist may, e.g., adopt a representational theory of perception, and thus deny that we ever immediately perceive physical objects. Or he may arrive at the conclusion that a great deal of what we believe to be found in reality is actually a contribution of our mind. What we experience is thus given a new interpretation, without the beliefs that served as a point of departure losing their function as the basis of the whole inquiry. On the other hand, a philosophical ethics that would essentially change the beliefs implicit in our moral consciousness would degenerate into a mere intellectual exercise, without plausibility or practical significance. In other words, normative ethics as a branch of philosophy should be conceived as being essentially a refined version of common sense morality.

This conception of ethics is admittedly vague, as it would be very difficult to give a precise description of the morality of common sense, even if we confined ourselves to our culture, and perhaps not less difficult to explain with precision in what the process of refinement consists. We will, however, attempt to clarify a few points.

First, to adhere in one's doctrines to common sense morality does not mean to close the door to innovation and improvement in our moral thinking. There is an important difference between the moral beliefs actually accepted by the common man, and those he would adopt as a result of a better knowledge of the relevant facts and of reflection. Factual knowledge enters as an ingredient of moral reasoning in various simple and complicated ways. The simplest function of a factual proposition in such a reasoning is to serve as the minor premiss of a practical syllogism. Facts may also be appealed to in order to justify the fundamental principle of a system, as it happens in Mill, or *a philosopher may cite alleged facts about human nature,* to explain the meaning, as it were, of the whole moral enterprise. As the role of factual knowledge in moral reasoning is so manifold, an improvement of this knowledge cannot be neatly separated from moral reflection.

However, the latter, as conceived here, is mainly concerned with *eliminating inconsistencies* in our moral thinking. One may, e.g., without learning new facts about man, realize that it is inconsistent to condemn individual acts of murder, and accept mass killings in a war for which there is no compelling reason.

The question arises why eliminating inconsistencies in one's moral thinking should lead to a higher level of ethics. Could one not, to take the above example, become consistent by approving of all murder instead of disapproving of war? One could of course. However, it is wrong to assume that *for our ordinary moral consciousness* all judgments which have the appearance of ultimacy are equally compelling. E.g., even extreme chauvinists are often anxious to justify their killing of the enemy in a war, but they would not find it necessary to justify the maxim that one ought not to kill outside of the war.

If we accept the view that there is a great difference between the "mixed bag" of the ordinary moral consciousness and those moral principles which can be elicited from that consciousness as a result of improved factual knowledge and of reflection, it would seem that, *logically,* common sense morality could provide us with a basis for an enlightened ethics of a very high order. Of course, this leaves open the question to which extent people can, *in fact,* be led to an acceptance of a higher ethics by freeing them from false factual judgments and from inconsistencies. Also, to accept, in theory, an ethical doctrine is by no means a guarantee that one is going to live by it. Nevertheless, it is of great practical significance not to underestimate the potentialities of our ordinary moral consciousness, especially since nothing else is available to us as a foundation for something better. The appreciation of the essential role played by presuppositions in ethics may also have a more specific practical result. If we become more acutely aware of the fact that a great deal must be presupposed in order to make an ethical discussion possible, we may also pay more attention to the values the great majority of us shares, and this includes our opponents. It is true, *exclusive* emphasis on shared values might blunt the needed criticism of social evils. But we should beware of ignoring the elements of human unity. And among such elements, the ordinary moral consicousness is, *potentially,* one of the most important.

NOTES

1. *Republic,* Jowett translation, 508-11.
2. *Philosophical Works of Descartes,* Haldane and Ross translation, Vol. I, p. 149.
3. *Op. cit.,* p. 222.
4. *Op. cit.,* p. 158.
5. *Op. cit.,* p. 147.
6. *Ibid.,* also op. cit., pp. 101 and 220.
7. *Phenomenology and Existence,* Harper & Row, New york, p. 10.
8. *Op. cit.,* p. 12.
9. *Gorgias,* Jowette translation, p. 491.
10. *Ibid.,* p. 513.
11. *Nichomachean Ethics,* Translated by D.P. Chase. 1095 b. Cf. also the comment on this passage by H.H. Joachim, *Aristotle : The Nichomachean Ethics,* Oxford, Clarendon Press, 1951.
12. *Groundwork of the Metaphysic of Morals,* Platon's translation, p. 64.
13. *Op. cit.,* p. 70.
14. John Stuart Mill, *Utilitarianism,* Chapter I.

HUSSERL : FROM NATURALISM TO THE PHENOMENOLOGICAL ENCYCLOPEDIA [1]

Enzo Paci, University of Milan

IN A RECENT BOOK,[2] Reck points out that Marvin Farber, the philosopher who introduced Husserl's thought in the United States, ends up with a criticism of phenomenology and existentialism in his polemical work, *Naturalism and Subjectivism.*[3] Farber's work exhibits a decisive naturalistic and materialistic orientation that invites us to study the relation of Husserl's philosophy with dialectic materialism. The reader of Reck's book finds himself a little uneasy in front of such synthetic judgments. In reality, Farber's overall contribution is much broader than his own work and the publication of *Philosophy and Phenomenological Research* suggest. Certainly one can say that Farber is a naturalist and a materialist, but all this is not at all obvious. In general, American philosophy is realistic and pragmatic. Matter is out there and there are no doubts about it. As for the subjects, they too are material and the problem of the relation between the subject and the object, or between the subjects themselves, is given as resolved. American philosophy thus finds itself in a strange situation where the solutions are actually already given. Farber's materialism suggests a comparison with Marx's dialectic materialism : this is something that we consider not only useful, but also necessary. Yet both phenomenology and naturalism on one hand, and dialectical materialism, on the other, are vague and not too well defined. Being, Reality, Matter, Existence are only words : what do they really mean? The possible perspectives require a phenomenological analysis that cannot be undertaken without rigorously applying the *epoché*. We are speaking of an application, and therefore of a praxis. It is only after the *epoché* that one can speak of material or of spiritual entities, or even of other worlds or structures (or, in Husserl's words, of other "ontologies").

Furthermore, in the context of what has been said so far, it is possible to distinguish a plurality of problems. Whether we speak of matter or of spirit, it has to be pointed out that it is more a matter of perspectives than of ontological realities. On the other hand, if philosophy aims or should aim at an ideal of purity, it does not follow that it can forget about human reality – the reality that Husserl, in the *Krisis,* presents as precategorical and realizable through operations aiming toward a *telos.* Obviously, philosophy is always historically conditioned, in the same way that it is always limited by passivity, i.e., from those syntheses that Husserl considered to be passive. Nevertheless, the limit, passivity, the economic structure, and materialism, are all elements that tie philosophical thought to man and do not prevent philosophy from moving according to a *telos* which, after all, is the *telos* of history. This *telos* can be defined as a society in which no man is exploited and in which all the subjects are, in the intersubjective conjunction, active subjects reciprocally aware and actually recognized. Philosophy is motivated and has purpose : in this sense not only is it historical, but it gives us the sense and the *telos* of our life and of the world's history. I do not know whether Farber would accept this. Yet, there is a passage at the end of one of his most recent books where he seems clearly to agree with the humanity of philosophy as we have indicated. The ideal philosopher has to have a human foundation and a motivation. In our language, it must be founded in the *Lebenswelt* as explicated in the *Krisis,* and on the motivation mentioned in *Ideen II.* Farber writes : "The entire procedure must have its motivation, since the ideal of unmotivated inquiry is as impossible as it is indefensible. But the motivation should be made explicit so that it can be appraised. It may be purely rational; or it may be concerned with the human welfare. A complete philosophy must be both 'pure' and 'applied'. This does not mean transcending the existing social conditions or the human realm, which in fact could never be done and should not be done if one wishes to serve and (hopefully) to change the world. In important respects, philosophy will always be historically conditioned."[4]

Philosophy is always motivated and always has a direction and, therefore, a *telos.* It is always both theory and praxis, and never a purely categorial discourse because it lives in the human realm. Its duty never is neutral and never should be neutral, in as much as it reveals the transformation of the world and society toward an end which, in our language, appears as a society of subjects where technology is at the service of man and not vice versa.

Obviously, phenomenology is always a transformation of the world. The *epoché,* in the Greek sense of *askesis,* transforms man. The phenomenologist does not write for the sake of writing. He writes in order to transform himself. He is suspicious of the written word which lacks the speed of living thought. From this viewpoint, Husserl thinks like the pharaoh of Plato's *Phaedo* who is happy with Theut's discovery of written characters (Theut is the god depicted with a baboon's head, almost to remind that characters are but monkeylike imitations of life). Yet, the pharaoh points out that, if men come to rely too much on writing they might come to believe that what counts is the written word and not the truth living in it. This is why we find such an intense vitality in Husserl's manuscripts. It seems to me that those manuscripts will be considered in the future as real philosophical and human masterpieces even more than his other great works.

The previous discussion can help us understand how ambiguous are words such as "Being," "Reality," "Matter," "Existence," and so on. When I was younger I was sure that the phenomenological introduction, both in the Husserlian and Hegelian senses, can allow us to talk of different ontological levels.[5] As already indicated, Husserl himself speaks of ontology as the problem of being in such a way that it can be considered fundamental. Nevertheless, Husserl's philosophy *is not actually an ontology.* Husserl's problem is not the relation of being to time, but the problem of things themselves in relation to their meaning and their truth. In other words, it deals with truth to the extent that it can live in concrete history.[6] We must not forget that phenomenology is the "return to the things themselves." If we want to call the things themselves with the name "ontology," we can do it, but we should not think that there is a concrete "thing in itself" which is being. This problem is not limited to phenomenology. We can only point out that when we deal with abstract terms such as ontology and being as if they were concrete, we fall in what Whitehead called "misplaced concreteness." Quine gives us a wonderful criticism, (which is also an elegant account) of Carnap's work. Quine understands very well that positivism must come out of its own formalism in order to penetrate into reality (and maybe transform it). Yet, Quine calls "ontology" that reality that positivism lacks. He knows of all the difficulties of this word and he is certainly aware that we cannot speak about what there is or about abstract being by making it concrete. Here Quine's work has two aspects. In attacking positivist dogma he reveals himself as a disciple of Whitehead and as such he realizes that even a realist ontology is inadequate. In so doing he unwittingly opens one of the possible paths that can lead to a new phenomenology.

Let us now state the purpose of our essay. We feel that the phenomenological problem is not the ontological one, but the problem of the foundation of an encyclopedia of all the sciences. This encyclopedia must be such as not to reiterate the dualism between the theoretical and the practical. If we avoid this dualism, which turns out to be a dialectic between the abstract and the concrete, we are faced with an horizon of a science founded on the precategorical operations of the *Lebenswelt.* These operations give rise to what we could refer to as various scientific domains. For technical reasons these domains, e.g., the mathematical, the physical, the biological, the psychological, and the social, can be studied separately. Yet, we should never forget that the separation is abstract. The awareness that the abstraction can never be considered concrete, forces us to see in the things *themselves* an indivisible *plenum.* Things are in human operations and human operations in things. Therefore, the various domains must be always brought back to a conception of man whereby man himself is both nature and spirit. Husserl often runs into difficulties with this problem. For example, in relation to such a problem, the position he took in *Ideen II* is extremely instructive. At any rate, in *Ideen I* (section 55) Husserl had already pointed out that the return to the subject is not at all a subjective idealism. In the first section of *Ideen II,* Husserl deals with material constitution. However, by "material things" he means the physical thing, i.e., the thing as conceived by physics. The physical thing is part of nature in general : it enters into the dialectic between spontaneity and the passivity and, on the other hand, to the extent that it is a physical thing, it has to have some particular characteristics.

These characteristics are substance and causality or, in Husserl's sense, circumstantiality. In other words, they are the cause and the substance which *give reality* to the things themselves. Materiality becomes substantiality, but this is possible only if it is founded on man's aesthetic body *(Leib).* Nature in general goes beyond the physical thing which can constitute a domain of its own, and arrives at a psychophysical conditioning, to animal nature, and to the animate subject. As Husserl points out, the real thing can be constituted only by means of sensible localizations of the body understood as *Glied des Kausalzusammenhanges.*[7] All of this indicates that the subject is corporeal, and that the concept of nature in general cannot be constituted separately from the sensible subjectivity of the organic human body (or, at any rate, of animate organic bodies). Usually this line of reasoning leads to the question whether a nature without life, without a body *(Leib),* without animate animal or human reality is at all possible. It is important to point out that *it is always ourselves,* and *only ourselves,* who can speak of a lifeless world. This does not mean that the lifeless world does not exist. Admitting that the moon does not support life, it remains the case that this statement can only be made by a living being. In the last manuscripts of the group D, Husserl speaks of possible spaceships which, even if far from the earth, carry with them the terrestrial corporeal environment. Hence, the inhabited worlds, along with our material world, are nothing more than the physiconatural bodies of human and nonhuman subjects. There is a living nature, but there is also an unconscious nature. Living nature is our body *(Leib),* and unconscious nature is our physical body, which is ours even though we do not know it. It is difficult to grasp Husserl's position which demands an analysis of temporality much deeper than Heidegger's. In a sense, nonliving worlds are the physical bodies of living beings which either have vanished or have not yet been born. Therefore, they are either the purely material premises of life, or the cadavers of a life already lived which have left only the *geologic sedimentation* which might be recognized by a new possible humanity. Today, no one among us is surprised if, when we find certain fossils, we reach the conclusion that there was life in that given geologic era. All of the astronomical and geological world is nothing more than the physical body of a subjective life which could have existed, could exist, or that will exist. This can be understood through the analysis of temporal modalities. We always begin from the present. If we say that once this human present did not exist, it does not mean that, in a rigorous empirical and materialistic sense, we are the ones who consider a past in which we did not live. The beginning from the present after the *epoché* is not a possibility : we can challenge anyone to do otherwise and no one will be able to do it. The present, which today is the actual historical life of the planet Earth, is necessarily the living body and the physical body of humanity. Husserl spoke of a crisis. It can be pointed out that it is not accidental that, at the very moment when man can destroy himself and his environment (his own *Umwelt),* man becomes aware of the impossibility of clearly distinguishing not only a material from a spiritual domain, a physical from an historical intersubjective ontology, but he also realizes that the present is the meeting point among the geological, the astronomical, and the social. It is a decisive moment in which man must decide whether to move toward an intersubjective socialist society, or if he wants to destroy himself by making the present into a geological past, as the past of other eras is for us. In this way the past is constituted as a historicophysical past. This is not the only way to constitute the past. The physical body of the whole universe is the physical body of animated subjects and of human societies sleeping and not yet awake. *It is in the actual present that man wakes up.* But this ideal of awakening becomes for Husserl the attaining of human responsibility for social and physical animated reality of the whole universe.

When Husserl wrote *Ideen II,* he found himself in an ambiguous situation. He is overcome by the German problem of the division between *Geisteswissenschaften* and *Naturwissenschaften.* But if one looks very closely, he does not accept the German cultural situation of the time. Thus he both agrees and disagrees with Dilthey. Later, in 1925-26, Dilthey's importance seems to grow through Heidegger's influence. This influence however, threatens to transform phenomenology into psychology in the sense of a psychology of being, i.e., a psychology in need of an ontology. Probably it is the assertion of an ontology of this kind that offends Husserl. He goes so far as to declare that existentialism is nothing but his philosophy without its foundation. The reaction of ontologism leads him to the conclusion that actually there is no distinction between the

Geisteswissenschaften and the *Naturwissenschaften.* At any rate, the founding operations are based on the *Lebenswelt.* Galileo's mistake is to have misunderstood the scientific abstractions for reality. His great discovery is the return to the human operating in the natural environment in a search that *even though it is infinite,* gradually attains *finite degrees* of perfection. This theme of the relation between the finite and the infinite must be remembered in reading the *Krisis.* Cantor's influence is not extraneous to this, in the same way that Husserl's influence is not extraneous to the further elaboration of Cantor's set theory. In the *Krisis* the problem is to prevent a break between a psychological and a naturalistic ontology. Closed domains no longer exist as regional ontologies of various sciences : there are only different ways whereby man operates in nature, and nature in man. Through a rigorous analysis that we cannot undertake at this point, we arrive at the conclusion that, in that given past, i.e., the past of a nature in which man and life are yet to appear, there was a future which later became life and humanity. Also warranted is the observation that a future is present in us which operates independently of our knowing it. Yet, this future posits itself as the *eidos* of a free human society of free cosmology and psychology and, in a dialectical and nonidolatrous sense, of a free function of religions.

The conclusion we have reached should be seriously considered. If it is elaborated we reach a strange result : Husserl reintroduces psychology, cosmology, and theology, understood in Wolff's and partly in Crusius' sense. However, the three ontologies reappear by renouncing their status as ontologies and by renouncing any dogmatization and every idolatrous interpretation of matter, nature, psyche, and truth which can have a sense only to the extent that it is not a divine truth transformed into being. This conclusion is extremely paradoxical. If we want to talk about God, in the sense of Kant's transcendental ideal, this God is not a being but truth. As truth it lives in the world but is never reducible to the mundane. A comparative analysis with Ricardo and Marx in this respect might be even more interesting. Ricardo is the first to realize that if there is a value, this value is not real. Marx follows him when he points out that in the exchange relations the concrete man is forgotten and the exchange price considered as concrete reality is substituted for it. This transformation of value into misplaced concreteness corresponds perfectly to the fetishization of commodities and to the degradation of the divine (which is not a real being) to the worship of the golden calf. Thus, we witness a strange genesis of capitalism. Of course, Husserl, even though he hints about it in his manuscripts, did not see this. In *Ideen II* he speaks with aloofness about the ontological superiority of mind *(Geist)* in relation to nature. In the second part of *Ideen II* the soul is constituted through the body *(Leib),* i.e., it seems as if only spirit can give rise to something animated. Yet the soul is also corporality and animality. What Husserl actually carries out is the demonstration of the inseparability of nature and spirit as indicated by the very *Seele.* Then, what happens to the spirit? Not only does it become society, but it is consciously identified with the whole personality, i.e., with the *Ich-Mensch.*[8] In this fashion the physicalist thing that Husserl sought is no longer separate, he himself admits : "Physics requires both psychology and physiology."[9] At any rate, these sciences are not objective in the sense in which objectivity is the fetishization of the subject and of the subject's activities, including these activities of work which produce commodities. Even though Husserl does not say it, the criticism of objectivism in the *Krisis* is very similar to the Marxian criticism of alienation. More specifically, nature is not reducible to the objective world already constituted, but is always *natura naturans* in process.

Living nature, like living labor, are the functioning of unreal truth in the mundane. Truth or, if we prefer, the vectorial and temporal direction aware of wanting to realize a social future (a transformation of man, history and the world) is not a simple application of the second principle of thermodynamics as the inevitability of entropy. In fact, mankind in its entirety lives precisely in the inevitability of the principle, in the consumption and degeneration of matter and of energy. Man in his presence, and the society of men in their presence, are real and whole if we do not divide the sciences and if we use all of the sciences as an encyclopedic unity which allows us to meet the requirements of consumption and the inevitability of wear and of degradation. But what do we really mean by this? We mean that the present is never fully present. *Something is always missing.* It must function in order to obtain what it lacks. From a consumed system it must find recourse to another system. If it were a matter of an astronomical system it would die if it did not obtain the needed energy from another astronomical system. This also entails a paradoxical conclusion. Since the universe continues existing, this means that a system in the process of exhaustion can always turn to another system, and so on. This tòo is substantially a cosmological translation of Cantor's set theory. However, this is not all. We shall try to elaborate this as simply as possible. What characterizes man and constitutes his human essence is not presence alone, but the consumption of presence and the continuous *need of new presentations and new values.* But if man can be so characterized in his essence he is not different from nature which also always needs to pass from one system to another. The world of needs that we are discussing is also Marx's and Ricardo's economic world.

Here we begin to discover that the passage from phenomenology to materialism is actually the discovery of the structure of needs and, therefore, of the economic structure common to both man and nature. This is why spirit and nature are identified in the soul *(Seele)* or, better, in animation. But essentially, what is animation? It is the answer to the increase of entropy that presents itself as *work* and that can continue as human and natural history only to the extent that, even in its finite parts the universe is infinite. Husserl scholars must notice how often Husserl mentions the "infinite." What is more difficult to notice, however, is that this infinite is essential to the finite : in fact, it is internal to it.

Husserl was not aware of it, but the life-world, the *Lebenswelt,* not only is a set of constitutive operations, but it is also a structure of needs which require work so that ultimately all of the sciences are founded on work. Psychology and economy are interpenetrated in the same way that in the soul *(Seele)* both mind *(Geist)* and nature meet.

These indications are not in Husserl, yet it is hazardous to say that they are not there. The great fecundity of Husserlian thought consists in the fact that such thought does not allow anyone merely to repeat or to remain content with Husserl's analyses. For example, let us look at *"Beilage IX"* of *Ideen II.* Husserl concludes that there is "a passage from exteriority to interiority since, as I am, I am not only nature but also I am able to take a position."[10] What does this mean? The deciding I is *the I which works in nature in order to transform both the world and society.* As a matter of fact, here the mind *(Geist)* becomes praxis. Ultimately, the passage to spirit is a passage to the will and to the action which *decides rationally* with labor and with a plan not only conditioned, but also always renewed by all the sciences, by all the technologies, and by all human behavior. The I of decisions is *motivated praxis.* To use Kantian language, motivation is a working transcendental scheme both practical and ethical. It ought to be pointed out that motivated and oriented praxis was already present in the idea of intentionality. It follows that the will requires an *ethos* not yet realized and is always to be realized anew. In other words, the will requires the unreal and its essence (what Kant called the transcendental ideal, or God) as ethical concreteness or as ethical *plenum.* Realization presupposes the nonrealization of the present situation (what Sartre leaves to the imagination). More precisely, nonrealization leads to values, to work, to the *telos* of history, to the meaning of the world as a precise *vision,* in the present, of a process which is actually infinite.

Husserl talks of regional ontologies in *Ideen III* contraposed to *Formale und Transzendentale Logik* and gives the impression that he believes that every science has its own closed region. It is as if a complete axiomatization were possible for every science. And it amounts to a denial of Gödel's proof. Actually, with the exception of some passing hints that we have mentioned, Husserl ultimately realizes that what allows a theoretical and practical encyclopedia, i.e., a philosophy in progress and a transformation of the world, is not the scientific ontologies. What really counts is the foundation of all the sciences in the *Lebenswelt.* Thus the problem of psychology becomes crucial : in fact, it is the problem that Husserl leaves open in the *Krisis.* Something was missing : the economic. Following Husserl, we must arrive at the *foundation of the economic,* i.e., to the precategorial sense of economy itself, in the same way that we must arrive at the foundation of language in human operations and in the *Sprachleib* of humanity.[11]

The move from phenomenology to materialism raises all the problems which we have suggested, and more. For example, it requires that Marx's *Capital* should not be considered as a *scientific book* of political economy. Rather, it should be seen as the *critique of political economy which considers itself scientific,* but which is not founded. Furthermore, it requires that we should not believe that man exists because it is possible to formalize language, but that language is always alive and realistic thus always an operation and an effort – precisely because there is man's presence which testifies to his *telos* and to a need which always has to be satisfied anew because, ultimately, it is identical with value and with the meaning of life.

NOTES

1. Translated by Paul Piccone of the State University of New York at Buffalo.
2. Andrew J. Reck, *The American Philosophers : An Exploration of Thought since World War II,* Baton Rouge : Louisiana State University Press, 1968, p. 160.
3. Marvin Farber, *Naturalism and Subjectivism,* Springfield, Illinois : Charles C. Thomas Publishing Company, 1959.
4. Cf. Marvin Farber, *Phenomenology and Existence. Toward a Philosophy within Nature,* New York : Harper and Row, 1967, p. 240.
5. Cf. my *Principi di una Filosofia dell'Essere* (Mondena, 1939) – a work that Farber mentions in his *The Aims of Phenomenology,* Evanston : Harper & Row, 1966, p. 157.
6. It is not by chance that I have entitled my book *Tempo e Verità nella Fenomenologia di Husserl,* (Bari : Laterza Editore, 1961).
7. Cf. Edmund Husserl, *Ideen II,* (The Hague : Martinus Nijhoff, 1952), p. 159.
8. Ibid., p. 38.
9. Ibid.
10. Ibid., p. 32.
11. This topic is fully dealt with in my work, *Funzione delle Scienze e significato dell'Uomo* (Milano: Il Saggiatore, 1963), pp. 219 ff.

TEMPORAL DESCRIPTION OF HUMAN LIFE[1]

Augusto Pescador, University of Concepción

FEW TIMES in my life have I managed to establish such a broad and affectionate philosophic communication as that which I experienced with Marvin Farber. In the month of October 1966 I reached Buffalo, after travelling several thousand kilometers, with the sole purpose of knowing the thinker to whom we are now doing homage. I shall never forget our talks over a cup of chocolate after his classes. We achieved an exchange of ideas and a mutual comprehension which was possible only thanks to the great simplicity of Marvin Farber, a simplicity which made it possible for me to be able to transmit my ideas despite my very poor knowledge of English. The unity of our philosophic preoccupations was greater than the diversity of our means of expression.

In this study I propose to combine two themes which have been a permanent concern of Marvin Farber : that of phenomenological description and that of human existence. I shall attempt a phenomenological description of man.

One defect of the phenomenological method is that it reduces itself to the description of essences, which as such are timeless and therefore cannot be applied to events, whose description must be that of their temporal development. Human life is constituted by a body of events which have an irreversible temporal direction. The only description of man which is possible is like that of thermodynamic processes, which cannot be two-directional as can simple mechanical ones, since it is impossible to invert the course of the process.

"Man is a continuous succession of successive discontinuities," a Spanish professor once said. To describe the successive discontinuities which constitute the life of each man is a task alien to philosophy, since it is not possible to describe the life of each and every man. But it *is* possible to attempt a description of those fundamental moments through which every human life must pass.

That knowledge must begin with a description of the phenomenon we seek to know is not only a demand of the phenomenological method for philosophic knowledge, but also of the scientific method for physical knowledge.

Because of this, I believe that when speaking philosophically of man one should begin by describing him. But this description cannot be spatial in the manner, for example, of a geographic description, for then we would only be describing the human body which is, precisely, the least human aspect of man. Nor can it be an eidetic description of the phenomenological type, since man is not an essence we can abstract from his formation and temporal transformation. The only possible description of man is a temporal description in the historic manner. This is what we propose to attempt here.

Human life begins with conception. Life is originated by two human beings, each of them of a different sex. But the life of a fetus is not strictly human life, since its life is like that of a plant; it is a vegetative life absorbed into the mother's womb, as the plant is absorbed by the place where it is found. The fetus is a passive being which receives its nutrition from another, doing nothing to live nor defend its life. When in the maternal womb it lacks sufficient sustenance, it perishes, without being conscious of its life nor of its death. The fetus is only a possibility of life and an indispensable condition for it. Besides, the fetus, although it is a real being, has no relationship with the world except indirectly. It is an entity entirely dependent on another; its life depends on another being and all its relations are only with this being who is its link with the world.

The first activity of human life is being born. To be born is to enter into the world in order to live. In conception each man is conceived by others. One is conceived, but on the contrary man is the one who achieves birth. I was conceived, but I was not born, but came to life.[2] Evidently, one is born of others and needs others in order to be born, but they do not bear me as they conceive me. It is I who am born. Man's birth is not dependent on others, as is his being conceived, since for conception the activity of two beings is necessary and neither of them is the conceived person nor does the latter enter into the act of conception, since he does not yet exist and will only exist through conception. In the act of birth the protagonists are the being who is born and the being of whom he is born, since prior to birth there exists a life which is that which is born, while in conception there existed only the lives of those who conceived a new life, but not the latter. Besides, although birth can be prevented by the decision of others, this decision is necessary to prevent birth but if there is no action to prevent it, the being will be born; whereas conception will not exist without a decision nor an action, since positive decision and action are necessary for the act of conceiving. Moreover, the man who is born has no conscience of being born, nor is his birth a wishing to be born, but he is born by a biological process which puts the fetus in a position to be born, but this does not remove the fact that being born is the first act of life.

As soon as one is born one begins to live. Up until birth, human life is passive; it depends on another life for everything, feeds on that life, limiting itself to receiving what it gives it. From the time of birth, man is no longer indissolubly linked to another life, so that if that other life which fed him when he was a fetus disappears he can go on living. But this does not mean that he does not go on depending on others. In the first years this dependence is still vitally necessary, since the child needs others in order to subsist. But he is no longer a merely passive receiver, for he needs to act, to do something for himself, like eating, etc. As time passes, from birth on, he acquires a vital independence in relation to others. He no longer perishes if others do not take care of him, since he can do by himself what others did before. But he is dependent on others in another way : his formation is determined by the men among whom he lives, by the environment in which he develops, and by the circumstances which surround him. We can say that every human formation, both organic and spiritual, is dependent on others, but in the act of living this dependence is not a mere passive reception but requires activity on man's part. What is most strictly human, the spirit, is received from others, from the human community in which one develops, from the spiritual environment in which one lives, that is, from what has been called objective spirit and what I have labelled "collective spirit."[3] The language man speaks, the customs he acquires, his ethics, religion, tastes, prejudices, all of this he receives from those who surround him, from what was already common property of the men among whom he was born. His parents, his friends, his teachers, if he has any, keep transmitting to him these common cultural riches. But he is an active receiver, he needs to assimilate them, to learn them; spirit is acquired by effort. He needs his senses and his consciousness in order to be able to make these common riches his; he needs to listen to learn a language and to speak it. If because of some physical defect he cannot hear he will not learn the language which is spoken around him, but if his hearing is normal, the language he will speak will necessarily be the language spoken by the men with whom he lives.

In spite of his dependence on others and the limits of space and the spiritual environment which surrounds him, at a certain stage of his formation man can oppose his environment and attampt to overcome it. He can learn languages which are not those spoken by the men among whom he is living; he can know cultures and forms of life which have already disappeared and live them in his imagination and with his thought more intensely than the living culture of his time and his environment. He can even turn out to be a stranger to his time and to the city in which he lives. Man is the only being in this world who, despite his dependence on the world and on other men, has the power of self-determination. He is the only animal who not only lives but can live in different ways, who transforms or can transform his mode of existence, who can attain the world of ideal objects, apprehend and realize values, leaving his imprint on this world to which he can bring something which was not there before. This power is unique, and the importance of men in the world is not lessened just because most men lead lives which are channelled by the environment in which they live.

Formation by others, the acquisition of knowledge through transmission, that is to say, the acquisition of a spirit, is needed only by a being capable of directing his activity in different directions, who is capable of choosing and who is doing so may be right or wrong. Animals, who are guided by instincts and act always in a predictable manner, do not need spiritual formation. The dependence on others in man's formation is an indispensable requirement for his self-determination. But what we acquire without our choosing it from the common spirit never disappears nor can we erase it from ourselves. In our actions, in our words, and in our thoughts and feelings there is always a penetration of the past, in which we were formed, into the present, just as the future also affects our present decisions.

To live is the fundamental activity of life. Man's life which goes from his being born to his dying, is a temporal succession of perceptions, sentiments, passions, joys, sadness, loves, hates, knowledge, errors, beliefs, aspirations, fear of death and hope or despair of survival after it.

But life has a third activity, which is dying. Dying is an activity of life, not of death, since dying is not being dead but alive, but being alive is not acting for life, but for death. To live is the activity of life for life, on behalf of life. To die, on the other hand, is not an act of death, since death does not act. Dying is an act of life against life. Hence, dying is an act of life on behalf of death. To live, life is necessary, but to die, death is not necessary. On the contrary, it is necessary that death do not exist, because dying is previous to death. To die is not to be dead, but is the activity of life which leads to death. To live is the activity of life in life and for life. To die is not an activity of, nor in, death, but an activity of, and in, life, but for death, not for life. Dying is life dying and life dying is not death, but neither is it living; it is dying. To die is to be alive, but not to live, because to live is the opposite of to die and one cannot live and die at one and the same time.

Summing up, we can say that life begins before birth, because to be born is only to enter the world, obtaining life independent from that of the mother. After entering the world we begin to live, because to live is to be in the world, acting in it and upon it. But we leave the world, we leave life to enter death. At death we enter life's exist, but death is not a prolongation of life but the contrary, the lack of life. In order to enter death it is necessary to have left life. Hence, death does not finish life; what finishes life is dying. But as dying is an activity of life, what finishes life is life itself. Death has no activity; it does not even struggle against its opposite, life. What struggles against life is life itself in the vital action of dying.

From the time which is, living derives one instant, dying, and from that instant derives eternity, death. Living is time, dying a moment; life is limited, death eternal. But even though each man has his death, death is no longer man. Man disappears with death; when he dies, he does not last on in death, for in death man is no longer man, no longer life. In man's death, human life ceases to be, to exist. What man is after dying, in death, is the opposite of man, of life. I die, but I do not enter death. What enters death is what is mine : my soul, my body. I, as I, disappear; man, as man, disappears. The history of man terminates with dying.

Attitudes Towards Death

What is the attitude that man should assume in the presence of the inevitable fact of death? The present study attempts a description of human life that implies no evaluation and no duty : in mere description one should pose no problems about what should be, but simply analyze what is as it appears to us. But the activities and attitudes of man are not what they should be but what they are, even if it can be maintained that they should be different from what they are. It is evident that man can adopt different attitudes towards death and these depend largely on whether he believes or does not believe in survival after death.

In the first place, I think that usually man does not adopt any attitude towards the inevitable fact that he must die. The average man is usually too busy solving the problem of how to live to worry also about his attitude to death. He knows that he must die just as everybody else knows it and says so and regarding the problem of the death of others he adopts the attitude which is usually adopted, repeating the ritual phrases in such cases. That is to say, in this case, as in almost all else, man is dependent on the community and acts in accordance with the norms that prevail and which have been established by custom. He has his sentiments and his grief in the presence of the death of loved ones. As far as his own death is concerned, he usually is prepared for it and adopts measures with regard to those who will continue living after his death and also accepts, out of inertia, many measures which are established for such cases. But his attitude is not related to death but to the life of others and to his corpse, which is what remains from life. Generally, the average man does not in his lifetime ask himself whether or not he should adopt an attitude towards the inevitable fact of death.

But other men do adopt an attitude towards this fact. The attitude depends principally on whether or not they believe in another life after death; whether they believe that human consciousness persists or does not persist after death. The attitude of those who believe in another life must be, if the belief is sincere and strong, that of preparing for that life. It is the attitude of the religious man of the Middle Ages, for whom the world was a vale of tears. It is also that of the mystics and can reach a vital attitude which revolves around death and desires it; it can go as far as the "I die because I do not die" of Saint Theresa. Life would thus be only a preparation for death, that is, a passage to another life. Because the attitude of the believer is not an attitude towards death; for him death does not exist. His is an attitude to the next life.

Most men do not adopt this extreme attitude, which is found only in mystics and which leads to a life dependent on the next life. Man changes his attitude towards death according to the circumstances of life, and there are moments in which the faith of the firmest believer weakens and others in which the unbeliever believes.

In present philosophy, existentialism, especially in the thought of Heidegger, adopts a position regarding this aspect of the attitude towards death. Existentialism takes as a starting point the radical finiteness of man, and on the basis of the consideration that there is no other human life than the worldly, poses the problem of what man's attitude should be. For Heidegger there are two positions. One is that of dissipation in pleasure and in the "one" ("one says," "one does"), which is in reality the position of the man who does not ask himself the question of what position he should adopt towards a fact which will inevitably present itself. For, man thinks tacitly or explicitly, if it is inevitable it is not necessary to adopt any position, since in any event death must come just the same. This for Heidegger is inauthentic existence, because it does not face the problem of death itself, which is personal, but only speaks of "one's" dying, of "one's" having to die, and that "one" is no one. The other existence is that which he calls authentic, that which permanently faces the supreme possibility of death. It is the attitude which in another article I have called "the desire to embitter one's life." What is authentic for Heidegger would be what we could call the personal and intransferable, that which necessarily must happen to me or which I must do, and that no one else can do for me. "To die my death," he says, "is the only thing no one else can do for me." My death is mine, it is what is most characteristic and personal. Hence, authenticity will consist in not stifling the anguish of death but in supporting it and facing it alone, even though I am defenseless in its presence. The acceptance of death must be a constant waiting for it, not a flight from it. But for Heidegger "man is an entity between two nothings"; when man dies he goes into the void. And as the one who lives authentically sees everything *sub specie mortis,* he must take things as they are : as nothing. The person of authentic existence endures permanently the anguish of death and takes his life and his actions as nothingness.

In view of this position we can ask : Is death the only thing that is authentic, personal and intransferable, as Heidegger asserts? I ask : Can another be born for me? If another is born for me, I am not born; the one who is born is that other. We can also ask : Can another live for me? It is obvious that what another lives for me, I do not live. Therefore, if what is authentic is what is most personal and intransferable, to be born and to live are as authentic as dying. Moreover, to die I need to have been born and therefore to have lived, long or little. To die is, then, more conditioned than being born or living, since dying is conditioned by my existence and assumes my having been born and having lived.

Contrary to Heidegger, I think that the most important and authentic of the three fundamental activities of our life – being born, living and dying – is living, since living is the only one in which I have possibilities, the only one in which I can choose, since dying is not a possibility but a necessity, and what I am and do is what I am and do during my life.

Heidegger forgets that there is a second possibility beyond that of taking things and life as valueless, even assuming the basic position of the radical finiteness of life (which I do not propose to discuss, since for me this is not a philosophic problem, at least not of philosophy as we understand it today), and that is to give value to life precisely because one has to die. Since we have only one life and this is limited, it must be lived; we must make of it something that justifies our having lived. If life were eternal, it would have no value nor importance, since everything could be done and undone, without much ado, for there would always be time ahead of us. Giving meaning to life and assuring values to it is possible only in a limited life. Since there is only one life, let us live it with the dignity of men, giving it sense and filling it with human values.

If it was once said that to learn to philosophize it was necessary to learn to die, we can now say the opposite : to philosophize one must learn to live.

NOTES

1. Translated by Leon Livingstone, State University of New York at Buffalo.

2. The original wording, "yo no fui nacido, sino que naci" is impossible to render into English, which does not possess an active, as opposed to a passive, form of the verb. What the author means is that birth is an active occurence, not a passive event. One can "be" conceived, according to the Spanish terminology (*ser concebido*), but he cannot "be" born (*nacer, not ser nacido*). (Translator's note.)

3. This point has been discussed in my study : *Ontologia* (Editorial Losada, Buenos Aires, 1967), pp. 34 ff.

AMBIGUITIES OF HUSSERL'S NOTION OF CONSTITUTION

Nathan Rotenstreich, Hebrew University

I

IT IS an established fact that in Husserl's thought – and, more exactly, in his late thought – the notion of constitution occupies a central place. Yet there is an inverse proportion between the centrality of the notion and the establishment of its meaning and function. The ambiguities which this notion carries, leave room for the question whether its centrality can be taken for granted from the systematic (as distinguished from the textual) point of view.

The term *konstituieren* may connote, *inter alia,* "to establish something." This, in turn implies (1) to create something and to make it such and such, and (2) to acknowledge that such and such is the case. An additional nuance of *konstituieren* is : to bring about, to organize things *together.* It is because of this nuance that we speak of constitution as an establishment of a certain order.

Because constitution connotes an establishment of things or of an order, we speak about something as being constitutive to things or for things. This nuance in turn introduces in our discourse an aspect of a basis : a thing is constitutive if it serves as a ground or a basis for another thing. It is the origin of things as in the case of constituting a team or a group of people. Origin connotes by the same token the principle of establishing that which originates from the act of founding, as in the case of bringing together people by way of assuming an objective for their togetherness, rules of one's behavior, etc. In this sense constituting may connote either a basis in an act that occurs in time – the constitution takes place at a certain date – or a grounding in a principle or reason, as, for instance, when a group is constituted by people who adhere to certain rules or objectives. These two aspects of constitution may be combined or – methodically, at least – separated.

We speak in addition about one's "physical constitution." In this case we refer less to the *act* that creates one's physical character than to one's character or nature. To be constitutive does not refer here to the grounding or founding *of* a state of affairs, but rather to that which is considered to be essential *in* the state of affairs.

Among these various meanings of the term constitution there are affinities, but there are also different nuances within each group of connotations. Therefore, when a philosopher refers to a term which has a meaning in everyday discourse he either transfers that meaning into the body of his system and thus uses the term vaguely, or else he establishes – or constitutes, as it were – a fundamental meaning related to that which is known in current discourse, but is made in his system more precise and defined.

II

It is plausible to assume that Husserl introduced the notion of constitution in his thinking under the influence of Kant. Yet, from the point of view of the position which this notion occupies in the Kantian system, the situation is even more perplexing.

In Kant's use, too, the term constitution is related to the various components extant in its current meaning. Thus, for instance, Kant relates constitution to the notion of order. The order referred to is the order of nature and as such it is related to the time-order.[1] The aspect of ground or origin comes to the fore in Kant's system when he refers to reason as being the origin of the general order of nature.[2] However, in the Kantian system the term "constitutive" has still a more defined meaning and function.

A constitutive principle is a principle of the possibility of experience and of empirical knowledge of the object of senses.[3] To be constitutive requires a relation to sense perception or to a corresponding schema of sense perception. Where the relation to sense perception is lacking, there can be only regulative principles[4] establishing the systematic unity of knowledge,[5] which stands against experience proper as related to objects of senses. Where there are only concepts, their unification is regulative or systematic; where there are sensuous data, their unification is constitutive or cognitive, i.e. empirical.

The difference between mathematical and dynamic principles and categories, makes this distinction even more prominent. Mathematical categories refer to objects of intuition (*Anschauung*); dynamic categories to the existence of these objects either in their interrelation or in relation to reason.[6] The a priori conditions of intuition are necessary from the point of view of possible experience, while the conditions of the existence of objects are accidental because we cannot establish a priori the very existence of things or objects.[7] We could explain at this point that the dependence of the principles of perception on the a priori structure of the forms of intuition enables us to assume their necessity. As against this the appearance of things or their existence does not depend on the a priori structure of knowledge and cannot therefore be necessary; it is defined as dynamic, as against mathematical. Dynamic principles refer to intuition; their validity is therefore intuitive, while the validity of principles which refer to things related to reason is discursive.

The relation to intuition which is characteristic of constitutive principles, becomes prominent in the nature of mathematical knowledge, as distinguished from philosophical knowledge. Constitution is related to construction. To construct concepts amounts to exhibiting the concepts in intuition a priori, without reference to experience. We exhibit in intuition the object which corresponds to our concept.[8] Demonstration as an apodictic proof is possible only because of the element of intuition.[9] Construction leads to demonstration and both are possible in mathematics and are not possible in philosophy. Philosophic definitions, in contradistinction to mathematical ones, are only expositions of given concepts, while mathematical definitions are constructions of concepts created originally.[10] Exposition is the process of making a meaning of a concept clear,[11] while construction is an embodiment of a concept in intuition. Hence exposition is analytic while construction is synthetic.[12] Being discursive, philosophical thinking is thinking in predicates,[13] while mathematical knowledge, being constructive, is thinking in relation to intuition. Hence Kant's concept of constitution refers to the relation between thinking and data and points to the exhibition of thinking in data. It clearly does not put forward the idea of creation of any data.

III

The ambiguity of the notion of constitution in Husserl has been recognized by his most authoritative commentators. Marvin Farber points to one meaning of constitution as referring to a whole being composed of simpler elements;[14] another meaning of constitution refers to a reduction of a sphere to an elementary stratum.[15] Eugene Fink points to several possible meanings of constitution as bringing together *(zusammenstellen):* establishing an order of things, creating and fixing of things, the ordering of our images and representations about things and the establishing of the meaning of the object. Fink acknowledges that in Husserl these meanings blend.[16]

A different interpretation or a rather different direction of interpretation is presented by R. Sokolowski. According to this interpretation constitution appears as an inquiry into the sources of primitive concepts and forms. This inquiry results in the discerning of three main spheres constituted out of the sources : (1) The logical or categorial forms which are constituted in categorial acts; (2) Meanings which are constituted in intentional acts; (3) Objects of reference, which are constituted.[17] The three spheres listed by Sokolowski could be classified as comprising meanings and objects. Yet Sokolowski's description points to an act as constituting the two first spheres (categorial forms and meanings) and does not mention acts as related to the sphere of objects of reference. It seems to be correct that the notion of constitution is related to the sphere of acts; while these acts are given this relation.

Though we are about to take the theme of acts as the most fundamental aspect of Husserl's theory, we cannot be oblivious of the fact that Husserl employs the term "constitution" or "to be constituted" as pointing to the relation existing between a thing and its nexus. Thus he says that a thing constitutes itself as unity of schemes, or more properly as unity of the causal necessity in the context of dependencies.[18] He also seems to use the term constitution as connoting the essence of a thing, as, for instance, when he says that the body constitutes itself originally in a twofold way : as matter, in terms of extension, in color, heat, etc., and also as in one's finding body feeling such as heat on the back of the hand, and cold in the feet.[19] There is no reference here, at least not a patent one, to an act constituting the construction of the body. Constitution connotes here the essence of the body, as this essence appears as a neutral matter on the one hand and as related to one's own sensitivity on the other.

Having said this, and without trying to suggest a unity in the diversity of meanings of the notion of constitution where this unity is lacking, we shall concentrate on that aspect of constitution which Husserl himself characterized as the constitution of objectivities of consciousness.[20] To speak about objectivities of consciousness presupposes the character of consciousness as expressing itself in objectifying acts *(objektivierende Akte)*.[21] Supposing that objectivity connotes that which subsists in itself, we may say that Husserl is interested (1) in discerning the character of acts by virtue of which we may refer, mean and grasp that which subsists in itself, (2) in analyzing the question whether the relation to the act is external to that which subsists in itself or else alters the character and the meaning of that which supposedly subsists in itself.

A literary observation might be appropriate at this point. Husserl uses the term *objektivierend,* or generally : *Gegenständlichkeiten des Bewusstseins.* We find in Goswin Uphues the term *Objektivationstheorie* which he introduced by way of opposition to the *Vertretungstheorie,* that is to say, the theory of representation. We project, he says, the ideas *(Vorstellungen)* from ourselves into the space and we make them into objects *(Gegenstände)* or we hold them as objects.[22] It is not relevant for our analysis to go into the details of Uphues' treatment of the theory. What matters here is the use of the term *objektivieren* and what is more essential, the fact that Husserl faces the question of assuming constitution as *objektivieren* without falling into the pitfalls of projection.

IV

A representing consciousness cannot be constituting. After all, constitution is an activity towards something and not just mirroring of something. Consciousness engaged in constitution is bound to be at least intentional. Intentional acts refer positively and actively to an object. Intentionality is a contact with an object created by the consciousness itself, since intentionality means eventually this contact entertained by consciousness due to the very nature of consciousness. This is the meaning of consciousness as objectifying. But is it constitutive? Is intentionality an activity of *reference* or an activity of *creation?* In an intentional experience there is the noetic ingredient, or moment, as Husserl has it, qua act; and there is the noematic moment, i.e., the meaning to which the act refers. Is the noematic moment constituted by the noetic one? Here lies the fundamental dilemma of Husserl. One may venture to put forward the thesis that he was led astray by his own findings as to the intentionality of consciousness by pushing intentionality forward to the point of constitution. Yet constitution considered to be an extended intentionality, as it were, uproots the basic notion of intentionality.

If the world is a meaning of reality constituted in infinitum,[23] one may wonder whether Husserl is referring in his description to the fact that the meaning of that which is in the world has to be entertained in acts of intentionality, or whether he considers that the sphere where this meaning is placed is constituted by intentionality. To put the question differently : Did Husserl think that were it not for the understanding of the notion or of the idea of the world this notion or "world" would not appear inside the horizon of consicousness which entertains it through its inherent intentionality? The first interpretation points to constitution understood as awareness, the second, to constitution as creation.[24] Yet if the first interpretation holds good, one may wonder why Husserl uses the term constitution at all. The interpretation of his view as pointing to the realization of a meaning by way of awareness of that meaning cannot, and does not, suggest the notion of creation of the noema or of that which is grasped in awareness and by it.

Reality as entertained by consciousness is a meaning not created by consciousness but discerned by it. It is understood precisely as a reality in contradistinction to phantom, or numbers or a fairy tale. The meaning of reality is the locus of that which is understood and discerned by consciousness. Consciousness understands what reality connotes, or gropes for its understanding. Reality appears within the horizon of consciousness through awareness of the former's meaning. But the meaning of reality carries the moment, to use here Husserl's terminology, that reality is not an inner aspect of consicousness though it is grasped by it. Hence one may wonder whether the enigmatic statement of Husserl that a true abyss yawns between consicousness and reality,[25] can validly be maintained. One may say just the opposite : the meaning is the bridge between consciousness and reality because consciousness grasps itself and is reflective, and also grasps that which is not itself, i.e., consciousness is referential. In both cases it is intentional; the intentionality is of its own character; it emerges out of its own spontaneity.[26] One may thus formulate the dilemma : either intentionality is enough, or else even constitution will not solve the problem which intentionality failed to solve. Consciousness entertains the idea – the sense or meaning – of reality because consciousness is aware of its antisolipsistic character. It does not create the idea of reality but it understands it. The creation of an idea of reality would have to be justified within the orbit of the process of creation,[27] while the intentional grasp of that idea has its justification in precisely the attempt on the part of consciousness to understand adequately that which is. Transcendences are not hidden, as Husserl says;[28] they are referred to and hence their character as transcendences has to be duly formulated.

Intentionality is not an empty activity creating the pole of the noema to which to refer. In order to be intentionality proper it has to create its own correlate. Yet, once he has pointed to the active character of intentionality *(Leistung),* Husserl is inclined to talk in a Fichtean vein. Thus he speaks about the activity of positing reality *(Seinssetzung),*[29] as if the Ego were Fichte's Ego. In Fichte the Ego *(das Ich)* posits the non-Ego through the act of his own limitation. In another content Husserl says that the pure Ego, being identical with itself, can be objectively posited *(gegenständlich).* He seems to imply here that the Ego has the capacity of self-awareness thus becoming an object for itself. But this does not mean that it becomes an object opposed to itself, as Fichte implied. The notion of constitution lends itself to an interpretation in Fichtean terms and thus may result in a confusion of the distinction between the activity of intentionality and that of constitution. Fichte's Ego is self-contained and all-embracing in its initial position. Out of its own self-awareness which is a perpetual act it creates the non-Ego. Husserl's Ego is *ab initio* related in and through the active intentionality. Intentionality refers to a content or to a sense. Consciousness, the intrinsic nature of which is intentionality, has enough sense to distinguish between itself and reality and to grasp reality as reality and not as consciousness, even without having to take advantage of the notion that the Ego is limiting itself to provide room for the "material of duties," as Fichte has it.[30]

V

What led Husserl to this view which amounts to a slip from intentionality to constitution qua production? A possible explanation might be that Husserl imposed on the structure of consciousness as objectifying the problem of transcendence and immanence which as such is related to a somewhat different logic of philosophical argumentation. Consciousness as objectifying transcends its sphere of acts by the very nature of the acts; by entertaining senses and meanings it is *transiens,* to use a term which was current in philosophical descriptions before the introduction of the term *transcendent.* Husserl seems to speak about a sphere of transcendence, or about transcendence as a sphere where the world is constituted. And he goes even further when he states that that which constitutes the world cannot be world.[31] To be sure, Husserl points to the aspect of intersubjectivity or cosubjectivity *(Mitsubjektivität)* which is an essential aspect of world. If he means to say that intersubjectivity is an indispensible feature of world, then he is certainly correct. We distinguish between a "private" world and *the* world; the world is not private and hence it is intersubjective by definition. It is doubtful whether intersubjectivity, which constitutes world in terms of being a feature of it, also constitutes world in terms of being the productive factor of world, because we define *the* world from the very beginning as being intersubjective; world comprises many subjects. World is also the noema of many acts of intentionality of the self-same subject and of different subjects. These subjects are of the world and the world is the ultimate horizon of their different thematic noemata. But all this does not warrant the statement that the factor constituting world cannot be of the world. The theological metaphor which creeps in here is more than misleading : the creator of the world is not of the world because the creator connotes the origin of the world in terms of its very existence. But the subject entertaining the meaning of the world is of the world and does not create the world by positing it as existing. Were it not for the fact that the subjects possessing consciousness, the inherent nature of which is intentionality, are of the world, one would wonder whether their intentionality would entertain the meaning of "world" altogether. The subject or subjects are in the world and hence in their intentionality or intentionalities they are aware of it on the level of the sum total of acts of awareness, that is to say, on the level of their respective consciousness. The harmony of monads to which Husserl sometimes refers is the harmony of monads "with windows," all of them related to the ultimate horizon of things and meanings – that is to say, to the world. The characteristic feature of human consciousness is that it is consciousness of a being belonging to the world and engaged in the activity of understanding, which is an activity *vis-à-vis* the world and not just a mere part or occurence in the regular course of events of the world-order.

VI

Husserl imposed on the intentionality of consciousness not only the aspect of transcendence but also symmetrically that of immanence, or what he calls subjectness *(Subjektsein).* When outward experience is taking place we do not know about the subjective modes of appearance. In the experiencing of things every subjective character is missing. Only through reflection do we direct our view from experiences of things and qualities related to things, to ourself.[32] Once we direct our attention to the realm of subjectiveness we discern that the activity of constitution is addressing itself not only to constitution of transcendencies and of ideal forms or logical shapes but also to the constitution of the subjectivity of the immanent experiences. Within the domain of immanent subjectiveness there is a stratum of *Urauffassung* which in turn is not constituted as an *Auffassung* within the flow of temporal variations of the manifold *(Abschattungsmannigfaltigkeiten)*.[33] Once we reach the ultimate stratum of subjectiveness we reach the stratum of original consciousness *(Urbewusstsein)* which is supposed to be subject only – or as Husserl says : is not in this sense content or object within phenomenological time.[34]

There seem to be two reasons for this concern with the subjective activities directed towards the subjectness. One reason is in the very fact that this subjective domain is discerned as a sphere; once it is discerned it seems to be the task of the phenomenologist to inquire into the dynamic rhythm of subjectivity. This leads Husserl to deal with the subject matter of subjectivity as *Egologie*.[35] We come back here to the original intentions. This sphere of subjectiveness is called the sphere of transcendental life. To be sure, life does not have here a naturalistic meaning rejected in *Philosophy as Strict Science*. Subjectivity is a realm of a kind of dynamics; it is called – and should be looked at as a metaphoric expression or as simile-life. By entering into this line of description Husserl is led to discern in subjectivity a messianic note. Once we discern the whole richness of the sphere of subjectivity, we dwell on the level of spirit. The natural child of the world is turned into the phenomenological child, the child in the kingdom of pure spirit.[36] This redemptive meaning of immanence, with all its Buddhistic associations, has nothing to do with the problem of reference to the transcendent object. The only element it has in common with the theme of the transcendent object is the fact that intentionality is not only characteristic of consciousness referring to an object but also of consciousness referring to itself. When consciousness refers to itself it discerns the original stratum of consciousness. Yet Husserl does not imply that this original stratum is an Ego in the Fichtean sense, which posits the non-Ego. Husserl tends rather to show that not only intentionality is characteristic of the self-referential consciousness, but constitution too. The difference between the various acts of constitution is to be found in the fact that within the sphere of consicousness we find ultimate acts or *Urbewusstsein*, which constitutes and is not constituted. But does this discernment solve the problem of the transcending consciousness? We learn here a great deal about consciousness; this part of Husserl's writings is clearly the richest part of his philosophical opus. When we start asking about consciousness transcending itself we discern that consciousness is immanent to such an extent and intent, that it is endowed with such a plenitude, that adherence to or immersion in it is, in a way, redeeming. Hence we have to ask how and why consciousness can and should go out from its own sphere and become involved in reality or in the world, an involvement which makes us not only children of the world but, to be sure, children of darkness, too.

Husserl assumes that in addition to his interest in the sphere of immanence for the sake of immanence, he can also go back from the world we live in to the subjective activities out of which this very world emerges. How it emerges is not clear and cannot be made clear by posing and describing the sphere of subjective activities. The fact that the immanent world is constituted also as the transcendent world does not make the two worlds parallel. On the contrary, there emerges the dependence of the transcendent on the immanent. This raises the question : Why is there transcendence at all? It seems thus that where Husserl is most illuminating in terms of his phenomenological findings, there he leaves us with the fundamental puzzle with regard to the functional relation of the immanent to the transcendent, or the functional transcending of the immanent in the first place.

This part of Husserl's system is made even more prominent through the imposition of the distinction between the absolute and the relative on the duality of consciousness and its intentional object. Immanent being is without doubt, in this sense, the absolute being. Experience is merely the grasping *(Erschauen)* of something which is given in perception *(Wahrnehmung)* as absolute.[37] In what sense can Husserl attribute absoluteness to consciousness? If he wants to convey the fact that consciousness creates itself and is not an effect of the processes of the world, then he is certainly correct. Yet if he wants to establish the position of consciousness – in the direction that its position can be asserted without its primordial or original relation, or intentionality to the object – then he seems to be wrong. Consciousness itself establishes the contact with the object but by the very same act it separates itself from the object. The subject understands his subjectivity by his constant reference to the object. Without reference to the object we would not be aware of our own inwardness; inner time is established through the constant pointing to transcendent time. Consciousness is self-originating but not absolute. It is relative to the object – either to the transcendent object or to the object of its own reflection. Again : Husserl does not assume that consciousness is self-contained or all-embracing. Hence he cannot assume that it presents an absolute realm. We have to distinguish between the self-originating character of consciousness related to its spontaneity and its alleged absolute position. The grafting of these two aspects or components on consciousness weakens Husserl's point because of the meaning of the terms themselves, and because of the consideration of the functional transcending of consciousness to objects with which we dealt previously.

VII

It seems that the stress laid on the absolute character of consciousness and its inward activities overshadows an important consideration present in Husserl's theory of constitution. The aspect in question is the place occupied by experience *(Erlebnis)* or intuition *(Anschauung)* on the level of consciousness vis-a-vis contents and meanings entertained intentionally by consciousness. The theory of intentionality, as it appears prima facie, stresses only the active character of acts of consciousness or else, from the other end, it stresses the fullness of consciousness, since consciousness is always consciousness of something. The theory of constitution adds another aspect : What is present on the level of consciousness is due to the acts of consciousness, that is to say, these acts intentionally entertain contents, be they related to transcendence or to the inward "life" of consciousness itself.

Husserl was concerned with the problem of how to provide clarity and distinctness for concepts and propositions of pure logic. He took the position – and this is the central aspect of his theory of constitution – that no clarity can be provided unless we explore the acts on the part of consciousness which accompany these contents or are their subjective correlates. The theory of constitution amounts here, as Walter Biemel says, to the restitution of the acts of consciousness which provide completeness on the level of acts and to what may be called the objective meaning of the contents. The best example for this direction of Husserl's theory is the theory of inner time. Husserl is concerned with what he calls the time-constituting flow of consciousness[38] which he characterizes as being absolute, in the sense explained previously as an experience of flow which is his view precedes the experience of objective time, and which can be understood as the primary experience. The reference to objective time is not a formula or a constructed method but an activity rooted in and supported by a real experience. This is an experience of consciousness on the level of consciousness on the one hand, and the root-experience providing immanent essence to all subsequent experience, on the other.

The systematic reason for this view of Husserl's lies in his position that the given is the ultimate factor. The ultimate given is the given experienced by consciousness within its own boundaries. The given is encountered not by way of thinking, let alone by way of construction; but through experience or even through *Wahrnehmung.* Hence Husserl speaks about the pure Ego as having the possibility of primary *Selbsterfassung,* or *Selbstwahrnehmung.*[39] The pure Ego is not encountered through the medium of knowledge which is the organ of perceiving as, e.g., in Kant *(Wahrnehmung).* The given has been shifted from the sphere of sense perception to the sphere of that which is originally given for reflection of the Ego itself.

It follows that (a) logical concepts necessarily have their origin in intuition and have to emerge on the basis of certain *Erlebnisse;*[40] (b) there is an *Erleben,* i.e., mathematical *Erleben* which is the correlate in terms of psychic character to pure logic or to pure mathematics;[41] (c) the principle of all principles is the primary giving intuition *(Anschauung),* which is the origin of the legitimacy of all knowledge. It is the primary origin of that which is given as it were in all its bodily reality;[42] (d) what is called evidence is eventually an experience either in the sense of *Erfahrung* or in the sense of *Erlebnis.* Hence the category of objectivity *(Gegenständlichkeit)* and the category of evidence *(Evidenz)* are correlates. The experience of the evidence is the experience of the Ego possessing that which it gives to itself *(Selbsthabe).*[43]

It is clear that Husserl himself oscillates between the view of consciousness as having an absolute position vis-à-vis contents which are relative and the view of consciousness and of its acts as correlates of objectivities. Being a correlate is a position which defies absoluteness. If we accept Husserl's theory as to the correlative position of consciousness, then consciousness is fundamentally dialectical. It is both self-originating and thus independent, and by the same token correlative. But we cannot accept the concept of the absolute position of consciousness.

What led Husserl to this view, or to this drive to find the corresponding acts on the level of consciousness even for pure forms of logic and mathematics, let alone for individual experiences – haptic perceptions, etc.? Why did he not let the form or forms be disconnected from acts? This aspect of Husserl's theory can be best explained by two considerations, one being of (1) a systematical and the other of (2) a historical character.

(1) Suppose we read a piece of poetry. We find there symbols, descriptions of landscapes and experiences, etc. We ask, Is this poetry genuine? Did the poet entertain the described experience? Does the symbol have a meaning within the orbit of his poetic imagination or experience, or did the poet take the symbol out of the dictionary and acquire the expression from another poet, i.e., does he, as a matter of fact, indulge in a poetic phraseology and not in an authentic expression? One may wonder whether such questions or criticisms as may be raised on reading poetry are always valid, as in the case of taking the view that the piece of poetry is self-contained and does not call or allow for criticisms or evaluation based on the restitution of the poet's experience. Husserl, within the sphere of philosophy, is concerned with the genuine character of thinking. He is opposed to the play of thinking for the sake of thinking, which amounts in his view to manipulations and constructions with pseudoconcepts. The genuine character of thinking is safeguarded when the construction has its correlate in an act of intuition and experience. Forms and contents without supporting acts are empty – this might be a way of summing up Husserl's view. This philosophical position as a total justification is difficult to maintain because it can lead to a questioning of the law of contradiction – unless we find an experience which is a correlate of the law. Even when we find the experience we still may wonder whether the fullness of the content or meaning safeguards the validity of the law, or else whether validity is warranted by the self-giveness which allegedly war-

rants authenticity of the content. At any rate, Husserl's is a very serious memento to philosophical constructions.

(2) At this point we have to consider a comparison with Kant's Metaphysical Deduction, as opposed to Transcendental Deduction. The point of departure of Kant's doctrine was the assumption that the function of unity is primarily exhibited in judgment or in proposition, i.e., in the logical functions as present in formal logic.[44] The form of the proposition creates the categories which are further exhibitions of the function of unity and which run parallel[45] to moments of passing judgment or propositions. The functions as exhibited in the realm of logic are pure concepts of reason while the categories refer a priori to objects in intuition in general. The transition is legitimate because of the fundamental identity of the function of the forms of logic and the categories of empirical knowledge.

It can thus be said that the functions of Formal Logic constitute the categories of empirical knowledge. The position of being constituted depends on the function of unity exhibited in the first place within the realm of formal acts of unifications. What is characteristic of Kant's view is that reason can depend only on reason, i.e., that the categories of empirical knowledge as categories of reason can depend only on the forms of Logic which in turn are forms of reason. Kant regards unity as unification and hence as the exhibition of the activity of reason while intuition *(Anschauung)* or perception *(Wahrnehmung)* are related to the manifold. The manifold is receptively absorbed through modes of contact with data, the data being given but not initially unified. In Kant there is the fundamental dichotomy between being given and being actively approached. Corresponding with this dichotomy is the dichotomy between intuition and reason. Husserl is concerned to eliminate this dichotomy. In his system there is givenness on the level of consciousness, which is self-givenness. Here we encounter a mutual dependence between activity and modes of passivity. Intuition, *Anschauung, Wahrnehmung* or *Selbstwahrnehmung* are not doomed to passivity. They are constitutive in acts of understanding according to Husserl's extreme view as founding transcendence; in his mitigated view they are correlates of acts of understanding of contents. Concepts relate to acts of experience qua *Erfahrung* and *Erlebnis,* and these acts are activities *(Leistungen).* Husserl bases the cognitive approach to the world on basic acts of *Anschauung* which are activities though not acts of reason in its formal and functional expressions as embodied in judgments and propositions. Intuition is active, and hence can be the point of departure or play the role played in Kant by the formal unification which is the basis and axis of Kant's Metaphysical Deduction. We encounter here a fundamental difference between Kant and Husserl, which cannot be obliterated in spite of the hesitations present in Husserl in his conscious relation to Kant. Kant thought that the transcendental ground is thinkable only by pure reason[46] (we have to stress in this context both reason and the quality of being thinkable). For Husserl the transcendental domain is not the domain of the thinkable in terms of reason. It is *eidetic* and opens up for investigation of the vast field of essential connections between the noetic and the noematic, between the *Erlebnis* of consciousness and the correlate of consciousness.[47] With all the interesting and illuminating elaborations of the concept of the transcendental it seems that this fundamental description of the concept has been retained throughout Husserl's development and it is clearly indicative of the difference between his and Kant's doctrines. This difference will become clear in the last part of our analysis, which deals again with the difference between Kant and Husserl in terms of the notion of constitution.

VIII

As we have seen before, in Kant constitution is the constitution of experience brought about by the categories or principles which apply to data; categories are of a constitutive validity for the data or for experience. Kant is not concerned with the acts of the transcendental ego beyond the fundamental act of Transcendental Apperception, Apperception being the ground of the possibility of the categories. Transcendental synthesis is *ab initio* the synthesis of the manifold of presentations *(Vorstellungen)*. The forms are of a constitutive character and Kant does not refer to the acts of grasping meanings. Here one discerns the main difference between Husserl and Kant in terms of their respective theories of constitution.

Kant approaches from the very beginning two different strata (reason and data) and his problem, i.e., the problem of constitution, is that of affinity between these two strata in spite of their difference. The affinity is accomplished by virtue of the validity of the forms of unification. Kant knows in a way what has to be united, i.e., the manifold of data, and he knows what is the unifying factor, i.e., the logical forms transformed into transcendental forms, i.e., categories and principles. Wherefrom does Husserl know the meanings which have to be constituted, i.e., reinstituted immanently on the level of consciousness? The acts know the meanings when the meanings are grasped within the flow of original consciousness. Here there is actually no difference between the acts of grasping and the content grasped, except for the very ego which can only grasp and not be a content of grasping. This is virtually the meaning of self-givenness of self-origination. But wherefrom do we know the meanings which are beyond the sphere of consciousness? One way for Husserl to solve this problem is to point to the constructive or productive character of the constitutive acts. We do not know, in the first place, the meanings beyond consciousness because they are not there, except when consciousness creates them and makes them relative to its own fundamental absoluteness. Creation provides for fullness as emanation. In Plotinus it provides for the manifold of the world, which is not the world in its purity but on the contrary, the world in its darkness, because of the material stratum of reality present in the world.

Yet when Husserl takes advantage of the noncreative component of constitution, i.e., when he points to the correlative aspect of it in terms of the correlative and hence mutual relationship between acts and meanings, he faces the question of the first knot, i.e., the question of where we encounter primarily, or let us even venture to say primordially, the sphere of meanings. It is here that the theory of *Lebenswelt* emerges. *Lebenswelt* is encountered by our prepredicative contact with it. On the basis of this primordial encounter all conceptualization is established, or constituted. We are immersed in the world which is from the very beginning grasped in its meaningful position and in the correlate components which constitute its meaning. Hence we may always refer to this world and we are called to refer to it. Space and time are not forms or pure forms of a constructed experience of science. Spatiality and temporality play a privileged role in the pretheoretical experience of the *Lebenswelt* and they provide the correlates from the very beginning. Additional meanings are thus conceptualizations or idealizations of the fundamental meanings.[48] The question of the first step towards contacts and meanings does not occur because meanings are encountered from the very beginning. What intentionality provides for the characterization of the structure of consciousness, the *Lebenswelt* provides for the description of the fact that there is no intentional moment without meaning and there is no encountering the world without encountering meanings. Kant's theory of constitution is concerned to create the synthesis; Husserl's theory of constitution attempts to discern and to articulate the primordial synthetic character of consciousness. Hence the synthesis need not be created; it is given.[49]

This important finding of Husserl's philosophy is obscured to some extent by the ambiguities of the term "constitution" and by the fact that he puzzles us by naming the prereflective synthesis of acts and meanings based on the correlation between the two as constitution. This term carries the association of a productive synthesis brought about for the sake of establishing a contact between factors which from their own respective position do not create this contact.

It seems that the understanding of Husserl's systematic intent calls here for a winnowing of his chaff from his genuine wheat.

NOTES

1. *Critique of Pure Reason,* B243.
2. *Prolegomena,* λ 38.
3. *Critique of Pure Reason,* B537,692.
4. *Ibid.,* B692.
5. *Ibid.,* B699.
6. *Ibid.,* B110.
7. *Ibid.,* B199 ff.
8. *Einl. III.*
9. *Critique of Pure Reason,* B762.
10. *Ibid., B758.*
11. *Ibid., B38.*
12. *Ibid., B758.*
13. *Prolegomena,* 46.
14. *The Foundation of Phenomenology. Edmund Husserl and the Quest for a Rigorous Science of Philosophy,* Cambridge, Mass., 1943, p. 579.
15. *Ibid.,* p. 556-557.

16. E. Fink, "Operative Begriffe in Husserl's Phänomenologie," *Zeitschrift für philosophische Forschung* XI (1957), p. 34.
17. R. Sokolowski, *The Formation of Husserl's Concept of Constitution,* The Hague, 1964, pp. 38-39.
18. *Ideen zu einer Phänomenologie und phänomenologischen Philosophie,* ed. H. L. Van Breda, II : *Phänomenologische Untersuchungen zur Konstitution,* ed. M. Biemel, The Hague, 1952, p. 127.
19. Ibid., p. 145.
20. *Ideen zu einer reinen Phänomenologie und phänomenologischen Philosophie,* ed. H. L. Van Breda, I : *Allgemeine Einführung in die reine Phänomenologie,* ed. W. Biemel, The Hague, 1950, Ch. II, p. 212.
21. II, Halle a.d.S., 1913, p. 493.
22. *Erkenntnistheoretische Logik, Leitfaden für Vorlesungen,* Halle a.d.S., 1909, p. 45 f.
23. See the quotation in Alwin Diemer, *Edmund Husserl, Versuch einer systematischen Darstellung seiner Phänomenologie,* Meisenheim am Glan, 1956, p. 18, n. 10.
24. On this consult E. Fink's various interpretations of Husserl.
25. *Ideen...,* I, p. 117.
26. See the present author's *Spirit and Man, An Essay on Being and Value,* The Hague, 1963, pp. 7 ff.
27. The creation of the world in monotheistic religions has to be justified in terms of the creator.
28. E. Husserl, *Die Idee der Phänomenologie, Fünf Vorlesungen* (Husserliana, II), ed. W. Biemel, The Hague, 1960, p. 11.
29. *Cartesianische Meditationen und Pariser Vorträge* (Husserliana, I), ed. S. Strasser, The Hague, 1950, p. 102.
30. *Ideen...,* II, p. 101.
31. Diemer, *op. cit.,* p. 35.
32. *Phänomenologische Psychologie* (Husserliana, IX), ed. W. Biemel, The Hague, 1962, p. 147.
3. *Vorlesungen zur Phänomenologie des inneren Zeitbewusstseins,* ed. M. Heidegger (Halle a.d.S., 1928), p. 44 (78).
34. *Ibid.,* p. 437 (71).
35. *Cartesianische Meditationen...,* p. 15.
36. *Erste Philosophie, 1923/24* (Husserliana, VIII), ed. R. Boehm, Zweiter Teil: *Theorie der phänomenologischen Reduktion,* The Hague, 1959, p. 123.
37. *Ideen..., I* 44,49.
38. *Vorlesungen...,* pp. 373 ff (7 ff.).
39. *Ideen...,* II, pp. 347 ff.
40. *Logische Untersuchungen II,* p. 5.
41. Quoted in W. Biemel, "Die entscheidenden Phasen in Husserl's Philosophie," *Zeitschrift für philosophische Forschung* XII (1959), p. 201.
42. *Ideen...,* I, p. 52.
43. *Formale und transzendentale Logik,* Halle,Saale 1929, p. 14.
4. *Critique of Pure Reason,* B159.
45. *Prolegomena,* 21.

46. *Critique of Pure Reason,* B124.
47. *Ideen...,* I. p. 245.
48. Consult A. Gurwitsch, "The Last Work of Edmund Husserl," *Philosophy and Phenomenological Research* XVI (1955/56), pp. 380-399.
49. Consult also J. Kern, *Husserl und Kant, Eine Untersuchung über Husserls Verhältnis zu Kant und zum Neukantianismus,* The Hague, 1964.

3

NATURAL EXISTENCE

THE NATURAL RIGHT TO AESTHETIC SATISFACTION

John P. Anton, Emory University

I

IN DEVELOPING my theme, I have tried to utilize the recent findings in role theory and apply them to political problems. The purpose is to kindle interest in the study of what may well prove to be one of Western man's most urgent concerns : how to effect a science of the Good Life and how to create a modern ethic. Preliminarily, I should like to note that I am not prepared to equate the concept of the good life with that of the affluent life. Wealth and goodness have been contrasted and their differences analyzed in ethical discourse since the days of Socrates. Similarly, it is important to maintain the boundaries that enable us to differentiate between efficiency and excellence. Failure to do so leads to misorienting the former and compromising the latter, and when either happens, the pursuit of happiness inevitably falls into disrepute. This, however, is a lesson which in modern times has repeatedly gone unheeded. That such ethical shortsightedness suits the designs and exclusive goals of the industrial and technological components of modern societies is a special problem, too vast to be given here the attention it deserves. Yet, it remains a fact that the persistent and, one suspects, cultivated discrepancy between limited goals and long-range objectives, between means and ends in our culture, which contemporary theorists and planners of technological society still refuse to remove from the ethical and political spheres of action, is perhaps one of the main sources of the paradoxes and contradictions of the Modern Industrial Age. Conceivably no paradox stands out more annoyingly than that which defines the state of irresoluteness between our aesthetic and ethical demands, and the meager returns in institutional reconstruction. We are now discovering that even planned change is not enough to guarantee progress.

II

It is useless to undertake an inquiry into the foundations and aims of democracy without pressing at the same time the principle that demands from each and every institution that it employ democratic procedures for the clarification and implementation of its own ends on the one hand, and for securing cooperativeness and beneficence on the other. Whether human beings have ever formed a society which observed this principle is not the question. What really matters is whether the communities that claim to have democratic structures and functions actually operate in accordance with the principle. What we must do, then, is use the principle as a criterion to test the veracity of the claims human societies make to being democratic, and explore the consequences that follow from its infractions.

It has been customary in the discussions of political theorists to characterize human societies as democracies when one of the basic dimensions of public conduct is so organized as to meet the stipulations of universal franchise, majority rule, equality of opportunity, freedom of speech, property rights, equality before the law and due process. We have also grown used to calling "democratic" those human communities which provide the public with opportunities to participate in the process for the continual reconstruction of institutions, the remaking of standards and reformulation of policies for domestic and international action. Yet there is another area of directed conduct which men have seriously meant to make part of the core meaning of the concept of democracy, but not with full success. I mean here the area of institutional balance and development which calls for coordinated progress in all the enterprises of man.

It is the failure to mark progress in this area that has alerted me to the need to revisit the problem of the adequacy of our current concepts of democracy. If democracy is the most viable model for organizing community life, and if, as Aristotle observed, men do not form communities simply to live but to live the good life, then we must make sure that the factors that secure the happiness of men remain functional and fully operative. The issue, then, is to decide not only whether the institutions of a given democratic society are "democratic," but also whether the pattern of their interrelationship satisfies the same condition. I shall refer to this latter demand as *the principle of institutional balance.* Ultimately this principle gives meaning to the idea of *cultural justice.*

Let us try to approach our problem with the aid of institutional analysis. We may start out by saying that human communities can be viewed as clusters of individuals, organized together as a public through the binding power of institutionalized concerns. The recent theoretical debates about the definition of "institutions" need not concern us here. Suffice it to note that whether we regard institutions as "standardized solutions to the problems of collective life," with Martindale, or as "procedures by which societies organize and regulate their social and cultural activities to meet the necessities of individual and collective existence and to persist through time," with Sirjamaki, neither their efficacy nor their plurality can be seriously questioned. What is of high relevance to our quest is the pattern of institutional interrelations because of its pertinence to a hidden dimension of the concept of democracy. More specifically, what concerns us at this juncture is the hierarchical arrangements of institutions within given sociopolitical orders, especially of the democratic type. Professor John Sirjamaki, among other sociologists, has given a summary of the situation : "Within the social order, institutions are held in a hierarchical arrangement, with some institution or set of institutions dominant in it, and the others of lesser status. Groups and organizations associated with paramount institutions have larger access to wealth, prestige, and social power, which enables them to maintain stability and integration in Society. In the American social order, economic and political institutions dominate, and educational institutions, despite their manifest importance, have smaller importance."[1]

The problem that must be raised is whether such practices are congruent with the general framework of democratic theory. G. H. Mead has made the following observation : "The institutions of society are organized forms of group or social activity – forms so organized that the individual members of society can act adequately and socially by taking the attitudes of others toward these activities."[2] By leaving the expression "adequately" unspecified, Mead was able to bypass what we regard as one of the most pressing needs in modern life : the need for a thorough critique of institutional ideology and its effects on axiological theory. Social psychologists, for instance, have identified certain salient features of institutional ideologies but have not pushed far enough the exploration of the implications of their findings for the broader principles of democracy.[3]

Although the social phenomenon of the hierarchical organization of institutions has been sufficiently recognized, a full account of the phenomenon through the application of the historical and comparative methods of sociology is still a task for future research. It should hardly surprise us if the results of such investigations were to lead intellectual and cultural historians to revise many of their assumptions and interpretations of political patterns and values. Be that as it may, the study of the symbiotic relations of human beings and institutions, namely the field of human ecology, must recognize that as long as it conceives its problems in terms of "competitive cooperation," it will remain tied to a set of value-assumptions that reach beyond the simple acceptance of the fact of institutional hierarchies.

If the investigations of hierarchical phenomena are themselves not altogether free from elements of some hidden "institutional ideology," the social realities are even more so and continue, with all the force of uninhibited habit and privilege, to remain imbedded in the practice of preserving the patterns of established hierarchies. When such realities succeed in persisting unaltered long enough to enlist the approval of several generations, they give rise to a determinate *cultural ethos.* The political efficaciousness of such an ethos is a separate issue and is best studied in the context of social dynamics. Its endurance, however, is a matter of internal flexibility. One such malleable case is the ethos of modern Western man. Not only has this ethos remained stable in its hierarchical arrangement of institutions since its early formation; it has proved capable of radical readjustments in the redistribution of manipulative power among the topmost institutions when changing conditions so demanded. The modern ethos proved amazingly able to maintain the stability of place it assigned to institutions vying for top position in the hierarchy of power, just as it displayed special powers to generate, as well as tolerate within its scope a whole family of political and economic systems, from communism and fascism to social democracies and constitutional monarchies. Such internal flexibility may be regarded as testimony to the inherent creativeness of the ethos, but it can hardly be appealed to for vindication of its claim to cultural supremacy. The inherent flaws become apparent as soon as we begin to apply to this ethos the criterion of cultural justice and to investigate all consequences it has for the formation of the self-conceptions of its bearers. In order to see this issue more clearly, we must introduce the notion of self-image or self-conception.

Until now we have been referring to institutions as though they were entities in themselves. The impression is highly misleading. In the last analysis, societies and institutions have no existence whatever apart from the human beings who comprise communities and through whose complex interactions they are sustained. We must, therefore, make certain that there is no intent here to hypostatize institutions and endow these societal units with the same ontological status that persons have. For this reason and this alone our quest must ultimately bring us back to human individuals and their patterns of institutionalized conduct. The components of such conduct, social scientists tell us, consist of (1) dominant beliefs, attitudes and behavior patterns; (2) symbolic cultural elements; (3) utilitarian and material content; and (4) written or oral codes that articulate specified conduct.[4] All these ingredients receive their organization within the structure of an activity consummating in a distinctive role. The logic of the concept of role, and the nature of the dialectical relationship between roles and situations, are topics far too broad to be discussed in this paper. What needs to be emphasized for our purposes is the fact that the human self is the locus of roles, and that in the plurality of institutions in a given society there is a corresponding plurality of roles.

The next important point is this : the hierarchical stratification of institutions, initially effected through leadership and priorities of interest, elicits eventually a parallel stratification of roles in the members of a society and seeks to ensure the preservation of that order through the employment of appropriate learning devices. The fundamental role of education as an institution for the preservation of any given institutional order, including the place and status of education itself in the ethos, hardly needs emphasizing. But to return to the issue at hand, the dynamics of institutions is a key to understanding the dynamics of roles and the motivational priorities of the individuals who accept the responsibility to guard and preserve the ethos. Given this commitment, the standard – bearer of any ethos founded on some special hierarchy of institutions are unlikely to tolerate behavior that threatens to alter the structure of accepted priorities. The limits of such tolerance define the limits of legitimate and approvable political action. In this respect it is almost axiomatic to say that even the most liberal social organizations contain restrictive ideological components, just as the most opentextured concept of *person,* when viewed as a totality or roles, is duty-bound to the social context that undergirds the ordained set of ordered values. Ralph Linton remarks that "Every individual has a series of roles deriving from the various patterns in which he participates and at the same time *a role,* general, which represents the sum total of these roles and determines what he does for his society and what he can accept from it."[5] It is important to add that the presence of hierarchical orders in roles and institutions raises some profound issues, particularly in relation to the concept of democracy.

III

Let us start with the simple observation that not all members of a given society can be or are willing to subscribe to the established pattern of role priorities. What makes this statement true is the fact that there are (1) differences in class status among individuals, (2) differences in ability and opportunity to identify with the pattern of value priorities, (3) differences in temperament and occupational drive, and (4) differences in emotional propensities. What is puzzling here is not whether the members of a given society can assume the number of responsive roles needed for survival and satisfaction of needs. The deeper issue is whether the imposition of a special hierarchy of institutions on all the members of the community is culturally beneficial and consistent with the democratic principle of the freedom of the individual. The answers that we give to these problems will throw light not only on the legitimacy of such impositions but, even more significantly, they will help us re-examine certain fundamental ethical considerations that pertain to the right to personal identity and the struggle for authenticity in self-conception.

Let us assume – and not without good reason – that the dominant institutions in a given society demand of its members that they recognize the hierarchical pattern and display in practice a personalized arrangement of roles that publicly confirms the corresponding dominance of certain institutions. Let us also assume that some members of that society find it difficult to comply with this demand. When reluctance to conform approaches defiance, serious maladjustments become inevitable. Fortunately, in most advanced societies, the limits of tolerance of deviant arrangements in role priorities are quite flexible. But this does not alter the fact that social imposition and compliance may interfere forcefully with the process of the forming of one's personal self-image. Such imposition is hardly avoidable in such cases where the circumstances of personality development require both an intimate identification with the values of *a lower grade institution* and the need to display publicly conduct fostered by the appropriate corresponding role. When this happens the experience of conflict is unavoidable.

The implications of the transformations in the diverse types of self-image of persons in modern society can be readily appreciated when brought to bear on our efforts to understand anew the vital relationship between persons and institutions. It is no doubt the case that whereas hierarchical stratifications of values and interests appear unavoidable and, under proper conditions, beneficial, particularly when persons arrange their corresponding roles consciously and reasonably, such is not necessarily the case when hierarchies of stratified interests are arbitrarily projected into the cultural body. The fundamental difference between a hierarchy of roles and that of institutions is best expressed through the distinction between *personal ethos* and *cultural ethos.* As persons we can always reflect on our conduct and adjust our plural interests, not only within *vertical and hierarchical* patterns, but also within *horizontal and intrinsic* frameworks. However, when the human response is one of conditioned learning to serve the hypostatized entities of the cultural ethos, behavior becomes passive and the power of ideology gains control over the freedom of decisions. That is why self-consciousness is fundamental to attaining a liberal ethos. Comparably, in the case of cultural ethos, its mode of existence, its *mythical* status, requires the highest form of reflective statesmanship to keep it within the boundaries of justice. The task of clarifying and defining in context the meaning of cultural justice, that is, to arrive at balanced organizations of institutions, is perhaps the supreme function of social criticism.[6] The expectation that such criticism cannot acquiesce with any of its temporal recommendations if it is to retain its dialectical character, may be regarded as part of the evidence in favor of the belief that, ultimately, the concept of *cultural democracy* and the hierarchical ordering of institutions are incompatible ideas. If further support is needed, we may furnish it by appealing to the frustrations we experience when our social enterprises are caught in the snares of paradoxes.

Consider, for instance, how contemporary society has been unable to bridge the gap between the demand for aesthetic satisfactions in the everyday affairs of life and the grand promises of our technological exploits. It is a gap which persists most annoyingly in the face of a growing concern for the arts and an open acceptance of the revolutionary character of contemporary art. Two conflicting attitudes seem responsible for this stubborn discrepancy : an attitude that acknowledges the goodness and usefulness of the arts in private enjoyment, education and public celebration; and one which objects to admitting the artist as an equal partner in the business of social planning and policy-making in governmental affairs and urban problems. An examination of the social dynamics that sustain this discrepancy reveals two basic factors at work : (a) The unequal distribution of social and political power, backed by steady technological advance, which in turn has legislated ways to maintain a disequilibrium in institutional values; this is noticeably a characteristic of both communist and noncommunist societies and is responsible for the hierarchical stratification of human values. (b) The presence of an ideological factor operating on the assumed primacy of the politicoeconomic concerns; so far this factor has proved to be inherently incapable of removing the discrepancy between artistic values and technics. Being a conservative mechanism, this ideology has failed to anticipate the axiological anomalies that were generated from the mishandling of technological applications.

IV

The message behind the diverse recent protests seems to be that the last vestiges of human spontaneity and aesthetic sensibility have already been replaced by artificial needs and regimented tastes. We have come to realize that what we have gained in luxuries and leisure we have lost in psychic serenity and sensitivity. True, we are trying frantically to keep abreast of the sprawling slums and deterioration of congested neighborhoods. So pervasive is the feeling that the physical aspects of our culture have got out of hand that even the people of pure profit are now showing signs of concern. The time has come for us to face bravely and realistically the paradoxical situation which threatens the technological culture of contemporary man and its democratic foundations with slow death from qualitative corruption. To state the matter bluntly, we have come to realize that what we have worked out for ourselves is a highly organized pattern of social life thriving on the output of an expanding and efficient technology but one that has been allowed to become indifferent if not oblivious to the need for beauty in daily chores, in our cities and natural surroundings, and above all a genuine democratic pattern of values within the broader framework of the concept of the good life.

It is not my purpose to say that technology is in and by itself an evil thing, and that it is erroneous to declare or inadvertently make technology the end of human pursuits. Hence, the root of the problem must be sought in the outlook that selects the aims. In this case we must look for the source in the value assumptions of the dominant institutions that are truly responsible for determining the uses of technology. They are the ones that dictate the manner in which the spectacular enterprise of massive research will find its place in our everyday lives. What is being criticized here, then, is not the services technology offers, but the limitations of institutional ideology of modern Western man in general and its implications for a general theory of democracy. This ideology is inherently incapable of foreseeing that the cultural quality of technology, when left unattended, will eventually generate serious axiological discrepancies. Most of its supporters today still refuse to believe that our real problem is a crisis in values. The unfortunate fact that modern society, especially that of America, has become artistically extravagant, and although the quality of life in our cities has deteriorated aesthetically, this feature is not generally interpreted as a serious cultural anomaly. As is the case with all diseases, no remedy can be hopefully found until the basic cause can be identified. What is suggested here is that it would pay dividends to look for the trouble in the dogmatic value system which the dominant institutional forces have grafted upon the body of modern democracy.

Despite the factuality of art as a cultural institution, the place of the arts in the structure of a democratic culture is open to controversy. If we may return to the paradox mentioned at the beginning, the position this essay takes it that the paradox, which is indicative of the presence of a cultural discrepancy, originates in the unequal distribution of institutional power itself due to the prevalence of an uncritical framework of values that permits the facile conversion of means into ends. Briefly put, it is the disequilibrium in our institutional values that has created the incongruous dissatisfying pattern of relationships between the theory and practice of democracy. The result is that our expectations for constant and genuine aesthetic satisfactions continue to be short-changed. It is this divorce of the demand for aesthetic satisfactions from all human engagements and the relative indifference of technology and other institutions toward such expectations that has generated the invidious cleavage between beauty and the applications of technology for social consumption.

Perhaps in a more sane and more balanced society such gaps between ends and means and the inversion of their place in the order of values would not be allowed to go undetected. We know that we cannot function, to say nothing about surviving, without the great services of a highly developed technology. The main issue then is whether we have acquired enough wisdom to reconstruct the axiological framework of democracy within which we permit technology to operate in relation to our complex institutional concerns. It is precisely in this area that

Western man's democratic way of life is about to face cultural bankruptcy unless we advance to more adequate conceptions of the good life. On this score then the social sciences have a far more important task to perform than that of gathering the facts and describing them in the spirit of value-free methodologies. The time has come for us to be aware of the need to raise some difficult questions about the cultural adequacy of our Western patterns of democracy. One of the urgent tasks of social inquiry is to alert us to our deeper problems and to initiate a bold policy to construct the tools for intelligent action and a more complex philosophy of democracy.

NOTES

1. "Education as a Social Institution," in *On Education : Sociological Perspectives,* edited by Donald A. Hansen and Joel Gerstl, New York : Wiley, 1967, pp. 36-68.

2. *Mind, Self & Society; from the Standpoint of a Social Behaviorist,* Chicago, 1934, pp. 261-262.

3. D. Katz and R. L. Schank singled out the following features : (1) belief in the institution as a reality transcending its members; (2) belief in the superiority of one institution over other institutions, or the fiction of institutional greatness; (3) belief in the absolute righteousness of its aims and purposes; and (4) belief in the inevitability of its success. *Social Psychology,* New York : Wiley, 1938, pp. 175-186.

4. See F. Stuart Chapin, *Contemporary Social Institutions,* New York : Harper, 1935, p. 6.

5. *The Study of Man,* New York : Appleton-Century, 1936, p. 114.

6. Plato's *Republic,* if read in this light, is the first and major philosophical treatment of the interrelationship of personal ethos and cultural ethos; furthermore, his theory of Forms can be seen as meant in this case to furnish the criterion of adequacy for any effort at social criticism.

AESTHETIC FUNCTION

Arnold Berleant, C.W. Post Center, Long Island University

I

EVER SINCE the eighteenth century when aesthetics finally discovered that it had an identity of its own, the hallmark of that identity has been disinterestedness. Concerned as it is with sense perception, aesthetics must somehow enjoin against the possibility of renewing the earlier subservience of the arts to religious, moral, political, or cognitive purposes. No longer is art significant solely for its contribution to the princely purposes of church or state. It must rather pursue its own course, fulfill its own ends, and offer its own contribution to modern civilization unhampered by outside obligations. It seemed clear that both identity and protection could be found in the notion of aesthetic disinterestedness. Thus the writings of most philosophers of art from the eighteenth century British[1] down to the present day have taken disinterestedness and the host of related notions it has spawned – isolation, contemplation, autonomy, intransitivity, dehumanization, and psychical distance, to name a few – as aesthetic axioms, or, perhaps, aesthetic dogmas. In one fashion or another our encounter with art must be kept from being confused with the world of practical affairs. To use Kant's influential formulation, we must exclude interest, with its concomitant desire for the pleasant and the good, for "taste in the beautiful is alone a disinterested and *free* satisfaction;. . . no interest, either of sense or of reason, here forces our assent."[2]

Yet the notion of distinterestedness has not enabled aesthetics to achieve the autonomy for which it was searching. As a concept, disinterestedness is actually derivative, for it embodies the classical model of the cognitive attitude as a contemplative ideal.[3] Furthermore, it shares this derivativeness with nearly every other theoretical concept in aesthetics. In fact, conceptual dependence and metaphor have been so prevalent in aesthetic theory that it is useful to describe such proposals as surrogate theories, theories which misrepresent art and our experience of it with substitute concepts and half-truths. Such is the case with notions of meaning, symbol, and feeling, and with theories of art as communication, imitation, form, and expression.[4]

Moreover, this freedom of aesthetics was a dubious freedom. Emancipation meant isolation, and until recently the arts, for the most part, have pursued their own course, unmindful of the role they played in the social dynamic. Yet art acts oblivious of philosophical decrees. And in each successive age, various arts, despite the proclamations of independence, explored new regions of sensibility and achieved new types and levels of human and social awareness. It has in fact become increasingly clear that disinterestedness is an overextended idea, and that the independence of aesthetics cannot be attained at the cost of isolation and general irrelevance. It has been the modern arts that have tended to reaffirm the connections and involvement of art, and this has occurred largely by means of a newly developed notion, the idea of function. Function here, however, is not identical with utility. Rather it becomes a description of the role of art in the full context of human activity. Indeed, function is more than a revision of disinterestedness as the proper aesthetic attitude. It signifies the radical shift from an aesthetics of contemplation which characterizes the appreciative observer by a psychological attitude, to an aesthetics of engagement that points to somatic, multisensory involvement in the aesthetic field. By examining the concept of function more closely, it will be possible to see how this has come about.

II

Perhaps the narrowest, most literal case of function is that of an object adapted to a limited task which it performs with a maximum economy of movement and a minimum of wasted effort. The paradigm of this is the machine, and we can describe function in this limited sense as *mechanical function.* At the same time as it exemplifies function, the machine, by virtue of the demand for efficiency that is placed on it, appears to be the ultimately unaesthetic object. By meeting its obligations for activity that is maximally economical, the machine is, by that fact, the exemplar of use and practice. No thought is given to imagination, delight, or any other quality for its own sake, but every attention is devoted to its external end of productive results.

Yet by a strange irony this very fact of the machine's extrinsic value has contrived to generate intrinsic qualities of an aesthetic sort. Instead of having been quarantined for its dirty hands and mundane thoughts, the machine has succeeded in penetrating the sanctity of our art houses and demanding our aesthetic attention. We find that it is impossible to turn back the clock and confine our aesthetic regard to the final products of the artist's craft. The machine, particularly the industrial machine, has pierced the very heart of our human activities to the point of transforming the arts themselves.

The machine has come to play a multifaceted role in art. It appears as a subject-matter in art, as in Leger's industrialized human forms, Honegger's aural locomotive, "Pacific 231," and the work of such groups as the Italian Futurists and the Russian Constructivists. Here the image of the machine, the movement of the machine, the transforming power of the machine, and perhaps, as with some of the dadaists, the criticism of the machine, become the basis of the perceptual object. Again, the machine serves as a supplier of parts and materials for art and at times collaborates with the artist in producing his work. It provides thin marble slabs and large plywood sheets, steel girders and prestressed concrete modules for the architect, tape recorders and electronic music synthesizers for the composer, sheet metal and acetylene torches for the sculptor, and moving stages and elaborate lighting and set changing devices for the playwright. Then there is mechanized art where the machine serves as a dynamic model for the artist to emulate. Sometimes these mechanical objects are parodies of the machine, often reaching the height of inefficiency when, ironically, they are out of order. At other times they are assimilations of the machine, from cubism's geometrization of nature which is a kind of mechanization, to the classically controlled kinetic sculpture of Jose de Rivera, computer graphics, and cybernetic sculptures.

Moreover, these uses of the machine as artistic subject matter, as a course of materials, as a creative force, and as an artistic model lead with little effort to the machine product and the machine itself as an art object. This is not only the case with the influence of the Bauhaus on design and graphics but also with recent stylistic movements like optical art and minimal art that derive their aesthetic dimensions from the simplicity, regularity, and repetitiousness of mechanical patterns. It is the case, too, with artists like Francis Picabia and Max Ernst, many of whose drawings and paintings look like engineer's blueprints, with the ready-mades of Duchamps, the playful machines of Tinguely, the automobiles of Bugatti, and the wide range of mechanical and electronic devices that populate recent movements in the plastic arts.

What, then, are the qualities that the machine and its products embody? They offer accuracy, exactness, precision of operation. They provide dependability of performance and a uniform, standardized product. Their effort to achieve ever greater efficiency of operation produces a simplicity of design that leads to regularity, to the use of repeated patterns, and to reproducibility in both the machine and its product. Finally, there is the search for suitability that strives for perfect adaptation of the mechanical object to its assigned task in the name of economy of operation. Moverover, all these features can be encompassed by the notion of functionality.

What is significant about all this is that mechanical function possesses a double appeal : It is eminently practical yet at the same time eminently pleasing in its own right. Regarded from the standpoint of production, mechanical function is perfect utility; regarded from the standpoint of perception, it is an aesthetic ideal. Thus an aesthetic of function emerges out of the principle of the machine. Such an ideal is embodied in syntheses of production and perception like the functional operation of the sailing vessel and the airplane, the excellence of performance of the watch and the engine, good form in the race horse and perfect timing in the trapeze act. The aesthetic of mechanical function finds its greatest application in design, in architecture, and in city planning.[5]

III

A rather different sense of function is based on a biological model. *Organic function* involves more than a collocation of parts designed to work together to fulfill an external task. It is characterized by an integrity in which all the component elements adapt reciprocally to each other in order to maintain a harmonious equilibrium. Organic function goes beyond mere interrelatedness; it requires cohesion, a mutual responsiveness which makes the function of the whole something over and above the action of the parts. This sense of function, then, cannot be described analytically by its elements alone but only in terms of reciprocal relationships. Moreover, unlike mechanical function where the ends are imposed externally, organic function has the important characteristic of generating its own ends. There is an internal dynamic force which impels the organism along its own course to fulfillment.

As the machine epitomizes mechanical function, so the human body epitomizes organic function. Little has to be said at this stage of biological science for the functional unity of the human organism. The puzzles that still remain have to do with the few exceptions to the functional standard rather than with its instances, and these probably have an evolutionary explanation. When the human body is taken as the subject matter or the material of art, its functional qualities usually demand to be acknowledged. Often they determine both the direction of development that an art takes and the quality of particular styles. The history of painting in the Renaissance illustrates how different organic features of the body are taken as subjects for artistic handling that impose requirements of their own upon the painter. The discovery of its mass by Giotto, of its muscularity by Michelangelo, of its linear extension by El Greco, of its vital sensuousness by Titian all reveal qualities of the human organism which find their fullest realization through the "insatiable appetite for the nude" in the sixteenth century.[6] Indeed, the nude as a subject of art, or as a form of art, as Kenneth Clark would call it,[7] can never abandon the functional necessities of the human body in seeking the ideal. Shape, proportion, and the disposition of the figure all demand to be taken account of.[8]

It is in the dance, however, that the organic functionalism of the body receives its fullest artistic exploitation. Here the human organism and its movements are not only the subject of dance but the material from which the art is fashioned as well. Just as formal imbalance in a sculpture produces a sensation of physical imbalance in the onlooker, so in dance there is somatic participation by the audience. We join with the dancer in a common activity, moving in empathetic harmony through the same space and sharing a common significance of gesture. Choreographers and critics alike agree that the appreciative experience of dance requires a sympathetic kinesthetic response.[9] Here is the body functioning as an organism at its fullest and freest, and yet it is a functioning that explores not just the biological dimension through twisting, turning, stretching, and leaping, but the biosocial range of human organic relationships through bodies lifting, carrying, embracing, and moving with each other in a shimmering iridescence of interrelationships. As the successful nude in painting must evoke at least a trace of erotic feeling,[10] so in the dance pure form and line are impossible. The human body has so powerful an attraction and reaches us on so fundamental a level that the art that uses it cannot help but invoke the full reach of mood, emotion, motive, and function.[11] We perceive the body aesthetically precisely through its ability and ease in performing its functions.

The organic functionalism of the body as the subject and material of art has, as I have already suggested, a parallel in the perceiver. The perception of art has its own organic unity of function. Ours is a multisensory involvement in which all the bodily senses participate in a cooperative and undifferentiated way. This includes the tactile sense, which tradition in aesthetics excluded because it has too close a practical relation to objects and impedes the attitude of detachment.[12] Furthermore, the functional unity of appreciative perception is not just biological and sensory; it also involves the psychological and intellectual. This has a parallel in the unity of subject and form that the art object possesses, and in their dynamic integration in perception. Moreover, all this suggests that there is perhaps a still more inclusive unity of perceiver and object in a phenomenal field, a possibility which yet other kinds of function have explored.

IV

The most common fashion in which men relate to things is in practical situations, and it is precisely here that art has always parted company. *Practical function* is one of use in which the relation of object to person is a relation of means to ends. Things do not delight in themselves; their attraction lies wholly in the uses to which they can be put. This is the interested attitude in its most unalloyed form which aesthetics has always taken pains to exclude, for it seems to deny the intrinsic qualities of aesthetic experience in a clear and unequivocal way.

Still, it is interesting to notice how difficult it has always been to keep aesthetic involvement unsullied by practical interest. Before the eighteenth century it was common to see the arts as participants in cultural celebrations. Music, dance, painting, and literature were important contributors to religious worship, state ceremonies, and the many other ritualistic observances that mark the significant occasions in every culture. Even after it proclaimed its autonomy, art continued to make its social contribution, often in the form of critical commentary, from the comedies of manners of Congreve and Wilde to the satirical paintings and sculptures of Goya and Daumier.

Yet it is precisely the discrimination of the fine from the practical arts that must be questioned. Is practical function as sharply removed from aethestic as it is generally thought to be? If disinterestedness can be challenged as the proper aesthetic attitude, perhaps its correlate, interest, also must. And so, then, too, must we question the antithesis of fine and practical art. "Beauty," as Emerson once pointed out, "must come back to the useful arts. The distinction between the fine and the useful arts must be forgotten." In fact, in the domain of function, he claimed, the beautiful rests on the foundations of the necessary. Nor was Emerson the first to note this. Hume had already observed that utility in certain practical objects becomes the source of their beauty.[14]

It is worth remarking here that the distinction between the fine and the practical arts is a philosopher's distinction, not an artist's. The activity of artistic creation is itself a synthesis of the aesthetic and the practical, where skill at fashioning art objects fuses with perceptual involvement in a mutually responsive way. Furthermore, in their work artists observe no such boundaries, freely crossing and recrossing the lines between literature and journalism, painting and illustration, sculpture and design. Moreover, there are many instances in which practical and aesthetic interests are so combined as to be inseparable, as in clothing, interior decoration, and simple tools and utensils. The cheap symmetrical hand pliers, for example, achieves its aesthetic qualities precisely from the ease with which we can grip and use it.

However the most outstanding instance of the creative amalgam of the practical and the aesthetic lies in architecture, where the function of the one is coextensive with the achievement of the other. Mies van der Rohe has observed that "Wherever technology reaches its real fulfillment, it transcends itself into architecture."[15] Together with Mies, Pier Luigi Nervi believes that the correct structural solution is the basis of good design and is the best aesthetic solution.[16] And Louis Sullivan's famous maxim that form follows function has become the starting point for virtually all of modern architecture, although its inherent ambiguity makes it a difficult guide to follow.

What is particularly pertinent here about architecture as the exemplar of practical function is that it brings together the art object – the building, and the perceiver – the building's inhabitant in the interest of complete utility. But this is more than a practical unity of perceiver and object, for when a building works well, in the fullest sense of the term, it achieves artistic success. When an office building, a school, or a house becomes a structural environment within which we can carry on with the fullest ease the kind of activities for which it was designed, there occurs a beauty of operation which is at the same time a beauty of living. Moreover, architecture is not just an art of interior spaces; it is an art of exterior masses as well, and here, too, function plays an integral part. A building must work well in relation with its environment, and consequently architecture must combine with landscape architecture and city planning to achieve a fuller and more coherent function. Further still, like other separations in aesthetics, the division in architecture between interior and exterior is disappearing as new materials and techniques provide greater strength with less bulk, and masonry walls fall before steel and glass. With the successful attainment of its practical function, architecture achieves its fullest artistic success. Moreover, the architectural environment illustrates at the same time how the mechanical function of a building and the organic function of the human body are absorbed and synthesized by the practical function.

V

By pursuing the role of function in the arts we have come to recognize traits of aesthetic experience which have often been overlooked or denied. Central to these is the notion of art as a kind of activity, an activity that infuses both the art object and its perceiver, bringing them together into a transactional relationship of mutual fulfillment. Although such examples as those of the machine, dance, and architecture may not be representative of the varied modes of the other arts, they do challenge traditional models of disinterestedness, isolation, and permanence. They stand, in fact, as perhaps more satisfactory illustrations of what the experience of art does involve. For not only is art an activity; it is an activity that embraces qualities of our world that tradition in aesthetics has often ignored – its mechanical and industrial features, its biological and sensuous elements, and most of all the intimate participation of the arts in the cultural environment that is man's special distinction.

Thus it is difficult to isolate the art object and view it disinterestedly when its force comes from the profound significance with which we imbue it. There is, in fact, some kind of contradiction between isolation and import. Yet it does not suffice merely to dispense with aesthetic disinterestedness. Something positive must take its place.

Now while each art creates its own characteristic qualitative situation, some general observations on how we experience the arts do seem to be possible. The sequence of aesthetic functions we have explored is not a series of alternatives; it is rather an order of subsumption in which each kind of function includes and develops what has come before. Thus organic function adds elements of vital harmony and self-generation to the austere efficiency of mechanical function, and practical function embraces both in a fuller context of interrelation and dependence where art object and aesthetic subject, engaging in a creative exchange, are functionally inseparable. In moving beyond the description of aesthetic appreciation as an attitude to an analysis of it as a function, we come finally to recognize a kind of setting which is most inclusive and offers the most satisfactory account – humanistic function.

Humanistic function includes the practical yet goes well beyond it. Here the interest in the object as a means to an external end is replaced by the object as a *medium* in relation to which we can function with the fullest range, intensity, and purity of experience.[17] Yet humanistic function describes not just a relation but the entire setting, the aesthetic field, within which there is an experiential merging of the perceiver and the object of art in a creative perceptual exchange. Here function becomes an active participation that combines the mechanical, organic, and practical features of the aesthetic perceiver and the art object in a living movement of intrinsic, primary experience. From this there emerges a synthesis of human fulfillment, social relevance, and aesthetic perception in which each not only encompasses the others but becomes inseparable from them.

Here many recent developments in the arts bring forth what has always existed, although in a dormant state, as action painting makes central Roger Fry's perceptive observation decades earlier that "the drawn line is the record of a gesture." Art as a functional process fuses the artist, the object, and the appreciator in a rich unity of common activity. From the "functional image"[18] of optical art to relief sculptures that require the reflected image and movement of the spectator to complete them; from theater which absorbs the audience into the performance, as in the Living Theatre, the Open Theatre, and the Polish Lab Theater, to the film which has "re-established that dynamic contact between art product and art consumption," molding the opinions, taste, language, dress, behavior, and physical appearance of an immense public;[19] from the religious experience of the medieval cathedral which creates a multimedia sensory environment that fuses architecture, sculpture, painting, poetry, drama, and music and even extends to the senses of taste and smell, to the art of community planning which offers the most inclusive setting for a cast composed entirely of actors in an environment with neither stage nor walls to provide a way of living that will allow men to become fully human[20] – out of these and more has art emerged as a vital and inclusive activity toward which the full range of human experience converges to attain its greatest self-realization and most complete consummation. This is aesthetic function at its most complete, the condition of being most human.

NOTES

1. Cf. Jerome Stolnitz, "On the Origins of 'Aesthetic Disinterestedness'," *Journal of Aesthetics and Art Criticism,* XX, 2 (Winter, 1961), pp. 131-143.

2. *Critique of Judgment,* 5.

3. Cf. A. Berleant, *The Aesthetic Field,* (Springfield, Illinois : C. C. Thomas, 1970, Ch. III.

4. *Ibid.,* Ch. II.

5. Cf. A. Berleant, "Aesthetics and the Contemporary Arts," *Journal of Aesthetics and Art Criticism,* XXIX, Cf. also M. Dufrenne, "The Aesthetic Object and the Technical Object," *JAAC,* XXIII, 1 (Fall, 1964), pp. 113-122.

6. Kenneth Clark, *The Nude, A Study in Ideal Form,* (Winter 1970) New York: Pantheon Books, pp. 155-168.

7. *Ibid.,* p. 5.

8. *Ibid.,* pp. 20 ff.

9. Cf., for example, Walter Terry, *Ballet, A New Guide to the Liveliest Art,* New York : Dell Publishing, 1959, pp. 11, 24; and John Martin, *Introduction to the Dance,* New York : Norton, 1939, p. 10.

10. Clark, op. cit., p. 8.

11. Martin, op. cit.

12. Cf. A. Berleant, "The Sensuous and the Sensual in Aesthetics," *The Journal of Aesthetics and Art Criticism,* XXIII, 2 (Winter, 1964), p. 188.

13. Cf. M. Merleau-Ponty, *The Phenomenology of Perception,* Routledge and Kegan Paul, 1962, pp. 150-151. Also p. 119 n.

14. *Inquiry concerning the principles of Morals,* Sect. V, "Why Utility Pleases," New York : Hafner, 1948, p. 207.

15. Quoted in "The City," Santa Barbara, California : Center for the Study of Democratic Institutions, 1962, p. 31.

16. *Ibid.,* p. 18.

17. Cf. John Dewey, *Art as Experience,* New York, 1934, pp. 197, 256.

18. William C. Seitz, *The Responsive Eye,* New York : The Museum of Modern Art, 1965, p. 43.

19. Erwin Panofsky, "Style and Medium in the Moving Pictures."

20. Cf. Percival and Paul Goodman, *Communitas,*New York : Vintage Books, 1960, pp. 19-21.

AN EMPIRICAL NATURALISTIC ACCOUNT OF METAPHYSICS AS METASCIENCE

Tad S. Clements, State University of New York at Brockport

"METAPHYSICS" is not a univocal term and the boundaries of the discipline the term ostensibly designates is not at all clear. Some thinkers, for example, those in the Aristotelian and Thomistic traditions, have viewed it as a kind of a posteriori discipline; whereas others, for example, certain Rationalists, have viewed it as an a priori science. Again, some of the fundamental problems, for example, the problem of whether universal determinism is true, false or meaningless, actually cannot be disentangled from the concerns of moral philosophy and other fields of human intellectual activity.

However, there have been certain central emphases, certain generally shared conceptions of the nature and goal of metaphysics, and a consideration of these conceptions suggests, at least in part, both the reason for the appeal and the disrespect metaphysics has had among thoughtful men throughout human history.

There is something exceptionally appealing and exciting in the conception of a discipline whose object is to study the "ultimate" nature and structure of "Reality"; a kind of super-science whose concern is not with this or that kind of being, as these may be revealed through "ordinary" or scientifically controlled experience, but with "being-as-such," with "being qua being"; a unique sort of speculative inquiry whose results are not established by grubbing observation and experimentation, but rather on the grounds of "intuition" or by "pure reason"; a study which is not limited to partial aspects of limited domains, but rather one which holds out the promise of full "cosmic understanding." Probably all men would find satisfaction in having adequate answers to the kinds of seemingly profound questions metaphysicians have dealt with. Does the world logically require, and hence necessarily presuppose, a sustaining first cause? A reason for being, or for being specifically what it is? Is man free or determined? Is there a kind of personal immortality? Is there a reality behind all appearances? Is there something eternal and immutable transcending the ephemeral? What is the status of universals and what is their connection with particulars? Does the world manifest a cosmic purpose, a universal telic principle? And so forth. What man would not like to possess completely adequate, reliable answers to questions of this sort? No wonder, then, that metaphysics has so powerfully attracted the consideration of so many great intellects.

But these very claims – of a superlative *via cognitiva,* of a transcendent knowledge of cosmic scope, of answers which are beyond the scope of ordinary or scientific experience to attain – unfortunately bear within themselves the seeds of their own destruction. Grandiose aspirations and claims lead, perhaps inevitably, to profound disillusionment and doubt. Skepticism and agnosticism are frequently the fruit of the metaphysical quest. The creation of imposing metaphysical edifices produces also those who are unable or unwilling to inhabit those edifices. Critical inquiries, since the days of the Sophists, have brought nearly every part of the metaphysical quest into serious question. From thinkers like Kant and Spencer, who would maintain that metaphysics seeks to know an ultimate reality which is hidden from man because of the limitations of his cognitive apparatus or methods, to the descendants of Hume and Wittgenstein, who question whether metaphysical utterances are real statements at all, there is a widespread and profound disenchantment with the whole enterprize.

Thus modern man finds himself in a dilemma. On the one hand are questions which seem to possess the greatest of significance, while on the other hand there is widespread disillusionment and distrust concerning the questions asked, the methods employed to answer them, and with the alleged answers themselves. It seems natural, therefore, to ask : Is there a satisfactory way out of this dilemma?

The answer, of course, depends on what one is willing to accept as "satisfactory." Pandora's box is opened as soon as one asks : Satisfactory in what sense? Satisfactory for what kinds of reasons? The crux of the problem is that different thinkers accept, implicitly or explicitly, different, frequently incompatible criteria determinative of meaning, truth, value, and reality – in a word, for what is satisfactory. Hence, if adjudication among rival metaphysical claims is to become possible, it becomes necessary to determine why different criteria are adopted and whether these criteria themselves can be evaluated in ways which can, at least in principle, command the respect of the general philosophic community.

Logically prior to attempts at answering these questions, are the questions : What are criteria? and What sense of "evaluation" is appropriate to them? These are not simply idle questions; they are fundamental. Different sorts of things frequently have unique roles in human experience and thought and the appraisal of these roles therefore can, and frequently does, involve distinctly different sorts of procedures. To see the truth of this, one has only to consider the ways in which we attempt to assess the functions performed by mathematical concepts as contrasted with empirical concepts or of legal rules as compared to scientific laws.

What, then, are criteria? As soon as the question is asked, we become aware of a profound difficulty. Not only do different thinkers accept different, frequently incompatible criteria of meaning, truth, value and reality; they do not even agree on what a criterion is. Of course, there are synonyms which are generally accepted, such as "standard." "regulative ideal." "rule of procedure," etc.; but, as should be expected, these suffer from the same ambiguity, that is, different thinkers do not agree on what they mean. For instance, some mean by such terms concepts which emerge within, guide, and are themselves testable by reference to ongoing inquiries. As such, they are viewed as useful conceptual devices in guiding experiential processes. For others, the terms designate arbitrary stipulations simply reflecting the purposes of the thinker. Still others seem to mean by criteria rules of procedure forced upon us by the nature of human reason or by the nature of reality or both and therefore in no sense to be construed as merely convenient, arbitrarily chosen stipulations. And there are other conceptions as well.

Now, is there any rationally justifiable way in which these different conceptions of the nature and function of criteria as well as the specific criteria proposed and adopted by various thinkers can be evaluated? This poses a serious dilemma. If we do attempt to evaluate conceptions of criteria or particular criteria, the attempt itself must involve criteria we have adopted (for evaluation involves judging something according to an accepted standard). And our problem then becomes : which criteria should be used to evaluate criteria? Why? Are these evaluative criteria themselves open to evaluation? If so, in terms of what sorts of criteria? We are led, in other words, into either the adoption of certain criteria which are, arbitrarily, treated as ultimate or into an infinite regress. But if we do not attempt to evaluate conceptions of criteria or the particular criteria proposed and utilized by different thinkers, we must rest content (or discontent) with a kind of skeptical relativism. In such cases we must say something such as : Mr. A understands by criteria "X," whereas Mr. B understands by criteria "Y," both propose and employ criteria for truth, meaning, value and reality in accordance with "X" and "Y," and although "X" and "Y" are incompatible, they are both acceptable as long as one confines himself to the universe of discourse of either A or B, i.e., as long as one does not mix his frames of reference. Both of these courses seem to me to be clearly undesirable, but one or the other must be chosen. Hence, the question involves a destructive dilemma. There may, however, be a way in which ontological criteria can be evaluated and I shall turn to this possibility after a short digression.

Now to the digression. Instead of dealing with the epistemic problem, let us ask : Where do criteria come from? What is their source? What sorts of factors cause or influence thinkers to choose one rather than another criterion? These are, of course, empirical questions which require careful studies to be adequately answered, but perhaps we can accomplish something without such studies by merely suggesting some plausible views. It should be noted that this procedure will not involve the Genetic Fallacy, for I am not making the claim that the source or alleged source of criteria has any logical status, but merely that such sources or alleged sources cannot serve as adequate justification for ontological criteria.

Some thinkers would probably trace criteria choice to temperamental differences. It is doubtful, of course, whether any careful philosophic thinker would go so far as to assert that *only* temperamental preferences are determinative of such choices, but some reputable philosophers have adopted a view which in practice tends to amount to the same thing. The names of F.C.S. Schiller and William James come to mind in this connection. Now it is true that even these men admit that temperamental preferences alone are insufficient as bases for determining what is true or real. James, for instance, was careful to insist that a person is warranted in believing something to be true only on the basis of its "cash value," i.e., on the basis of its experiential, testable consequence. However, he does adopt the criterion that if in fact alternative beliefs have the same cash value – i.e., there is, pragmatically speaking, no advantage to believing one rather than another of the alternatives – then one is free to choose the one he prefers. Since in many cases there will be no greater pragmatic utility for one rather than another alternative, in practice James' criterion does, in such cases, make personal preference ultimate.

F.C.S. Schiller, while accepting the Jamesian pragmatic criterion, goes even further down the road toward the Sophistic dictum : "Man (the individual man) is the measure of all things." In making experiences private and unique, in his insistence that each individual creates his own truths and his own realities out of the structures of his own unique experience, in his desire to see each man as the final judge of what is true or real on the basis of how well ideas work for him, Schiller has come very close to the position suggested, i.e., the attempt to trace criteria choices to temperamental differences. However, even he puts some limitation on this approach by insisting that many of our ideas must meet the test of social utility.

Existentialism, at least in some of its major expressions, seems to involve much the same sort of appeal to individual subjective preference as the final court of appeal. This certainly appears to be the case as far as values are concerned, for existentialists generally assume that men freely create values through their undetermined choices. It is not, however, so obvious that this holds also for ontological criteria. They usually accept, as given, the ontic world, i.e., the world of facticity, the realm of other, nonhuman beings, and this certainly does not seem to be a concession to a subjective preference basis for ontological judgments. But when it is noted that such thinkers make the individual subjective human world, as revealed in phenomenological analysis, the only significant one for human beings and thus relegate the world of other beings, together with its relations and processes, to an inconsequential status, it becomes clear that individual preference is the regnant ontological criterion. Now it may be that this treatment does not do justice to such thinkers, but this is really not very important in terms of the present purpose, for it is here intended merely to illustrate a possible view concerning the source of ontological criteria and of conceptions of the nature of such criteria. If there are no thinkers who actually hold such a view – which I think is dubious – the position attributed to them is still a possible one which some thinker might maintain.

However, if anyone does hold such a position, he is on dangerous philosophic ground; for surely the criteria chosen to answer questions foundational to a *theory of reality* must be logically irrelevant to one's personal preferences. If metaphysics is to be viewed as a respectable cognitive enterprise, the way in which the term *theory* must be understood in the expression *theory of reality* is in the sense of a consistent set of conceptual principles which form a general frame of reference. And, in the same context, the *general frame of reference* must be intended as an adequate delineation of what *is* the case, not merely what one would *prefer to be* the case. If one adopts, deliberately or through some form of self-deception, criteria for reality for which there is no better "reason" than personal preference, one cannot hope to avoid the charge of wishful thinking, of philosophical daydreaming; and one's resultant "theory" is at best a kind of disguised autobiography, a sort of introspective psychological description, expressed in inappropriate categories.

Instead of tracing the adoption of ontological criteria to personal psychological factors (preferences), it is possible to view such criteria as being the results of stipulations, as being arbitrarily chosen conventions, whose justification is to be found in the use to which they are put, i.e., in the conceptual frameworks which they make possible. From this point of view, it seems to be the case that a large number of alternative metaphysical syntheses and solutions to metaphysical problems are possible and are, in one sense at least, equally acceptable. Metaphysical systems are, thus conceived, simply different conceptual models, each of which is (ideally) internally consistent and capable, through its own set of presuppositions and categories, of organizing diverse aspects of experience in terms of its own frame of reference. So conceived, metaphysical systems are analogous to different art styles or to alternative geometries. Though there are certain conditions which any geometry must meet (e.g., internal consistency) and (presumably) which any work of art must possess if it is to be capable of producing "aesthetic experience," there is no reason why all geometries or all art works must satisfy completely identical sets of criteria. Indeed, we know that this is not the case. In like manner, it might be argued, though all metaphysical systems, if they are to be acknowledged as such, must satisfy *certain* criteria, it does not follow that they must adopt an *identical set* of criteria. Freedoom to stipulate, within certain limits, is an option open to the metaphysician. It is apparent, I think, that the adoption of such a viewpoint would place metaphysical speculations, together with the criteria they involve, very largely above critical evaluation; metaphysical speculations, if only they meet certain fundamental conditions, can be understood as systems, but not criticized from without. The result is much the same as that which follows from the adoption of personal preference as ultimate justification.

However, there is a serious weakness in such a view : the analogies involved simply will not hold. Alternative geometries are after all simply formal systems. As such, they do not claim to be about reality, but merely about certain conceptual entities and their ideal systematic relationships. Metaphysical syntheses and the elements which enter into them, in contrast, do not claim to be merely formal. Works of art, it should certainly be conceded (whatever else might correctly describe them) must, if they are to be judged as being artistic, be capable of producing certain kinds of responses, i.e., those usually designated as "aesthetic experiences." But on what conceivable ground could one demonstrate the justification for assuming that reality must be portrayed in an aesthetic manner? Reality is whatever it is and aesthetic appeal or lack of such appeal is not logically relevant. If metaphysics is the study of reality, as it has nearly always been defined, and if any metaphysical theory is therefore meant to be a theory of reality, then reality must be portrayed as it is, if this is possible. Aesthetic impact is relevant to art works, not to metaphysical systems.

In other words, the criteria employed in the construction of metaphysical theories must be guided by the actual nature of the object of its concern, if this is possible; the metaphysician is not free to stipulate arbitrarily and still call the result a theory of *reality*.

Traditionally, some philosophers treated ontological criteria and the judgments they make possible as though they were intuited, self-evident truths or a priori synthetic truths of reason. In view of the devastating criticisms philosophers and other thinkers have levelled against such opinions, there is some question whether any further comment is needed. Perhaps a few questions will suffice. What is to be understood by the vague and ambiguous term *intuition?* What decision procedure is open to those who use the criterion of intuited self-evidence or the requirements of reason when they happen to disagree ? When, as has happened in the past, a metaphysician reaches a conclusion, using criteria based on intuited self-evidence or the a priori requirements of reason, which conflicts with well-established experience, is it not then simply dogmatic to continue to espouse criteria of the former types? An examination of the kinds of judgments made and categories adopted by metaphysicans ostensibly on the basis of such conceptions of criteria reveals clearly that such judgments and categories are either (1) those which reflective experience would suggest or (2) empty tautologies or (3) mere preferences of the metaphysician. But if they are (1), what is to be gained by saying they are the result of "intuition" or "pure reason." If they are (2), what could they tell us about the natural world, without being interpreted along lines suggested by experience? And if they are (3), the criticisms previously suggested apply.

The expression "a priori synthetic truths of reason," as used in the preceding paragraph, refers to one of the traditional interpretations of a priori; the sense intended in the metaphysical speculations of Parmenides, for example. Currently, of course, the term, a priori, has taken on a different meaning. In the writings of certain thinkers, e.g., P.F. Strawson in his work *Individuals,* the term, a priori, means *necessary* in terms of the logic of discourse. Thus, such thinkers insist that we are entitled to make certain existential (ontological) claims simply because the denial of such claims commits the person who attempts to deny them to an inconsistency. For example, to express doubt as to the reality of other individuals.

But the adoption of such a criterion as ultimate ontologically seems plausible only if one fails to note that such discourse and all of the elements essential to it are pragmatically warranted, i.e., only if one fails to realize that human discourse itself emerges within and ideally serves instrumentally to make coherent human experience and practice possible. In other words, in some sense, it is the nature of whatever experience reveals which is ultimately determinative of the truth or falsity, appropriateness or inappropriateness, of our conceptual (linguistic) requirements, Linguistic consistency is epistemologically warranted and applicable to metaphysical researches only if reality is such that it is itself isomorphically consistent, but whether it is or not cannot be decided solely by reference to our logical and linguistic requirements. To repeat, the criteria employed in the construction of metaphysical theories must be guided by the actual nature of the object of its concern (reality), if this is possible.

Viewed from a different perspective, the criteria adopted by metaphysicians and their opponents can be traced to various contexts which condition human intellectual enterprises, including the metaphysical enterprise. It should be realized that even though a metaphysical system - a *Weltanschauung* - seeks to be all-inclusive and this to serve as the widest of all contexts, it is itself always context-dependent. The categories and principles employed in its world account, indeed, the very problems and questions it considers, have wider cultural, historical and intellectual uses and dimensions. After all, the metaphysician is not a pure intellect concerned with completely insulated problems; he is an acculturated being, a being influenced in diverse ways by the cultural fabric of the groups in which he participates. As such, he will tend to adopt, to a large extent, criteria of meaning, truth, value and reality not too much at variance with those accepted within his social milieu. To do otherwise would be to give up the desire to communicate, and obviously metaphysicians do wish to communicate their thoughts to others. To deny this would amount to the claim that metaphysicians seek to do exercises in futility and this could hardly be defended.

But it is clear to anyone versed in cultural studies that social groups are seldom very self-critical or articulate. All cultures contain numerous nonrational assumptive elements. It is indeed rare for social groups adequately to comprehend the subtle ways in which mere prejudice, traditional and conventional habits of thought, shape their notions of what is real.

The metaphysician can hardly avoid bringing some of these unexamined cultural criteria into his metaphysical inquiries. What he thus introduces may be innocuous. Such seems to be the case in appealing to a two-valued logic. On the other hand, the criteria may be quite pernicious. Such certainly seems to be the case when appeal is made to some allegedly absolute authority.

So much, then, for criteria – the rules and regulative ideals employed by metaphysicians in making ontological judgments – assumptive, unjustified (and perhaps unjustifiable) criteria do enter into metaphysical inquiries.

Surely the same sort of conclusion must be reached in connection with other kinds of assumptive elements, the axioms or other primitive elements found in systems of thought. Every universe of discourse, every level of analysis and description, and every kind of explanation presuppose (as unproved, indeed, unprovable) within the system certain primitive elements. Aristotle was quite right when he noted that not all things can be proved. Nor can we avoid this conclusion by appealing to meta-disciplines. For, even though it may be true that what is taken for granted, unproved and unprovable, within a given intellectual framework may be revealed, critically examined, and proved by means of principles employed in a meta-discipline, the meta-discipline itself also presupposes unexamined elements, elements which cannot be established within the meta-discipline itself. Whether one conceives of the meta-discipline as ultimate or as merely one step in either a finite or an infinite series of meta-disciplines, the result will be the same : there must always be certain unexamined presuppositions.

Does this mean that the rational appraisal of assumptions is impossible? Perhaps not, because such primitive elements as well as the criteria previously discussed play their roles in the thought frameworks they make possible, and these thought frameworks may be open to various conceptual and experiential tests. It is generally acknowledged that certain critical evaluative techniques are effective in understanding and testing certain kinds of intellectual frameworks. Scientific methods, educational and guidance procedures, psychological techniques, propaganda, analyses, logical treatments of fallacies, linguistic analyses, as well as many other sorts of critical evaluative activities, are grounded in the belief that it is possible to become more self-critical, to think clearly, rationally and realistically. If human beings were completely unable to attain an awareness of their own presuppositions and to appraise these presuppositions in terms of testable conceptual and experiential consequences, then the belief underlying such procedures would generally lead to lack of success. But, though none of these activities has had indubitable successes (and some of them are in fact more or less open to suspicion), many of them have been pragmatically successful. By modus tollens, it seems to follow that if metaphysical investigations belong to the class of intellectual frameworks amenable to one or more of the sorts of procedure suggested, some of the uncritical assumptive elements they contain can be assessed. Are metaphysical systems intellectual frameworks of this type?

If one denies that they are of this type, i.e., denies that they are amenable to certain logical and critical evaluative procedures, two serious difficulties face him. First, he must then accept a kind of relativism in terms of which it becomes impossible for genuine disputes between metaphysicians or between metaphysicians and nonmetaphysicians to take place. Both metaphysicans and nonmetaphysicians should find this result deplorable. Secondly, he must give up any claim that metaphysics is concerned with developing theories of reality which are true or accurate; for there would be no such thing, even in principle, under such conditions, as a *true* or *accurate* theory of reality. *True* and *accurate* are applied to assertions or systems which have successfully met some sorts of critical tests.

To summarize briefly : though it is not possible to develop an assumptionless metaphysics – one which does not take for granted certain criteria and primitive elements – it may always be possible to expose some of these presupposed elements and guiding principles, and perhaps even eliminate or modify those which critical scrutiny indicates are unwarranted. And, finally, refusal to follow up such clarificatory and critical possibilities has very undesirable cognitive consequences.

However, the claim that metaphysical inquiries should be scrutinized and evaluated in terms of testable conceptual and experiential consequences implies that there is or ought to be a particular purpose and context relevant to metaphysics, so let us return to the question of what sorts of considerations ought to determine the criteria chosen by metaphysicians.

Now, even though personal preferences, in the sense previously discussed, are logically irrelevant to metaphysical inquiries, I think something roughly analogous to them is logically relevant, namely, purposes proper to metaphysics conceived as an intellectual discipline concerned with the accurate portrayal of reality. By this I mean simply that if metaphysics is to become a respectable *cognitive* enterprise concerned with the nature of what is *real,* the purpose of the metaphysician ought, logically speaking, to be the attainment of a *true* view of reality and this is only possible, if at all, if his methods are epistemologically sound. In terms of this regnant purpose, metaphysical knowledge must be pursued as dispassionately as science pursues its knowledge. Of course, scientists are not free of bias; but the methodological criteria involved in scientific conceptual activities serve, at least to some extent, to correct and eliminate the results of such bias. It is just such sorts of safeguards which must become regulative in the conceptual activities of metaphysicians.

Not only must the metaphysician, as a respectable theoretician, seek to eliminate his biases by assuming as starting points of his inquiries only what other metaphysicians would grant as epistemologically warranted; he must also, if he is to reach warranted conclusions, not seek to answer (or even pose) unanswerable or nonsensical questions (such as, why is there anything at all? or How can the Absolute, which is nontemporal, enter into the temporal?). The metaphysician must, in terms of this ideal, ask real rather than pseudoquestions and ones which can, at least in principle, be answered and tested effectively; for otherwise we have counterfeits in place of knowledge.

This means, for example, that a metaphysical knowledge of reality must not be understood as implying an ultimate, final, complete knowledge of reality; for such a conception of metaphysical knowledge is doomed to failure. If metaphysics is conceived as a discipline which gives or seeks to give a knowledge of "being qua being." on a "cosmic scope," it is doomed to failure not only because such a conception fails to recognize that all human intellectual constructions necessarily involve assumptive elements, as previously suggested, but equally because it fails to recognize that human knowledge of reality is always limited to what can be inferred from human experience and that both of these – human inferences and human experience – are always limited and partial. Both human empirical experience and human inferences involve references to *some* kind of being or beings viewed in terms of *some* kind or kinds of relationship(s) within *some particular* kind of specifiable context about which certain assumptions are made.

The goal of metaphysics ought, therefore, to be newly conceived. Instead of seeking complete knowledge, it should seek plausible conceptual syntheses limited to what can reasonably be inferred or extrapolated from tested (logically and scientifically controlled) inquiry. Instead of seeking immutable, absolute truths, it should seek provisional constructions, responsive to critically developed transformations in human thought. Instead of being a web of fancies reflecting the hopes and preferences of human beings, it should seek to portray the cosmos and man's place and possibilities in it as objectively as possible. Instead of seeking to portray a realm which completely transcends human thought and experience, it should seek an admittedly human and testable perspective. If such goal revision is accepted, metaphysics will of course no longer be as grandiose an undertaking as it has frequently been thought to be, but it will gain immeasurably in what it is able to accomplish and in the respect accorded to it.

It is clear, however, that to attempt metaphysical inquiries in this new spirit will not free the metaphysician from the necessity of adopting certain epistemic and ontological criteria as well as certain fundamental conceptual categories. Which criteria and categories should be adopted? In attempting to answer this question, let us begin by noting that the proposed goal revisions for metaphysics largely coincide with the regulative ideals which guide theory construction in the natural sciences also. This raises two interesting questions : How, in terms of this conception of metaphysics, does metaphysics differ from the sciences? and do not the natural sciences themselves presuppose a metaphysical perspective which is in need of clarification and justification? Or, to bring all questions together, we may ask : Why and to what extent should the sciences serve as models for metaphysics?

Now the natural sciences, through adherence to certain criteria of meaning, truth, evidence, etc. have been able to develop more dependable accounts of nature than any alternative methods. By "dependable accounts of nature" I mean accounts which are logically consistent and which are capable of bridging, conceptually, gaps between ascertained and logically related experiential data; accounts which are, as a result, confirmable through controlled experience. If any belief systems whatsoever have a valid claim to be entitled knowledge of reality it is scientific accounts. The only defect in such accounts appears to be that they involve *restricted* studies of *selected aspects* of the world. They are too limited, in themselves, to serve even the toned down purposes proposed for metaphysics.

Since the accounts of the natural sciences are, at present, the nearest thing men have to a *knowledge* of reality, metaphysicians should look to these sciences and their basic methodological principles for guidance; but metaphysics must be something more than these sciences taken individually or collectively. It must seek a more comprehensive and a more profound vision that that afforded by the natural sciences.

What I recommend is that metaphysics should seek to become a kind of science, but one which seeks to formulate a theory of reality which goes beyond the accounts of the natural sciences. It should seek to "go beyond" these sciences in at least three senses: (1) in the sense of viewing these natural sciences themselves in a broader cultural and intellectual framework or perspective; (2) in the sense of extrapolating from and generalizing the limited scientific accounts; and (3) in the sense that, while seeking to remain as consonant as possible with the goals, criteria and basic categories of the sciences it would, at the same time, probe their foundations and utilities, that is, seek to find epistemic and pragmatic justifications for them.

To accomplish such a task the metaphysician must be able to exist simultaneously or alternately in two intellectual worlds : he must be able to view science sympathetically and still seek to view it in context. To do so implies the ability and willingness to accept and use scientific procedures and accounts as probably reliable and at the same time to recognize the sorts of things such procedures and accounts assume, the logical relationships exemplified, and the connections (real as well as ideal) between the sciences and other relevant segments of human experience and thought. The metaphysician must, in other words, become a kind of metascientist and his discipline a kind of metascience.[1]

What kind of metaphysical system is most appropriate, if we proceed along this line? One might be tempted to think this is an absurd question, since almost any metaphysical system is compatible with the natural sciences : that any well developed, logically articulated, philosophic synthesis must be able to accept, as reasonable and useful, scientific procedures and accounts. Such a view I do not wish to dispute. The history of intellectual thought makes it clear that this contention is correct. Many different, incompatible metaphysical theories are compatible with science.

What I do wish to dispute is the claim that all well developed metaphysical systems are equally acceptable metascientific disciplines. By employing gratuitous assumptions and making required conceptual distinctions, etc., a metaphysician can bring his speculations into at least apparent harmony with the sciences. He can then, for example, assert that time is unreal, that there is a realm of scientifically unverifiable realities, etc. without apparently encroaching on the domain of science in any way. However, absence of contradiction is not sufficient. If one is to proceed in the way I propose – which seems to be the only way in which metaphysics can become respectable in the way science is intellectually respectable – one must develop metaphysical constructions which accord with the fundamental cognitive criteria and principles of the factual sciences better than all other alternatives. That there are such criteria and principles presupposed by all of the sciences I believe I have shown in my work, *Science and Man.* And I have there argued that the metaphysical system which accords maximally with these criteria and principles is an Empirical Naturalism. Let me summarize briefly the treatment of these points in *Science and Man.*

A study of the various factual sciences reveals that their different universes of discourse, which employ quite different explanatory constructs, such as *quanta* in physics, *biogenesis* in biology, *culture* in anthropology, etc. presuppose at least six fundamental explanatory principles which these sciences share: (1) a realist thesis – that there is an independently existing world having "objective" structures and properties; (2) the principle of the uniformity of nature – that what occurs under a specified set of natural conditions will occur again under a sufficiently similar set of conditions; (3) the organic or ecological principle – that the proper understanding of anything requires reference to some relevant contextual features; (4) and (5) the belief in universal lawful changes – that everything in nature undergoes transformation and that underlying these transformations are laws; and (6) the nonteleological principle – the belief that the real causes of goal-directed processes are antecedent, efficient causes.

In addition to such fundamental beliefs and principles, all of the natural or factual sciences presuppose various epistemic criteria. Analysis of scientifically acceptable meaning-situations reveals that the criteria scientists adopt reflect, primarily, the scientific purpose of testing accounts in such a way that they are shown to be logically relevant to the system of scientific notions (conceptual schemas, laws, concepts, etc.) generally accepted on the one hand and on the other hand so that they will serve as "reliable guides to the empirical context, as determined by the social context." (*Science and Man,* p. 16). The "empirical context" refers to the phenomena the scientist is concerned with in his investigation and the "social context" refers to the group of scientific investigators engaged in related projects who will, ultimately, judge the scientist's work by reference to the "rules of the game," the accepted criteria.

The epistemic criteria adopted by the scientific community serve to differentiate between purely individual subjective experiences and those which, because of their constancy, uniformity and public character, can be taken as "objective" in reference. Criteria of repeatability and/or intersubjective agreement function in this way. However, the desire to distinguish between pure individual subjectivity and "objective" experience is only one scientific desideratum. Scientific accounts must, as already noted, be testable. The desire for testable accounts has led the scientific community to adopt criteria which are supposed to enable investigators to recognize and eliminate, from the scientific domain, various kinds of untestable accounts – those which are empty, i.e., those which, because they are consistent with any state of affairs, are neither confirmable nor disconfirmable; those whose sole justification lies in "intuition" or a priori principles or authority; those which employ *essentially* mysterious, vague concepts; and those which utilize unnecessary ad hoc assumptions.

To what extent do the chief rival metaphysical systems seek to establish their conclusions in accordance with such principles and criteria? Existential speculations fail to meet the requirements imposed by certain of the fundamental principles, notably numbers (3), (4), (5) and (6), i.e., they fail to recognize the fundamental importance of the natural context in adequately understanding the human consciousness and its projects and they do not admit that human life and behavior are best understood in terms of natural laws of the efficient type. In tracing meaning, truth and values ultimately to an individualistic subjectivity rather than to intersubjective agreement; in maintaining an essential yet unverifiable freedom for men – a doctrine which runs counter to the warranted conclusions of all of the factual sciences which take men as their proper subject matter; and in their use of certain essentially mysterious categories, such as "being-in-general," "Nothingness," etc., they fail to meet some of the fundamental scientific criteria.

Objective Idealism infers from nature's (partial) intelligibility, cosmic intelligence; from order, the reality of a cosmic ordering principle or mind; from life, mind and values, as these are found in the biotic and human domains, the presence of such things in the nonhuman universe. All such essentially anthropomorphic tendencies violate the principle of parsimony and other criteria regulative for inductive and analogical inferences. And, of course, these inferences are not fundamentally consonant with principle number (6).

Subjective Idealism, in making the reality of things depend upon acts of perception, reverses the causal order, a unidirectional order for the natural sciences. Idealisms of this type fail to agree with principle (1), the realist thesis of science. Also, science admits as probably real entities and processes not available to the act of perception; entities which, without the God notion (which violates the criteria pertaining to testability), Subjective Idealism cannot allow.

Neo-Thomism is guilty of assuming gratuitously, as truths of faith, many essentially mysterious and unverifiable entities and processes, such as the "soul," "transubstantiation" and "the trinity"; of ignoring criteria of intersubjectivity in accordance with the cannons of logic and experimental procedures in appealing to faith; of violating principle (5) in the doctrine of creation *ex nihilo* and principle (6) in tracing natural events to final causation.

Ordinary Language Philosophy fails to serve as a good metascience primarily because it fails to recognize the importance of principle (3) : linguistic or conceptual frameworks are either separated from (treated independent of) the broader encompassing experiential behavioral contexts or are at least taken as fundamental in order to account for the features of human life, thought and action. A moral-legal linguistic framework (certain principles of linguistic interpretation) is taken as ultimate in dealing with human action. In terms of this framework, values are treated as stipulations or are said to be assumed as a characteristic only of men. In narrowing their concern in this way, Ordinary Language Philosophers separate philosophy, more or less effectively, from the wider, relevant contexts within which the sciences function.

All other rival metaphysical systems violate one or more of the principles and criteria discussed. Only empirical naturalisms, philosophies which begin with two fundamental categories – experience and nature – and seek to develop their picture of reality in accordance with the fundamental principles and criteria of the sciences can hope to develop an adequate metascientific metaphysics.

NOTES

1. There are, of course, a number of different, albeit more or less closely related, conceptions of Metascience. Cf. for example, *Ways of Looking at Science : On a Synoptic Study of Contemporary Schools of "Metascience"*, published by the Institute for the Theory of Science, University of Gothenburg, Gothenburg, Sweden (A Preprint from *Scientia*), 1969.

NATURALISM, AND THE SENSE AND NONSENSE OF "FREE WILL"

C. J. Ducasse, Brown University

THE WORDS, Natural and Naturalism, have been used by philosophers in various senses. I do not propose to review them but only to make thoroughly clear at this point what in this paper I shall mean by those two words.

It is that whatever exists or occurs is capable of being explained *scientifically;* i.e., in a manner that yields *knowledge* as distinguished from groundless or inadequately grounded opinion. This is the only ontological commitment of what I shall mean by Naturalism, which, aside from it, is ontologically neutral; its meaning being thus wholly methodological.

This meaning of Natural and Naturalism does, I believe, wholly accord with the account of Naturalism contributed by Professor Arthur C. Danto to the *Encyclopedia of Philosophy* published in 1967.

My finding his account congenial, and hence my adopting it, is itself natural in view of convictions of mine long antedating that *Encyclopedia,* that what philosophers seek concerning the questions they discuss is answers having fully the status of knowledge.

For instance, more than thirty years ago, in an article entitled "Is Scientific Verification Possible in Philosophy? "[1] I pointed out that both philosophy and the sciences seek not mere opinion but knowledge; that the sciences have won a vast body of knowledge and daily make positive additions to it notwithstanding their theoretical controversies; whereas in philosophy the same great problems are discussed generation after generation with meager results other than multiplication of theories and schools of opinion; so that one is moved to wonder whether philosophy is forever doomed to inconclusiveness, or whether on the contrary knowledge and definite progress are possible in its field in the same sense of these terms as in the physical and biological sciences.

Again, that such knowledge and definite progress are possible in philosophy and are aimed at there was contended in 1941 in my book, *Philosophy as a Science.*[2] And in 1944, in my Howison Lecture at the University of California, *The Method of Knowledge in Philosophy,*[3] I described that method and gave illustrations of its employment.

What I shall attempt in the pages to follow is, in accordance with that method, to define in a precise and nonarbitrary manner the terms that are key terms in a knowledge-yielding discussion of the common assumption that Determinism is inherently incompatible with possession by man of the freedom postulated when he is said to have "Free will."

If my attempt is successful, it will make evident both what sense and what nonsense are latent in the would-be magical term "Free Will."

That man has "Free Will" is a belief prized by plain men because of the eulogistic connotation of "free," as contrasted with the depreciatory connotation of its opposites. The belief is prized by moralists because they think "Free Will" is indispensable for moral responsibility. And the monotheistic theologians who hold that man has "Free Will" do so because they believe that ascription of the evil men do to misuse by them of their "Free Will" exculpates their God of responsibility for it – although, in so believing, they overlook the statement by Jehovah to be found in Isaiah 45-7 in the unexpurgated editions of the Old Testament, that "I form the light, and create darkness; I make peace, *and create evil;* I am Jehovah, that doeth all these things." (Italics mine)

Moreover, no contradiction would be involved in the supposition that men had been created not only free to do good or evil as they chose, but created also good instead of partly good and partly evil; in which case they would simply prefer not to do the evils they nevertheless had the power to do.

Anyway, plain men, moralists, and theologians, and the persons with whom they dispute, are usually much more *sure* that man has "Free Will" than *clear* as to what exactly they mean by the term – their discussions thus generating more heat than light.

As a first step, then, toward a responsible analysis of what sense and what nonsense there is in the contention that man has "Free Will," let us list a few simple instances of what could commonly be regarded, respectively, as exercise by him of "Free Will," and of things which on the contrary man is not free to do.

Instances of the first would be that, in my present circumstances, I can, "at will," raise my arm or not raise it; frown or not frown; move or not move my pen. On the other hand, instances of human impotencies would be that I am *not free* to look at the back of my head *directly* (vs. at a mirror-reflection of it), nor to look *directly* at my eyeballs; nor am I free to fly through the air by moving my forelimbs as does a bird; etc.

These few instances are enough to make evident that what a person *can,* "at will," do or abstain from doing always has limits. The freedom he has is always freedom only inside some "jail," be that "jail" more or less spacious or cramped.

The next step in my analysis of the sense and nonsense of "Free Will" is to call attention to the following basic *three fold equation :*

I. That a person P *"can,"* under circumstances K, do A or abstain from doing A, means exactly the same as :

II. That the person P, under circumstances K, *"is free to"* do A or abstain from doing A. And this in turn means exactly the same as :

III. That the person P's *willing* (i.e., deciding, choosing) to do A, or not to do A, would, under circumstances K, *suffice to cause* respectively his doing A, or his not doing A.

Moreover, the above equations to "Person P *can*" are valid, *mutatis mutandis,* also concerning Person P *"could have,"* and concerning Person P *"would be able to."*

I turn now to the question why it is so widely regarded as evident that Determinism, taken to mean that every event is caused and has an effect, is inherently incompatible with possession of "Free Will." Two erroneous assumptions are what explains the prevalence of this opinion.

One is that Determinism, as meaning that every event is

caused and has an effect, entails that every event is theoretically predictable. This assumption mistakenly identifies causation with causal law.

The other erroneous assumption is that being *caused* to perform or not perform an act of some specified kind, or to believe or disbelieve a specified proposition, or to entertain or not entertain some specified feeling is, inherently, to be *compelled to* or *compelled not to* do so.

The truth, however, is that causation is compulsion *only in cases where what one is caused to do is something to which one is averse,* such as handing one's money to a holdup man who threatens : "Your money or your life." If, on the other hand, one is hungry and this causes one to eat, and one eats something one likes, then one's eating it is a case not of compulsion but on the contrary of gratification of the desire to eat which caused one to eat.[4]

In the light of all that has preceded, I now submit as evident that the *Sense* (i.e., the *good* sense) of "Free Will" is that there are some things which, at will, one is free to do or to abstain from doing.

On the other hand, the *Nonsense* of "Free Will" is that human volitions (i.e., decidings, choosings) have no cause and that this is necessary for moral responsibility – the truth concerning this, I have contended, being on the contrary that, without some determinant (some reason, motive, or ground) for one's volitions, they are then morally irresponsible; so that psychiatric treatment is what one then needs.

NOTES

1. *Philosophy of Science,* Vol. 2, No. 2. April 1935.
2. Published by Oskar Piest, New York, 1941.
3. *University of California Publications in Philosophy,* Vol. 16, No. 7, 1945.
4. Concerning what I take Determinism to mean, it is necessary to bear in mind that, in addition to meaning that whatever occurs is caused and has an effect, I have contended in various published articles that the terms of the causality relation are always *events;* that events are either changes or "unchanges" (i.e., endurings); that the causality relation is irreducibly *triadic,* to wit, of the form "Occurence of single difference C in a state of affairs S was what then caused occurence of E"; and also that, in some cases, *the causation relation itself* is perceivable *as literally as* are the events between which it obtains.

THE REJECTION OF NATURALISTIC ETHICS

Rollo Handy, State University of New York at Buffalo

MARVIN FARBER'S long-standing interest in the possibilities of a scientific, empirical approach to value problems makes the present topic an appropriate one for this *Festschrift.*[1] Through the years, an impressive number of students have received a healthy introduction to a scientifically informed and naturalistically oriented value theory in Marvin Farber's classes. Although doubtless he would disagree with much that I say here, I think he would at least accept my views as being on the "right side of the fence."

Although naturalistic value theory had vigorous and influential supporters not so long ago in American philosophy, the main philosophic tendency has been to reject naturalism. In Mary Warnock's survey of ethics since 1900, for example, all of the people discussed in detail (mainly English and European authors) shared "an interest in refuting ethical naturalism."[2] As is common in the history of philosophy, however, views that have been regarded as disposed of once and for all have a way of surviving refutation, and even some analytic philosophers recently have expressed dissatisfaction with previous wholesale rejections of naturalism.[3] My paper is concerned with certain aspects of the rejection of naturalistic ethics, and I will suggest that naturalism is far from dead. Rather than being outmoded, it is the approach offering the most hope for the future.

A complicating factor is that often those who oppose naturalism have been more concerned with specifying what ethical naturalism consists in than have the naturalists themselves. Naturalists have often argued in a context established by their critics, and as a consequence have barked up some wrong trees.

Specifically, the strong metaethical emphasis of the critics encouraged naturalists to focus too narrowly on certain language issues; i.e., abstracted from the sociocultural situation in which value language is used. Many of the controversies occurred in a heavily epistemological setting, when in view of the main drive of naturalistic theories, the emphasis should have been methodological and empirical.

Not only is there disagreement about the precise specification of 'naturalism,' but there is disagreement even on the level of roughly identifying naturalistic theories. From time to time English philosophers find themselves almost totally baffled by the label 'naturalism,' and sometimes seem to regard it as the prototype of an unhelpful category. Perhaps much can be said in favor of their suspicion of the usefulness of that term. On the other hand, the thoroughly ingrained aversion of many recent English academic philosophers to a scientifically oriented mode of inquiry may also be a factor in their inability to understand what has been advocated under the rubric 'naturalism.' In this country, where the label has won higher acceptance, there is also considerable disagreement as to what it stands for. If we take 'naturalism' in general as referring to views that reject the supernatural or nonnatural, some writers have been willing to include among the ethical naturalists almost any philosopher writing on ethical theory whose general philosophic orientation is naturalistic. Thus sometimes emotivists and good-reason theorists are considered as ethical naturalists, along with writers taking views of the sort urged by Ralph B. Perry, John Dewey, and Stephen C. Pepper.[4]

Since I believe that the methodology chosen in value inquiry is one of the key questions, I find it helpful to distinguish between what is sometimes called 'classical naturalism' (and is exemplified in many respects by Perry, Dewey, and Pepper) and various other value theories held by those who adopt a generally naturalistic approach in philosophy. But how to specify most adequately what is called classical naturalism is also a controversial topic. For some time, a frequently chosen mode of differentiating value theories was in terms of their metaethical differences. Although I think that such an approach does not take us very far, a review of some of the issues may be helpful.

In the period in this country when battles raged among the

naturalists, the intuitionists, and the emotivists, some of the key metaethical issues concerned questions as to whether ethical statements were descriptive or nondescriptive, cognitive or noncognitive, and capable of being true or false or not. Issues also arose as to whether or not ethical predicates name simple, unanalyzable, and nonnatural characteristics. In contrast to a variety of other metaethical theories, classical naturalists tended to regard ethical statements as descriptive, cognitive, and as in principle either true or false, and to deny that ethical predicates name simple, unanalyzable, and nonnatural characteristics.

As the emphasis came to be more and more on "our language," the classical naturalistic metaethics came to seem less and less appropriate. Although analyses of "ordinary usage" sometimes differed rather remarkably from each other, it was obvious enough that in our culture many uses of value language are quite unlike our uses of scientific language. Such differences were regarded by many writers as well-founded and as not subject to serious challenge. Naturalists were faced with the alternatives of trying through ingenious ways to show that "our language" is more descriptive than it appears to be, or to give up the naturalistic metaethics, or to challenge the soundness of relying on "ordinary language" as a fundamental basis for ethical theory.

In my opinion, naturalists should have pursued the third alternative more vigorously than they did, for it not only offers the greatest hope, but indirectly is implied by much of the history of naturalistic value theory. Indeed, the marked tendency to carry on the discussion along epistemological lines not only gave too much ground to the nonnaturalists, but tended to distract attention from the major theoretical strengths of naturalism.

Rather than trying to specify 'ethical naturalism' primarily in terms of metaethical categories, then, I suggest that another approach would be more useful. In attempting to generalize about the line of development followed by people such as Perry, Dewey, and Pepper, I think the following points have considerable significance :

(1) An emphasis on viewing human valuations as behaviors;

(2) An emphasis on those behaviors as natural and biosocial;

(3) An emphasis on scientific inquiry into the relevant behavior and on finding scientific ways of resolving value disputes and differences.

A host of diverse problems is raised by the three points just mentioned. For one thing, naturalists vary as to the relative emphasis they put on various aspects of what I have just said. Perry, for example, stressed the biological much more than the social, and Pepper stresses the social less than does Dewey. And subtle methodological issues are involved as to whether it is best to see the biological and the social as separate phenomena that interact, or whether it is better to begin with the biosocial matrix as a transactional whole. There is no lack of conflicting positions taken as to what 'behavior' encompasses; one can make behavior central without endorsing the most popular current versions of behaviorism. And what constitutes a scientific approach to human behavior also is a matter of dispute.[5] Still and all, the family similarities among naturalists are impressive and in marked contrast both to many traditional approaches in ethical theory and to contemporary linguistic modes of attack.

My point is *not* that if the main drift of naturalism as roughly indicated above is grasped, the critics will cease criticizing; for I suspect that to the extent naturalism is thus understood it will encounter the most hostile reaction. Rather, I am suggesting that many criticisms really do not get to the root of the issue. The issue can only be productively discussed when the radicalness of naturalism is appreciated. In my opinion, many of the objections to naturalism stem from a fundamental belief that the language of moral discourse is somehow very special and is unlike that of scientific discourse, and that what moral discourse expresses is different in kind from what descriptive discourse expresses. I think such issues are more important, and go more to the heart of the matter, than the usual criticisms and replies emphasizing the naturalistic fallacy, the open question, the "illicit" derivation of *ought* from *is*, the "confusion" of logical and causal analyses, etc.

The handling of language issues perhaps constitutes, at least in recent Anglo-American philosophy, the greatest gulf or impasse between naturalists and nonnaturalists. At least two major issues are involved, one concerning the most profitable path to follow in value inquiry, and one concerning language in general.

Naturalists of the kind I am describing tend to take human valuing behavior as the basic unit of analysis, with the language aspects of that behavior being viewed as only one (extremely important) part of that behavior. This involves naturalists in issues that their opponents tend to regard as nonphilosophic or as philosophically trivial. And, at least to the extent I grasp the situation, naturalists tend to have far less reverence for conventional language in general than do some other philosophers; e.g., instead of assuming that well-established linguistic patterns of behavior are to be taken with the utmost seriousness, they tend to be somewhat suspicious of those patterns and attempt to test them against warranted results of inquiry into human behavior.

I have described this as an impasse because often neither side seems to be able to take the other seriously. To illustrate, W.D. Ross suggested that many specifications of 'right' could be disposed of because, after reflecting on them, it was clear that those specifications bore no resemblance to what we mean by 'right.' And A.C. Ewing proposed that we should judge any proposed specification of 'good' by asking, after hearing the proposed specification, whether this was what we meant all along, even if we had not previously succeeded in stating the matter so clearly. By such tests, typical naturalistic analyses of value terms were quickly ruled out, and naturalists indeed seemed remarkably obtuse. Naturalists, in turn, often had great difficulty in comprehending that their opponents were serious about all this. Perry, for example, in replying to such criticisms, pointed out that different people mean different things in different contexts, and held that the problem is not to discover a present meaning, for there are too many such meanings. Rather, the task is to *give* a suitable meaning to a term, either through a selection from existing uses, or by developing a new one. And Pepper argued that the use of a term in the empirically most productive way "would never, or almost never, correspond exactly with a common sense definition or with traditional usage."[6]

What has been missing, in my view, is both a thorough attempt by naturalists to explain their approach to others, and a consideration of the merits of that approach. Although obviously on this occasion a detailed treatment is not possible, I think at least the main outlines of what seems implicit in the naturalistic approach can be given.[7]

Naturalists of the type I am discussing would be quite sympathetic to the remarks of the sociologist, George Lundberg, who was always on watch for an uncritical reliance on folk language. He said :

> "Man has always stood in awe of his verbalizations, especially when they are in written form and are traceable to ancient sources. No feeling is more widespread than that the structure of our language, that most fundamental repository of our culture, *must* represent, and closely correspond to, the structure and nature of reality. When, therefore, we find deeply engrained in our language different types of sentence structure, we are sure that the phenomena, the events, or the processes these sentences purport to describe are fundamentally of a different order."[8]

But just that certainty is what needs to be challenged, according to Lundberg.

More generally, implicit or explicit in the work of naturalists is a view that can be roughly described as follows. Ordinary uses of various terms often are not in accord with the best available evidence. In scientific inquiry we see a constant development and correction in our use of terms. There is a complicated process of rectifying the use of terms not only to make them accord with available evidence, but to help achieve the most productive forms of further inquiry. Over time, there can be a great shift of "meaning," but this is not to be lamented or discouraged, for inquiry is thereby aided. Typically, we begin with certain data that at the time seem well-grounded; the use proposed for a term is presumably consistent with that data. As inquiry proceeds, we may find that some of the data are more erroneous than was assumed, or that what seemed to be well-chosen applications of a term were poorly chosen. Hence we may find good reason to modify both the intension and the extension of a term. We do not begin either with data assumed as sacrosanct or with "meanings" assumed as unchangeable for all time, but our views about both shift as inquiry proceeds.

Many naturalists, then, hope that the progressive rectification just described would be applied to value language. Pepper, for example, in his *Sources of Value,* explicitly traces some of the terminological changes he finds advisable as his inquiry progresses. Although he insists that he wants 'value' to be specified in a way that will apply to the general field we ordinarily take as comprising value situations, he holds no brief at all for keeping traditional "meanings." What he looks for is improvement in our language as inquiry proceeds; he does not test his value theory in terms of its conformity to "what we mean" or to how we traditionally use value language.

Although ordinary language philosophers often object, observers sometimes see a close connection between a methodological emphasis on ordinary language and a support for conventional morality. John Ladd, for example, uses the terms 'revisionist' and 'conservative' in discussing views toward conventional morality. He lists Dewey and Perry among the revisionists, and contemporary intuitionists and emotivists among the conservatives. And Walter Kaufmann says : "ordinary language philosophy is well on its way toward succeeding Idealism as the prime apologist for Christianity and bourgeois morals."[9] The issue is a complex one, since it is clear that some ardent defenders of ordinary language are in general neither ideological conservatives nor supporters of considerable portions of conventional morality. Although logically there need be no connection between a support of conventional morality and viewing the task of philosophers as primarily the exploration of ordinary language in morals, behaviorally there often may be a strong connection. And there does seem to be a marked tendency for those opposed to an emphasis on ordinary language in value theory also to hold reformist views about conventional morality.

This issue, too, turns partially on the question of where we begin in value inquiry and what we take as well-supported data and conclusions. Personally, I would find much of the ethical theory of the past few decades almost unintelligible if something like the views of W.D. Ross were not widely held. Ross said :

> "We have no more direct way of access to the facts about rightness and goodness and about what things are right or good, than by thinking about them; the moral convictions of thoughtful and well-educated people are the data of ethics just as sense-perceptions are the data of a natural science."

In the same book, he also says that the "main moral convictions of the plain man seem to me to be, not opinions which it is for philosophy to prove or disprove, but knowledge from the start." I would think there might be considerable difference between the "thoughtful and well-educated" and the "plain man," but in any event the role of the philosopher is clearly indicated.[10]

Much of what Ross says is so enlightened, so humane, and so thoughtful that it may seem churlish to suggest that the attitude exemplified in the quotations above is rather parochial and insular. But, at least from a naturalistic point of view, that is the difficulty with much ethical theory; no matter how personally enlightened and nonchauvinistic philosophers are, they tend to posit a kind of autonomy of ethics from its biosocial and historical matrix that cannot be justified. One does not have to cast a very broad net to see that the "main moral convictions of the plain man" have often been woefully far from the mark. To take them as "knowledge from the start" is exactly what we should not do. Historical, class, and cultural differences (usually minimized or doubted by philosophers) should occupy more of our attention, not in an attempt to amass entertaining examples of human diversity, but in order to grasp why certain moral convictions are what they are, given certain sociocultural circumstances.

Naturalists, then, tend neither to start with traditional moral convictions as given nor to judge value theories in terms of their conformity to such data. Rather, valuational behavior is the focus of attention, and one important aspect of that behavior is the verbalized account that is given of the process by those involved. I am inclined to view 'behavior' as an adjustmental process that is best understood in biosocial or transactional terms. From that point of view, morality, as one type of behavior, is viewed in human terms, not as something superhuman or nonnatural. As the social connections of individuals vary greatly, so do the moral aspects of their behavior. Our reflective processes may be subject to great error even under favorable circumstances, but to abstract from the full range of human behavior and focus only on that of a particular sociocultural group is almost guaranteed to make our value theory parochial and culture-bound. Further, once we begin to get highly warranted information about the links between particular biosocial structures and processes and the values involved, we have some hope for a better way of handling disputes and disagreements about values.

In summary, the naturalistic value theorists I have been discussing tend to view value phenomena as empirical patterns of behavior. This is in marked contrast to those who view morality, or the language of moral discourse, as something very unlike other patterns of behavior that may be explorable using scientific inquiry. Once the general naturalistic approach is accepted, the door is opened to a scientific resolution of many value disputes. Human valuations, if taken as important aspects of behavior, can be studied in approximately the same way other aspects of behavior are studied. The mainstream of recent criticism of naturalistic value theories fails to come to grips with such issues, and assumes just what the naturalists deny. Naturalists share much of the blame for this situation, for they often have failed to make clear just how radical a departure their approach is from widespread philosophical assumptions about language and conventional morality.

Obviously, almost any topic mentioned in this brief paper is complex and deserves much fuller treatment. My paper is intended only to suggest the importance of a somewhat different kind of look at the issues between naturalists and nonnaturalists than is usually taken.

NOTES

1. A brief overview of Marvin Farber's views is found in the section on value theory in his *Basic Issues of Philosophy,* New York, Harper & Row, 1968, Ch. IX, and in *Phenomenology and Existence,* New York, Harper & Row, 1967, Chs. VII, VIII.

2. Mary Warnock, *Ethics Since 1900,* 2nd. ed., London, Oxford University Press, 1966, p. 140.

3. For example, William K. Frankena has recently shown some sympathy toward aspects of naturalism in his "On Saying the Ethical Thing," *Proceedings and Addresses of the American Philosophical Association, 1965-66,* Yellow Springs, Antioch Press, 1966. And L. W. Summer, after noting that since G. E. Moore most major contributors to moral philosophy have held the conviction that naturalism is fundamentally mistaken, makes some telling points against alleged refutations of naturalism, in "Hare's Arguments Against Ethical Naturalism," *The Journal of Philosophy,* Vol. LXIV, 1967.

4. For example, E. M. Adams includes among naturalistic ethical theories many views that I regard as opposed to naturalism. He does this on the ground that the theorists involved hold that both value language and the experience expressed through that language "have no unique ontological significance distinct from that of the language of modern science or its common-sense counterpart." *Ethical Naturalism and the Modern World-View,* Chapel Hill, University of North Carolina Press, 1960, p. viii.

5. I have discussed such methodological matters at length in my *Value Theory and the Behavioral Sciences,* Springfield, Thomas, 1968. Chapters are devoted to Perry, Dewey, and Pepper. Discussions of various uses of 'behavior' and of 'science' and my own views on those topics can be found in my *Methodology of the Behavioral Sciences,* Springfield, Thomas, 1964, especially chapters 1, 2, and 3.

6. W. D. Ross, *The Right and the Good,* Oxford, Clarendon Press, 1930, p. 11. A. C. Ewing, *The Definition of Good,* New York, Macmillan, 1947, p. 43. R. B. Perry, *Realms of Value,* Cambridge, Harvard University Press, 1954, p. 2. S. C. Pepper, *The Sources of Value,* Berkeley, University of California Press, 1958, p. 9.

7. I have attempted to give a much fuller story in my *Value Theory and the Behavioral Sciences,* especially chapter 2.

8. George A. Lundberg, "Semantics and the Value Problem," *Social Forces,* Vol. 27, 1948, p. 114.

9. Walter Kaufmann, *Critique of Religion and Philosophy,* New York, Harper, 1958, p. 2. John Ladd, *The Structure of a Moral Code,* Cambridge, Harvard University Press, 1957, pp. 36-37; p. 438, note 11.

10. W. D. Ross, op. cit., pp. 40-41, p. 21n.

ETHICAL NATURALISM AND THE EVIDENTIAL-VALUATIONAL BASE

Paul Kurtz, State University of New York at Buffalo

I

THE central issue that I want to focus upon in this paper is the question as to whether naturalism is committed to the doctrine that value judgements are *logically deducible* from factual premises – which is the basis of Hume's attack. The answer that I would give is negative; first, because value judgments in their distinctively normative sense are not wholly or primarily descriptive in function, but prescriptive and evaluative; and second, because although the naturalists would insist that there is an important relationship between facts and values, the relationship is not one of deductive entailment, but of practical decision.

Value judgments :

An assumption about naturalistic ethics which critics assert without proof is that naturalism is committed to the doctrine that value judgments are *in toto* descriptive, because naturalists have claimed that value judgments may be tested empirically. On the contrary, many naturalists have insisted that value judgments are primarily prescriptive and directive in function. The writings of John Dewey, a leading naturalist, bears out this interpretation. For Dewey considered value judgments to be at root *practical* and to concern means-ends in relation to action. Indeed, Dewey went so far as to maintain "that the *entire* use and function of ethical sentences is directive and practical."[1] "A judgment of value," he held, "is simply a case of a practical judgment." And a "practical judgment" he defined as "a judgment of what to do, or what is to be done." "Practical judgments," he said, "do not therefore primarily concern themselves with the value of objects, but the course of action demanded. . . The question is of better or worse with respect to alternative courses of action, not with respect to various objects."[2] Thus value judgments are not primarily descriptive, as Hare charges, but "prescriptive," "directive," and "imperative," in that they function to recommend or advise a course of action as based upon evaluation and appraisal.

The key logical issue for naturalistic ethics is the relationship of evidence or reasons to judgments of value and decisions. It is important to point out that naturalistic inquiry has not focused exclusively upon ethics, but also has seen fit to deal with the theory of valuation, the logic of judgments of practice, and decision-making theory. Naturalists have thought it important to investigate the logic of practical judgments in general and not simply the logic of ethical judgments, because moral decisions are only part of the broader class of practical valuations and decisions. Most analytic philosophers have eschewed this kind of inquiry and have concentrated instead upon the logic of moral language; for they have not appreciated the necessity of investigating valuation theory and decision theory separate from classical moral philosophy. I must concede that many or most of the questions that naturalists have chosen to deal with under other headings do eventually emerge in one form or another in ethics; though I do think there is some merit in a division of labor. In any case, the whole point of naturalist inquiry is that there is a continuity between the methods of practical decision-making in ordinary life and in the experimental sciences on the one hand, and the way we frame ethical decisions and judgments on the other. The naturalists claim, on the basis of their inquiry, that both practical judgments and ethical judgments, in principle at least, are amenable to some degree of objective determination. Thus the naturalist thinks that he has uncovered an implicit "logic of the judgments of practice," in which there are rational principles guiding choice, and that these principles also apply to ethical matters.

In so far as this is the case, there has been an important reunion in ethics and valuation theory between recent analytic ethics and naturalism. Analytic philosophy has developed an appreciation for the "objectivity" and "reasonableness" of moral decision, based upon a detailed analysis of ordinary language and the ways we reason in morals; and naturalists have reached a similar conclusion based upon an examination of the judgments of practical behavior and the hypotheses in the applied sciences.

The significant contrast which still exists in metaethics today would be between either naturalists and subjectivists on the one hand or naturalists and absolutists on the other. In answer to the subjectivists, naturalists do not think that ethical judgments are meaningless or incapable of verification, nor do they depend in the last analysis upon taste and caprice. And in answer to the absolutists, they do not think that ethical judgments are absolute, necessary or universal.

The present-day union between analytic philosophy and naturalism in ethics is shown by the fact that they have both returned to the Aristotelian tradition.[3] Both agree that there is a kind of practical wisdom in life. Even though we cannot be as precise in ethics as in the sciences or mathematics, nevertheless some degree of ethical objectivity is possible.

The essential point that the naturalist today would still wish to maintain is that practical judgments may be *supported* by reference to evidence, though again I do not know that analytic philosophers need disagree. Perhaps it is only a matter of emphasis. The questions to be raised, however, are first, what kinds of evidence, and second, what is the relation between the range of evidence and the ethical (or practical) judgment?

In all processes of practical judgmental reasoning or decision-making there is, I submit, an *evidential base,* in terms of which the judgment functions. A judgmental inquiry is related to decision or choice and this is connected to action. In a problem of decision we are faced with a number of alternatives, one or more of which we wish to select. Our choice is teleonomic, intentional, purposive in the sense that there is some end in view, some goal or aim that we wish to achieve.

The judgment or decision is practical in that it is related to praxis or conduct. Only those decisions which are connected to action and which are voluntary are the subject of ethical inquiry. Some responses of human organisms are causally determined by physical-chemical or psychosomatic factors. Some responses, however, are conscious and rational and may be modified or influenced by reflection and deliberation.

Practical decisions (as distinct from theoretical decisions) spill out into the world of objects and events, in the form of behavioral interaction. Practical decisions are relational; they are situational and contextual. In so far as the problem of decision is to motivate the person to act, the decision involves passion, feeling and desire, and has its roots within the conative and biochemical soma. In so far as the decision involves social policy, its content and reference is social and cultural.

The question that especially concerns the ethical philosopher is the kinds of evidence that we appeal to in the deliberative process, and by means of which we may say that our decisions are "adequate," "correct," "wise," "judicious," or "prudent." Certain fairly basic kinds of evidence are immediately presented as relevant to the ordinary man, who reflects on how he makes choices in everyday life : To be meaningful, a decision must be related to (a) his practical action; hence it is by its very nature prescriptive and directive; (b) his decision must also have some reference to the context or situation in which it arises and in terms of which it applies and to the objects and events within it; hence it has a descriptive aspect. Thus his decision has both a prescriptive and descriptive element and it must take into account certain empirical factors as "givens" within the range of practical behavior.

Choices which are not capricious or irrational and have some basis in our intellectual judgment must have some reference to an evidential base. The appeal to an evidential base in ethical deliberation is analogous to the use of an evidential base in ordinary life and the experimental sciences when we are concerned with establishing certain descriptive hypotheses; it differs in *what* is contained within the base.

One part of the evidential base is relatively "value neutral", i.e., it includes knowledge on the part of the agent(s) within the situation of the particular facts that confront him, i.e., the objects and states of affairs immediately at hand, the circumstances and other agents involved. We may say then that a rational decision is possible only if one is fully aware of the relevant particulars.

The evidential base also includes to some degree knowledge of relevant causal conditions, regularities and generalizations. If an agent is to act, his action is limited by causal conditions within the encountered situation. Knowledge that "if I do *a*, then *b* will most likely follow" is, according to C.I. Lewis, an elementary instance of a causal regularity which is essential to any kind of intelligent behavior.

That we must have knowledge of both particular facts and general conditions should be rather obvious to anyone who reflects upon the way we frame judgments in practical life. Frequently the commonplace is overlooked. Naturalism has claimed that full attention to the range of descriptive and explanatory knowledge is an essential condition for any kind of ethical knowledge. Naturalists have argued that our ability to frame practical judgments is functionally related to our factual knowledge, and that insofar as we are able to expand our knowledge of man and his world, we are better able to resolve the complex problems that arise. (In the evidential base, I would include data from biology, psychology and psychiatry about human needs and requirements – what I call "natural" or "normal needs.")

However, in no sense does naturalism stop here; and it would be ludicrous to think that one's normative judgments may be derived or deduced in any way from a neutral descriptive account of the situation, the particular and general facts of our world (or the nature of man). What is essential to the evidential base in ethics, unlike science, is that it be extended to include what Abraham Edel has called a *valuational base;*[4] that is, among the important or crucial "evidence" to be considered in a decision procedure is the whole range of value experiences, value judgments, principles, norms and ideals given with the situation. Indeed, far from claiming that what "ought" to be the case may be derived from what "is" the case in any antiseptically pure value-free sense of "facticity," the naturalist would insist that any normative conclusions drawn, can only be developed on the basis of those already intrinsic to the valuational base. The charge of Protagorean relativism no doubt applies; for the naturalist wishes to relate practical judgments to an existing set of de facto value prizings, principles and rules. This is where decision begins, with an existing body of norms; though this is not where it need end or remain.

There are two sets of "factors" to be considered within the evidential-valuational base. First, it refers to the interests, and felt needs of human beings, the things that they desire, prefer, or appreciate. That is, it applies to the value experiences and judgments of the things that are considered good and bad, as based upon previous inquiries. One's preferences, likes and dislikes, have been inherited, or imbibed, but they have also been modified in the light of experience. Second, it refers to the principles and ideals to which human beings are committed and to which they appeal in justifying their decisions and acts. These principles (whether legal, political, social, religious or moral) are conditioned in individuals and become embedded in social habits and conventions. Thus, there is both an individual and a social basis for value judgments and normative principles.

I have used the term "evidence" here to describe value judgments and principles because I do not find them to be mysterious psychic or ontological entities. They are, in my view, natural modes of human experience within nature, having both psychobiological roots and social-cultural dimensions.

The question of which decision should be adopted and acted upon in a given situation is always related to the set of antecedent value judgments and principles that are implicated within the situation. They are the "data" to be examined as to their adequacy. One cannot consider problems of judgment and decision without taking into account the existing valuation commitments.

Where decisions are practical, real, urgent, they always have prospective orientation. To choose, means that there is a course of action which is open and that there are alternatives. This presupposes that there are instruments and tools at our disposal. In other words, action which strives to attain objectives involves means-ends considerations. Critical judgment is intrinsically related to the means that we are able to use. Decision is dependent upon the range of possibilities open to us. What we can do is always a function of the means. If our means are limited and impoverished we are limited and impoverished. If our means are many, our opportunities are increased. The extent to which we can expand our technological resources as means enables us to expand the alternatives before us. Creative thinking in practical decision is not simply linear or additive, but novel and seminal. Choice depends upon invention, which is a form of creative imagination. The extent to which we can think up new instruments to implement and further our interests is the extent to which we are liberated from our limiting animal environment. Technological imagination has a profoundly emancipating effect upon human life. Accordingly, naturalism emphasizes the need to develop the technical arts and policy sciences as important contributions to creative decision-making. If we cannot solve a problem in traditional ways, we can experiment by going around or over it, by adventurously leapfrogging in new departures. As Sartre has pointed out, man is in a sense able to recreate himself; for his future life is pregnant with possibilities.

A central factor in practical methodology is the means-end continuum. It is not the end that justified the means, rather our ends presuppose and are contingent upon the means at our disposal. Decisions are a result of weighing means on a comparative scale, strategically calculating costs and expenditures, as well as inventing and bringing new ones into being.

However, there is still another important criterion of choice. Inasmuch as decisions display themselves in action, we may observe and evaluate what we do in terms of the effects of our decisions upon our lives. We continually learn from experience. We discard old methods because they no longer serve us and adopt new ones because we think they will. Some judgments are well tested in practice, are generalized and become social guides to conduct. Indeed, they may eventually become enshrined within tradition and are supported by religion and morality. A whole body of moral duties and responsibilities may develop to support them. Great efforts are made to stabilize and institutionalize social rules and to base them upon universal moral principles. We eventually discover that all rules and principles have exceptions and that they must be modified in the light of new conditions. Thus rules and principles, introduced to assist individuals within society in making decisions, are themselves fallible, tentative, hypothetical. They are continually being evaluated by reference to their observable *consequences,* by how well they serve our desires and our needs.

In the above, I have only touched on *some* of the factors that I think go into the evidential-valuational base, as materials for consideration in any judgmental decision process : particular facts, general conditions (including statements about human nature), de facto value judgments, principles, means, consequences. There are no doubt others.

What is the relation of a judgment or decision to the evidential-valuational base? It is, I submit, practical, teleonomic, functional. A decision is considered fitting, appropriate or adequate to the present situation. The decision cannot be deduced from "the facts," it is not entailed by them. It does relate to them; but it is drawn by reflecting upon them in a creative decision procedure. The decision drawn is not a mere summary generalization; it is not tested inductively. Its relationship to the evidential-valuational base is not necessary, as is the case of formal inference; it is not probabilistic, as in the relationship between a scientific hypothesis and the data to be explained. I have elsewhere described the relationship as "act-ductive" to indicate that it involves a special kind of practical logic;[5] though I admit that term commits a barbarism; and I am not at all surprised that it has not been taken up.

I am not denying that inferential procedures enter at some point into practical reasoning, but this does not provide either a decisive or complete account of the deliberative process. The deductive aspect enters when we are concerned with general rather than particular judgments, and when general rules and principles are applied to particular cases; though even here whether to use a specific principle in a situation cannot be determined solely by a priori deductive rules of inference. Inductive procedures also enter into a decision process, as factual claims are made and tested in the process of investigation. But in the last analysis the logic of judgments of practice has its own kind of autonomy and rationale. Objectivity and the logic of deliberative thinking in ethics and life is practical, not formal or inductive.

One should be clear that in any decision process we start in the *middle,* not at the beginning. This means that we do not have in most cases to justify our decisions by reference to "first principles." If called upon to defend any one principle of the many that we hold, we may do so at the appropriate level of discourse. Though here we have a new situation of inquiry in which we appeal to a new evidential-valuational base. We deal piecemeal and contextually with our principles and value judgments, and we do not need deductively to demonstrate their "truth" a priori; nor can we. Indeed, we assume a body of principles as given. Justification emerges only when a particular principle or judgment is criticized or attacked and thus requires special justifying reasons. It is a mistake in metaethics to look for one or more basic principles (for example the greatest happiness principle or the categorical imperative) on the basis of which all others are deduced. As a matter of fact there are any number of principles and rules, value judgments and commitments, and I might add, responsibilities, obligations, duties which we hold and which may have to be considered in any decision procedure.

The above model of decision-making is based upon an analysis of how we reason about our choices in practical life, and how we refer to an evidential-valuational base in supporting our decisions. It does not claim that all problems of decision may be resolved. One's decisions may be such that there seem to be nothing but *un*desirable consequences available (the Vietnam war for example). There is both an optimistic and pessimistic appraisal of decision-making. Some optimism is warranted, because given a commitment to the rational methods of practical judgment, at least many or most of our decision-problems may be resolved. Yet there is a tragic aspect to decision, for we are limited by the materials with which we work and the range of actualities before us, and in some human situations there seem to be no available solutions.

The above model also does not presuppose that all objective and impartial inquirers will necessarily agree as to what is good, right or wise within a given situation. They are likely to agree only if they operate from the same evidential-valuational framework. If the evidential-valuational base from which two or more individuals or groups operate differs, then the decisions drawn may differ. Although the fact that there are common human problems and needs, and that men of different backgrounds share many similar interests and principles, suggests that in many situations we may be able to reach common conclusions. We live in the same world, a world in which traditional barriers are breaking down, and in which an individual may be influenced by normative principles from several traditions at the same time. We can argue and disagree, inquire and dispute, and out of the process, we may hope that some consensus on common principles may emerge. But we have no guarantee.

One basis for disagreement no doubt is the fact that some moral systems presuppose mistaken facts or theories about nature or man – thus evidence and valuational principles in the base are closely related. Given a detailed factual inquiry, we may be able to modify those principles which are incorrectly related to mistaken facts. In a dispute with a racist, for example, if his beliefs about blacks are based upon his view that they are "inferior" in talent and ability, then we can show that he is mistaken, and hope that his judgment may be modified. In a dispute between a Thomist and humanist, we may empirically investigate whether a fetus may be said to have a "human personality" as preliminary to our judgment about whether or not it should be aborted. In arguing with a Marxist we can examine his claim that there are dialectical laws of history, since this influences his judgment about social policies. A dispute about birth control is dependent in some sense upon empirical data about trends in world population growth. The principles of men, whether racists, Thomists, humanists or Marxists, I take to be human commitments; and accordingly they are available to careful scrutiny and critical analysis. Such analyses hopefully may assist us in modifying elements within our given evidential-valuation base. The naturalists believe that the more we can critically examine our inherited principles, the better able we are to build common bridges. However, no one can guarantee that we will succeed. And the emotivists may be correct; for there may be basic disagreements in *both* beliefs and attitudes which it is hard to resolve or to change. Still one has no other alternative than that of reliance upon reason as the best guide to man's practical and ethical life.

II

The above is a statement of a naturalistic theory. It is a theory in metaethics, which argues for one key point : namely, that although normative conclusions may *not* be deduced from factual premises, judgments of practice (including ethical judgments) are amenable to some objective treatment, by reference to the operative evidential-valuation base. Does the above metatheory itself presuppose any normative principles? The answer is a qualified, Yes. I do not think that one can do pure metaethics without some normative commitment; and it is self-deception to think that this is possible. What I have done in this paper is to try to analyze and uncover the logic of practical reasoning that I think is embedded in ordinary life when we deliberate about our decisions; I would go further and recommend that we use this logic as a guide. Deductive and inductive logic are also normative. If one wants to be consistent, then he must abide by the rules of formal inference; and if one wants explanatory and predictive hypotheses, then he must abide by the criteria of scientific methodology and inductive logic. Similarly, if one wants wise judgments of practice (following Aristotle), then there is a model for practical judgment which we may use. The analytic philosopher who seeks to uncover the rules of use of value language, or wishes clarity and the avoidance of confusion also presupposes certain normative principles. The very commitment to philosophy itself is normative. Therefore, I think that metaethics cannot be sharply distinguished from normative ethics; for there are at least minimal normative standards implicit in any act of philosophical analysis – though there is surely some difference between a dispassionate philosophical analysis on an intellectual level and the actual recommendation of a course of action in concrete moral situations.

In this latter regard, I think that it was a fundamental mistake for philosophers of the last generation to withdraw from the area of normative ethics to a linguistic meta-sanctuary. This tendency is now being reversed. Philosophy has had many missions besides analytic clarification, and among the most significant is the Socratic mission which not only attempts to define what we mean by certain key moral concepts, but also recommends the adoption of a set of moral principles and a way of life.

I have not tried myself in this paper to move beyond the analysis of certain meta-issues in ethics to my own substantive normative principles, though perhaps at times they were implied, if only minimally, in what I have said. If I were to lay bare my own normative position, the valuational base from which I operate, I would label it "humanistic ethics" rather simply than "naturalistic ethics." What I would try to show is that although most Anglo-American philosophers may dispute on the meta-level concerning their theories of meaning and truth, they nevertheless share in their own lives certain common normative principles, principles which are perhaps naturalistic in their metaphysical foundations, but are humanistic in their application to man.

NOTES

1. John Dewey, *Theory of Valuation,* Chigago; University of Chicago Press, 1939.
2. John Dewey, "The Logic of Judgments of Practice," *The Journal of Philosophy, Psychology and Scientific Methods.* XII, No. 19 (September 1916), pp. 505-23.
3. See especially P. H. Nowell Smith, *Ethics,* Harmondsworth, England; Penguin Books, 1956.
4. Abraham Edel, *Ethical Judgment, The Use of Science in Ethics,* Glencove, Illinois; The Free Press, 1955.
5. Paul Kurtz, *Decision and the Condition of Man,* Seattle: University of Washington Press, 1965, Chs. 14, 15.

THE CONTRIBUTIONS OF CHARLES S. PEIRCE TO LINEAR ALGEBRA

By V.F. Lenzen, University of California, Berkeley

I

CHARLES S. PEIRCE (1839-1914) deserves a place in the history of science for his contributions to astrophysics, spectroscopy, gravimetry, geodesy, and mathematical logic. A major contribution to the latter field was his logic of relatives. Peirce's memoir, "Description of a Notation for the Logic of Relatives" (1870), was described by Whitehead in *Universal Algebra* (1898) as the most important contribution to the algebra of logic after Boole's *Laws of Thought* (1854). Through his work on relatives Peirce was led to make important contributions to linear algebra and the theory of matrices. Thus E. Cartan in his article "Nombres Complexes," *Encyclop. des Sciences math.*, Tome I, Volume 1, fasc. 3 (1908), states concerning "systèmes de nombres à multiplication associative," p. 369, "leurs rapports avec le calcul des matrices ou des substitutions linéaires, déjà pressentis en 1858 par A. Cayley le fondateur de ce dernier calcul, mais seulement mis en évidence par Ch. S. Peirce en 1870, contribuèrent d'ailleurs beaucoup au développement de la théorie de ces systèmes."

Peirce described in a manuscript of 1909 the manner in which he became interested in the field. "About 1869 my studies of the composition of concepts had got so far that I very clearly saw that all *dyadic* relations could be combined in ways capable of being represented by addition (and of course subtraction), by a sort of multiplication... and by two kinds of involution... But I found my mathematical powers were not sufficient to carry me further... I therefore set to work talking incessantly to my father (who was greatly interested in quaternions) to try to stimulate him to the investigation of all systems of algebra which instead of the multiplication table of quaternions,... . had some other more or less similar multiplication table. I had hard work at first. It evidently bored him. But I hammered away, and suddenly he became interested and soon worked out his great book on linear associative algebra." As we shall see, Peirce's contribution arose from the application of the theory of relatives to his father's work.

II

The *Linear Associative Algebra* (1870) of Benjamin Peirce was a pioneer contribution to the extension of the concept of number. In the search for solutions to quadratic equations, there had been introduced the ordinary complex number, a + bi, where a and b are real and i is the imaginary unit, the square root of -1. If the unit "1" is also introduced, the complex number may be expressed as a.1 + b.i. Upon the acceptance of the ordinary complex number, which can be interpreted by a point or vector in the plane, efforts were made to find numbers of three or more units which would admit interpretation in space. In 1843, Sir William Rowan Hamilton introduced the quaternion, a quadruple number which is expressible in terms of four units, i.e., $q = a_0 + a_1 i + a_2 j + a_3 k$. As defined by Hamilton, 1, i, j, k, are the units, and a_0, a_1, a_2, a_3 are the respective coefficients, which were assumed by Hamilton to be real. The multiplication of quaternions is defined by, in addition to the associative and distributive laws, the laws of multiplication for the units :

$i^2 = j^2 = k^2 = -1$; $ij = k$; $jk = i$; $ki = j$; $ji = -k$; $kj = -i$; $ik = -j$.

The laws of multiplication for the quaternion units may be expressed by a table in which the multiplier is at the left, the multiplicand at the top, and the product is at the intersection of a row and column :

	1	i	j	k
1	1	i	j	k
i	i	-1	k	-j
j	j	-k	-1	i
k	k	j	-i	-1

Benjamin Peirce defined a linear algebra as "one in which every expression is reducible to the form of an algebraic sum of terms, each of which consists of a single letter with a geometrical coefficient." If e_1, e_2, e_3,. . . . . . e_n are the letters which designate units, and a_1, a_2, a_3,...... a_n are the coefficients, which for Benjamin Peirce may be complex, then an expression in the algebra, that is, an n-dimensional number, is expressed by $q = a_1 e_1 + a_2 e_2 + a_3 e_3 + \ldots\ldots a_n e_n$. The product of two expressions in an algebra is again an expression in the algebra. Further, the algebras considered are associative in the sense that "the associative principle extends to all the letters of its alphabet." Benjamin Peirce was the first to offer a classification and enumeration of linear associative algebras with a small number of units. Several decades later, H. E. Hawkes evaluated and perfected the method of Benjamin Peirce. In "Estimate of Peirce's Associative Algebra," in *Amer. Jl. of Math.*, Volume 24, 1902, Hawkes stated that Peirce sought to develop as much of the theory of hypercomplex numbers as would enable him to enumerate all inequivalent, pure, nonreciprocal number systems in less than 7 units. "Peirce solved the problem completely. His theorems are correct, although some proofs are invalid." E. Cartan, in his Encyclopedia article, *op. cit.*, p. 423, has stated that Peirce has determined "not without some errors of reasoning, all the systems up to the fifth order inclusive, and has given indications for the determination of systems of the sixth order."

An example of an algebra found by Benjamin Peirce is his g_4, which is a form of quaternions : indeed, Henry Taber in "On the Theory of Matrices," (*Amer. Jl. of Math.*, Volume 12, 1890), called this form of quaternions canonical. If we use Benjamin Peirce's letters for the units, i.e., i, j, k, l, and the symbols w, x, y, z, for the coefficients, respectively, so that a quadruple number is $q = wl + xi + yj + zk$, then the multiplication table is

	i	j	k	l
i	i	j	0	0
j	0	0	i	j
k	k	l	0	0
l	0	0	k	l

Benjamin Peirce's "canonical" form of quaternions is an example of a type of algebra that was termed a quadrate algebra by W. K. Clifford. In a letter to his father in February, 1870, Charles Peirce showed how the preceding multiplication table can be expressed in terms of his relatives. This result appeared in his paper "Description of a Notation for the Logic of Relatives," which was published in the same year, 1870, as was *Linear Associative Algebra* by Benjamin Peirce.

III

In the just cited paper of Charles Peirce, he introduced the concept of elementary relative as a set of terms in relation. I shall restrict the discussion to simple, or dual, relatives which are pairs in which individuals of two mutually exclusive classes are in dyadic relations. Two such classes would be "body of teachers in a school" and "body of pupils in a school." Then "teacher." more explicitly, "teacher of ," is a dual relative, since it consists of one individual from the body of teachers in relation to one individual from the body of pupils. Similarly, the relative "pupil," more explicitly, "pupil of ," is a dual relative, since it consists of one individual from the body of pupils in relation to one individual from the body of teachers. If we denote the individuals of the body of teachers by u_1, and the individuals of the body of pupils by u_2, then we can define four relatives:

colleague $c = (u_1 : u_1)$ teacher $t = (u_1 : u_2)$
pupil $p = (u_2 : u_1)$ schoolmate $s = (u_2 : u_2)$

Peirce called these relatives "vids," also capital pairs, since he also used the notation (A : B). The above relatives may be arranged in a square array:

$$\begin{matrix} (u_1 : u_1) & (u_1 : u_2) \\ (u_2 : u_1) & (u_2 : u_2) \end{matrix}$$

The rules for the multiplication of a relative into an individual are:

$$(u_i : u_k)\, u_k = u_i$$
$$(u_i : u_k)\, u_l = 0.$$

I offer an interpretation of the first rule in terms of a concrete example: If u_1 denotes an individual from the body of teachers, and u_2 denotes an individual from the body of pupils, then the relative teacher multiplied into an individual of the body of pupils equals an individual of the body of teachers, $(u_1 : u_2)\, u_2 = u_1$; this may be interpreted to mean that the teacher acting upon an individual from the body of pupils transforms him into an individual of the body of teachers, that is, he may

become a teacher. But if a teacher acts upon an individual other than one from the body of pupils, the result is null.
The rules for the multiplication of relatives are :

$$(u_i : u_k)(u_k : u_l) = (u_i : u_l)$$
$$(u_i : u_k)(u_l : u_m) = 0.$$

Charles Peirce in his paper of 1870 gave a multiplication table for the relatives : colleague, teacher, pupil, schoolmate, as follows,

	c	t	p	s
c	c	t	0	0
t	0	0	c	t
p	p	s	0	0
s	0	0	p	s

The preceding table for the multiplication of Charles Peirce's relatives agrees with the multiplication table for Benjamin Peirce's algebra g_4. The interpretation of the rules stated in the foregoing table may be illustrated by a number of examples. (1) The product of c and c equals c states, the colleagues of the colleagues of any person are the colleagues of that person. (2) The product of c and t equals t states, the colleagues of the teachers of any person are the teachers of that person. (3) The product of c and p equals zero states, there are no colleagues of any person's pupils. In view of this correspondence between the table of Charles Peirce for his dual relatives, and the table of Benjamin Peirce for his form of quaternions, Henry Taber (*op.cit.*, p. 385) declared, "The discovery of this form of quaternions, is due to Benjamin Peirce; it received its full significance only after the discovery by his son, Charles Peirce, of the unlimited system of quadrates formed from the system of vids (A : A), (A :B), etc., when it appeared that quaternions was only the first of this system of quadrate algebras, and the identification of quaternions with the theory of dual matrices was virtually accomplished."

In the foregoing example, we considered only two classes of individuals, body of teachers and body of pupils. We may have several classes of individuals which may enter into relations with one another. Given mutually exclusive classes of individuals designated by u_1, u_2, u_3,. . . u_n. Then we obtain the relatives :
$(u_1 : u_1)(u_1 : u_2)(u_1 : u_3)$. . . . .$(u_1 : u_n)$

$(u_2 : u_1)(u_2 : u_2)$. . . . .
. . . .
. . . .
$(u_n : u_1)(u_n : u_2)$ . . . . $(u_n , : u_1)$
The previously stated rules of multiplication apply. Since we have n classes, there are n^2 dual relatives, and this complete system of dual relatives constitues a quadrate algebra of order n.

Charles Peirce, by his systems of vids, discovered the possibility of constructing an infinite number of quadrate algebras. In particular, he discovered the quadrate algebra called nonions, for which he published the multiplication table in his paper on "Notation" of 1870. We have three mutually exclusive classes of which the individuals are designated by u_1, u_2, u_3. Since $n = 3$, there are $3^2 = 9$ vids :

$$\begin{matrix} (u_1 : u_1)(u_1 : u_2)(u_1 : u_3) \\ (u_2 : u_1)(u_2 : u_2)(u_2 : u_3) \\ (u_3 : u_1)(u_3 : u_2)(u_3 : u_3). \end{matrix}$$

If these vids are designated

$$\begin{matrix} i & j & k \\ l & m & n \\ p & q & r, \end{matrix}$$

the multiplication table is

	i	j	k	l	m	n	p	q	r
i	i	j	k	0	0	0	0	0	0
j	0	0	0	i	j	k	0	0	0
k	0	0	0	0	0	0	i	j	k
l	l	m	n	0	0	0	0	0	0
m	0	0	0	l	m	n	0	0	0
n	0	0	0	0	0	0	l	m	n
p	p	q	r	0	0	0	0	0	0
q	0	0	0	p	q	r	0	0	0
r	0	0	0	0	0	0	p	q	r

In a paper "On Nonions," Peirce states that he or his father discovered the form of nonions, for which the units are nine cube roots of unity, in analogy to Hamilton's form of quaternions, for which the units are square roots of unity. This special form of nonions was first published by Sylvester, but Peirce had the opportunity to insert his claim to the discovery in Sylvester's paper. Upon objections from Sylvester, Peirce wrote the just cited paper in which he claimed authorization from Sylvester for the insertion.

IV

Charles Peirce's vids may be represented by matrices. If there are two types of individuals which are designated by u_1 and u_2, respectively, the vid ($u_1 : u_2$), for example, is represented by the dual matrix, in which the entry in the first row and second column is one, and the other entries are zero. Thus the set of vids for g_4

$$(u_1 : u_1)(u_1 : u_2)$$
$$(u_2 : u_1)(u_2 : u_2)$$

is represented by the set of matrices

$$\begin{bmatrix}1 & 0\\0 & 0\end{bmatrix} \begin{bmatrix}0 & 1\\0 & 0\end{bmatrix}$$
$$\begin{bmatrix}0 & 0\\1 & 0\end{bmatrix} \begin{bmatrix}0 & 0\\0 & 1\end{bmatrix}, \text{ respectively.}$$

To the law of multiplication of vids,

$$(u_1 : u_1)(u_1 : u_2) = (u_1 : u_2),$$

corresponds

$$\begin{bmatrix}1 & 0\\0 & 0\end{bmatrix} \cdot \begin{bmatrix}0 & 1\\0 & 0\end{bmatrix} = \begin{bmatrix}1.0 + 0.0 & 1.1 + 0.0\\0.0 + 0.0 & 0.1 + 0.0\end{bmatrix} = \begin{bmatrix}0 & 1\\0 & 0.\end{bmatrix}$$

The above example illustrates that the rules of multiplication for the matrices are identical with the rules of multiplication for the vids which are represented by the matrices, respectively.

The nine vids of nonions :

$$(u_1 : u_1)(u_1 : u_2)(u_1 : u_3)$$
$$(u_2 : u_1) \text{ etc.,}$$
$$(u_3 : u_1)(u_3 : u_2)(u_3 : u_3),$$

are represented by the matrices :

$$\begin{bmatrix}1 & 0 & 0\\0 & 0 & 0\\0 & 0 & 0\end{bmatrix}\begin{bmatrix}0 & 1 & 0\\0 & 0 & 0\\0 & 0 & 0\end{bmatrix}\begin{bmatrix}0 & 0 & 1\\0 & 0 & 0\\0 & 0 & 0\end{bmatrix}$$
$$\begin{bmatrix}0 & 0 & 0\\1 & 0 & 0\\0 & 0 & 0\end{bmatrix}\begin{bmatrix}0 & 0 & 0\\0 & 1 & 0\\0 & 0 & 0\end{bmatrix}\begin{bmatrix}0 & 0 & 0\\0 & 0 & 1\\0 & 0 & 0\end{bmatrix}$$
$$\begin{bmatrix}0 & 0 & 0\\0 & 0 & 0\\1 & 0 & 0\end{bmatrix}\begin{bmatrix}0 & 0 & 0\\0 & 0 & 0\\0 & 1 & 0\end{bmatrix}\begin{bmatrix}0 & 0 & 0\\0 & 0 & 0\\0 & 0 & 1\end{bmatrix}$$

In view of the identity of the rules of multiplication of the vids and the representative matrices, Henry Taber declared (*op.cit.,* p. 351), "the matrix of order ω whose non-zero constituent is in the rth row and sth column is identical with the vid occupying the same place in the quadrate system of order ω."

The concepts introduced by Charles Peirce made possible the linear representation of a matrix. If, for example, we have the dual matrix

$$\begin{bmatrix} a & b \\ c & d \end{bmatrix},$$

it can be expressed as

$$\begin{bmatrix} a & 0 \\ 0 & 0 \end{bmatrix} + \begin{bmatrix} 0 & b \\ 0 & 0 \end{bmatrix} + \begin{bmatrix} 0 & 0 \\ c & 0 \end{bmatrix} + \begin{bmatrix} 0 & 0 \\ 0 & d \end{bmatrix},$$

since the sum of two matrices is the matrix whose elements are the sums of the corresponding elements of the summand matrices. Then, since the product of a number and a matrix is the matrix each element of which is the product of the number and the corresponding element of the multiplicand matrix, we obtain

$$\begin{bmatrix} a & b \\ c & d \end{bmatrix} = a\begin{bmatrix} 1 & 0 \\ 0 & 0 \end{bmatrix} + b\begin{bmatrix} 0 & 1 \\ 0 & 0 \end{bmatrix} + c\begin{bmatrix} 0 & 0 \\ 1 & 0 \end{bmatrix} + d\begin{bmatrix} 0 & 0 \\ 0 & 1 \end{bmatrix}$$

Thus the representation of a matrix in linear form is accomplished by the use of the matrices which represent Charles Peirce's vids. These latter matrices have been called the units of a matrix, in the present example, the units of a dual matrix, and represent the units of a quadrate.

In 19th Century expositions, the foregoing method was attributed to Charles Peirce. Thus, W.H. Metzler in "On the Roots of Matrices," (*Amer. Jl. of Math.,* Volume 14, 1892) states, p. 356, "The linear form representation of a matrix is due to Charles S. Peirce, and the notation employed is virtually his." The example given by Metzler is

$$\begin{bmatrix} 0 & 0 & 1 & 0 & 0 & 0 \\ 0 & 0 & 0 & 1 & 0 & 0 \\ 0 & 0 & 0 & 0 & 1 & 0 \\ 0 & 0 & 0 & 0 & 0 & 1 \\ 0 & 0 & 0 & 0 & 0 & 0 \\ 0 & 0 & 0 & 0 & 0 & 0 \end{bmatrix} = 13 + 24 + 35 + 46.$$

That is, instead of writing $(u_1 : u_3)$ or its representative,

$$\begin{bmatrix} 0 & 0 & 1 & 0 & 0 & 0 \\ 0 & 0 & 0 & 0 & 0 & 0 \\ 0 & 0 & 0 & 0 & 0 & 0 \\ 0 & 0 & 0 & 0 & 0 & 0 \\ 0 & 0 & 0 & 0 & 0 & 0 \\ 0 & 0 & 0 & 0 & 0 & 0 \end{bmatrix},$$

Metzler writes 13, to indicate that the vid is the one in the first row and third column, and the matrix is the one in which the entry is 1 in the first row and third column while all other entries are 0. From the rule of addition for matrices, the given matrix is expressed as the sum of the unit matrices of the sixth order.

Metzler also states, "This canonical representation of a matrix was virtually given by Buchheim in *Proc. London Math. Soc.,* Vol. XVI, but was first explicitly given by Weyr in *Comptes Rendus,* Volume C." J.J. Sylvester, however, in his "Lectures on the Principles of Universal Algebra," (*Amer. Jl. of Math.,* Vol. 6, 1884), entitles one section of his memoir, "On the Linearform or Summatory Representation of Matrices, and the Multiplication Table to which it gives rise," and states, "This method by which a matrix is robbed as it were of its areal dimensions and represented as a linear sum, first came under my notice incidentally in a communication made some time in the course of the last two years to the Mathematical Society of the Johns Hopkins University, by Mr. C.S. Peirce, who, I presume, had been long familiar with its use. Each element of a matrix in this method is regarded as composed of an ordinary quantity and a symbol denoting its place, just as 1883 may be read 1⊖ + 8h + 8t + 3u, where⊖, h, t, u, mean thousands, hundreds, tens, units, or, rather, the places occupied by thousands, hundreds, tens, units, respectively." Sylvester assumes that a matrix is of the form

$$a\lambda + b\mu + c\nu + d\pi .$$

and expands the product of two matrices so expressed. The condition that the product is expressible in terms of the unit matrices λ, μ, ν, and π, yields equations from which the multiplication table for the units λ, μ, ν, π, is derived, which table agrees with that set forth by Charles Peirce for the vids.

The contributions of Charles Peirce to the methods described in the preceding account have been recognized by N. Bourbaki, *Eléments de Mathématique* I *Les Structures Fondamentales de L'Analyse* Livre II *Algèbre* Chapitre 8 *Modules et Anneaux Semi-Simples, Note Historique,* p. 169 (1958), "L'idée générale de représentation régulière d'une algèbre est introduite par C.S. Peirce vers 1879 (IVa); elle avait été pressentie par Laguerre dès 1867 (IV), p. 235)."

Note on developments subsequent to C.S. Peirce. Quadrates have been investigated by Th. Molien (*Math. Ann.*, 41 (1893, p. 93), who calls them "ursprünglich," and by E. Cartan (op. cit., p. 427), who uses the term "simple." In the language of Cartan, a linear transformation, a matrix, and a bilinear form determine a system of complex numbers of higher order, that is, a linear associative algebra. The linear transformation in m variables is expressed by

$$y_k = \sum_{i=1}^{i=m} a_{ik} x_i \quad (k = 1, 2, \ldots\ldots m).$$

From this one obtains the bilinear form

$$A = \sum_{i=1,\ K=1}^{i=m,\ K=m} a_{ik} x_i u_k .$$

For the quadrates, the linear transformation which determines the relative units e_{ik} is $y_k = x_i$, $y_p = 0$ ($p = 1, 2, \ldots\ldots k\text{-}1, k+1, \ldots\ldots m$).

$$e_{ik} e_{lm} = 0 \quad (\text{when } k \gtrless 1),$$
$$e_{ik} e_{km} = e_{im}$$

The unit e_{ik} corresponds to Peirce's vid ($u_i : u_k$), and corresponds to the matrix of which all elements are 0 save the element which is at the intersection of the ith row and the kth column, which is equal to 1; it also corresponds to the bilinear form $x_i u_k$.

In comparing contemporary notation with that of Peirce, it is necessary to distinguish between first and second regular representations.

V

We have thus far considered among linear associative algebras only the quadrates, such as Benjamin Peirce's form of quaternions g_4 and Charles Peirce's nonions. In these special cases the units are individual relatives, the vids, or representative matrices. As a step toward the general case let us next consider Charles Peirce's representation of ordinary complex numbers and Hamilton's form of quaternions. In each case the units of the algebra are expressed as linear functions of a set of vids.

If u_1, u_2, u_3, ... u_n are nonrelative units which correspond to the original units, the general form of a relative unit may be given by

$$e = a_{11}(u_1 : u_1) + a_{12}(u_1 : u_2) + \ldots\ldots a_n(u_1 : u_n)$$
$$+ a_{21}(u_2 : u_1) + a_{22}(u_2 : u_2) + \text{etc.}$$
$$\ldots\ldots\ldots\ldots\ldots\ldots\ldots\ldots\ldots\ldots\ldots\ldots$$
$$+ a_{n1}(u_n : u_1) + a_{n2}(u_n : u_2) + \ldots\ldots a_{nn}(u_n : u_n).$$

Charles Peirce gave the relative form of the algebra of ordinary complex numbers as a double algebra. The complex number x + iy may be expressed as x.1 + y.i. Then if X, Y are mutually perpendicular vectors in the x, y plane, Peirce wrote

$$1 = (X : X) + (Y : Y)$$
$$i = (X : Y) - (Y : X).$$

The rules of multiplication for the original units, 1 and i, namely : 1.1 = 1; i.i = -1, are satisfied by application of the rules for the vids.

For example,

$$i^2 = ((X{:}Y) - (Y{:}X)).((X{:}Y) - (Y{:}X))$$
$$= (X{:}Y)(X{:}Y) - (X{:}Y)(Y{:}X) + (Y{:}X)(X{:}Y) + (Y{:}X)(Y{:}X)$$
$$= -((X{:}X) + (Y{:}Y)) = -1.$$

The matrix representation of the ordinary complex number is readily obtained. Since the matrices corresponding to (X : X), (Y : Y), (X : Y), (Y : X), are

$$\begin{bmatrix}1 & 0\\0 & 0\end{bmatrix}, \begin{bmatrix}0 & 0\\0 & 1\end{bmatrix}, \begin{bmatrix}0 & 1\\0 & 0\end{bmatrix}, \begin{bmatrix}0 & 0\\1 & 0\end{bmatrix} \text{respectively,}$$

$$1 \rightarrow \begin{bmatrix}1 & 0\\0 & 0\end{bmatrix} + \begin{bmatrix}0 & 0\\0 & 1\end{bmatrix} = \begin{bmatrix}1 & 0\\0 & 1\end{bmatrix}$$

$$i \rightarrow \begin{bmatrix}0 & 1\\0 & 0\end{bmatrix} - \begin{bmatrix}0 & 0\\1 & 0\end{bmatrix} = \begin{bmatrix}0 & 1\\-1 & 0\end{bmatrix}$$

Hence, from the rules for the addition of matrices and the multiplication of a number and a matrix,

$$x + iy \rightarrow x\begin{bmatrix}10\\01\end{bmatrix} + y\begin{bmatrix}01\\-10\end{bmatrix} = \begin{bmatrix}xy\\-yx\end{bmatrix}$$

Thus, Charles Peirce gives the matrix which represents the ordinary complex number as $\begin{bmatrix}xy\\-yx\end{bmatrix}$

Charles Peirce expressed Hamilton's form of quaternions by q = w + xi + yj + zk. He expressed the units 1, i, j, k,as relative units in terms of nonrelative units X, Y, Z, W, of which the first three are three rectangular components of a vector, while W denotes numerical unity (or the fourth rectangular component, involving space of four dimensions). The vid

(Y : Z), for example, denotes the operation of converting the Y component of a vector into its Z component.
Peirce expresses Hamilton's units as functions of the vids :

$$
\begin{aligned}
1 &= (W:W) + (X:X) + (Y:Y) + (Z:Z) \\
i &= (X:W) - (W:X) - (Y:Z) + (Z:Y) \\
j &= (Y:W) - (W:Y) - (Z:X) + (X:Z) \\
k &= (Z:W) - (W:Z) - (X:Y) + (Y:X).
\end{aligned}
$$

Hamilton's rules for the multiplication of his units also apply to the units as expressions in terms of the vids, as may be verified readily by carrying out the indicated operations and applying the rules of operation for vids.

We may readily obtain the matrix representations :

$$(w:w) \longrightarrow \begin{bmatrix} 1 & 0 & 0 & 0 \\ 0 & 0 & 0 & 0 \\ 0 & 0 & 0 & 0 \\ 0 & 0 & 0 & 0 \end{bmatrix}, (x:x) \longrightarrow \begin{bmatrix} 0 & 0 & 0 & 0 \\ 0 & 1 & 0 & 0 \\ 0 & 0 & 0 & 0 \\ 0 & 0 & 0 & 0 \end{bmatrix}, (x:w) \longrightarrow \begin{bmatrix} 0 & 0 & 0 & 0 \\ 1 & 0 & 0 & 0 \\ 0 & 0 & 0 & 0 \\ 0 & 0 & 0 & 0 \end{bmatrix}, \text{ etc.,}$$

$$1 \rightarrow \begin{bmatrix} 1 & 0 & 0 & 0 \\ 0 & 0 & 0 & 0 \\ 0 & 0 & 0 & 0 \\ 0 & 0 & 0 & 0 \end{bmatrix} + \begin{bmatrix} 0 & 0 & 0 & 0 \\ 0 & 1 & 0 & 0 \\ 0 & 0 & 0 & 0 \\ 0 & 0 & 0 & 0 \end{bmatrix} + \begin{bmatrix} 0 & 0 & 0 & 0 \\ 0 & 0 & 0 & 0 \\ 0 & 0 & 1 & 0 \\ 0 & 0 & 0 & 0 \end{bmatrix} + \begin{bmatrix} 0 & 0 & 0 & 0 \\ 0 & 0 & 0 & 0 \\ 0 & 0 & 0 & 0 \\ 0 & 0 & 0 & 1 \end{bmatrix} = \begin{bmatrix} 1 & 0 & 0 & 0 \\ 0 & 1 & 0 & 0 \\ 0 & 0 & 1 & 0 \\ 0 & 0 & 0 & 1 \end{bmatrix}$$

$$i \rightarrow \begin{bmatrix} 0 & 0 & 0 & 0 \\ 1 & 0 & 0 & 0 \\ 0 & 0 & 0 & 0 \\ 0 & 0 & 0 & 0 \end{bmatrix} - \begin{bmatrix} 0 & 1 & 0 & 0 \\ 0 & 0 & 0 & 0 \\ 0 & 0 & 0 & 0 \\ 0 & 0 & 0 & 0 \end{bmatrix} - \begin{bmatrix} 0 & 0 & 0 & 0 \\ 0 & 0 & 0 & 0 \\ 0 & 0 & 0 & 1 \\ 0 & 0 & 0 & 0 \end{bmatrix} + \begin{bmatrix} 0 & 0 & 0 & 0 \\ 0 & 0 & 0 & 0 \\ 0 & 0 & 0 & 0 \\ 0 & 0 & 1 & 0 \end{bmatrix} = \begin{bmatrix} 0 & -1 & 0 & 0 \\ 1 & 0 & 0 & 0 \\ 0 & 0 & 0 & -1 \\ 0 & 0 & 1 & 0 \end{bmatrix}$$

Similarly :

$$j \rightarrow \begin{bmatrix} 0 & 0 & -1 & 0 \\ 0 & 0 & 0 & 1 \\ 1 & 0 & 0 & 0 \\ 0 & -1 & 0 & 0 \end{bmatrix}, k \rightarrow \begin{bmatrix} 0 & 0 & 0 & -1 \\ 0 & 0 & -1 & 0 \\ 0 & 1 & 0 & 0 \\ 1 & 0 & 0 & 0 \end{bmatrix}$$

From the rules for operations upon matrices, it follows that the quaternion is represented by the matrix given by Charles Peirce :

$$\begin{bmatrix} w & -x & -y & -z \\ x & w & -z & y \\ y & z & w & -x \\ z & -y & x & w \end{bmatrix}$$

VI

We have seen that for quadrates, ordinary complex numbers, and Hamilton's form of quaternions among linear associative algebras, the units of these algebras can be expressed as linear functions of the vids introduced by Charles Peirce. In his paper on relatives of 1870, Peirce gave the relative form of a number of the linear associative algebras in his father's work. Subsequently, in 1875, he gave a proof that every linear associative algebra may be expressed in relative form, that is, represented by matrices. He stated that "the actual resolution is usually performed with ease, but in some cases a good deal of ingenuity is required. I have not found the process facilitated by any general rules." After the death of Benjamin Peirce, Charles prepared a second edition of his father's work which was published in *American Journal of Mathematics,* Volume 4, 1881. In footnotes the son gave the relative form of practically all the algebras in Benjamin Peirce's work. In an important addendum Charles Peirce published two significant contributions : (1) A proof of the theorem that every linear associative algebra can be expressed in relative form, i.e., in terms of matrices; (2) A proof of a theorem concerning division algebras, which had been published earlier by G. Frobenius in 1878, but for which Peirce is also given credit in the literature. Thus E.Cartan (*op. cit.,* p. 409) states, "Le Système des quaternions jouit,. . . ,de la propriété qu'un produit de facteurs ne peut s'annuler que si l'un au moins des facteurs s'annule; G. Frobenius et C.S. Peirce ont démontré que parmi les systèmes de nombres complexes à multiplication associative le système de quaternions est le seul, avec le système des nombres complexes ordinaires, qui jouisse de cette propriété." Peirce's statement is that "ordinary real algebra, ordinary algebra with imaginaries, and real quaternions are the only associative algebras in which division by finites always yields an unambiguous quotient."

I shall now outline Charles Peirce's proof that every linear associative algebra can be expressed in relative form.

Given : an associative algebra with units of which the letters are i, j, k, l, etc., and for which multiplication is determined by :

$$
\begin{aligned}
i^2 &= a_{11} i + b_{11} j + c_{11} k \text{ etc.}\\
ij &= a_{12} i + b_{12} j + c_{12} k \text{ etc.}\\
ji &= a_{21} i + b_{21} j + c_{21} k \text{ etc.}\\
&\text{etc.}
\end{aligned}
$$

Peirce introduces a number of new nonrelative units, one more in number than the original units, and every one except the first, A, corresponding to a particular letter of the algebra, i.e., I, J, K, L, etc., corresponding to i, j, k, l, etc., respectively. He then forms the vids :

$$
\begin{array}{llll}
(A : A) & (A : I) & (A : J) & \text{etc.}\\
(I : A) & (I : I) & (I : J) & \text{etc.}\\
(J : A) & (J : I) & (J : J) & \text{etc.}\\
\text{etc.} & & &
\end{array}
$$

These vids are subject to the rules of operation as previously set forth.

Finally, Peirce assumes a number of complex operations denoted by i', j', k', etc., corresponding to the units i, j, k, etc., of the algebra, and determined by its rules of multiplication as follows:

$$
\begin{aligned}
i' = (I{:}A) &+ a_{11}\,(I{:}I) + b_{11}\,(J{:}I) + c_{11}\,(K{:}I) \text{ etc.}\\
&+ a_{12}\,(I{:}J) + b_{12}\,(J{:}J) + c_{12}\,(K{:}J) \text{ etc.}\\
&+ a_{13}\,(I{:}K) + b_{13}\,(J{:}K) + \text{etc., etc.}\\
j' = (J{:}A) &+ a_{21}\,(I{:}I) + b_{21}\,(J{:}I) + c_{21}\,(K{:}I) \text{ etc.}\\
&+ a_{22}\,(I{:}J) + b_{22}\,(J{:}J) + c_{22}\,(K{:}J) \text{ etc., etc.}\\
k' = (K{:}A) &+ \text{ etc., etc., etc.}
\end{aligned}
$$

Peirce proceeds on the principle that any two operations are equal, which being performed on the same operand, invariably give the same result.

He supposes that i'j'A = k'l'A, then expresses the equality in terms of the nonrelative units, and by application of the rules of multiplication cited above, finds in the original algebra ij = kl. Hence, if m is any letter, ijm = klm.

Peirce then expresses ijm as a function of the original letters, i, j, k, etc. He expresses i'j'm'A as a function of the nonrelative letters I, J, K, etc. The latter function has the same coefficients as the former. A similar relation holds for klm and k'l'm'A as expressed in terms of the letters i, j, k, etc., and I, J, K, etc., respectively. Then from the equality of ijm to klm, he infers i'j'm'A = k'l'm'A. Hence, i'j'M = k'l'M. Thus, if i'j'A = k'l'A, then i'j' into any nonrelative unit equals k'l' into the same unit, so that i'j'= k'l'. We thus see that whatever equality subsists between compounds of the accented letters i', j', k', etc., subsists between the same compounds of the corresponding unaccented letters i, j, k, etc., so that the rules of multiplication of the two algebras are the same. To quote Charles Peirce : "Thus, what has been proved is that any associative algebra can be put into relative form, i.e., that every such algebra may be represented by a matrix."

In a manuscript, dated 1909, and previously quoted, Peirce explains in detail how to determine the relative units of an algebra for which the multiplication table is given for the original units. If the original units are designated i_1, i_2, i_3, etc., and the corresponding nonrelative units are designated I_1, I_2, I_3, etc., one labels the rows at the left i_1, i_2, i_3, etc., consecutively, and similarly labels the columns at the top. Then one selects row i_i, for example, and examines the entries in the places of intersection of the row with the columns. If an entry occurs in the column labeled i_b, then the second letter of a vid is I_b. If the letter at the intersection of the column and row is i_c, then the first letter of the vid under consideration is I_c. If the entry has a scalar coefficient s, this becomes a coefficient of the vid. In this way a vid is constructed from the multiplication table in the *Linear Associative Algebra.* Other entries give new vids for the result. The first vid is (I_i : A), where A is the nonrelative unit added to the ones corresponding to the original units, in the final expression for the relative unit as a linear function of the vids.

$$y_s = \sum_{K=n} \gamma_{kis} \; x_k \quad (s = 1, 2, \ldots\ldots n)$$

or the bilinear form, k = 1

$$A_i = \sum_{(k,s)} \gamma_{kis} \; X_k \, U_s$$

The corresponding formula in Peirce's notation is

$$e_i = \sum_{(k,s)} \gamma_{kis} (u_k : u_s).$$

The present paper on the contributions of Charles S. Peirce to Linear Algebra may be concluded with a quotation from N. Bourbaki. In the previously cited *Eléments de Mathématique,* in *Algèbre,* Chapitre I *Structures Algébriques* (1942), *Note historique,* p. 156, there is offered a selected list of contributors to the field at the end of the 19th and beginning of the 20th centuries : "en Angleterre (Sylvester, W. Clifford) et en Amérique (B. et C.S. Peirce, Dickson, Wedderburn) suivant la voie tracée par Hamilton et Cayley, en Allemagne (Weierstrass, Dedekind, Frobenius, Molien) et en France (Laguerre, E. Cartan) d'une manière indépendante des Anglo-Saxons, et en suivant des méthodes assez différentes."

NOTES

Bibliography of C.S. Peirce's contributions to linear algebra.

1. Description of a Notation for the Logic of Relatives, resulting from an Amplification of the Conceptions of Boole's Calculus of Logic. *Mem. Amer. Acad. Arts and Sciences* ns 9 (presented 26 January 1870) 317-378.
2. "On the Application of Logical Analysis to Multiple Algebra."*Proc. Amer. Acad. Arts and Sci.* ns. 2, ws. 10 (presented 11 May 1875) 392-394.
3. "On the Relative Forms of the Algebras," *Amer. Jl. Math.* 4 (1881) 221-225.
4. "On the Algebras in which Division is Unambiguous," *ibid.*, 225-229.
5. "On the Relative Forms of Quaternions," *Johns Hopkins University. Circular* 1 (February 1882) p. 179.
6. "On a Class of Multiple Algebras," *JHUC* 2 (November 1882) 3-4.
7. "A Communication from Mr. Peirce (On Nonions)," *JHUC* (April 1883) 86-88.

The above items have been republished in Volume III of *Collected Papers of Charles Sanders Peirce,* Volumes I-VI (1931-35), Volumes VII-VIII (1958) Harvard University Press. No. 1 at 3.45-149; 2 at 3.150-151; 3 at 3.289-305; 4 at ibid.; 5 at 3.323; 6 at 3.324-327; 7 (On Nonions) at 3.646-648. I am indebted to the bibliography in Vol. VIII by Arthur W. Burks.

I wish to express my thanks to Professor Max H. Fisch for assistance with the Peirce Collection, and to the Houghton Library for permission to quote from the Ms. L224.

THE FEAR OF FREEDOM*

Franco Lombardi, University of Rome

1. *The planet earth and the history of man.* Beings that one day were to be called human appeared some 150,000 years ago on a planet that had been in existence for a time estimated to be between three and four billion years. These beings descended from the trees where they lived and, in order to better dominate the plains they assumed an upright position. This made possible the development of the encephalon and the articulation of their hands. When they were to use purposefully their hands, they discoverd how to light a fire. Fire enabled these beings –– the weakest of them all –– to escape beasts; led to the development of the Fireside and thereby laid the groundwork for man's self-domestication; it led him to pass from warmer to colder environments, and thereby forced him to cover himself with skins; furnished him with a way to cook food, and resulted in a reduction of the jaw and in the development of the human mouth thus making speech possible.

When human civilization had already produced enumeration and the Phoenician alphabet, the temples of Luxor, the treasures of Crete and Mycenae, the wisdom of Confucius and India's religions, a great thing happened. Men began to discuss how it was possible to justify the concept of truth. This great event took place in a small city called Athens. The man who in eminent manner most embodied this revolution was called Socrates. He had a faun face, and he used to talk freely about gods (in whom he apparently did not believe), and of asses, horses, etc. that were about the market-place where he liked to spend his time. Philosophy as we know it today dates from then, and it is since that day that preoccupations with "Logic" have arisen.

The length of mankind's existence with regard to that of the earth has been compared to the thickness of a sheet placed upon a column as tall as the one in Trafalgar Square, and the duration of the life of civilization with respect to the life of mankind with a section very much thinner of that sheet. Our distance from our ancestors such as Cicero, Lucretius, or Socrates (notwithstanding the problems raised by these geneologies) is still less.

Considering the many civilizations through which man has passed, the civilization that arises with Greece in the ninth century B.C. and can be traced up to the First World War, is only a thing of yesterday. Thus, it is not surprising that we find ourselves still using terms and concepts coined in Plato's and Aristotle's Greece. Notwithstanding the glorious path that he has been trod so far, man changes much slower than our historicists claim. Yet, he changes enough to show that our historicists have not changed at all: they are still operating within Plato's and Aristotle's thought to a much greater degree than they think. We must acquire thus a better awareness of what has happened in the meantime and on the other hand, of what has not changed.

2. *Athen's society and civilization and Greek philosophy.* The peoples that initially gave rise, with Athens and Greek-civilization, to European civilization, lived in the indented area that extends from the coast of Asia Minor through the Greek Archipelago, up to the promontory of the Greek Peninsula and, from there, to Sicily. To the great expanses of Asia a civilization had corresponded which had been, with the static character of its society, the cradle of religions, and which had given expression to systems that set off Being against Appearance, Unity against Multiplicity, Eternity against the Belief in the existence of man (existence seen as suffering and death from which the human soul longs to escape so as to reach the eternity of the All-One). In contrast to it a new continent (Europe, the land of the Gods) was now emerging, a land whose sea-line is continually broken where mountains and seas continually alternate, where climates are changeable but always temperate and whose population of mixed racial origins is composed of sea-faring and trading people. This land in turn produced a civilization whose distinctive features are the interplay of thought and action, the

delight in the drawing of distinction and *nuances,* the cultivation of art and experience, in short thepursuit of intellectual freedom and critical thinking.

If in Miletus investigations, largely on navigation, had given rise to physical and cosmological investigation, the type of critical thinking which was being developed in the Greek world of Athens, where the greatest variety of professions and of attitudes was to be found assembled in a restricted location, and the clever race of the Ionians was to be found in contact with other races and in active cultural exchanges and maritime trading, it was naturally turned from the very beginning to the human world of the arts. However, by making linguistic skill the major and most sought instrument of power in the assemblies, Athenian democracy furnished the maximum incentive for the appearance of the sophists who came from all parts of Hellas. Not only this, but the main "direction" of this movement (however divergent its manifestations) consisted in the questioning of tradition by submitting everything to examination and criticism. This trend was taking place under the implusion of the new "bourgeoisie" constituted by the craftsman class.

In fact, a new spirit of initiative and of adventure encouraged by the new traffic and relations with different cults and civilizations, and the very intimate relationship with the more lively Ionic world of the coasts of Asia Minor, had come to be substituted, and finally prevailed with the victory over Persia, to the patriarchal character of Athen's more ancient life. The more daring and enterprizing sea-faring and trading groups (who would eventually constitute Themistocles' party) had already begun to challenge the supremacy of the landed gentry and of the peasants, and that already by the time of Aristides. From the 7th to the 4th century B.C. indications of the belief in the survival of the soul, that can be discerned in the care with which the tombs of the dead were honored, become increasingly dimmer, conventional, and uniform. The weakening of traditional faith, along with the democratization of the Greek world, can be seen in the evolution of the tragedy, within the span of a few years, from Aeschylus to Sophocles and Euripides. Euripides' uncertainty concerning the fate of the soul, even if mixed with pantheistic hints or with the hope of a final annibilation of consciousness, is confirmed by the words of his friend Socrates as they have been transmitted to us through Plato's *Apology.* [1]

The intellectual movement that has Socrates as its chief representative, reflects the work of a generation to find again on the base of *reason* the foundation of life that it no longer finds immediately in tradition and faith. In its constructive as well as in its destructive aspects, this movement belongs within the general *enlightening* movement whose major spurt can be found, with singularly analogous traits, in the self-assertion of the modern bourgeoisie, departing from literary "humanism", through Bacon's and Locke's "philosophical" enlightenment, up to the French political and social enlightenment, and, finally, in Kant.[2]

The philosophers that advanced in such a new world of thought were, however, the citizens of a society of which it is all too natural that they would end up by wearing and upholding the customs not only in civil life, but also in their very modes of thought. Every civilization has its own spiritual vibration and therefore its focus or spermatic center whose repercussions can be found in all of the manifestations not only of its civil life, but also, of religion, architecture and, in general, of the arts and of thought. Thus, those thinkers drew from the society and civilization that they represented the stimulus to assert in the world of thought those characters that have since opposed Western European thought if compared to the practical interest for it, prevailing in other civilizations. It is not surprising, therefore, that they carried, along with the critical spirit, the limitations of such a society.

Actually, we could still use the term "form" that Socrates derived from his father's occupation (he was a potter), and that Plato found in the arts of his own youth. Furthermore, those arts were called "liberal", (with a term class conscious *avant la lettre*) –– that were properly of free men and did not appear bound to the slavery of matter or of work aimed toward an end. And it is perhaps not altogether arbitrary to recognize in the very contraposition of "pure", rational, and apriori thought to "sense" or to matter (and even Kant will vindicate for thought an origin "nobler" and other than that "vulgar of the senses", properly of experience) distinction, akin to the relation of conquerors with conquered populations, between the intellectual classes with the proletarian masses (one could almost say the different biological species), whose destiny would be that of insuring, with the sweat of their brows, the survival of a superior class.

Thus perhaps it is not wholly accidental if to the crisis of "speculative" philosophy that comes about immediately after Hegel's death with the fall of the Hegelian School, there corresponds in civil life the first cracks in the liberal and bourgeois order and almost the first hint of that wave from below which announced about a century ago, advances, with the reaction against the ideology of universal and "rational thought", through the very blooming epoch of 19th-century Europe, and finally surfaces today in the civil and political order as well as in culture and in thought.

The ideal type in "culture", that ideal type and "classical" concept of culture which was valid for Goethe or was valid up to Croce, has collapsed. And we must at least ask ourselves if it was not bound accidentally to a certain type of civilization or of Western society which today is in crisis: thus the crisis of that culture is connected with the crisis of bourgeois-artisan European society; and it is at the same time the crisis of the West in a world in which there appears a different type of Totalitarian society and civilization whose external dimension is, meanwhile, the continent.

If, however, the doctrine of a pure universal and rational thought, as against the Socratic dialogue was asserted in Greece, and in general if the claim of true "thought" against the many "opinions" is introduced, there is a deeper reason.

This reason (and we can recognize in the first elements of logic and European spectulative thought as introduced by Plato), is the *fear of freedom.*

3. *Fear of freedom, and the determinations of logic and of traditional metaphysics.* Man was born only yesterday. Yet we cannot picture the line of development of humanity from the "savage" to the so-called civil man, as a railroad line where the accent falls upon the term "line", and the stations that the train has passed are left behind our backs to disappear into the night. That development could perhaps be better compared to the growth of a plant where the graft made on it does not prevent its continuously throwing out new buds in which its old "savage" nature lives again. We are unknown and, so to say, savages to ourselves. We do not know the thousand eyes of the

species that continuously open themselves in us, and that inhabit that republic of beings — monads, as Leibniz would have called them — that constitute the dark and profound night that each of us calls "I".

When we surprise ouselves in not daring to advance our arm in a dark and deserted house in which we "do not know what" seems to hover in it through the thickness of the shadows in the air; if we curse, even as grown-ups, the chair that we stumble against, or we ask, with James, which *sin* have we committed if the earthquake surprises us in our sleep, so that it seems as if *someone* shakes the room and the bed; if my three year old baby says that he knows his mother's shcool because he *has seen it in his dreams,* and he is not yet able to distinguish reality from the image that appears but is not real; if I tell him that three years ago, when we came to this house, he wasn't here since he was not yet born, and he asks me, since he *cannot* imagine *not* being, "where was I"; or if he stops to observe in the *pupil* of his brother his own image: we reproduce once again, at a distance of millennia, the path and the ways of primitives. The primitive man from the experience of things that fall apart and thus end, is led to think of something that, so as not to be without an end, is not material because it must not be material, or at least is a finer and smaller substance which can be gone through but cannot be hit, as the shadow of the body that follows us but that cannot be stepped on, as our image in the pupil, or as the shadow of the friend that has visited us in the dream, but who does not leave any traces in the sand.

So he comes to transcribe, beyond the reality of this thick — yet breakable — material world, a more diaphanous reality not any less tenacious, in which he can find refuge even if he does not yet lift his sight to the concept of an immaterial and *eternal* reality. Thus, he can hover a little longer in this life similarly to the way in which souls of the dead are supposed to hover around the house if cherished and fed until such time as they will suffer a second death, so to speak, in the affection and memory of those left behind.

But along with the escape from the fragility of living and with the craving for a reality in which man can continue to live (since man will give weight as Kant writes, to that side of the scale with the word "Hope" written upon it) the escape from freedom asserts itself accidently in an event clearer way in the very doman of logical thought.

Our experience in fact shows us a world of many, or rather of an infinity of men, individuals made of flesh and bones like us, each one doing his own thinking, even if it cannot be claimed that each one of them formulates equally valid thoughts.

How is it then, that instead of accepting the fact that since there are many individuals, many thinking beings after Plato and Aristotle, or rather *with* them, when we begin to philosophize we are led to pose "thought" and "concept" as "true" since it cannot be other than true, against the many "opinions" which are, because of their nature, other than and different from "thought"?

Obviously the answer is this: only the fear of having to face many truths. Or, as it must be clear, fear in the face of freedom, not any lesser of one's own thought than of the many thoughts of others whose freedom appears as individual arbitrariness.[3]

This is the path that takes us directly to true concepts and true thought as against the multiplicity of opinions.

But how will this thought distinguish itself from the numerous opinions? Because the first is allegedly *objective,* where the second is only *subjective.*

But what does it mean to say that the first is *objective?* The very reason that has led man to establish such a doctrine helps also to explain how the objectivity of the concept is to be distinguished from the subjectivity of opinions. The distinction consists in the fact that the subject does not introduce in the concept any trace of his individual free thinking (any trace of the arbitrariness of his individual thinking), to use the terminology of that doctrine. The "concept" will then be objective to the extent that, by itself and without the intervention of the subject that changes the substance of the thing, it is *exchangeable* and *one* with the object.

But how can it be imagined that man's "concept" can be exchanged or be one with the object? Only by granting that the object, it not itself what could be called its *essence,* be *ideal* in nature.

This is how, starting with Plato, the *metaphysics* of *idealism* becomes established, that metaphysics whereby it is asserted on the one hand that the essence of things is given by *ideas* (at the same time it is claimed that the ultimate reality is not the individual but the universal from which the individual is to be deduced); and on the other hand, that there is not, as the only reality, a thinking individual (as Kierkegaard will begin to say in more modern times), rather, that there is in man the "concept" which would be *in* the individual although it is not *of* the individual. This pure or rational thought has with material and sensible experience no better relationship that the "soul", which knows eternal ideas, has with the "body" or with matter (where it descends, although its nature and origin are supposed to be different from those of the body).

Thus Plato, not without being influenced by a patrician family origin, was led to couple the generically and mediately religious tendency of his theory of knowledge (to the extent that he sided with an objective thought and truth, against arbitrariness or, rather, against the freedom of the many thoughts of many men) with the immediately religious and mystic tendency of his philosophy. Thus he drew inspiration from mysteries.

In both cases it becomes clear how traditional logic, to the extent that it is the logic of the pure concept or the logic of universal and rational apriori thought, is based upon a motive which is not logical in character but rather is connected, in the short or long run, with the fear of freedom.

4. *The principle of salvation and critical reflection, Oriental metaphysics and critical European philosophy.* Socrates' problem is still that of *moral autonomy.* In Plato, on the other hand, the problem of *salvation* begins to come to the fore.

This point is important, not only in order to understand the whole of Plato's philosophy, but also in order to understand the subsequent development of European speculation.

In fact, it can be claimed that metaphysics, through Plato, penetrates again in Western speculation — a metaphysics (which is in itself typical of the fundamentally religious and oriental frame of mind) is reintroduced through Plato, into Western philosophy —— the metaphysics of Being and Appearance, of Being as the One, of Multiplicity are mere appearance, of Eternity as reality and of Time as transitoriness and nothingness.

This multiplicity is understood as mere appearance *(feno-*

menia), of eternity understood as reality, and of time understood as shortcoming and as nothing. Against this stands the opposite tendency which is the tendency of Western philosophy to the extent that we could say it is properly *Western* and *modern,* to value activity and experience, to uphold science, logic and the individual; in other words, the leaning toward a critical and scientific philosophy and the activity of the individual.

In the field of morality that contrast between the principle of autonomy and the principle of salvation, with the consequent authoritarian solution even in regard to the moral problem, can be seen exemplified in the experience of Julian the Apostate in Mereskowsky's novel.[4] There, faced with the master who believes he has educated Julian and supposes therefore that the latter is now mature enough to be told that the tables of the law do not "exist" and that, for what regards his moral and practical conduct he must be self-responsible, Julian vacillates. Hence the master understands that Julian is not yet mature enough for freedom so that he confirms him once again in the belief, not only of the laws, but also of the *tables* of the law: i.e., in an objective situation rather different from the freedom and the *arbitrariness* of the individual, upon which he can lean thus renouncing, or at least deluding himself to be renouncing, his own moral judgment.

Although hints concerning the idea of the autonomy of morality, whereby virtue becomes its own reward, had already been given at the end of ancient times by the Stoics, it was Pomponazzi in modern times who, obviously going back to Averroistic doctrine of those who "would have the soul die along with the body" (to use Dante's phrase), advanced it. But it was Immanuel Kant who stated the principle of the autonomy of morality in the clearest form.

Yet Kant connects and binds moral conscience to a principle, both transcendental and apriori, which rests *in* the individual (at least in the empirical individual) without, at any rate, being *of* the individual. He binds it to a noumenal reality of Reason which in fact reproduces (even if in the peculiar forms of Kantian philosophy) that very same dualism of an immaterial noumenal reality and for the fleeting material body, which was already present in Plato's metaphysics and ethics, and was derived from the metaphysics of mysteries.

The difficulty of such an ethical doctrine consists in explaining how man's moral freedom and responsibility, proper to man is to be explained, given that the noumenal, will as such, can neither make mistakes, nor want evil while, on the other hand, as Kant put it, the "pathological" will, vitiated by the senses, is or should be radically bad. What is difficult to understand is how the noumenal will which, according to Kant, should be "the" reality, can be won over or placed in doubt by a reality such as that of the senses which are, or should be, merely phenomenal. A further difficulty (not to mention others) is the one already indicated by Schopenhauer: how, and, so to speak, in what non-temporal instant, can the noumenal will which is free from the laws governing matter insofar as its nature is different from that latter, or better, because that will has swept away matter by a philosopher's proclamation can be introduced in the realm of necessity which is valid, even if only phenomenally, for the world of experience.

The contrast between the two principles mentioned at the beginning of this section, i.e., of the principle of a philosophy (and of an etics) based upon freedom and aimed at justifying the multiplicity, experience, and the activity of the individual, and of a philosophy (and of an ethics) based on the principle of salvation and, mediately or immediately, upon the fear of freedom, can be followed even more clearly throught the development of Western speculation.

We have already said that, in the twenty five centuries of the history of European cilivization, there has also been an attempt (unlike what is the case in oriental thought) to give a justification of experience, and at the same time of producing a metaphysical picture of the universe synthesizing not only the results of critical or phylosophical reflection, but also those of the scientific researches of the times. This has happened, even if in different measure according to the different times, with Aristotle, with Descartes, and with Kant. For each one of these thinkers, however, difficulties have arisen because of the interference upon the spirit and principle of Western philosophy, of a logic of pure concepts or of the apriori universal thought, of a metaphysics of being and appearance that could be defined as of oriental origin and, in the ulitmate analysis, considered of a religious nature.

The contrast is already present in Aristotle. This scion of a family of physicians is more *modern* and Western than Plato, both for the "scientific" form of his "treatises", and the multiplicity of his interests. Yet his metaphysics, although aimed at justifying the reality of the individual as against Plato's distinction, founders against the persistence of a logic of forms or of universal concepts. In fact, from this logic it is impossible to derive the *principium individuationis* and to understand how thought belongs to *this* man, that is I, and not to universal reason.[5]

Analogously, the same can be said about the growth of Cartesian *rationalism,* or better, of *criticism.* Cartesian rationalism consists in the rational reappraisal of all the data of tradition and accompanies, both in France and in England, the growth of modern society, and explains how a set of ideas was transported from Calais, and returned again, became French "materialism" to finally end up in the French Revolution. Now the demands of reason are, in Descartes, cut short by the limitations imposed by the principle of innate ideas, a principle which is extraneous to his demand for a justification of *sciences.*

In an even clearer way Kant, whose positive role in the history of philosophy continues to be distorted by our idealist historians on the strength of some mistaken opinions of the Hegelian Kuno Fischer, stops the effort of reappraising man's thinking that he had himself had initiated. This process tended to vindicate man's thought and at the same time a *human* thought that Kant calls "phenomenal" against objectivistic gnoseology that anchored it in a truth outside and before our thought.[6] But Kant halts that process to the extent that he takes from traditional logic the doctrine of universal and rational apriori "concepts" to which experience remains hanging as from a hook. For, if experience *depends* on some such apriori principles and concepts, and experience turns out to be shaped by them, it is clear that its validity cannot be extended outside of our very thought and thought in this case, can be said to be "subjective" in the negative sense of the term.[7]

In this way Kant, while trying to justify man's experience and science in a world that he wants to be taken as real, is led to what can be considered his great misadventure: namely transcendental *idealism.*

5. *Continuation. The contrast of those two principles in Italian neo-idealism.* Let us now consider two more examples, closer to us, where it can be seen how fear of freedom seems to halt the process of modern thought in its effort of gradually conquering anew, against Plato's gnoseology and logic, a justification of the multiplicity and of the individuality of men's experience.

At the beginning of the century, Benedetto Croce, polemicizing with Gröber, argued that we do not communicate and understand other people's discourse because there are unique general terms equal for everyone, at least in a certain time; rather, because each one of us creates and re-creates within himself the words used by others as an individual word. In fact (as Bergson had said a little earlier) no word could be rightly repeated without the subject's being conscious of making such a repetition and uttering therefore a different word. Thus the word will always be different.[8]

With this, Croce (without being fully aware of it), began a revolution. It would have been easy to extend his argument to overcome, after many centuries of Western speculation, the Idea or the Spirit are necessary insofar as the validity of thought depended on the necessity of that unique universal concept almost arithmetically reproducible by all but not belonging to the individual. The necessity of a metaphysics of universals or, better yet, of universal ideas is, in the ultimate analysis, bound to this.[9]

Yet, after having written on that basis his *Estetica come Teoria della Espressione e Linguistica Generale (Aesthetic as Theory of Expression and General Linguistic),* Croce works out a logic where he once again finds recourse to the doctrine of pure universal "concepts" that inhere *in* words, although not being identical with them, for reasons that no one knows.

Better yet, we know very well why Croce does not identify thoughts with words,[10] Because, counter to the principle that he put forth in the *Estetica* the freedom or on the *arbitrariness* of the critic outside of any preconceived scheme concerning what is beautiful and what is ugly, Croce is flabbergasted when faced with the perspective of losing or trading "the" one and only thought for the many thoughts of the many, rather, of the infinity of individuals.

Against the spirit of his philosophy (or at least against the new principle of his philosophy which is, in this respect, the new principle of his *Estetica* as general linguistic), Croce is thus led back into talking about only "one" true concept and thought which would be *in* the individual even if it is not *of* the individual. In developing the internal logic of such a doctrine, Croce will be led from this to conclude (against the metaphysical position of the first *Estetica* where the individual has a reality or, rather, *is* reality) that the individual is not real since thought – or at least Spirit, of which thought is a moment – is the only reality.

For the same reasons, every other thought and concept that does not happen to be in accordance with the concept of the "Philosophy of the Spirit" was declared not only to be untrue, but also no thought at all. Furthermore this conclusion was defined as the principle of a philosophy that was to be called (as *lucus non lucends),* historicism.[11]

Gentile, in turn, has argued that we are *bewildered* at the variety of men's thoughts i.e., the variety of truth, only if we lose sight of the act of thinking in virtue of which we pass a judgment on whatever we are saying. In fact, it is possible to talk about something, only in virtue of that act, since without it or without us it would be altogether impossible to either talk or judge.

This argument according to which we are made aware of that principle which is almost the hinge of all experience, i.e., that we must think of and judge everything we treat as reality, can no longer be ignored. It is the positive and valid principle of "actualism".

Gentile, however, adds to this claim a metaphysical thesis according to which the act of thinking *(pensiero in atto)* in virtue of which we think about anything is only thought and reality in the world. This is what constitutes the literal sense (and at the same time the *paradoxical* meaning) of "actualism". But he reaches this conclusion through a *petitio principii* – which he obviously does not admit and, in fact, is contrary to the spirit of his philosophy. It is the claim that only a *thought,* assumed as *metaphysically* absolute, i.e., unique in an arithmetical sense, can be *transcendentally* valid. In other words, he reaches such a conclusion to the extent that, even if unaware, he does not base the conclusions of our experience upon the principle of the critical validity of our act of thinking *(pènsiero in atto)*, rather – once again and counter to the more valid principle of his philosophy –– he bases the validity of thought upon a metaphysical presupposition. This is what I have elsewhere defined as the Gentilian paralogism.[12]

Let us examine in the following pages, the general picture of the world that the previous considerations afford us. And at the same time let us consider the strength that fear of freedom has in trying to stop our investigations.

6. *Fear of Freedom and the modern Totalitarian State.* Fundamentally, man is afraid of freedom. As will be shown, this is not valid solely in relation to truth. On the contrary, it is valid in relation to truth only to the extent that the motives that have led to a distortion of logic and of traditional metaphysics are a function of a more general attitude and at the same time of a deeper fear of man in relation to freedom.

On the front page of very recent history one could quote a page of *The Brothers Karamazov* where, after Christ has returned to earth to start the Great Inquisitor's discussion finds him among the mass that gathers around him. He recognizes Christ, yet he has him arrested and goes to visit him in his cell in the middle of the night. He tells him: Why did you come back on this earth? Men *do not* love freedom. We had established order in this world. Why did you come to upset it? "You have now seen these 'free' men. For fifteen centuries we have tormented ourselves with this freedom, but now the work is finished. You must know that today these men, who have brought us their freedom and humbly laid it at our feet, are more than ever convinced of being free. They will bring us all the most bothersome secrets of their consciences, and we will resolve every case. They will have faith in our decision, because it will free them from the grave bother and from the terrible contemporary torment of having to personally and freely decide. And these millions of beings will all be happy, with the exception of some hundred thousands of leaders. Only us, those who keep the secret, will be unhappy."

It is difficult to relate this page to the more ancient tradition in which religion is explained as the escape from fear, or maybe even with that tradition (cf. Bruno) where the Church is presented as the instrument of domination – or at least as the brake – of the instincts of the masses.

No matter what Dostoyevski means to say concerning a defense of the individual's responsibility and liberty in relation to God, this page is actually the beginning of an epoch. Nowadays astonishment seems to have taken hold of the individual faced with the disarray of the established order. The institutions of organized society, from the Church to the State, seem to intervene as givers of salvation on earth from such a fear (recall Thomas Hobbes' *Leviathan,* where he wrote of himself as having been born with fear). Today, however, we are not in need of resuscitating Christ in order to start a discussion concerning the Great Inquisitor. The new saviors of society against the fear of freedom have persuaded us (with Hegel) that "true" freedom consists in the chaining of the individual in the State.

Recent experience has made us aware of how naive was the faith that our fathers had in freedom and in progress. In fact, sometimes it appears that history is dominated, not by the search for freedom, but by the fear of freedom. It seems furthermore that there is only a small minority who fights for a freedom. Thus, they must first of all defend themselves from those for whom they want to obtain greater freedom. This reminds us of Shakespeare and the roar of the Roman masses immediately after Brutus had knifed Caesar : "Let us make him Caesar! " It also reminds us of the dictator who "goes to the people" and of the ancient wisdom of the tyrant who distributed *panem et circenses,* or the more modern wisdom of him who distributed feasts, flour, and the hangman. What is tragic in recent history consists in the realization that it was not always necessary for the dictatorship of our "modern" totalitarian States forcibly to overcome the people's resistence : on the contrary, it was very often the people who threw themselves enthusiastically singing into the hands of the "liberating State."

Yet the experience of modern totalitarian states is closely connected with the search for *security,* both material and psychological, of an isolated and therefore atomized individual in a society where he no longer has the connections that he had in the Greek polis or in the medieval commune. In this sense, fear of unemployment or lack of work in the modern human situation are not a danger greater than free time resulting from the shortening of working hours and the diminishing of the worries of life. There is no sufficient interest in the latter as there was for the *otium* of the Roman patrician or of the *virtù* of the Renaissance. The result is a collective infatuation with mass sport and gambling, not too different from the infatuation in the lower empire with the games of the Circus. In the epochs of the great crises of humanity, such as at the crumbling of the classic *polis* and, following the Napoleonic wars, during the romantic age, the thirst and hope for salvation reappears and increases. With the end of the faith in the beyond, however, the solution is sought in placing oneself in the hands of the State, or of the Church, or of a Party, where one abdicates his freedom in favor of the comfort of accepted opinion or the consecration of conformism.

This has resulted in an epoch without myths, or perhaps only with modern myths of the perfect State and of the "plan" which, however, leave no room for *heresies.*

Must we conclude from this that in religion, in politics, or in philosophy, man necessarily rejects freedom by becoming bound, from time to time, to the doctrine of a universal truth in the person of a tyrant or, beyond the limitations of this earth, in a being conceived to be extremely powerful and perfect in which he can renounce his own freedom (or his own arbitrariness) in order to obtain salvation? The answer is no since we have already mentioned two different spirits and principles (the principle of salvation and the critical principle of scientific investigation); they do not seem to run through European civilization.

Even if we no longer know how to have the immediate and naive faith of our fathers in the "magnificent and progressive destiny" of mankind, in the metaphysical faith of our historicists in the incarnate God of Progress; even if sometimes we ask ourselves whether in the ultimate analysis, humanity is freer today than when Epicurus preached the freedom of the individual from the fear of the Gods; we can nonetheless notice the deeper motives underlying the "involution" of present humanity in the path of the search for freedom.

The *cupio dissolvi* of the individual against the savior State in a society where a structure that has lasted for centuries or milenia fails and the individual finds himself almost torn out from the habitual living connections (as already once before at the end of antiquity or, more recently, with the end of the Napoleonic wars) arises out of fear of unemployment and from insecurity – this cancer of present society that corrodes it in its depth. On the other hand, the traits of the new epoch are a result of this : that the masses, risen upon the historical stage, no longer need to work twelve, fourteen, or more hours, and they remain spiritually unemployed during those leisure hours. Intensified by the crumbling of old faiths, this spiritual unemployment acts in unison with the fear of material unemployment, although at first sight the two appear to clash.

What can be said of the destiny of freedom under these conditions?

Must we despair of the destiny of freedom? Must we think that the very concept of freedom is mistaken and that, as a matter of fact, history marches towards slavery rather than towards freedom?

In speaking of concepts we must consider whether this is the source of the equivocations that we face when we speak of freedom : that not only has the traditional structure of society entered into a crisis, but so have our traditional concepts and, with them, our traditional concept of freedom.

7. *The crisis of the traditional concept of freedom.* What this means is only that today's crisis of the concept of freedom is much deeper than it appears at first to be. Actually, it is not only a matter of criticizing the "theological" concept of freedom given to us, for example, by Hegelian Idealism. Rather, it is a matter of integrating the sociopolitical concept of freedom that has been valid up to now in the order of traditional European society. The critique and at the same time the crisis of that concept of freedom has accidentally proceeded throughout the nineteenth century, both in theory and in fact.

What we might call the civil concept of freedom has been gradually broadening through the centuries. The polis knew only the liberty of the "free" with respect to slaves on the one hand, and of Greeks with respect to barbarian on the other. The Renaissance had known the *vir.* Very often, in the Italian society, we have not yet reached the concept of "citizen" in which France's bourgeois revolution broadens that aristocratic and Renaissance concept of an individuality which is both social and moral at the same time. After Hegel, and throughout the nineteenth century, there is a tendency further to broaden that concept of freedom. What is demanded is a reintegration of thought with life, and of the citizen or of "political" freedom with man.

The concept of freedom that traditional philosophy offered us, however, was not any less one-sided and abstract than the civil or political concept of freedom. From what we have said concerning Plato's philosophy it can be seen that freedom appeared there as independence of a reality (of spirit) that defined itself as *immaterial* against a matter assumed to be of a different nature. Consequently, Plutarch's hero appeared as superior – in the ultimate analysis as independent – in regard to the dangers and the temptations of matter, of sickness, of riches, and of the senses.[14] So-called modern idealism has lastly sublimated this freedom by making it the freedom of a God that creates as he wills and wills as he thinks. Of course, modern idealism's freedom was nothing other than the power of a theatrical king.

When, however, beginning with post-Hegelian movements, the attempt was made to bring back to the human condition and connect with the theological freedom of idealism, it was also believed that an overturning of the concept was necessary. At any rate, the various environmental conditions of individual action, were thought of as relevant. Thus the individual could not *act* any longer, other than in that sense whereby one can talk of "action" as of one of the many phenomena of a wholly determinate nature. The choice was between the abstract concept of freedom (of a theological type) on the one hand, and determinism on the other. In either case, man's freedom was incomprehensible.

Nor would it be possible to understand this freedom by making a compromise between that abstract and irrelevant freedom, and the determining conditions. In fact, if these conditions are conditions in the philosophical and rigorous sense of the term, freedom is illusory. The same is true, contrariwise, if one begins with the theological type of freedom.

That abstract concept of freedom (falsely absolute) of a spirit abstractly conceived as immaterial reality and placed, not any less abstractly, in front of an atemporal truth, cannot be corrected by taking only a slice of it (since, in this sense, the concept of freedom cannot be divided). Rather, it can be remedied only by changing that very concept of freedom.

8. *Continuation. Critique of the traditional concept of freedom. Freedom as crisis, or "heavy" freedom.* One obtains the impression that through those earlier theories what is sought is to salvage "spirit," so as to make it immune from matter and sin. In the same way, "thought" is saved so that it is true and cannot err. If man makes mistakes, or sins, this is his fault. In the meantime, however, something is saved independently of the freedom and arbitrariness of the subject.

In actuality things proceed quite differently.

If I utter even the simplest word, if, for example I answer "yes" to those who question me, I must formulate or almost choose my word among the infinite number of words that I could utter. I do not utter any other word since none of them would be appropriate. That is to say, the word that I utter when I succeed in formulating an appropriate answer is one with which I not only answer my interlocutor, but at the same time forestall the many objections that could be opposed to it. There are the various doubts that I could raise remembering past experiences, or the suspicion of a different interpretation of what I thought of remembering, that crosses my mind in the very moment that I open my mouth. Thus, if I in fact utter the word, I formulate it and utter it only because it succeeds in checking those latent objections and in capturing the world of my past or only possible experience, so that it appears as possible. In this way the word in which I enclose and at the same time by which I understand that experience is posed as the concept of it.

If thinking does not consist in this effort of comprehending each time my total experience of a word, which, as such, poses itself as more or less appropriate and well chosen, or more or less superficial and vain, if there is originally a "thought," true in itself, that is followed by the "will," which must depend on that thought, man's freedom cannot be saved or defended otherwise than in the sense of claiming to act against reason or without any reasons whatsoever. Rather than being absurd, this turns out to be an illusion.

Instead, man's freedom and responsibility can be vindicated only if one begins to vindicate them by starting out at the most elementary manifestations of thought, or better, as soon as sensations are interpretated and apprehended.

Yet, I cannot formulate words other than to the extent that I apply myself to lip processes, functions of the brain and of the whole organism for which, if I want to think, I must employ all the energies of the body and spirit. Instead if I am tired, if I am preoccupied by various worries, if an inferiority complex misleads me or, more simply, if I am sick, I am unable to think and to formulate even a brief word.

Concluding, if even the activity (of the brain and of the organs is voluntary and intelligent since I think through it) although I am unaware of it except in so far as I think while engaging in that activity (but I do not have a scientific notion of it), then the notion of organic intelligence or rationality becomes understandable.[15] What we call logical thought and, before that spoken and discursive thought, constitutes only a very small island of the great obscure sea of life. This thought is even obscure to itself since not only does life know more than we do, but we come to grasp the motives and hidden truths of the thoughts that we put forth only gradually.[16]

Therefore we could say that we are immersed in matter, almost saturated with it. Only within such a human condition can we exercise our freedom as individual finite beings, in flesh and blood.

9. *The courage to be free.* We exercise our freedom even when we formulate just a "yes" as an answer to whoever asks us. And we exercise our freedom to the extent that we summon, according to what we remember, all the forces of the body and of the spirit. We exercise our freedom to the extent that we make an effort to understand the meaning of our interlocutor's words. In doing so we examine that word so that its meaning can be part of the context of the discourse not unlike the key that, turned several times in the keyhole, finally fits, catches on, and opens the door. Thus I understand others, to the extent that I understand them, in virtue of my effort to do so. In the same way others understand me if they want to and if they know how to renovate the sense of the words that they hear or that they have used in a different sense. Thus, they must be able to become

adult in their thoughts so as to have a wider experience of the world, but also remain young enough, almost virgin, so as to know how to be open to new interests and loves.

There are in the world many truths or, better yet, many and different thoughts of infinite men. Yet, each time there is only thought in terms of which I must think and judge everything, and which I can trust if I have faith in the truth that I have helped to construct. And, if I have no faith in it, I simultaneously begin to work to construct a different concept more valid than the actual one, in which I can trust. In fact, it is a delusion to think that man could disinterest himself of truth, almost unburden himself of it, and that left to his own devices he could construct truth of his own.

Man must know what truth is, even in order to live. If he does not, he must ascertain it for himself and not because he is so commanded from outside. Otherwise he would not even be sure of the ground under his feet, and of the society and world in which he lives. But, in order to live as a man, he asks to know increasingly more, to become certain in the world in which he feels that he does not want to live as a brute, but as a follower of virtue and knowledge.

This is why he also asks to test the truth in which he believes with other truths. In this way, he comes up, sooner or later, with a concept that does justice to the objections advanced by others, and to the demands mentioned above, that the concept be the meeting ground of present experience, of my past experience and that of other people. This is the only possible criterion of truth.

Things are not any different if we consider moral experience. The latter, in fact, does not hold because there is in me, or maybe outside of me, an imperative or almost a moral commandment which would force or pull me half-heartedly to be "moral." No one can be moral unless *he* so chooses. Here also, it is only an illusion to hold that, left and abandoned to himself, man would stop being *moral.* Actually, the very principle of a modern morality must be that of the *dignity* of our life where by we not only do not tolerate living a life that we consider not worth living; but we also do not tolerate living a life that would not be morally worthy.

The moralities of the imperative do not succeed in practice in giving reasons for moral experience.[17] If these moralities can, or if they seem able to give a justification of the moral life, in practice they only succeed, at best, in speaking of a slave morality. What humanity in the course of its long evolution has come to consider as morally *worthy* cannot, to reiterate, be abstractly established. There are values that we swear by, which, for example were not such for the moralist Seneca, who had no scruples in demanding payment for every sexual intercourse with one of his slave girls. There are other values valid only for a primitive humanity. It has long been observed that everyone offers to his God what he considers an absolute value: Feuerbach pointed out that long before men devoted temples to the gods, they considered art to be divine.

Progress in the awareness of moral values, however does not necessarily entail *moral* progress. Thus, that perspective has progressed from Giotto to Vasari does not entail that Vasari was a better painter than Giotto, or that Giotto was not a great painter. Everyone must, within the situation and the degree of moral consciousness reached by humanity, resolve his problem, which is always individual in character and spatiotemporally defined. We know, however, that there is no responsibility in the abstract, as of a spirit created *sine matre,* outside of space and time, in front of a truth, or a value conceived as absolutes in the abstract.

In order to judge anyone, we must, as they say, fit in their boots. We must have at least enough moral sensibility to be able to understand whether we, in a similar situation, would not act similarly or whether we can and must ask for a different behavior – at least, if we want to judge in moral terms and not in the fashion of the judge who is only concerned to safeguard the constituted order and the observation of the law.

We never act as abstract individuals. Rather, we always act as that individual which each one of us is. We do so insofar as we carry with us (and lift up with us whenever we manage to lift ourselves up) the obscure reality of the generations that preceded us and of the species, the temptations of the flesh that are with us or are rather our very reality, the bites of need and the pinch of a misery endured at times through one's entire existence, or the power that we seek. In moving with every step of our walk, we lift the weight of this human condition. And yet, it is a free process nonetheless. In a similar way the process of evolution of the species – and I was about to say, of education – is free.

If from the times of Hegel's German and Prussian State the concept of right and of political freedom has changed, the philosophical concept of freedom has not changed. Rather, this concept of freedom, that we recognize as solely adequate, constitutes, on the whole, the principle of our consciousness as philosophers, as teachers, as political men, and as citizens.

The modern crisis of freedom, comes about as a result of a crisis of the traditional ordering of our society and civilization. And it is, at the same time, a crisis of the philosophical and traditional concept of freedom.

Let us hope that this crisis is a prelude to a society whose traditional values of this old Europe are not lost, rather, only reintegrated.

In the spirit in which we began to speak of the concept of freedom,[18] we can say that there is nothing that touches, in a smaller or greater way, an interpretation of the concept of freedom that does not become anachronistic in relation to our time; not even freedom from need and freedom from *fear.* In this fear, however, what in these pages we have defined as the *fear of freedom* does not play a minor part. I do not know whether he had in mind the same thing that today we call mental hygiene, but many centuries ago Epicurus wished for a humanity free from the fears of the unknown and the dread of the gods. Since then, humanity has not progressed very far on this path.

NOTES

* Translated by Paul Piccone, Washington University, St. Louis and Enrico Musacchio, University of Alberta.

1. Plato, *Apology*, 40 c and ff.

2. I have here taken the liberty to reproduce the two last paragraphs of my work, *Le Origini della Filosifia Europea nel Monde Greco* (Instituto di Filosofia del Universitia: Roma and Asti, 1953), pp. 14 ff. This work should be consulted for a more detailed treatment of the topic.

3. Where, to say I have the true concept and that others that do not agree with me have only opinions means to say that I am in the truth or, *tout court,* that I think and that the others do *not* think altogether.

This is not only Plato's doctrine, rather, it is also, after more than 2000 years, the doctrine of that thinker that presented himself as the benefactor of "historicism," i.e., Croce.

4. V. Mereskowsky, *La Morte digli Dei,* Italian translation (Milan, 1901).

5. Cf. the analogous development that, in the Middle Ages, contraposes Averroes to Aristotle and, more recently opposes Feuerbach to Hegel in the first Hegelian phase of his doctoral dissertation, whereby one similarly arrives at the denial of the immortality of the individual. For an identical process, cf. the development of Hegelian thought in the Italian idealism of Croce and Gentile.

6. Cf. Section # 2.

7. Cf. the already cited work, *Le Origini della Filosifia Europea nel Mondo Greco.* Cf. also my other work: *Nascita olel Mondo Moderno* (Sansoni, second ed. Florence, 1967).

8. For an elaboration or a clarification of this Crocian position in linguistics, see my work: "Noterelle in Tema di Linguaggio" in *Aforismi Attuali sull'Arte* (Florence: Sansoni, 1965).

9. In the so-called modern idealism of Croce the necessity of the Idea or of a Spirit is reiterated in the sense that the validity of thought and, with this, of our Knowledge, is founded only in this, that Knowledge itself constitutes the "theoretical moment" of that very Spirit whose reality, or the facts, constitute the moment of the praxis.

10. Apparently Croce would have considered it reactionary to reduce once again "words" to logical "thoughts."

At any rate, Croce could behave in this fashion since he continued to keep his eye on the (false) concept of a unique or bare thought and he rightly refused to reduce the words whose individuality and originality he vindicated to that mythical thought with bones but without flesh. Instead, he should have treated *thoughts* according to the new principle that he had already applied to words.

In fact (as Kierkegaard put it), there are no "thoughts" rather, there are only thinking individuals. The distinction between what we rightly call logical thought, and what we call art is based upon the different aims of the activities that we characterize respectively as critical knowledge or as art, and it is not distinction, or a division, between "forms" or "moments" of Spirit.

The supreme irony is that since these moments, according to Croce's own doctrine, cannot fail to be always all co-present in each particle or almost in every "atom" of reality (this is Croce's expression), in the ultimate analysis Croce cannot even justify the distinction that he considered to important between a work of art, a work of thought, or a practical fact. And his failure shows how inadequate is his starting point when trying to draw a distinction between man's different activities.

11. In this respect, cf. my article "Dopo lo Storicismo," in my work: *Il Senso della Storia ed Altri Saggi* (Florence: Sansoni, 1966), and my other work by the same title *Dopo lo Storicismo* (Instituto di Filosofia della Universita: Asti and Rome, 1955).

12. Cf. *Le Origini della Filosifia Europea nel Mondo Greco, op. cit.*, or *Nascita del Mondo Moderno, op. cit.* It goes without saying that an explication of the positive principle of Gentilian actualism on these lines implies a reexamination of what thought is. In other words, it implies the reexamination for the bases of experience made by the so-called empirical individual (the only real subject) advances in a world of real things.

13. Cf. section #3.

14. Of course, Plutarch's hero would be no "hero" at all if he were truly independent by nature in respect to those various temptations and dangers. If, notwithstanding everything, when and where he succeeeds in winning himself, he is a hero, he is so to the extent that he must win *himself* or, better, to the extent that he must win, in the name of a better and more deserving ego that humanity elaborates from within itself, that fragile reality which each of us is, in as far as he is an individual subject to sickness, temptations of the flesh, weariness, and, ultimately, death.

15. For an elaboration of this, see my recent volume, *Problemi della Libertà,* Florence: Sansoni, 1966.

16. The identification of that profound intelligence of living or, better yet, of the fuller and broader concept of rationality, with the processes of logical thought understood in its more restricted sense as a discursive and spoken thought, is therefore an error of traditional logic. Furthermore, traditional logic has identified intelligence with the concept of a thought wrongly understood as a "concept" that would be true since it could not be otherwise, i.e., a so-called pure rational, universal, rational or a priori thought.

17. For an elaboration of this point, see my work, *Il Concetto della Libertà. Ed. Altri Saggi,* Florence: Sansoni, 1969 .

18. For a broader political and sociological elaboration of the problem, see my work, *Nascita del Mondo Moderno,* 2nd ed., Florence; Sansoni, 1967.

A NATURALISTIC ONTOLOGY OF CAUSALITY

Edward H. Madden and William T. Parry
State University of New York at Buffalo

1.

THERE IS little point in looking for *the* meaning of 'cause' as if this term were always used in the same sense in the many different contexts in which it appears – though, as we shall see, the different ways in which it is used are not unrelated.

Consider the following cases of causal talk. "Running out of gasoline caused the car to stop"; "Removing the center beam caused the barn to collapse." Such talk, of course, makes perfectly good sense by drawing attention to some necessary condition for the occurence of the effect which was under the control of human intelligence. And the point of drawing attention to just these conditions is prudential in nature : check the gas tank before starting next time, and learn something about construction before you try your hand at remodeling. Sometimes the point of drawing attention to certain necessary conditions as the cause of an event is legal in nature : it is to ascribe legal responsibility in order to apply the resultant sanctions. The guide on a desert tour whose car runs out of gas and the contractor who pulls the wrong beam may well be liable for damages.

However, the word 'cause' might be used quite differently and yet equally sensibly in both these cases. We might say that it was friction that caused the car to stop when the gas ran out, and it was the attraction of the mass of the barn and the mass of the earth that caused the barn to collapse when the beam was removed. As long as gasoline was exploding in the cylinders, power was produced to overcome the normal operation of friction; and as long as the center beam was intact the attraction of the masses was kept in check. But as soon as the gasoline ran out or the beam was removed, the operation of those structural features of our physical universe known as friction and attraction had a chance to come into play. They finally produced the effect which had been held in abeyance by "interfering" conditions. By saying that friction and attraction are the causes of the car stopping and the barn collapsing, one is drawing attention to those pervasive physical features of our universe, formulated by the scientist in laws and theories, which are universally operative in producing certain effects provided certain conditions are met.

There is, however, a third perfectly sensible way in which the concept of cause is used which conflicts with neither of the previous two – as they do not conflict with each other – but incorporates both usages into a more comprehensive one. We sometimes ask "What was the cause of x? " when what we want is a *complete explanation of this particular occurence of x,* an explanation which shows, without taking anything for granted, why it is that x had to occur at t_1 rather than something else. In response to such a question as this, it would not be enough to mention either those conditions alone which have prudential or legal significance or those which have scientific significance, but it would be necessary to mention the whole set of conditions without which the effect at t_1 would not occur. To explain why the car stopped at t_1 it is necessary to mention both that the car ran out of gas and that friction was no longer overruled, just as it might be necessary at t_2 to mention both that the driver put on the brakes and that friction was reinforced. In the same way, to explain why the barn collapsed at t_1 it is necessary to mention both that the center beam was removed and that the attraction of masses was no longer counterbalanced, just as it might be necessary at t_2 to mention both that a hurricane wind hit the barn and that the attraction of the masses was no longer counterbalanced.

The two versions of the barn example are useful in helping to avoid a possible misunderstanding. It might be supposed that the necessary condition of a universal sort found by science is always made relevant in the complete explanation of a specific case by some other necessary condition best described as a "lever" condition – where, one might say, the collapsing of the barn by removing the beam is taken as a paradigm case. But, as the second example makes clear, what makes the "standing condition" relevant to the specific causal context may be another condition not appropriately described as a "lever" at all because it is not the result of intelligent agency – e.g., the attraction of the masses became operative because the wind blew the barn off balance.

This third notion of 'cause' is what a person has in mind when he speaks of the cause of some event or state of affairs as complex, and can be explicated in part by the following chain of definitions : 'the cause' = df. 'the immediately antecedent sufficient condition'; 'the sufficient condition' = 'the whole set of necessary conditions'; and 'necessary condition' = 'immediately antecedent condition without which the effect would not occur.' This definition must be construed, however, as giving a meaning only to 'the cause of x,' where x refers to some specific concrete situation, and not the concept of cause in general or in isolation. The whole set of necessary conditions is sufficient to produce that particular x, but another event or state of affairs (x') different from x only in point of occurring or being at a different time might have a different set of concrete necessary conditions sufficient to produce it. For example, there are two forces of specific magnitudes and directions acting on object O at place A at t_0. One force acting on O at A for one second would move it to C, while the other force acting on O at A for one second would move it to D. The two forces combine to move O to B in one second where AB is the diagonal of the parallelogram ACBD. The two forces and their directions exerted on O at A, we can say, are the set of necessary conditions sufficient to produce at t_0 the movement of O to B. However, at t_1 it might be the case that O is again at A, but that this time the set of constituent forces and their directions sufficient to produce the movement of O to B are different from what they were at t_0. Hence, the use of 'necessary condition' and 'sufficient condition' in the above definition of 'cause' must be understood to entail an essential reference to a specific context. 'Necessary,' as we use it, means 'indispensable in this context.' It must be kept in mind, moreover, that this definition explicates only one sense of 'cause' and is no more the "right" or "true" definition of this concept than definitions which single out certain necessary conditions as the cause of an event or state of affairs on prudential, legal, or scientific grounds. This definition does have the advantage of relating the family of causal concepts into an intensional whole as well as having a particular use itself, namely, referring to a reasonably complete explanation of a specific event or state of affairs.

2.

There is a current analysis of 'cause' which needs to be examined in some detail since it bears directly on all the senses of this concept so far discussed. This view, which Samuel Gorovitz calls the "differentiating-factor analysis,"[1] can be understood best as an effort to generalize the concept of cause when it is used to refer only to one member of the set of necessary conditions sufficient for the occurence of *e.* It is an effort to show what the different selections of one factor as cause have in common whether the grounds for such selection be prudential, practical, legal,or – presumably – of any other sort.

According to Gorovitz, the cause *c* of an effect *e* in situation S is that condition which, along with *e,* differentiates S from certain situations T with which it is compared by being present in the former and absent in the latter. Say that a man in a smoking car strikes a match to light his cigar : the striking of the match, on this view, is the cause of its lighting because the striking is the factor that differentiates that situation S from any situation T in which the matches are left unstruck and do not light. T is the "most natural" comparison class for S. However, which condition is called *c* of *e,* and what comparison class T is chosen, depends upon the context of inquiry and the point of interest. In another context, the lighting of a match might have another event than striking ascribed as its cause. Say that in a match factory match heads are being tested for hardness by being struck in a chamber from which oxygen has been evacuated and that a match nevertheless lights. Here one would say that the cause of the lighting was the (unexpected) presence of oxygen because the presence of oxygen is the factor that differentiates that situation S from any situation T consisting of striking matches that fail to ignite in the evacuated chamber – T being again the "most natural" comparison class for S. The crucial point in this analysis is that, though both examples reflect different practical interests and have different conditions chosen as cause, the condition chosen in each case is the differentiating factor. All cases of causal talk will be structurally similar in this respect.

Moreover, on this view, whenever we state a cause – that is, cite the factor which differentiates some S from some standard comparison T – we have adequately explained *e* in that context without providing an enumeration of the whole set of conditions necessary for *e* and hence without providing enough information to permit the deduction of the claim that *e* occured.[2] This sort of explanation is perfectly adequate and appropriate in ordinary contexts and in historical narratives. The scientist, however, according to Gorovitz, has a "deeper" sense of explanation than providing causes : it is his job to discover what differentiates an S not just from some particular standard of comparison T, but from all possible standards of comparison. It is his job not to produce the cause of an event but that whole set of conditions necessary for its occurence – in short, what Mill would have called the cause of *e*. Either the striking of the match or the presence of oxygen, depending upon the context, may be cited as the cause of the lighting of the match, but the striking of the match, its dryness, the presence of oxygen – and, no doubt, many other conditions – are all together a set of conditions jointly sufficient for the lighting of the match. Citing these conditions provides a scientific explanation of an event which is "deeper" than a causal one because it is more complete. A scientific explanation, moreover, is more general than a causal one and objective in a way the latter is not, since it delineates all possible differentiating factors and not simply ones that have practical import. Since causal explanations, unlike scientific ones, are not general and objective, "it comes as no surprise that the notion of cause tends to be replaced in theoretical science by that of jointly sufficient antecedent conditions." [3] Causal explanations, however, are still perfectly legitimate in ordinary and historical contexts where great detail is incompatible with the practical interests involved. Causal inquiry is admittedly nonscientific, but this fact does not detract from either its cognitive status or its usefulness.

Any estimate of the differentiating-factor analysis might well begin by acknowledging the usefulness of trying to discover what all selections of one condition as cause have in common. And it may well be that Gorovitz has managed to show what this is, though there may be some question about his success.

To begin with, though his formal conditions do not require it, Gorovitz, when he writes that causal explanations are not general and objective in nature, suggests that all selections of one condition as cause reflect practical, prudential, or legal considerations.[4] However, such a suggestion is misleading and even false. If one says removing the beam caused the barn to collapse and running out of gas caused the car to stop, then one clearly is selecting one condition as cause on practical grounds. However, if one says that the attraction of the masses caused the barn to collapse and that friction caused the car to stop, then one is selecting one condition as cause on theoretical and not practical grounds. The theoretical ground involved seems to be that gravity and friction are pervasive features of our universe and just as their effectiveness was forestalled by the presence of the beam and gasoline so it is their presence that produces *e* when the beam is removed and the gasoline burned up. There seems to be no prima facie good reason why one should be forbidden to select one condition as cause as a way of recognizing the scientifically fundamental nature of that condition any more than there are good reasons why one should be forbidden to select one condition as cause for legal purposes.

The question immediately arises whether Gorovitz's differentiating-factor analysis which works so well with conditions under the control of man applies equally well to those which are not. It would take a long analysis to answer this question in full, but that there are certain difficulties in the latter cases seems immediately obvious. We can evacuate oxygen from a chamber but we cannot produce a frictionless plane. What in principle could constitute the comparison class, natural or unnatural, when one is referring to pervasive features of our universe?

The next difficulty is that Gorovitz seems to commit the opposite error to that of J.S. Mill. Mill insisted that 'cause' "really meant" 'set of necessary conditions sufficient to *e*,' since selecting one condition and calling it the cause seemed to him an arbitrary and capricious procedure. But Hart, Beardsley, Gorovitz, and others show that there is nothing wrong with such procedures, since they serve perfectly legitimate practical and legal ends. Conversely, however, Gorovitz shows a curious reluctance to admit that 'cause' also can legitimately mean 'set of necessary conditions sufficient to *e.*' He refers to this definiens only as "what Mill would mean by 'cause' " and sharply contrasts this sort of scientific explanation with a causal one.[5] Only the former, he says, has the generality requisite for science and that accounts for the fact that it replaces the notion of cause in scientific explanations.

Rather than trying to quarantine one use of 'cause' as only "Mill's sense" it seems wiser by far to admit that when we speak of the cause of the Civil War as complex or the cause of a bowler's nervousness as involved, as we frequently do in historical and everyday contexts, clearly we mean by 'cause' 'set of necessary conditions sufficient to *e,*' and to put this sense of 'cause' alongside the other ones we have discussed as more inclusive than they, but wholly compatible with them and equally useful.

Moreover, in trying to separate scientific and causal explanations Gorovitz unwittingly gives a distorted picture of the former. Except in geophysical-type sciences like meteorology, the scientist is not concerned at all with explaining specific events or states of affairs. The scientist, as we have seen in our previous analysis, is eager to discover those basic structural features of our world which figure in many specific causal explanations, though rarely singled out for the appellation 'cause' on practical grounds. It is these features, moreover, which are crucial in those higher-order explanations of laws and unifications of theory that the pure scientist eagerly seeks. These unifying features are what the scientist has in mind when he talks about the generality of laws and model theories, rather than generality in the sense of providing a list of all possible differentiating-factors in a specific causal explanation.

3.

The causal relation, in one ordinary sense of 'cause' which is both useful and coherent, then, is between an effect and a set of necessary conditions sufficient to *e,* where 'necessary condition,' it will be recalled, entails, in our sense, an essential reference to a specific context. The question now arises what ontological status the terms of this causal relation have, an absolutely fundamental question to ask about any of the explications of 'cause' but one to which the answers in general have been discouraging. Different advocates at different times have claimed that only objects, or only events, or only facts, etc., can be the relata of the causal relation, and since none of them was willing to make concessions, the result was pretty much a stalemate. However, once one admits that there is no one "true" or "real" sense of 'cause,' but various notions which require explication, the stalemate situation disappears. It may well be that on the "lever" interpretation of 'cause,' e.g., the relata of the causal relation will always be events. The burning of the forest was an event, we say, and was caused by another event, namely, the careless disposal of a cigarette butt, which was under the volitional control of human beings. From this and similar examples grows the "lever" analysis of 'cause,' in which one of the necessary conditions of change y, say change x, under the control of intelligent agents, is fixed upon, for practical purposes, as the cause of y. But while this sense of 'cause' entails that the causal relation is between events, it is not the only legitimate sense of this word, and other senses, including the present one of 'set of necessary conditions sufficient to *e,'* do not require that either a cause or effect must always be an event. On the present interpretation of 'cause,' the cause may be a set of conditions, some of which are events, some states of affairs. To complete the ontology of causality, it is also necessary to recognize that the complete analysis of causes and effects must contain reference to objects (or particulars of some sort), properties of objects (or particulars), and relations between or among such entities. In some sense of 'fact,' facts also may be referred to.

Since it is impossible to analyze rigorously and in detail all of these fundamental notions on the present occasion, we will simply indicate the general lines we think an adequate analysis of 'particular,' 'property,' and 'relation' should take and shall concentrate our attention on 'event' and 'fact,' and the overall question of whether any of these concepts is eliminable as far as the sense of 'cause' we have in mind is concerned.

By a *particular* we shall mean some entity with a unique location in time and a position in some other specifiable order-system. The afterimage experienced by P at t_1 counts as a particular in this sense, since it has a unique location in time and is part of an ordered and understandable system of sensory experience. A physical object like a tree or chair is also a particular since it again meets both of these requirements, the position in the order system being in this case unique location in space. Occurring in an order-system alone is never a sufficient ground of particularity, though it does render the most general sense of 'to exist.' In the order-system of the irrational numbers it makes sense to say that the square root of 2 exists, while in the order-system of rational numbers it does not make sense, though even in the former case the square root of 2 is not a particular since the notion of having a unique location in time would make no sense if applied here.

By a *universal* we shall mean a property or relation that is repeatable in time and space (or applies to abstractions) and has some position in a specifiable order-system. Such a position itself gives some sense to the notion that universals "exist" independently of particulars, though not, of course, in the sense that particulars can be said to exist, since such existence entails uniqueness in time. Whatever the final ontological status ascribed to universals – and our task is not even to try to solve this complex problem – it seems clear that no description of any state of affairs would be possible without the uneliminable presence of universals in the language used. Whether the uneliminable presence of universals is accounted for in terms of a pragmatic a priori or a synthetic a priori makes no difference to the claim of descriptive irreducibility that we are making.

Though it is easy to give examples of relations and the formal properties of relations like symmetry, asymmetry, transitivity, etc., it is difficult to explicate the concept without circularity. 'x is before y,' 'x is to the right of y,' 'x loves y,' and 'x is the father of y' all express dyadic relations; while 'Aristotle is a philosopher' and 'Aristotle is rational' involve the heterogeneous dyadic relations *Being a member of the class K* and *Having the property P.* 'x gave y to z' expresses a triadic relationship, 'x bought y from z for p' a tetradic relation, and so on for other polyadic relations. It is of the essence of a relation (of the lowest type) that in each exemplification it must involve two or more particulars (or the same particular taken in two different ways). It should be quite clear that relations have no ontological status independent of the entities that may be related : that is, in a world without sentient life the relation of 'loving' is nonexistent; in a world without objects, 'to the left of' is nonexistent, etc. However, it should be equally clear that relations are not "reducible" in any of the senses of that word to particulars and their properties; specifically, there can be no description of a state of affairs without irreducible reference to relations. The very definitions of 'particular' and 'universal,' with their references to uniqueness and repeatability in time and space, depend themselves on concepts of temporal and spatial relations. Indeed, the concepts of 'particular,' 'universal,' and 'relation' are intimately interwoven and every separation of them, with attendant claims of "ontological priority," is gratuitous and pointless. The world is described in terms of this or that "state of affairs," and any description of a "state of affairs" concerns particulars, their properties, and the numerous relations between and among them.

Intuitively, the concept of an event is easy to grasp : what we ordinarily mean by it is a "happening," and this can be formulated technically, in our language, as a 'change in a state of affairs.' An example of an event would be the striking of a tree by lightning, the collapsing of a barn, a trip to Italy, and the recalling of a forgotten name. Such events occur "at" some time and place but are not themselves dimensionless points in space and time. A change in a state of affairs rather occupies a span of time and (usually) a region of space. However, since not all particulars involved in events are objects like trees, stones, and barns, but may well be mental operations like recalling or remembering, it follows that events strictly need occupy only a span of time. Only events involving objects must occupy both a span of time and a region of space. On the other hand, it would be convenient and apparently legitimate to refer to the order-system of psychological experience as "mental space," and hence permissible to say, even though partly metaphorically, that all events occupy a span of time and a region of space.

It might be objected that we have only a partial definition of 'event.' A change in a state of affairs is an event, to be sure, but, the argument goes, so is *the continued existence of a state of affairs* an event. For example, the question "What occurred then? " or "What happened then? " could be answered equally sensibly either by "He got up," a change in a state of affairs, or "He remained seated," an "unchange" in a state of affairs, and hence the latter qualifies as an event just as much as the former.[6] 'Event,' then, must be defined more inclusively as 'either a change or unchange in a state of affairs.'

This argument is not convincing, however, since it gives extraordinary meanings to 'occur' and 'happen' while supposedly using them in normal ways. These words have the general dynamic sense of "to take place" or "to come about," which suggests the basic notion of change in a state of affairs rather than unchange. The same suggestion is involved in the colloquial exclamation, "That was some event! " where 'event' means 'some change in routine of a dramatic sort.' So there is something quite artificial in saying that the man's continued sitting is an "occurrence" or "happening" and hence an event. It would seem more natural to say that in this case the man did nothing that could be construed as a happening and, in fact, nothing happened to him. To the question asked after a severe storm, "What happened to the barn? " it is correct to say that "In spite of what happened to it, the pounding rain and hurricane-force winds, the barn still stands intact." The continued standing of the barn, then, in spite of what happened to it, is not a "happening" itself, but the continued existence through time of certain particulars, their properties, and their relations. Events thus are legitimately still definable as only changes in states of affairs. We recognize, of course, that in the absence of a word ordinarily used for 'change or unchange in a state of affairs,' many philosophers, including Russell, have given 'event' this technical meaning rather than inventing a new name for the concept.

Events as changes cannot be construed as ontologically independent of particulars, properties, and relations, since these are the ingredients of states of affairs a change in which constitutes an event. Events in this sense are also ontologically distinct from particulars, properties, and relations, since they constitute changes in just such ingredients, and not another ingredient, of states of affairs.

4.

The meaning of 'fact' and the relation of facts to causality are both difficult questions and require close analysis. Such an analysis is forced on us especially by the carefully formulated but unusual view of Zeno Vendler that, when *f* is the cause of *e*, *f* must be a fact, not an event, though *e* must be an event.[7] On this analysis, the relata have – to borrow Marvin Farber's terminology – "causal unity" but not "substantive unity," the latter holding for things "analyzable into the same kind of components, or made of the same kind of substance."[8]

When we examine the meanings of 'fact' in dictionaries of the English language, excluding obsolete and legal senses, we find different categories involved. The basic meaning is that of reality, actuality, a state of things, something that happens or exists. More narrowly, it means that which is *known* to exist or have happened. Sometimes 'fact' specifically means physical actuality or practical experience as distinguished from imagination, speculation, and hypothesis. Shifting to a distinct category, a fact is a *true* proposition (or assertion or statement) – that which expresses or asserts a fact in the first sense. This sense may be "loosely" extended to the false : *"Your facts are false."*

The most distinctive and common philosophic use of 'fact' probably is to refer to that to which a true proposition corresponds. This use is in line with the dictionary's basic meaning of 'fact,' and we shall accept the latter as normal. In this sense, a fact is not distinct from a unique complex of particulars, properties, and relations. It is, in short, a state of affairs or an event.

Professor Vendler takes the words 'events' and 'facts' in "extended technical senses" that make events and facts mutually exclusive, and he holds that only facts or fact-like entities can be causes. His argument is based on syntactical features of English, especially the use of noun phrases. The noun phrases used for facts are imperfect nominals whereas the noun phrases used for events are perfect nominals. Since the noun phrases used for causes are also imperfect nominals, causes must be facts and not events.

Vendler explains his technical terms in this way : "The difference between these two kinds of nominal is . . . . [that] in the imperfect nominal the verb keeps some of its verb-like features : it retains the verb-object intact; tenses, modals and adverbs may be present . . . "[9] There are two main patterns of imperfect nominals. The first is the 'that'-clause type, e.g.,

that he sang the song,

while the second is exemplified by

his having sung the song.

(Note the past tense and the verb-object.)

On the other hand, "the verb in the perfect nominal sheds these verb-like features and behaves like a noun . . . " Examples of perfect nominals, naming events, are :

his singing of the song

the beautiful singing of the song heard

where 'singing' is completely noun-like.

According to Vendler, the following sentences are supposed to show that, since "the word 'cause' can be ascribed to or can replace imperfect nominals," "causes are facts and not events."[10]

The fact that the insulation failed caused the fire.

His having crossed the Rubicon caused the war.

His not being able to stop the cavalry caused the defeat.

(The artificiality of the last two examples is deliberate; Vendler wishes to illustrate the various peculiarities of imperfect nominals.)

We believe, however, that the same three propositions are being expressed whether it is done in fact-language or event-language, and we suggest that the above sentences could be reworded, with perhaps a slight increase in naturalness, as follows :

A sudden (*or* gradual) failure of the insulation caused the fire.

His sudden crossing of the Rubicon caused the war.

His prolonged (*or* sudden) inability to stop the cavalry caused the defeat.

We have inserted the gratuitous adjectives "sudden," etc., to emphasize the fact that our subjects name *events,* for on Vendler's view, only events and not facts can be sudden, gradual, or prolonged.

When not on guard and not involved in expounding his own sense of 'fact' and 'cause,' Vendler himself lapses into the more natural and stylistically preferable event terminology. He says that Hamlet's thought of failing his father caused his agony, and cites this as "one of the relatively few cases of something other than a fact, the thought of something, functioning as a cause."[11] But in other cases he clearly refers to physical events as causes, apparently without noticing the discrepancy. For example, "the explosion was the cause of the collapse of the house";[12] "a short circuit in the cellar caused the fire."[13] He indicates in a variety of sentences that "the explosion" names an event,[14] and indicates that "a short circuit" refers to an event.[15]

The "strongest argument" against saying that causes are events (and also against our contention that the same proposition can be expressed in either event or fact terminology) arises, Vendler says, from the fact that "the co-occurence set of 'event' (and its family) is alien to the word 'cause'," He asks : "If causes are events as effects are, . . . then why is it nonsense to say that a cause has occurred or taken place, that it began at a certain time, lasted for a while, and ended suddenly? Why is it that no witness can ever watch or listen to causes, . . . and that nobody has yet produced . . . a moving picture of a cause? "[16]

This argument, however, is something of a confusion. It might well be the case that the explosion which caused the collapse occurred at 11 : 01 a.m., though it would be unnatural to say : "The cause of the collapse occurred at 11 : 01 a.m." It might well be that a woman watched (or took a moving picture of) the accident which was the cause of her husband's death. She did then watch (or take a moving picture of) the cause of his death, though one would not ordinarily express the matter in that way. An event may be sudden and a cause, though one does not call it a "sudden cause"; just as – to take one analogy out of thousands – a teacher may be skillful and a sloven, but not a skillful sloven. We think Professor Vendler's methods throw light on the peculiarities of language, but not on the ontology of causality. As applied to ontology, his methods create what Marvin Farber calls "methodogenic problems." [17]

5.

The word 'fact' can be used both in the expression 'the fact that,' and in other expressions without 'that,' such as "Facts are stubborn things," where 'fact' is being used in what we called its basic sense. In the 'that'-clause use, a fact is necessarily propositional in character; in other uses it need not be propositional and may be an event, a state of affairs, or even an object. Though not the only use, the 'that'-clause use is perfectly legitimate. Vendler can be understood best, perhaps, as trying to show that the 'that'-clause has an ontological referent and that it is this referent which figures as the cause of events. We shall try to show how Vendler is mistaken and will be led, as a result, to a clarification of our own concept of a propositional sense of 'fact.'

Vendler holds that "the substitution of coextensive referential phrases preserves the fact. The statement that Oedipus married Jocasta is not a paraphrase of the statement that Oedipus married his mother. Therefore, they express different propositions, yet state the same fact."[18] Vendler concludes that 'fact' means "an abstract entity which indiscriminately contains a set of referentially equivalent true propositions."[19] It is facts in this sense that act as causes.

However, given this view, we do not see how Vendler can avoid a line of argument, similar to the one derived from Frege which Professor Davidson used (or rather misused[20]) in the same symposium, leading to the conclusion that all true statements state the same fact.

We assume the following two (empirical) truths :

(1) Oedipus married Jocasta.

(2) Nero fiddled.

Each of these is (intensionally and extensionally) equivalent to a statement that the universe U can be described in a certain way; i.e., to

(1') $U = \hat{x}(x = x \mathbin{\&} \text{Oedipus married Jocasta})$

(2') $U = \hat{x}(x = x \mathbin{\&} \text{Nero fiddled})$

respectively.

Using 'That' for 'The fact that,' 'Oe' for 'Oedipus,' 'J' for 'Jocasta', we would then have the following chain of identities :

That Oe married J

.=. That $U = \hat{x}(x = x \mathbin{\&} \text{Oe married J})$ [1 = 1']

.=. That U = U [by 1']

.=. That $U = \hat{x}(x = x \mathbin{\&} \text{Nero fiddled})$ [by 2']

.=. That Nero fiddled [2 = 2']

∴The fact that Oedipus married Jocasta is identical with the fact that Nero fiddled

The reduction of all facts to one (like Frege's "the True") would, on Vendler's view, also reduce all causes to one – something of an oversimplification. Even if causes are not facts, we would prefer to keep our facts distinct. The best solution is to reject the most questionable principle assumed above. namely, that substitution of coextensive referential phrases preserves the fact. Thus we would reject replacement based on the extensional identities 1' and 2.'

We also reject the (less implausible) identification of the fact that Oedipus married Jocasta with the fact that Oedipus married his mother. We accept the following argument as valid, with premises that may well be both true :

> Oedipus was aware of the fact that he had married Jocasta.
>
> Oedipus was not aware of the fact that he had married his mother.
>
> Therefore, the fact that he had married Jocasta is not the same as the fact that he had married his mother.[21]

As a result of the above considerations, we are forced to reject Vendler's concept of fact as an abstract entity which indiscriminately contains a set of referentially equivalent true propositions,[22] and which, upon the proper occasion, supposedly acts as cause. We must, however, make our own brief exploration of the ontology of facts in the 'that'-clause sense, sufficient for the present purpose.

We must recall, first, that there is useful sense of 'fact' in which all events are facts. Facts in this sense are simply events or states of affairs. However, there is a difference between an event – say, the beheading of Charles I of England – and the *fact that* the event occurred. The execution in question is an event that occurred, in living color, on January 30, 1649 (it is reported), and never before or since. At all other times, this event had only such reality as the future or past may have in the present. The *fact that* Charles I was beheaded, however, came to be a fact at the conclusion of the event, and has continued to be a fact ever since. The "life span" of the event was finite, but the *fact that* it occurred maintains its shadowy being indefinitely in one direction of time. Two quite different categories of being are involved here.

That a *fact that* should ever be a physical cause seems to us prima facie implausible – an unlikely form of Platonism. The formulations – especially by philosophers – often indicate the *fact that* as cause; but we are not convinced they should be taken literally. Even in the case of psychological causality, it is probably the *thought* of the fact, rather than the *fact that* itself, that may act as cause. No doubt the *fact that* may be an Aristotelian final or formal cause; but that it is a cause in other senses requires a better demonstration than we have as yet seen.

6.

In summary, we have done the following things: distinguished various senses of 'cause,' and shown how they all have a useful function to perform, whether the word refers to one of a set of necessary conditions, or to the whole set of jointly sufficient conditions. We criticized Gorovitz's effort to show what all selections of one condition have in common, as well as his reluctance to call a "complete explanation" a "causal explanation." We showed that in the 'jointly sufficient' sense of 'cause' states of affairs and events are the ontological entities involved in the causal relation, and that 'event' is most acceptably defined as 'change in a state of affairs.' A description of an event or state of affairs, we urged, involves uneliminable reference to particulars, properties, and relations and suggested that any effort to establish "ontological priorities" among the latter is fruitless. The overall result of our discussion of 'fact' and its role in the causal relation was this: 1) there are senses of 'fact' in which facts can be causes and effects, but in these senses a fact is an event or state of affairs – a complex of particulars and universals; and 2) there is a sense of 'fact,' the *fact that* sense, in which a fact is not an event or state of affairs but an indefinitely prolonged abstraction; but in this sense facts are not the relata of the causal relation.

NOTES

1. Samuel Gorovitz, "Causal Judgments and Causal Explanations," *Journal of Philosophy,* LXII (1965), pp. 695-711. Cf. Donald Davidson, "Causal Relations," *Journal of Philosophy,* LXIV (1967), pp. 691-703.
2. Gorovitz, op. cit., p. 706.
3. Ibid., p. 710.
4. The formal conditions appear in Part I; the latter claims in Part II.
5. Gorovitz, op. cit., pp. 709-711.
6. Cf. C. J. Ducasse, *Nature, Mind, and Death,* La Salle, Illinois: The Open Court Publishing Company, 1951, p. 108.
7. Zeno Vendler, "Causal Relations," *Journal of Philosophy,* LXIV (1967), pp. 704-713.
8. Marvin Farber, "Types of Unity and the Problem of Monism,"

Philosophy and Phenomenological Research, IV (1943), p. 42. Note that for Vendler the "causal relation" varies with the specific word used. Thus in "e_1 is the effect of e_2" and "f_1 is the result of f_2" we have substantive as well as causal unity, the relata being both events in the first case, and both facts in the second. *Op. cit.,* p. 705.

9. Vendler, op. cit., p. 707.
10. Ibid., pp. 708 ff.
11. Ibid.,p. 712, text and n. 8.
12. Ibid., p. 705, n. 3.
13. Ibid., p. 712.
14. Ibid., pp. 705, n. 4; 706.
15. Ibid., p. 705, n. 4.
16. Ibid., p. 709.
17. Marvin Farber has often pointed out an important distinction among philosophic problems between the methodogenic problems, which result from the method adopted, and the "empiriogenic problems," which arise in perceptual or conceptual experience. Cf. his "Experience and Subjectivism," in *Philosophy for the Future* New York 1949, p. 593; *Basic Problems of Philosophy,* Harper Torchbooks, 1968, pp. 83 f.
18. Vendler, op. cit., p. 711.
19. Ibid.
20. We say that Professor Davidson has misused his Frege-style argument, for the following reason : He has raised the question whether, as he puts it, the "logical form" of the sentence (1)

(1) The short circuit caused the fire

"would be given more accurately by" :

(2) *The fact that* there was a short circuit *caused it to be the case that* there was a fire.

Within the context of an argument purporting to show that (2) does not give the logical form of (1), he claims to show that we must accept the principle of extensional substitution for such sentences, as well as substitution of logical equivalents. Then he transforms (2) by both kinds of substitution into the absurdity

(2') *The fact that* there was a short circuit *caused it to be the case that* Nero fiddled.

Then, instead of "tampering with the principles of substitution" that led to this absurdity, he finds a "wholly preferable way out" : to "reject the hypothesis that (2) gives the logical form of (1)." But the transformation of (2) into the absurdity (2') in no way depended on the aforementioned hypothesis; it depended simply on the principles of substitution. If he wants (2) to be regarded as tenable, he has to reject the principle of extensional substitution. And he regards it as a tenable proposition, since he concludes the section by saying that "(1) entails (2), but not conversely."

21. The reader might inquire whether we must not also accept the following argument as valid :

Oedipus was aware of the fact that he had married Jocasta.

Oedipus was not aware of the fact that Jocasta had been married to him.

∴ The fact that he had married Jocasta is not the same as the fact that Jocasta had been married to him.

This argument is of the same form as that in the text above and is indeed valid. However, the premises are inconsistent, and so is the conclusion. For we ordinarily do not intend to – and do not – mean anything different by "*a* married *b*" and "*b* was married to *a*."

22. An abstract entity that "contains a set" must be a set. So he means perhaps that a fact is the set of propositions referentially equivalent to a given true proposition. A proposition, by the way, he says, is "an abstract entity which indiscriminately contains all the members of a paraphrastic set of imperfect nominals." Then a fact is an abstraction from an abstraction from certain noun phrases. We are glad we do not feel constrained to accept the view that all causes are "facts" in this sense. This might be called a doctrine of Linguistic Causality (or perhaps "Zeno's paradox"). We see this as another instance of the creation of methodogenic problems.

SELF-EVIDENCE AND PERCEPTUAL THEORIES

V.J. McGill, San Francisco State College

IF SENSE-DATA were "intuitively apprehended" and had "all those positive characteristics which they seem on careful inspection to have," as Broad claimed (*Mind and its Place in Nature,* London, Routledge & Kegan Paul, 1925, p. 181), one would expect them to become less controversial as time passes. Yet today perplexity and incredulity have increased to the point where the main interest seems to be to exclude sensa (also called sense-data and sense-impressions) from the perceptual process altogether. The theories of perception designed to eliminate sense-impressions have to answer the old questions about illusions, hallucinations, and direct evidence in new ways, matching the plausibility which the resort to sense-impressions had made possible.

In this paper we shall consider briefly two quite different theories of perception, both of which dispense with sense-impressions, and attempt to assess their success in answering questions which, in the empiricist tradition, were thought to require sense-impressions. The first theory to be discussed substitutes belief for sense-impressions and the second, appearing. In order to avoid complicating comparisons in discussing these theories we shall confine our attention, for the most part, to a recent book by D.M. Armstrong and the most recent one by Roderick M. Chisholm. We are mainly interested in showing that these theories come to grief because of their insistence on self-evidence in perception, and in conclusion recommend an alternative approach which rejects self-evidence.

Perception as Acquiring a Belief

For Armstrong perception "is *nothing but* the acquiring of knowledge of, or, on occasions, the acquiring of an inclination to believe in, particular facts about the physical world, by means of our sense" (*Perception and the Physical World,* New York. The Humanities Press, 1963, p. 105). A weaker formulation substitutes "belief " for knowledge in the definition. When it is stated in terms of belief we can make the following objection. Belief cannot take the place of the sense-impression since the latter, admittedly, confers evidence but needs none, whereas belief needs evidence or justification but does not confer any. The objection might seem to be weakened if we put knowledge in the place of belief, and say that perception is "the acquiring of knowledge . . . about the physical world by means of our senses," for knowledge does afford evidence or justify beliefs about the physical world. On the other hand, if the knowledge is to be more than a knowledge-claim it must, unlike the sense-impression, be supported by evidence. The parallel between the function of the sense-impression and the perceptual belief breaks down in this respect, even though the latter be called "knowledge." This knowledge, to be knowledge, must be supported by evidence, whereas the sense-impression is self-supporting.

Armstrong makes the usual distinction between immediate and mediate perception. When we hear the noise of a train going by, the train itself not being visible it is the noise which is perceived immediately, the rest mediately. The same distinction is made for perception in other exteroceptive senses, and the basis is laid for the traditional claim that immediate perception is entirely self-evidencing and incorrigible. Armstrong quotes with approval Hume's contention that our "sensations" or sense-impressions "must necessarily appear in every particular what they are, and be what they appear" (p. 37), and then makes the corresponding claim for beliefs acquired by means of the senses. "We cannot be mistaken about the nature of our sense-impressions at the time of having them," and similarly, "our conscious beliefs or inclinations to believe are also things about which we cannot be mistaken at the time of holding them" (*Ibid.,* p. 129). That is, we could be mistaken about its being a train but not about its being a noise.

The latter is true vacuously, since in Armstrong's definition of perception the noise, as distinguished from the physical sound waves, disappears : There is no noise immediately perceived but only the belief that we are perceiving it, and the physical noise which, according to the theory, is mediately perceived and is of course *not* unmistakable. Another way of putting it is that, in Armstrong's view, only physical things which stimulate our sense organs are perceived, the physical object in the present case being the sound waves, but neither on his nor on any other account are sound waves considered the kind of thing with regard to which error is impossible. Although one can sympathize with Armstrong's ingenious attempt to bypass the sense-impression, it is hard to see how it can be done while holding fast to the doctrine that there is such a thing as immediate perception, the basis of empirical knowledge, which is entirely self-evidencing and incorrigible. You cannot have self-evidence while removing the evidence. Armstrong's program seems to require a more radical break with tradition. If one wants to get rid of the sense-impression one must give up self-evidencing too. Having done so, it is possible to start off with perceptual beliefs or judgments as hypotheses to be tested, confirmed, vindicated by their consequences, and this program was, as is well known, carried out in broad strokes on a large canvas by John Dewey. Armstrong, however, is dead set against any such alternative.

He argues in accord with the *Theaetetus* that knowledge cannot consist of true belief plus good reasons for this belief, "because these good reasons must again be things that we *know,* and so, on pain of an infinite regress, we cannot produce good reasons indefinitely. There must be at least some truths that we know *without* good reasons" (*Ibid.,* p. 120). Since immediate perception is accepted as the final arbiter of facts about the physical world, it should also be accepted as the purveyor of some facts of the kind without good reasons. Yet at odds with this and what he has just said about the incorrigibility of immediate perception, he now admits that "error, that is to say, immediate perceptual illusion, may be always logically possible" (*Ibid.*). The point of his argument, nonetheless, is that only the a priori impossibility of error in a certain class of cases will save us from the infinite regress : where there is a possibility of error reasons would be called for. To avoid this snag Armstrong adds that though error is always possible, "in many cases we know that it has not occured" (*Ibid.*). This is true, of course though not because some self-evident immediate perceptions are more self-evident than others, and thus exclude error; but rather because some are consistent with and supported by a whole system of perceptions.

Armstrong's reply to this line of thought is reminiscent of the Argument from the First Cause for God's existence. If there are no empirical propositions which are entirely self-evidencing, so that knowledge of anything depends on knowing something else, then I cannot know that p without knowing that q, and cannot know that q without knowing that r, and so on *ad infinitum.* Thus, I cannot really know anything (Cf. *ibid.,* p. 134). The particular flaw in the argument that interests us is the assumption, very much like the conclusion drawn, that only knowledge resting on propositions which are entirely self-evidencing is really knowledge. One can of course take "knowledge" in this sense if one pleases, but if it is a question of knowledge of ourselves and of the world it would probably have only special philosophical uses.

Any account of perception which eliminates the sense-impression meets a crucial test in explaining illusions and hallucinations. Armstrong says that to have a sensory illusion "is to acquire a false belief or inclination to a false belief in particular propositions about the physical world by means of the senses" (*Ibid.,* p. 106). This formula includes those cases in which we "see through" the illusion, i.e., do not believe what we see, as well as those in which we are "taken in," i.e., do believe what we see. But though we do not believe in the former cases, we do have an *inclination* to believe what we see, and would "necessarily" believe it were it not for other beliefs we hold which contradict it (*Ibid.*). Thus to see the railroad tracks converge in the distance is to begin to *incline* to believe that they do converge. But for our belief that they are parallel we would necessarily believe that they do.

But does not this account leave out something very important, namely, *something* which converges and does so so convincingly that (if we were naive enough) we should take it for real? Armstrong replies that as the word "see" is used there is nothing converging which could be *seen,* i.e., nothing which could stimulate our retinas. Secondly, it could not be sense-impressions which converge since these admittedly do not have spatial properties and are not *in* space. If we suggest that the sense-impressions might have properties *analogous* to the spatial properties of physical objects, it would be open to Armstrong to reply that what people believe when they "see double," and are taken in, is not something analogous to double, but a real double physical object : What is going on is simply the acquiring of a false belief by means of the senses. If it is suggested that there is something else besides the false belief, namely, something that *appears* double, Armstrong's answer is, in effect : How would this differ from the false belief that there are two objects? Well, using "appears" in one relevant sense the following difference shows : We say the railroad tracks *appear to converge,* but meanwhile our perceptual belief (as opposed to the inclination to a false belief which it overrules) is *that the tracks are parallel.* Undoubtedly the language of appearing, though it has troubles of its own, could have added more fulness and credibility to Armstrong's gaunt picture of perception, but at what cost and gain may become apparent in the next section.

The explanation of hallucinations is similar to that given for illusions except that the kind of relevant stimulation of receptors present in the latter is absent in the former. Armstrong, however, makes the important point that the man who undergoes hallucination believes or at least is inclined to believe he is perceiving. He is in a position to perceive something in a certain region of space, and is receiving sensations from his eyes as he turns and focusses in a certain direction. It might be added that there is generally a framework of veridical perception which encloses the hallucinated object. The hallucinated cat on the mat, in Armstrong's example, is seen perhaps in familiar surroundings which lend it verisimilitude. But why a cat rather than a dog? If the cat, now deceased, has made a practice of sitting on the mat we may still expect to see her there, and sometimes do. Conditioned sensations, of course, are well established, and common sense does not hesitate to account for misperception in terms of expectation. In general, explanations and grounds of perceptual cognitions are found in biographies and the social milieu, not just in the perception itself.

Armstrong, to the contrary, carries over from sense-datum theory the conviction that at least what he calls "immediate perception" must explain itself on the spot. Sense-datum theory insisted that the man who hallucinates a cat on the mat must be sensing a cat-like shape. Otherwise he would not be fooled. How this shape which was not the shape of anything could possibly act on the nervous system to produce this result was seldom discussed, and one was not expected to press the question. Armstrong, while vigorously rejecting the dubious entities affirmed by sense-datum theory, thinks he must supply a substitute for them in immediate conscious experience. It is enough, he says, if the hallucinating man has a *belief* (or an inclination to a belief) that a cat is on the mat, and that corresponding to the cat-like shape, which is unmistakable according to sense-datum theory, there is an immediate belief which is unmistakable. But a belief in what? A belief that there is a cat-like shape on the mat? But this would be impossible on Armstrong's account. If the immediate belief is to explain why the man falsely perceives the cat on the mat, then it must be a true belief and the cat-like shape must exist and be immediately perceived. But to be perceived on his view it would have to stimulate his eyes, which it cannot do, and besides, Armstrong has rejected the existence of sense-data.

There are also some phenomenological questions about Armstrong's reductive theory of perception. We may ask whether, when we "perceive" the railroad tracks converging, (1) our inclination to believe that they do converge, (2) the belief that they do *not* converge, and (3) the belief, or inclination to believe, that we are set in the right direction and are actually perceiving the tracks, are supposed to be occurrent beliefs (or inclinations to believe) or dispositional'. It would seem they must be occurrents, since Armstrong thinks of perception as conscious and cognitive, and tends to restrict (unjustifiably, I think) the cognitive to the conscious. He states, however, that his analysis is consistent with both interpretations of belief, and this seems doubtful. For one thing, I cannot always, if ever, distinguish three concurrent beliefs or inclinations thereto when looking at railroad tracks. I do not seem ever to actively believe that they are *not* converging unless somebody raises the question, nor can I be sure that I am inclined to believe that the tracks themselves do actually converge. Perhaps I am inclined to believe in the sense that if I were to draw a picture I *would* show the tracks as converging, and *would* expect them to do so in a photograph, but this would be a dispositional sense of belief. Similarly, I would say that I am peripherally aware, via patterns of sensation, of my eyes being set in the right direction to perceive the tracks, but I cannot identify this awareness with a conscious belief that my eyes are set to perceive the tracks, or even with a conscious inclination thereto. The most that we can say, perhaps, is that it is *as if* we had these various beliefs, this being shown by our *readiness* to act and behave in certain ways, given motivation and other biographical particulars.

Appearing vs. Appearances

What Broad called the "Multiple Relation Theory of Appearing" (*Op. cit.,* pp. 178f.) got rid of appearances by introducing a unique triadic relation of appearing. When physical things are perceived they appear to the observer from where he is to have qualities. From the fact that "This looks red from here", however, it does not follow that "This *is* red", nor would the former, by itself, give us the slightest reason for believing the latter. The same would be true of other perceived characteristics: X appearing to have them from a certain place would give us no reason for supposing that x does have them, and in some cases we know that x could not have them. This theory could explain, with as much success as the sense-datum theory could, how the same physical surface of a coin can reasonably be assigned differed shapes by observers differently located in space, except that according to the sense-datum theory the sensum is really elliptical, whereas for the Multiple Relation Theory of Appearing elliptical belongs to the surface of the coin only triadically: It is in the coin only from a certain place. Whether for better or for worse interest in this type of theory has much declined. The reason may be the oddity of properties which inhere in physical things only triadically, and the difficulty of envisaging a world so structured, but this would seem to be a very weak objection. It might be a much more serious matter if, as Broad claimed, the theory entails the acceptance of absolute space.

Such objections do not apply to Chisholm's form of the theory of appearing, for whatever "appears" in his special sense may turn out to mean, it clearly does not stand for a triadic relation. Chisholm distinguishes three important senses of "appears" and "seems" which have sometimes been confused. "It seems to me I see a light," he says, (1) may simply report my *belief* that I see a light, or on another occasion, it (2) may be used to "hedge" or withhold any guarantee to others that what they seem to me is the way things actually are. There is also a phenomenological sense of "seems" and "appears," as in "This appears white to me," which (3) "may be used to describe a state of affairs which is not itself a belief" (*Theory of Knowledge,* Prentice-Hall. Englewood Cliffs, N.J., 1966, p. 31). (3) is distinct from (1), it is argued, since we can make the following statement consistently and without incongruity," viz :

"That thing appears white to me in this light, but I know that it is really grey." We shall call this statement (A).

If "appears" in (A) is used simply to express a belief that that thing is white, then, as Chisholm says, (A) would be either inconsistent or incongruous, which it is not. But the belief expressed here (if any), in our opinion, is rather the belief that that thing is white *in this light*; and this belief does *not* clash with the knowledge that it is really grey. For the perhaps intense light in which that thing is seen as white may not be a usual or standard condition for viewing colors. Thus I might sensibly say :

> (B) "In this light that thing is certainly white, but I know that it is really grey, i.e., would be considered grey under standard conditions of perception."

Chisholm also argues that the phenomenological sense of "appears" (3) must be distinct from the hedging sense of the term (2), since we may say without inconsistency or incongruity :

> (C) "It appears white to me in this light and I know that, as a matter of fact, it *is* white" (*Ibid.*).

"Appears" cannot be used in the hedging sense in (C), he says, since in that case the second half of (C) would give a guarantee which the first half withholds. The statement would be incongrous, but it is not. Now does it follow from this argument that "appears" cannot be used in a hedging sense in (C), or that it must be used in the purely descriptive sense (3)? It seems to me there need be no incongruity in (C) when "appears" is used in a hedging sense, for it should be noted that "in this light," is important in (C). It would not have been mentioned if the light had not been unusual. I might quite sensibly say :

(D) *"In this light"* it looks white to me and I know that, as a matter of fact, it *is* white, i.e., would be considered white under usual conditions of observation."

Roughly parallel would be the natural remark :

> "In the light of his present action alone I myself would call him a very brave man, and I know in fact (from past experience) that he is just that."

In criticizing these arguments designed to show that there must be a basic purely descriptive sense of "appears," we do not wish to deny that there *is* a descriptive sense of the word, but only to doubt that it is *purely* descriptive. Why should it be ruled out that descriptive utterances sometimes offer guarantees and sometimes withhold them? Chisholm argues quite rightly, in another place, against Austin, that "I know" can be *both* descriptive and performative :

> ". . . an utterance of "I know" may serve both to say something about me and to provide you with guarantees. To suppose that the performance of the non-descriptive function is inconsistent with a simultaneous performance of the descriptive function might be called. . . an example of the *performative fallacy.*" (*Ibid.,* p. 17).

Our suggestion is that "I am appeared to" can likewise serve to say something about me and also to withhold from you guarantees which would be risky.

Another suggestion in this connection is that there is, or should be, another sense of "appears" not mentioned by Chisholm, in which "It appears F to me" would carry the sense of "I appraise, estimate, size up, or construe it as F." It is hard to know whether this is one meaning of "appears," since the word is not commonly used except in the hedging, or perhaps descriptive-hedging sense. Terms like appraisal, at any rate, seem to express what goes on in ordinary goal-bent, learning-involved perception.

Chisholm also insists on the distinction and on the importance of the distinction between the comparative and the noncomparative use of "appears." Used comparatively "appears white" may be taken as an abbreviation of "appears in the way white things normally appear," he says. But it is a mistake to think that *all* appear-statements "involve some comparison with previously experienced objects, and hence, that what they express cannot ever be said to be directly evident" (*Ibid.*, p. 35). The phenomenological use of "appears," discussed above, does not involve a comparison of a present object with one previously perceived. In proof of this he offers a beautifully precise argument: "White thing," *may* be taken as short for "thing having the color of things that normally appear white." But if we now substitute for "appear white" in this formula the comparative explication of "appears white," which is given above (i.e., "appears the way in which white things normally appear"), the result is to reduce the formula to nonsense. Waiving the question whether substitution is legitimate in this case, it seems to follow that there is a noncomparative sense of "appears." But even without an argument it is clear to me on inspection that when I say "This appears white" I am not always carrying out a *conscious* comparison.

However, we also know that perceptual recognitions, estimations, examinations, construals, interpretations in terms of past experience, can proceed without the benefit of consciousness, and do so typically when success becomes habitual or there has been overlearning. To the extent that the way things look to people is influenced by their past experience of these things, as expressed in their appear-statements, to that extent the rationale and justification of these statements lies in past experience. It is known that people recognize things perceptually by way of their object colors, intensities, shapes and sizes, and that such habits are of great adaptive value. It is found also that people are influenced by the object qualities of things, which were of course learned in the past, even when they are urged to report only how the things *"look"* to them. When they are so instructed this influence diminishes, but does not disappear. A subject will report that the coin seen from one side look elliptical, but the width of the ellipse reported will be greater than the perspective size, more like the round shape of the coin which he has learned. The way colors, sizes, and shapes look to subjects represents a "compromise," as Egon Brunswik puts it, between phenomenal or perspective values and object values. Perceiving would thus be a continuous appraisal, in the light of cues and clues, not a finished givenness.

Another point about Chisholm's argument designed to show

that there is a basic, completely noncomparative sense of "appears," should be mentioned briefly. The conclusion is reached only by way of the equivalence of "white thing" and "thing having the color of things that normally appear white." But even if this kind of equivalence (or abbreviation) did hold for white, black, and cardinal colors, it would not hold for other sense-modalities. The color of objects, after all, is a special case. We do not know that, or when, physical things have this color or that, so we let the majority decide the distribution of colors in the common sense world or *Lebenswelt.* The shapes and sizes of physical things, on the contrary, are determined by scientific measurement. A man could certainly successfully recognize a thing as triangular without knowing much about normal perceivers and normal conditions of perception, so that it is doubtful whether "triangular thing" *could* be an "abbreviation of" "thing having the shape of things that normally appear triangular."

From this point of view, indeed, it is even doubtful whether "white thing" is a proper abbreviation of the phrase given by Chisholm. But perhaps he is using "abbreviation of" in some sense or other in which (1) the short expression could be clearly understood whilst the longer expression synonymous with it is vague, and in which also (2) it is legitimate to make the substitution for "appear" which Chisholm's argument calls for. However, our main objection to this argument is that the brain can make comparisons with past experience for which we can be held cognitively responsible, whether they are conscious or not. Often nobody, not even ourselves, can be really sure which it is, for conscious comparisons can become telescoped or disappear while the brain goes on with the same work alone, but much faster, a fact which is borne out by tachistoscopic studies.

The "primary truths of fact," according to Chisholm, report experiences which are immediate, "self-presenting," undemonstrable, and can be justified only by reaffirming them. That I am believing or thinking such and such is taken as paradigm cases of such truths, and another class consists of statements reporting immediate perceptions of "proper objects" of the various senses, as when we say "This appears white to me," or round, hard, loud, or smooth, etc. Such truths, known to us all, are "directly evident," and the touchstone which reveals them is our inability to cite any extraneous fact which could possibly justify them, though of course they themselves justify other beliefs which are *not* directly evident. They are thus self-justifying or, perhaps one could say, self-evident. They are a posteriori, however, and so one would assume they *could be* false, but if this question is raised it would seem that there would be no conceivable way of resolving the doubt by proving that they were true, after all, or really false. It is probably such considerations which lead Chisholm to state that directly evident propositions (these "primary truths of fact") can also be "paradoxically" characterized as propositions with regard to which it would be senseless to say of the man to whom they are directly evident that he knows they are true, though they give him evidence for other propositions (*Ibid.,* p. 30). The problems raised by this alternative formulation of "directly evident" are not explored by Chisholm.

We shall be mostly interested in directly evident reports of immediate perception, though we want to touch on directly evident havings of beliefs and thinkings first, and first of all to say something about "directly evident."

Chisholm takes great care in defining basic epistemic terms to avoid circularity, but the difficulties have often proved exorbitant. He defines "knowledge" in terms of "evident" : S must know h; h is true; and h is evident to S – all at the same time (*Ibid.,* p. 23). "Evidence," then, is defined in terms of "more reasonable," viz. : h is evident to S provided "(1) that h is reasonable to S and (2) that there is no proposition i such that it is more reasonable for S to believe i than it is for him to believe h." (*Ibid.,* p. 22). Finally, "more reasonable" is defined (or explained as follows : A choice between two attitudes would be more reasonable if it were made by a person who was "a rational being" whose "concerns were purely intellectual" (*Ibid.*). The only comment we wish to make here is that it is hard to see how these laudatory attributions could be defined or explained except in terms, such as "devoted to *knowledge,*" which would involve circularity. But the circularity may be unavoidable and the question does not seem nearly as important as the difficulties involved in the directly evident, which are avoidable.

Note that if it is directly evident to me that "This looks turquoise to me" (or "I am appeared to turquoisely"), according to Chisholm, there must be no other proposition in the world more reasonable for me to believe than it. And if I know that it is directly evident, then I must know that there is no other proposition more reasonable for me to believe than it, but how could I know this without knowing something that goes far beyond the proposition which is said to be directly evident and self-justifying. It is possible, of course, that I do assert directly evident propositions without *knowing* that they are so, but what use would this be?

But let us first consider the paradigm cases of directly evident. If a man is asked to justify his thinking he believes (say) that he will pay the debt on time if he is granted the loan, he can say nothing for himself, according to Chisholm, except something like "As I say, I believe it"; such beliefs differ radically from others in this crucial respect. But do they? The man who says he has the belief that he would repay the loan, can be challenged as follows : How can you believe that? Your record in meeting payments is very bad, you must admit. And you know you have no security in your present job, and no other funds to draw on in an emergency. Reminded of such facts and other telling circumstances the man may come to realize that he is mistaken in thinking that he believes he would make the payments on time. To believe this is to believe that he will have the financial competence to do it, and that he will have the "character" (say) to forego luxuries, to withstand the financial demands of the family, and so on. Maybe he has not considered all that is involved in believing that he will surely meet his obligations. So he cannot justify his thinking he holds *this* belief. He simply has not "thought the thing through." But he may be on stronger ground with respect to other beliefs, e.g., that he loves his wife.

Often a disparity is noted, by psychotherapists and the rest of us too, between profession of belief and conduct, and it is often concluded that actions speak louder than words. If, however, Chisholm is right in holding that the only justification a man can give for his thinking it evident that he believes he will meet the payments on his loan is to reiterate the belief, it will be pointless or "senseless" for him to cite his financial solvency, his sterling record in the business world, and his reputation as a man "who knows his own mind." For it will be said : This would be evidence of the truth of his belief, not of the truth of his holding this belief. Now what we wish to maintain is that evidence for the former, assuming a common rationality in men, can also be evidence for the latter. Thus if a man's behavior bears out his announced belief that he dearly loves his wife, I take his conduct as evidence not only for the truth of his belief, but also for his being earnest and meaning what he says when he announces it. The chances are it is the same with him. If a skeptic expresses some doubt about his really having this conviction (or thinking he has it), he unfurls evidence to show that it would be odd if he did not have this belief, the facts being what they are.

It seems to me that we all have the experience of being called on to justify our claim to have certain beliefs (or to really think we have them). When some one says : "How can you believe anything so foolish? " we respond by demonstrating that the belief is actually a very reasonable one, and hence acceptable to a reasonable man, or even such that a contrary belief or no belief, given the facts in our possession, would be silly or preposterous. The same seems to be true of intentions to do so-and-so, which Chisholm classes with thoughts and beliefs, as self-presenting and impossible to justify save by reiterating them. When our good intentions are questioned, when it is questioned whether we have at a particular time the intention that we profess to have, we point to our good actions. This provides some evidence that good intentions are at work, but also that we have them at the time we say we do.

Similarly, it would seem that we can also justify our thinking that what is experienced in immediate perception is what we report it to be. If someone should question whether the wine (which as a matter of fact tastes sweet to other people) *does* taste sour to me, as I claim it does, (where "tastes" is an appear-word used in the phenomenological sense), I can offer in justification evidence of the following kind : I am prepared to prove to you that I know the meaning of the English words I used, that in particular I am using "taste" in its phenomenological sense, that I am not the kind of man who would lie in such a matter or say things just to be different or funny. People will testify to the latter. Also I have learned to recognize a sour taste even when it is combined in all sorts of different patterns of other tastes, olfactory qualities, temperatures, and texture feels. Some people can confuse shades of sour with bitter when it is experienced in unusual combinations, or seem to detect it only because they very strongly expect it to appear, but a man like myself, who was once a wine taster, cannot be fooled. I will add that when I reported the sour taste there was no distraction; I was attentive and alert. I knew it was not some kind of delusion. I saw the glass with its red contents handed to me coming closer, felt its cool surface and somehow welcome weight in my hand, opened my mouth and felt the cool flow, just as it had happened hundreds of times before. Everything clicked.

In the case of immediate visual perception there is additional evidence. When I report "This looks green to me," I am aware that my head is set in the right direction to see the This, and that my eyes are properly focussed to see it. I have learned which sensations from neck, eyes, etc. are *proper* for different viewings of what is our common social space. But suppose now that, without warning, the proper positional and focussing sensations for seeing something *back there* occurred, instead of the proper ones for *in front of me*. With these cues all wrong, would it still be directly evident to me, as before, that "This surface in front of me is green? " Evidence should come also from the corroboration of our fellow men. If our reports of immediate perception were continually greeted by disapproving shakes of the head or incredulous eyebrow-raising, would we go on finding what our report expresses directly evident? If continued repudiation would make us falter, could not a lifetime of conciliation or understanding in the swapping of immediate experiences count as collateral evidence for these reports?

The quest of the directly evident has to face up to the fact of hallucinations. This leads Chisholm to make what amounts to a drastic revision of his description of what is directly evident in immediate perception. "The wine tastes sour to me" and "Something looks red to me" really include more than is directly evident. The existence of a physical object is assumed or taken for granted in both cases. To avoid this we must say : "I am appeared to sourly" and "I am appeared to red," and preserve this usage in all cases of the kind however awkward and cumbersome it becomes.

There are several consequences which might be mentioned. (1) Direct realism seems to have been abandoned in favor of something like representative realism. Physical things are not directly perceived in the sense of being given, but must be inferred on the basis of what *is* given, i.e., directly evident. (2) Although "I am appeared to red" does not imply that what is given is red, this kind of language does imply that there exists a realm of appearing-F-to-me (and to others, similarly) distinct from the objects of the physical world and their qualities, and quite as populous and complex as is the realm of sense-data. This is because "appearing" is nothing by itself, but is always hyphenated, viz., "appearing-yellow," "appearing-loud," etc., and there will be as many entities of this sort, as Roderick Firth once pointed out (*Science, Language and Human Rights,* Philadelphia; University of Pennsylvania Press, 1952), as there are sense-data according to the sense-datum theory. Appearing, after all, is no longer a *relation* between the subject appeared to and a physical object. Thus the claim of the theory of appearing that it avoids the multiplication of entities beyond necessity is put in question.

(3) According to this account the red, loud, sour, etc. which appear modify the appearing and are related to it adverbially. They tell the *how* or the *in what manner* of the appearing. In other cases of applying adverbs to a process, however, we can describe it adjectivally and know in advance what kind of adverbs would be appropriate to it. The process of appearing, on the other hand, has the peculiarity that we can give no adjectival description of it, or of a *kind* of appearing which could indicate what range of adverbs would be appropriate. Directly evident is only the redly-appearing, but nothing in the way of an extended surface to mark the appropriateness of the adverb. (4) The elimination of the physical object from what is directly evident, as in the formula "I am appeared red to," brings into special prominence the self-evidence of the I. The I which is directly evident in every immediate perception cannot be anything physical, nor can it be any pattern of sensations. On Chisholm's account it must be recognized as the *same* I, but by what characteristics could it be recognized on the spot as the same? What characteristics, if any, does it have? There is also the problem which we cannot consider here, how anyone can regard this recognition as more certain or "more reasonable" to

believe than my recognition of what appears to me now as a typewriter. I might be having an hallucination, but there are also such things as alienation and fugue states.

The difficulties cited above doubtless afflict other theories of perception than Chisholm's, and some may give trouble for any theory. In our opinion, however, a relinquishing of the ideal of self-evidence and a somewhat different *Fragestellung* will effect a considerable easement.

In Conclusion

G. Dawes Hicks' account of perception is regarded as a version of the theory of appearing, and yet it differs in the most fundamental respects from Chisholm's carefully worked out theory of appearing. (1) Hicks rejects appearing as an "ultimate . . . not further explicable" relation, and seriously questions whether we are aware of a relation so characterized. Appearing is largely explicable in the concrete contexts of perception, he says, for discrimination is the basic process. For him, indeed, discrimination is "the essence of any act of apprehension, however primitive and crude that act may be (*Critical Realism,* London, Macmillan & Co., 1938, p. 74). (2) Hicks also rejects both knowledge by acquaintance and (3) the infallibility of immediate sensory apprehension. "The crudest act of sense-apprehension," he argues, "is still an act of discrimination and comparing, an act involving, therefore, the characteristic that, in a higher form, is an act of judgment. And the presence of discrimination and comparison implies at once the possibility of error; indeed, the more purely sensuous the cognitive act, so much greater the liability to mistake and illusion. The capacity of discerning separately the sense-particulars, of which an object, that is always complex, consists, increases as discrimination proceeds." (*Ibid.*, p. 24-5).

We call attention to these three basic tenets in which Hicks' theory differs from Chisholm's -- and in the last two from Armstrong's theory as well – because they show the ground on which we have stood in making our criticisms in this paper, and indicate the line we would want to take, if space permitted us to develop an alternative account of perception.

It seems to me that the unending complexities in which the theory of acquaintance has involved us bear witness to a costly mistake, and that skepticism on this point has become simply heroic. The scientific temper will reserve the right to challenge any assertion, though not all of course can be challenged at the same time. The starting-point, as Peirce said, can be what we postulate or assume to be true, or is warrantedly assertible, and this seems to be present scientific procedure.

From this point of view the problem of accounting for illusions, and especially hallucinations, without recognizing sense-data, is not at all hopeless. The hallucination of a cat on the mat (Armstrong's example) becomes philosophically perplexing when we say : At the moment there is nothing in the man's visual field, not even a cat-shaped sense-datum, which he could have mistaken for a cat, nothing, therefore, to explain why he should "see" or report he sees a cat. Of course, the cat-shaped sense-datum could not really *explain* the error either; the causal agency of sense-data is either not assumed or left entirely unexplained, and remains at most a bare possibility, nor does anyone expect that any scientific breakthrough will change *this* situation. When sense-data are eliminated, however, and replaced by beliefs acquired by means of the senses, or by appearings F to me, taken as nonphysical occurents, and as incorrigible and self-justifying, explanation seems to be thwarted in the same way, and for the same reasons.

It is generally agreed that the more we know about other people's biographies, the better we can understand and appraise their responses, even the most intimate, and it is not clear why our own case must be radically different. It is true that I learn things about myself which other people have to be told (though the converse is true, too), but this is not too surprising since my receptors and autonomic nervous system are connected to my cortex and speech organs, but not with theirs, and again, I am more interested in the subject. Hallucinations are only semi-private, and are often shared as in mass hysterias and collective use of drugs where a common suggestion is operating. Their explanation, even in an epistemic regard, would hardly be found in the experience itself, but rather in cultural history or pathological data. And since stimulation of brain tissue at the right places could, presumably, bring about the drunkard's report of seeing pink rats, whether he has a private showing of rat-shaped sense-data or rat-like appearings, or not, and the very controversial question of what is "given" is incapable of confirmation, in any case, it is not surprising that many philosophers are now exploring different approaches. Study of the implications of developments and prospects in cybernetics and neurophysiology might in time, perhaps, lead to philosophical constructions which could be tested.

Behavioristic theory of perception is another alternative, and it does not seem to have had a fair trial in philosophical circles. A behavioristic theory which, while retaining Skinner's operant conditioning, accepts available physiological supports and certain hypothetical constructs, has hardly been heard at all. If perceptual reports are taken as learning responses as well as responses to present stimulation, we are well on the way to explanation in terms of observables and manipulables. If discrimination is the basic process in perception, as Hicks claimed, we can say that what is reported is discrimination of stimulus values in relation to learning and prospective responses. It is hard to see, as B.A. Farrell argued (in "Experience," *Mind,* LIX, 1950), what psychologists leave out when proceeding in this way, as they do; nor is it clear what would necessarily be lost to the philosophical enterprise either. If the objective reporting is many-sided and historically oriented it need not jeopardize the facts of individuality, but can secure them among confirmables. As Marvin Farber has persuasively argued, even the best insights of phenomenology could be accommodated within the growing scientific picture of the natural world which, he adds, must be accepted by the conscientious philosopher in any case.

A NATURALISTIC APPROACH TO PERSONS, DETERMINISM, AND EVIDENCE

Norman Melchert, Lehigh University

IS DETERMINISM compatible with freedom and responsibility? Certainly –– if you mean the right thing by «freedom» and "responsibility." Must determinism be false if we are free and responsible? Certainly – if you mean something else by "free" and "responsible."

The burden of this essay is to argue the following points: that the compatibilist[1] and the libertarian have in effect been working with different senses of the central terms in the debate, that one can get a new and useful perspective on the problem by viewing each side as proposing a partial specification of the concept of a person, and that when it is seen in this way it becomes clear that a crucial assertion on each side is a matter for empirical confirmation.

I shall assume for the purposes of this essay that those "hard" determinists who argue that no human is ever responsible for anything may be safely disregarded. Most of them reintroduce moral distinctions and responsibility anyway, so as to agree with the compatibilists or "soft" determinists.[2] I shall also assume that the recent attempt by "action theorists" to provide a priori, purely conceptual grounds for believing that determinism logically cannot apply to human actions is a failure.[3] It is, then, the two more traditional parties to the dispute who still have the field.

1

It will be useful to have some of the principal points of this debate before us. In the twentieth century, the dialectic has gone something like this (no pretence is made to historical accuracy).

Libertarian : At least some actions of men are freely chosen. It is these that we hold men responsible for. That men sometimes act freely can be shown in two ways : a) by paying careful attention to our *experience* in the act of choosing; b) from the fact that a man *is* morally responsible, which implies that on the occasions he is responsible he *could have done otherwise* than he did in fact do.

Compatibilist : It is true that men sometimes act freely and responsibly, but this is not at all incompatible with determinism. It is compulsion or coercion which is the opposite of freedom, not causation, which is quite a different matter. As to the libertarian's "evidence" :

a) Even if we grant that he gives the right description of the experience of choosing, it may be that (1) this experience is illusory, or (2) the experience *is just* the experience of not being compelled or coerced. It is not even clear what it would be like to experience the *absence of a cause.*

b) It is true that if a man is responsible *he could have done otherwise;* but what does this mean? The analysis of

C. "Jones could have done otherwise" is given by
W. "Jones would have done otherwise, *if* he had (chosen, wanted, tried...) to." Compatibilists differ over the best verb for the antecedent clause.

Since C is the condition for freedom and responsibility, and W is what C really means, and W is compatible with determinism, it follows that freedom and responsibility are compatible with determinism.

Libertarian : I agree that if C is true then W is true. But I don't agree that W is an analysis of C. For W might be true while C is false : if Jones could not have (chosen, wanted, tried. . .) otherwise than he did.

To get an analysis of C compatible with moral responsibility you must conjoin with W the following :

C' "Jones could have (chosen, wanted, tried...) otherwise." But C is not compatible with the deterministic thesis which holds that Jones' choosings, wantings, and tryings are an inevitable result of previous causal factors. What is needed is a *categorical* sense of "could have done otherwise" and more generally of "can."

2

The dialectic here, I wish to suggest, may be regarded as the development of two alternative conceptual schemes. These alternatives are in effect two partial specifications of *different concepts of a person.* It will be seen that these schemes are incompatible, so they cannot both apply to human beings. It will also become clear that the question of determinism is the crucial point in which they differ, and that *because of this* the key terms in each differ in meaning.

Before we turn to the specification of these person concepts, however, we shall need several definitions in hand. A preliminary definition of *determinism for human actions* will be helpful. It is human *actions* which are in question in the free will debate, not any of the varied *passions* humans are subject to. The actual definition I shall depend upon will be given later (in section 6), so this one is provisional. An action is *determined* if there is a series of antecedent conditions, each of which is the cause of a subsequent one, and some of which exist prior to the birth of the person doing the action, the last of which causes the action.

We shall furthermore say of any event or action which is determined in the above sense that it is *causally necessitated.* And finally, I shall use the word "power" in such a way that a person has a certain action in his power only if that action is neither causally necessitated nor causally impossible, given the actual series of states preceding the action.

3

The following seven theses are a partial specification of a certain conceptual scheme for thinking of persons. For brevity's sake, I shall refer to it as *Person-Concept-I.* And I shall occasionally refer to human beings who satisfy this concept, if there are any, as *Persons-I.*

1. *Determinism holds for human actions.* This means that a causal series of states traceable to a point before a person's birth exists for each of his deeds. Each of his actions is causally necessitated. If this is true, then it is causally impossible (relative to the actual series of antecedent states) that anyone should have done what he did not do, or not have done what he did do.

2. *No Person-I has any action in his power.* This follows from the first point and the definition of "power." If every action is causally necessitated, then no actions are in a person's power. Furthermore, no person ever has it in his power at a given time both to do *A* and to leave *A* undone (which is not, of course, to be confused with the *logically* impossible power to do both *A* and *not-A* at a given time).

3. *For any action that a Person-I does, there is a sense in which he could have done otherwise.* There may, in fact, be several such senses. In section 2 we saw the compatibilist arguing for a hypothetical sense in which he could have done otherwise : *if* certain causal antecedents *within him* had been otherwise, then he would have acted otherwise. These antecedents, we saw, were variously specified. To most of them there are objections of one sort or another.[4]

Recent attempts to formulate the sense, compatible with determinism, in which a person could have done otherwise have focussed on the concept of *ability.* One of the most interesting of such attempts is by Professor Wilfrid Sellars, who defends a hypothetical analysis in terms of what a person *willed* to do and what he was *able* to do.[5] As a first step in understanding abilities Sellars suggests that

> "Jones is *able* to do A at t"

means

> "It is causally necessary that if just prior to *t* Jones *wills* to do *A*, then he *does A* at *t.*"

Acts of will (which are not *actions,* in his view) are part of Sellars' sophisticated and complex philosophy of mind; their nature cannot be discussed here. If Jones is *able* to do *A* then it is *possible* for him to do *A*. But it does not follow from this that it is at *t* possible that he should do *A* relative to *every possible* state of the universe just prior to *t.* Suppose that just prior to *t* the universe had been in such a state that it causally necessitated Jones *not* doing *A*. Still, it is argued, it might nevertheless be that Jones was *able* to do *A* at *t* because the above hypothetical analysis could still be true.

The above sketch of the argument does not do justice to the network of distinctions made by Sellars, which includes also the concepts of being in a position to do something, circumstances which prevent actions, and others. All these are woven together in a defense of the claim that Jones' *ability* to do *A* at *t* is not incompatible with his being causally necessitated to do something else at *t*.

To the inevitable libertarian question, "But can Jones *will* to do A? " Sellars replies by distinguishing "real" circumstances from "deterministic pseudo-circumstances." It is of some importance, if one wishes to understand the reply, to notice that the former are taken quite common-sensically. "Real" circumstances endure throughout a period of time, and it is *in* those circumstances that one wills to act. It is circumstances of this sort which we ordinarily say can *prevent* us from acting; they can also prevent us from willing to act. (Being under the influence of hypnosis or drugs during a certain period might be examples). Antecedent states are clearly very different; they are not circumstances *within* which we are prevented from willing. And one can see why Sellars terms them "pseudo-circumstances." These do not render Jones "unable" to will *A*. And it is this sense of "able" which is crucial for Jones' having been able to do otherwise.

4. *A Person-I is free to do A when he is able to do A.* Implicit in Jones' being able to do *A* is the proviso that circumstances neither force him to do *A* nor prevent him from doing *A*. It is external circumstances we usually have in mind, and these may have different points of pressure. Here we could distinguish degrees of coercion and duress, but we will make just one point. There is a difference between my not leaving the room because I am tied to a chair and my not leaving because someone threatens to shoot me if I do. In the first case I may want to leave, may will to leave, and may try to leave. In the second I neither will nor try to leave. In the first case the circumstances work on what I do; in the second on what I will to do. But both are cases of my being *unfree* in the relevant sense with respect to leaving the room. The fact that the threat of death is counted as a circumstance making me "unable" to leave may seem a little peculiar. One might think that my *abilities* are unimpaired by such a threat. But it does mirror one common use of "able." It would not be odd for someone to explain to people who were expecting me that I was "unable to come because a madman had me cornered in a room."

The concept of circumstances preventing me from doing

something or forcing me to do something may also be internalized. Drugs may be such an internal circumstance. Any compulsions and psychic incapacities may also be included. These, too, may be thought of as circumstances existing for a time, during which time a person is *unable*.

Because of the way ability is understood, it should be clear that a person's being *free* with respect to a certain action is quite compatible with his being causally necessitated with respect to that action.

5. *A Person-I is responsible for what he does when he does it freely*. If Jones, a human being who satisfies this first model, signs a contract under no duress we hold him responsible for that act. By this we simply mean that its proximate source is to be found *within* him, that he was *not unable* with respect to it, and that no one but he himself did it. If all this is true of Jones, then (in the sense above defined) he could have done otherwise than to sign the contract. It is always possible, of course, that circumstances yet unknown should come to light which diminish or "defeat" his being responsible. These would be such as to indicate that he *was unable* with respect to the act, and so did not act freely.

In holding Jones responsible we also mean to imply that if a repetition of the act is not desired it is *Jones* (and not anyone else—not Smith nor his long dead great-grandmother, for instance) upon whom we must work.[6] *How* to work on him is a matter of strategy, of what will succeeed; suggestions range from trying for a personal religious conversion, to making him suffer, to readjusting the social conditions in which he lives. This is not the place to argue the appropriateness of these methods. But we may note that they all agree in taking Jones as the focus of concern; it is *his willing* that we want to change. If he did the action freely it makes sense to try. And that is what it means in scheme I to hold him responsible.

6. *A Person-I may be subjected to treatment so as to modify his future behavior*. Since no person, in this sense of person, has the power to do anything other than he does, it would be foolish at best and bad at worst to *punish* him for what he did. Punishment should be thought of as deserved or earned by a person, brought upon himself within a context of rules and sanctions. *It* has its justification in the *past*, in what the

person did. Treatment, on the other hand is *future*-oriented solely. If a person was responsible for an action in the sense of responsible defined above, then he had the ability to do otherwise. And then the application of persuaders of some sort may make a difference in his future behavior.

If the person was unable to do anything else than he did (e.g., an epileptic in a seizure), treating him in the ordinary way to prevent future repetitions is useless. This corresponds to our not holding him responsible and not considering it a free act. It is worth noting that this example brings to light a distinction between two sorts of treatment, that applied to the able and that used with the unable. We can treat a man's epilepsy so as to cure it. In this case we would be attempting not to modify the behavior of a person who is able to do otherwise, but to provide a person with an ability he is lacking. These two types of treatment must be kept quite distinct. Yet both are similar in that their justification is found in the expectations of future success.

7. *Any conviction on the part of a Person-I that his actions have their origin solely within him is an illusion.* This follows evidently from the truth of determinism for human actions, which entails that causal origins of any action can be traced back to a time before a person's birth.

4

The second alternative conceptual scheme will be called *Person-Concept-II.* Human beings who satisfy this concept, if there are any, will be referred to as *Persons-II.* There are seven theses here, too, paralleling the seven just given.

1. *Determinism does not hold for all human actions.* This means, according to the definitions given, that (at least) some human actions are not the last in a series of causal states traceable to a time before a person's birth. And that for these actions there is no antecedent causal condition necessitating their occurence, or at least that such a sequence of conditions does not extend to a time before birth.

Sheer indeterminism is not, of course, going to yield a satisfactory person-concept. It would construe actions as purely chance or random happenings; and that would destroy not only the applicability of the term "responsible," but the very notion of an action itself. There may be notions of freedom, responsibility and action which are compatible with determinism (as sketched in the above section), but there are no such concepts compatible with sheer indeterminism.

Recourse must then be made to a notion which has been in philosophical disrepute since Hume, the notion of an *agent.* What is necessary is to think of the person himself as the origin and sole author of these actions. They are not necessitated by prior events or states of the person in question; these leave it open whether the action will be done or not. But they are not *uncaused* either. The person himself is their cause.[7] We shall put this point in the following way.

2. *Some actions are in a Person-II's power to perform or not to perform.* These actions are such that the person has at a given time the power to do them and also the power to leave them undone. It is, quite strictly, "up to him" whether he does them or not. Neither the doing of the action nor leaving it undone is either causally necessitated or rendered causally impossible by previous states of affairs.

3. *For at least some actions, it is true that a Person-II could have done otherwise in the strongest possible sense.* It is not only *abilities* to do these actions which are at stake when we say a person can do them, but *powers.* Since in these cases it is wholly up to the person himself, there is no need for a carefully qualified or hypothetical analysis of "can."

It is possible, nevertheless, in this model to hold that there are causes for the movements involved in actions. Depending on one's stand on the mind-body problem, these may be of two sorts—mental or physiological. Consider the action of raising my arm. Let us grant that this is a basic action, so that there is no other action I must perform in order to do it. I simply raise my arm. And let us suppose it is one of those actions which was in my power to do, and so was not causally necessitated by previous events. It is not often noticed that this does not involve one in the foolishness of denying the physiological story of muscle movements caused by nerve excitations which can be traced back to the central nervous system. What this view does involve one in holding is that certain among these immediate causal antecedents are caused to happen not by preceding events, but by the person himself. There is, in this view, a whole "gestalt" of events I "make happen" when I perform the action of raising my arm. Some of these I know about, others I am ignorant of, but can study scientifically. They are not things I *do* in the proper sense of "do," though they are essentially a part of what I do. It is, I think, safe to say that this way of looking at actions is not contradicted by any physiological knowledge we have in our possession at the present time.

The same sort of move may be made for mental causes. Why did I raise my arm? Simply, let us suppose, because I *wanted* to. And there is no reason why, in this model, wants should not be thought of as causes.[8] Only they are *not actions.* And some among these wants *I* "make happen." Not, of course, in the absurd sense that I *do* them (for doing is appropriate only to actions) but in the sense that they are not causally necessitated by chains of factors beginning before my birth. (This point need not be construed as denying that some wants I have are *not* "up to me," e.g., the biologically based need for food). A want, too, is part of a whole "gestalt" which includes, if circumstances and opposing wants permit, an action. (This may account for the intimate tie noticed and made use of by "action theorists" between wants and actions without forcing us to deny that wants can cause actions).

When an agent, then, does what is in his power to do, a whole *pattern* of events occurs. And some of these events may be causes of other events in the pattern. But, considered as a whole, this pattern has no other cause than *the person himself.*

4. *A Person-II is free when what he does is in his power.* A person in this model may lack freedom with respect to a certain action in several ways. He may be coerced to do it or prevented by circumstances from doing it. *Or* the events involved in the performance of the action may be causally necessitated by events which were not in his power.

An obvious implication is that, since there is a great deal we do not know about persons yet, we cannot always tell whether a person was free to do an act or not. Simply getting straight about common-sense coercion and prevention will not suffice. If determinism were true, all action would be causally necessitated, and no person would be free – in this sense of free.

5. *A Person-II is responsible for what he does when he does it freely.* Suppose Jones makes a cutting remark calculated to hurt Smith. Provided what he said was in his power to say, that

he could have withheld the remark (and not just that he had the "ability" to withhold it), Smith may properly resent Jones for it. And we may be morally indignant over it. In fact, the *appropriateness* of these reactions seem to *presuppose* that it was solely *up to Jones* whether to make the remark or not. It seems that if it was not in his power to refrain from making the remark, then, though we may be angry, it is not appropriate to be angry *at Jones.* It is like being angry at a car that will not start. We may *be* angry at it, but we realize all the while that it is not strictly appropriate. It cannot help it, poor thing.

If determinism is true, then we might be angry or act resentfully or express our indignation as a matter of *policy.* These reactions might be calculated as useful in modifying a person's future behavior, as causes for change. We do, in fact, often use anger in this way with children. This fits with the fact that we do not consider children as fully responsible persons. Insofar as Jones is not fully responsible, does not have the action in his power, it might be appropriate to be angry *over* what Jones did, or resentful *because of* his remarks, but it is not appropriate to be angry *at* Jones.

To hold a person responsible in this model is to allow that with respect to some act these attitudes are appropriate. Praise and blame are *due* to Jones, then, depending on what he does. They are not simply tools to be used to manipulate him for the future.

6. *The concept of punishment is appropriate.* For actions that a person is the sole cause of, reward and punishment are quite appropriate. Persons in this model have in their power the setting up of rules to bind their own behavior, together with sanctions for breaking the rules. If a person in a society governed by these rules deliberately breaks one in order to gain a benefit at the expense of others, he – *by his own choice* – has made himself subject to the sanctions. Punishment, then, is brought upon a person by his own choice, and has its justification in the rules and the action done – not in expectations for future behavior. Insofar, of course, as a person is not responsible for what he did, punishment should not be applied – though he may still be *treated,* as for an illness or a pathological condition. Needless to say, there is no necessity that punishments in this scheme be barbaric, and no hindrance to their

being combined with education and training for the future.

7. *At least at some times a Person-II's conviction that his action originates solely with him is correct.* Persons may, of course, make mistakes here as well as elsewhere. And they may discover, to their surprise, that what they thought was in their power to do was causally necessitated. But there are, in this way of looking at persons, times when the person is quite correct in believing that it is solely up to him what he does next. This is something we all do believe very often, and it may be that we are very often right in so believing.

5

There seem, then, to be these two possible concepts of a person. The first is obviously patterned on the case traditionally made out by the compatibilists, the second on that of the libertarians. Each of them contains notions of freedom and responsibility, but each means something *quite different* by these terms, as can be seen by their relations to other terms in the set. We could tag the corresponding concepts so as to make obvious the differences.

action - I	action - II
freedom - I	freedom - II
responsibility - I	responsibility - II
treatment	punishment
anger over	anger at
etc.	etc.

There is a clear sense in which the difference in meaning between the two sets stems from the first postulate in each set, that concerning determinism. This can be brought out using the concept of *appropriateness.* Acting toward another human being in a certain way or having a certain attitude toward him may be appropriate or inappropriate. Each mode of action and each attitude has embedded within it certain assumptions about the nature of the object. (Think of the conscientious slaveholder in the Old South and what he was apt to say in justification of his practice : they are happier this way, they are subject to the curse of Cain, or even, they are not fully human). These assumptions embedded in practices and attitudes may be true or false. If they are false, we can say the practices and attitudes are *inappropriate.*

Thus it would be inappropriate to be angry *at* a human being (except as a calculated policy) if he were a Person-I. For then what he did would have been causally necessitated by events occurring before his birth. And it would be inappropriate to subject the doer of an action-II to *treatment,* for the action was not so causally necessitated. (Suppose there were a man who could instantly give himself malaria and cure himself again; giving quinine to him would not be appropriate).

In short, the other six points in each set of propositions depend on the first in this way : acting on them is appropriate only on the assumption that the first proposition is true of human beings. If it is false (i.e., if the first proposition in the *other* set is true), acting on them is inappropriate.

This point seems to me to be neutral with respect to the two alternatives. Proponents of each could, and at least implicitly do, agree to it.

If determinism is, in the above sense, the key to the choice between regarding human beings as Persons-I or as Persons-II, we are faced with the question of how to make that choice. I now wish to urge that the first proposition in each model is, in principle at least, subject to empirical verification.

The way here has been shown by Carl Ginet in an interesting article entitled, "Might We Have No Choice? "[9] I shall adapt his argument to my own terminology and purposes here. He uses the notion of a "complete first level description" of a person's behavior during a certain period. (We shall be content to consider only actions that involve overt behavior; suitable modifications could, I think, be made to cover also mental actions). Such a description contains the specification of all the places occupied by all the observable parts of a person's body during the period, together with the specification of all the sounds emitted by his body during that period. Call such a description *B.* Descriptions of antecedent states of the person, including descriptions of brain states and mental states (if these are not identical) we can call *A's.*

Determinism for human actions consists in the following thesis :

D. Every temporal segment of every human being's behavior has a complete first-level description B, for which there are antecedent states having the descriptions A_1 ,

A_2, A_3,. . . . A_n, such that :

(1) A_1 does not logically entail B,

(2) A_1 causally necessitates A_2,
A_2 causally necessitates A_3 ... A_n,
and A_n causally necessitates B, and

(3) the human being in question clearly had no power to determine whether or not A_1 would occur.

If *D* is true, then no human being ever has any action in his power, despite the fact that he may have countless abilities and that it may be true of him in a number of hypothetical ways that he could have done otherwise.

It might be objected that *D* concerns only *events* or *happenings, movements* – not actions. But while there may be good reasons for refusing to identify the concepts of action and movement – e.g., my raising my arm and my arm's going up – it is nevertheless clear that an action is the action it is only in virtue of the movements it involves. If my arm does not go up, then I do not raise my arm. So if *D* is true for all of my movements it turns the notion of an action into a fantasy to claim that *actions* are nonetheless in my power. If *D* is true it would be appropriate to think of human beings as Persons-I, with all that entails.

We ought to remark, however, that if *D* is false this does not automatically confirm the Person-II scheme. Indeterminism is a *necessary* condition for the libertarian view, but it is not *sufficient.* In addition the libertarian requires some sort of agency on the part of the person, so that undetermined actions do not turn into mere random events. Nevertheless the falsity of *D* taken together with the character of our experience in choosing and the general implausibility of a carefully thought out action being merely random, would seem to make it appropriate to hold that human beings are Persons-II.

There seems no great difficulty in seeing that *D* is in principle empirically confirmable, though the practical difficulties are enormous. If we were to get a series of theories which allow prediction of movements and utterances on the basis of antecedent conditions, the earliest of which the person obviously had no power over, *D* would be confirmed to some degree. As more and more actions became predictable on the basis of such theories, it would become more and more reasonable to accept

D. A point might certainly be reached where any rational man ought to accept *D* on the evidence attained.

Disconfirming *D* has the problems associated with negative hypotheses generally. It is always possible, if no causal chain of *A's* has been found leading to a *B,* that we have not looked hard enough, or persistently enough, or in the right places, or that we have not come up with the right theories yet. Nevertheless, it seems to me that we might reach a point where we ought to repair to theories of agency. These would not allow the kind of prediction that *D* would allow if true. But they would make human action *intelligible,* even if not causally explainable.

It is implicit in my remarks that I am convinced that we do not know whether *D* is true or not. If this is so, it follows that we do not know whether it is Person-Concept-I which is appropriate to human beings or Person-Concept-II. And in a rather important sense, *we do not know what human beings are.*

It also follows that the issue between compatibilists and libertarians has a crucial point (proposition 1 in each scheme) which the philosopher cannot resolve in his study. To resolve it will involve the confirmation of very sophisticated empirical theories, some of which are scarcely on the horizon as yet. The crux of the matter is not, it seems, a philosophical problem at all, but a scientific one.

7

If the argument presented above is correct, several further conclusions can be drawn. First, it is time for philosophers to stop worrying about whether free will and determinism are compatible or not. There are two answers to that question, each as good as the other : yes and no. It all depends on what concepts you are working with. If the question arises about which of these concepts applies to human beings, the answer is that we do not yet know.

Secondly, so long as we do not know whether *D* is true, there is a rather clear sense in which we do not know how it is appropriate to treat other human beings. This has obvious implications for morality and the law. Nonetheless, act toward others we must. And our only help seems to be in terms of what we *value* in the way of human community and institutions. Pending eventual settlement of the question about *D* it is in this area that debates over responsibility, treatment, punishment, and free will must be carried out. And the arguments should be offered without *presupposing* the truth or falsity of determinism. Arguments of this sort have of course been an ongoing concern of philosophy. The value-case for treating humans as Persons-I has been made repeatedly since the great utilitarians of the last century. Novelists especially, but some philosophers also, have pointed out dangers in that direction. Herbert Morris has recently stated the case for regarding humans as Persons-II with great forcefulness.[10] This is not the place to enter upon that controversy. But that it is largely in value terms that it must be carried on (for the present, at least) seems to follow from the conclusions reached earlier.

And finally, if we ever should reach the point where the truth of *D* is settled, we should again be faced with a value choice. We would then know how it would be appropriate to regard other people (and ourselves). But it is conceivable that we might then have to choose between a life-style based on the truth, which we value, and a life-style we value, which is not based on the truth, It is possible that in this situation we would prefer a life and a society grounded in an illusion.

NOTES

1. By "compatibilist" I shall refer to all those philosophers who in various ways believe that determinism and free will are compatible. They need not believe that determinism is true; indeed some of them profess not to know whether it is or not. But they hold that *if* it is true, it is consistent with a belief in free will.

2. See John Hospers, "What Means This Freedom? " in *Determinism and Freedom in the Age of Modern Science,* edited by Sidney Hook, pp. 126-142.

3. For devastating criticisms of this type of argument, see William P. Alston, "Wants and Actions," in *Intentionality, Minds, and Perception,* edited by Hector-Neri Castaneda, pp. 301-356, and Donald Davidson, "Actions, Reasons, and Causes," *The Journal of Philosophy,* LX (1963), pp. 685-700.

4. For objections to taking "choose" as the antecedent, see J. L. Austin, "Ifs and Cans," *Philosophical Papers,* pp. 153-180. For objections to "try," see Roderick M. Chisholm, "J. L. Austin's Philosophical Papers," *Mind,* LXXIII (1964), pp. 20-25, and Arthur Danto, "Freedom and Forbearance," in Keith Lehrer (ed.) *Freedom and Determinism,* pp. 55-60.

5. In "Fatalism and Determinism," in Lehrer, *Op. cit.,* especially pp. 161-174.

6. Responsibility need not be limited to cases of wrongdoing. Nor even to cases of right- or wrongdoing. I am responsible for so innocuous an action as wiggling my finger. Moral distinctions supervene; they do not create responsibility.

7. This notion of an agent is, it must be admitted, none too clear. But as Roderick Chisholm points out in "Freedom and Action" (Lehrer, *Op. Cit.,* pp. 20-22), the same may be said for Humean causality, despite the attention it has received. Some clarification of the notion can be found in Chisholm's article as well as in C. D. Broad's "Determinism, Indeterminism, and Libertarianism," in his *Ethics and the History of Philosophy* where he considers briefly "nonoccurrent causation of events" – and rejects it. C. A. Campbell's writings shed some small light on the notion, and so does "'I Can,'" by Richard Taylor, *The Philosophical Review,* LXIX (1960), pp. 78-89.

8. Though wants and desires may well be causes (see Davidson, footnote 2, above) they are not *interesting* causes, since wants can not easily be identified independently of what is wanted. This is the kernel of truth in "action theory" arguments that wants cannot be causes. The interesting causes will be those which can be identified independently of the behavior they cause, such as speculations in social psychology about aggressive behavior being caused by frustration.

9. In Lehrer, *Op. Cit.,* pp. 87-104.

10. In "Persons and Punishment," *The Monist,* 52 (1968), pp. 475-501.

ON THE MORAL WEIGHT OF DEONTIC STATEMENTS

Evangelos P. Papanoutsos, Athens, Greece

WHEN in a deontic statement ("ought..." - "ought not..." and their equivalents) one makes an assertion on a moral point, one is doing (since stating is a mental act) something different from what one does (also by stating) when he describes (ascertains, analyses, explains, etc.) a natural or historical fact to provide the required information to those who listen to him or read his writings. With the assertion "ought..." - "ought not..." which means "I approve" - "I disapprove," he openly acknowledges (as an outcome of inner acceptance) a moral value and, correspondingly, a moral nonvalue. This stands for a voluntary and responsible assumption of obligations, that is, for what in modern philosophical discourse is called "engagement," "commitment."

It is one thing to say :

1. Mercury is a metal in liquid form,
2. The laws of classical physics do not apply to the phenomena of the microcosmos,

and another to assert :

3. You ought to put self-respect above (material) interest,
4. I condemn ingratitude.

In the second case (propositions 3 and 4) you leave the impersonal neutrality of an objective outlook, and take a personal stand, the stand of a person directly concerned with a problem of life. By your judgment you are now committing yourself, you are assuming the obligations imposed by your own conscience. From this moment on you "serve" an idea, a scale of values. Should you, later on, refuse to comply with the rule that you have already formulated, this would constitute not simply a logical contradiction but a treason, a moral degradation.

But, more fundamentally, what does it really mean to assert :

Inwardly I accept and openly recognize value + A (and, conversely, non value -*A*)?

By expressing my judgment in terms of "ought" I take a personal stand on a problem of life as a person who is directly concerned?

I assume obligations imposed by my own conscience, voluntarily and responsibly?

When does the moral judgment ("ought. . . " - "ought not. . . ") constitute a real commitment on the part of the person who makes it?

In the explanations that moral philosophers give to this phenomenon they emphasize various of its elements, but they omit or do not stress what, in my opinion, is the most important one : That a moral statement carries its full weight, if and only if the person who makes the statement :

a. is *autonomous* in his judgment, i.e., he does not "rely anywhere," on any other person (authority) or institution (custom, tradition, law of the state) but charts his own course without any assistance or influence; and
b. is fully aware of the *consequences* of his judgment and proves by his actions (not just in theory) that he is ready to face all such consequences without any hesitation.

In this paper my purpose is to show that few, indeed very few, statements relating to aspects of moral life contain these two features, and, consequently, belong to the full type of deontic statements. Most of them are deficient (even though they may give, at first glance, an impression of completeness) precisely because they lack elements a. and b. (either one or, more often, both).

Let us now analyse two cases.

Suppose that at the time when a company is ready to engage in battle one of the soldiers insists on his original declaration that his religion forbids him to shed human blood under any pretext, and refuses to take up arms. All efforts to persuade him to change his mind having failed the soldier is courtmartialed, sentenced to death and, in accordance with military regulations, is executed at dawn the following day.

During the successive phases of this process, which had such a tragic outcome, many people must have judged the case from the same viewpoint, and must have expressed their opinion (presenting it in general terms, as it usually happens in such cases) as follows :

"A soldier who, even though he acts in accordance with his religious convictions, in the hour of combat refuses to make use of his weapons and fire at the enemy must be sent to the firing squad."

To mention only the persons who played a leading part in the drama, the following must have expressed the aforementioned opinion :

I. The commander of the military unit in making the prosecution.
II. The prosecutor making the charge.
III. The president of the courtmartial in issuing the verdict.
IV. The officer of the firing squad in explaining to his soldiers the necessity of the punishment, after the verdict was carried out.
V. The soldiers who participated in the execution in order to pacify their agitated colleagues, or calm their own consciences.

It is quite probable that all these persons used the same or approximately the same words in their statement. (In such cases clichés are easily formed and passed from mouth to mouth). Nevertheless, all these statements do not have the same connotations and, consequently, the same moral weight.

The first impression is that the only one which can be considered as perfect, that is a complete deontic statement, is that of the president of the courtmartial (he is the one who represents the "court"), while the statements of the others are deficient. Admittedly, this impression is not without some foundation. Even though by their judgment the others started the case or directed it toward its final outcome, it was the verdict of the courtmartial that gave the definite solution to the drama. The commander of the unit who brought the case to court and the prosecutor who demanded the condemnation of the culprit knew that they did not have the final word. They simply recommended that the accused should be punished in accordance with the letter of the existing law and the real facts of the crime. It is the "court," however, that has the final authority to judge and the responsibility to decide. Consequently, since the man had a chance of escaping death despite their recommendations, they did not hesitate to state that he had to suffer the death penalty. Much more deficient is the statement of the officer of the firing squad, as well as that of the soldiers who justified the verdict after the execution. The case had been judged, all that had to be done had been done, and all this without these individuals' initiative and responsibility. They were no more than mere instruments, since they had received orders to do what they did. Their approval, therefore, would have neither cut the knot of the problem nor brought about the outcome. That is why it could be offered safely.

In this light all the other judgments are deficient; they lack sometimes one and sometimes both of the aforementioned essential features. It is only the judgment of the jury, as pronounced by the president, that is complete. With their "ought" the others say :

"Let the accused be put to death" (I and II). or

"He deserved the punishment" (IV and V).

It is the president alone, as a representative of the court, who, by his own categorical "must," sets the rule, fully aware of its importance, and assumes the responsibility by ordering that the verdict, with all its consequences, be executed immediately. He asserts :

"He is guilty of an offence which is punishable by death. To the firing squad! " (III).

Yet, if we push the analysis further, we shall ascertain that even the judgment of the court is deficient. The judge does not legislate (he does so only on a very limited scale and under certain prerequisites). "Somebody else" makes the laws. The judge applies them by interpreting the letter of the law and its spirit and by trying, in every case, to determine which are punishable acts, the extent of their culpability, and the punishments that must be rendered, always in accordance with the will of the legislator. The court is not free to measure the action of the soldier in terms of its own standards, to evaluate it according to its own scale of values, to approve or disapprove it by setting, responsibly and by public statement, the correct rules of behavior in similar cases. The court is bound by the existing law. How then can we consider the judgment of its members as autonomous and forthright, burdened with the responsibility of all consequences? It is, of course, possible that there might be a judge who, during the trial, may undergo a deep "crisis of conscience," He may then rebel against the law which stipulates that a soldier who refuses to fight should be sent to the firing squad, without any discrimination or exception. Using another concept or another ideal of justice as a criterion, he may refuse to cast his vote for the verdict of condemnation, not because the facts do not persuade him that the action is one of the offences for which the law stipulates the death penalty, but because, in this case, he considers the law unfair, illogical, and inhuman. The statement of this judge :

"The soldier who (in obedience to his religious convictions) refuses to fight in the hour of combat must not be punished" has, of course, the weight that we are looking for. But it is not at all similar to the others mentioned in the example; on the contrary, it is diametrically opposed to them.

The remark above will be better understood by a second example.

As a physician who has specialized in the disease of my patient (I have long been engaged in its systematic study and have constantly followed the international bibliography concerning it) I stand at his bedside and watch his suffering. My patient is in the last stages of a cancerous ailment. In great pain he is struggling to die. There is absolutely no hope; this is not only my own view, but also the unanimous opinion of all the other doctors who have seen the patient. Analgetic drugs (I have used them all in maximum doses) cannot provide relief any longer. During his agony the unfortunate man repeatedly implores me to have pity on him and assist him to his death in order to relieve him of his unbearable suffering. I am alone with him, no one is interested in his death; and the injection that can offer euthanasia to this man is at hand. I consider the problem in a sober manner: "Do I have the right to take away even a very short time from the life of a man under these conditions? I am here to prolong life, not to shorten it"... And fully aware of my responsibility, as well as of the consequences that my action may have (be charged with homicide, condemned, and not only destroy my career, but lose even my personal freedom) I decide :

"An incurable and dying man must be relieved of the unbearable pain."

And I carry out my decision.

The same, and possibly with the same words, will probably be stated by some such individuals :

I. The relatives and friends of the patient.

II. The colleagues of that one who dared give him euthanasia.

III. The defenders in the daily press and in court, if the case is brought to court.

IV. The jury who will pronounce the accused physician not guilty.

Yet, although, they see the matter in the same light and use the same measures in assessing its difficulties, none of these people has, in his judgment, the autonomy and bravery of the physician who, on his own initiative and responsibility, gave the solution. For all of them judge an event already accomplished, a question whose solution was given by "somebody else." Moreover, now that they state "ought to etc.," they do not have the man, who will be put to death in consequence of their judgment, lying in front of them. Therefore, no matter how insistent they are in expressing their opinion; no matter how categorically they state that "if they had been in the physician's position they would have done exactly the same"; in their moral weight their judgments are deficient. For their supposed responsibilities do not have the same dimensions as the real ones; and the same applies with respect to the consequences of their supposed actions as compared with the consequences of the real ones. By their judgment ("ought. . . ") these people declare that they assume the obligations to behave in the same way under the same circumstances; this is certainly positive and noteworthy. Yet no one, not even themselves, can foretell with absolute certainty that they would carry out the promise they are now making – men are weak by nature and frequently unpredictable in their actions. The physician, on the other hand, acted according to his judgment without hesitation or delay. That is why it is only his judgment that is, in its moral weight, perfect.

The characteristics of a judgment which is complete in its moral sense are, according to the analysis given in the aforementioned examples, two :

a. that the person who made the statement was autonomous in his judgment, i.e., he did not accept the solution given by "somebody else," nor was he influenced, in his judgment, by an event already accomplished; and

b. that he is fully aware of and is determined to face all the consequences of his judgment – in fact and not in words only.

Now, is it possible to establish with certainty whether a deontic statement possesses these characteristics? That is not easy, although it is possible. To measure the moral weight of a deontic statement we must cease to consider it as a sentence with a definite logical content that derives its meaning from the sense and the structure of the words constituting it, in accordance with the symbols of a certain linguistic system. Instead, we must place it within the *situation* to which it refers. The term situation here denotes a network of facts and events within the framework of life (happenings, relations, behavioral patterns etc.). As basic elements, this framework includes the person who makes the statement and the person or persons to whom it is addressed. That is, in every concrete case one must pose and answer the following questions :

a. Who makes the statement in this particular case? In what capacity, by what right, and what are his intentions?

b. What implications does he want his judgment to have, or will his judgment have, intentionally or unintentionally, for those to whom it is addressed, as well as for those who will be informed about it in one way or another?

c. Within what life conditions, personal and interpersonal, is the statement made, and what is its relation to the chain of events which have given rise to it or will contribute to its direct or indirect continuation?

It is from the rates of these variables, to use the language of mathematicians, that the final product of the function to be estimated will be determined. The analysis above of the two examples (to the extent to which it has reached its target) is intended to illustrate the application of the method.

A last remark. Lofty ideas for the formation of individual and social moral life are usually expressed and projected in oral or written speech. This is because men aim at the easy effects of rhetoric, and also because the commitments made through words are not as weighty as those made through actions. Obligations "on paper," which one does not impose on oneself and which are not intended to be carried out immediately, are more readily undertaken. If, however, the verve of moral perfection is usually encountered in "inspired speeches," the much humbler, but genuine virtue is found in deeds only. "By thy deeds thou shall be known."

A NATURALISTIC INTERPRETATION OF AUTHORITY, IDEOLOGY, AND VIOLENCE[1]

Ch. Perelman, The University of Brussels

Authority and Power

The political demonstrations, the campaigns of civil disobedience and university strife which are widespread across the world during the last years, have been presented on all sides as a rebellion against authority, the latter being identified with power which, thanks to the public use of force, constitutes a continual threat as regards individual liberties.

It is in this way, as opposed to liberty, that authority was presented more than a century ago by John Stuart Mill in his famous study "On Liberty," from which I wish to the following passage:

> "The struggle between Liberty and Authority is the most conspicuous feature in the portions of history with which we are earliest familiar, particularly in that of Greece, Rome, and England. But in old times this contest was between subjects, or some classes of subjects, and the Government. By liberty was meant protection against the tyranny of the political rulers. The rulers were conceived (except in some of the popular governments of Greece) as in a necessarily antagonistic position to the people they ruled. They consisted of a governing One, or a governing tribe or caste, who derived their authority from inheritance or conquest, who, at all events, did not hold it at the pleasure of the governed, and whose supremacy men did not venture, perhaps did not desire, to contest, whatever precautions might be taken against its oppressive exercises."[2]

In the course of this account, Mill no longer uses the term "authority," and regularly replaces it by "power," as if these terms had been synonyms. But are these terms interchangeable? If one speaks of the holders of power by saying "the authorities," one wishes to mean by this that their power is recognized, adding a nuance of respectful submission or flattery, and, in this way, the two terms come to be considered as synonyms. It is this that Littré expresses in a note on the word "authority," where he admits that "in a part of their usage these two words are very close to one another"; but he adds this restriction: "as authority is that which authorizes and power that which empowers, there is always a nuance of moral influence in authority which is not necessarily implied in power."

Indeed, even in the 18th Century these two notions were thought to be as opposed as fact and law. It is in this way that the English Bishop and moralist Joseph Butler, in his second sermon, opposes the power of the passions to the authority of the conscience, that which is pursued for the sake of its control of the actual event, to that which is pursued for the sake of moral superiority itself.[3] *Auctoritas,* in Latin, is that which the guardian supplies to the will of the infant, and which the law validates : it transforms a juridically ineffective expression of will into a juridically valid action.

It is an opposition of the same type to which Jacques Maritain refers in the important essay entitled "Democracy and Authority," which is published in the second volume of the International Institute of Political Philosophy has devoted to a discussion of power. He there sets down two definitions:

> "Let us call 'authority' the right to direct and command, to be listened to or obeyed by others, and 'power' the force which one uses and by the aid of which one can oblige others to listen or obey. The just man, deprived of all power and condemned to hemlock, does not see his moral authority reduced but enhanced. The gangster or the tyrant exercises a power without authority. There are some institutions, the Senate of ancient Rome, the Supreme Court of the United States, whose authority seems the more manifest because they themselves do not exercise determined functions in the command of power... All authority, as soon as it relates to social life, desires to be completed (in any sort of way, which is not necessarily juridical) by a power, without which it risks becoming useless and inefficacious among men. All power which is not the expression of authority is iniquitous. To separate power and authority is to separate force and justice."[4]

Bertrand de Jouvenel, in his remarkable studies "On Sovereignty" and "On Authority," insists at length on the importance of authority in political matters :

> "I call authority the faculty of gaining the consent of others. Or again, and this comes to the same I call authority the efficient cause of voluntary association. When I observe a voluntary association, I see in it the work of a force, which is authority.
>
> Without doubt, an author has the right to use a word in the sense which he chooses, provided that he has given one warning. Nevertheless, one invites confusion if the bestowed sense is too removed from the usually recognized sense. It seems that I am putting myself in this position, since "authoritarian government" is readily being qualified, that one which largely has recourse to violence, in act and in threat, in order to be obeyed, a government of which it would be necessary to say, according to my definition, that it lacks an authority sufficient for carrying out its designs, so that it makes up the gap by intimidation.
>
> But this corruption of the word is altogether recent, and I am only replacing it in the correct way by its traditional sense."[5]

The same deformation, pointed out by de Jouvenel, is found again in those who identify the authority of the law with the fear of sanction, but, in fact, the police should only intervene if due respect to law is not by itself sufficient to prevent its violation.

Authority always presents itself with a normative aspect; as what should be followed or obeyed, like the authority of an adjudication, the authority of reason, or that of experience. In effect, those who possess power without authority can compel submission, but not respect.

In the Judeo-Christian tradition, authority is a nonjuridical but moral notion; it is linked to respect. The model of authority thus conceived is that of the father over his children, whom he educates and guides, to whom he shows what they ought to do and what they ought to abstain from, who initiates them into the traditions, customs, and rules of the familial and social environment into which they are to be integrated. Authority derived from that of the father is that of the teacher, who tells children the correct way to read and write, and what they should consider as true or false. The teacher said so, *magister dixit,* is an excellent example of the argument from authority.

Authority in the Family and in Education

In any case, the question of equality is impossible either in the relation between the father and the children submissive to his authority, or in that of the teacher to the children in primary school. In effect every variety of education, or instruction, no matter in what area, begins with a period of initiation in which it is absurd to concede the equality of the initiator and the initiated. It is indispensable that some authority be granted to whoever is responsible for the initiation, even if it concerns a relation between adults. If I direct myself to a teacher to instruct me in the rudiments of chemistry or Chinese, it is very necessary that during the period of initiation I conform to his directions and instructions.

All criticism implies the knowledge of the domain in which it will be exercised. This is the reason that primary instruction is usually more dogmatic than secondary, and that university instruction is characterized by the formation of the critical spirit. This is not, even, solely a matter of age and level of instruction, for it is the same in university education; for the subject matter unknown to the student, like Chinese, a period of initiation, of apprenticeship, will be inevitable; but the apprenticeship will occur on a base previously habited to the critical spirit making a clean slate of the past, Descartes had been led to suppose the existence of innate ideas in the mind of all reasonable beings, which led Rousseau in his *Émile* to the aberrant theory according to which there is no reason to teach the sciences to a child: since it is necessary that he discovers the facts in his own way. We know today that the methods, called active, necessitate the cooperation of a much more competent and more inventive teacher than the traditional methods, where the teacher, could if neccessary have been replaced by a manual.

The indispensable role of the authority of the father and the educator with regard to young children cannot reasonably be contested. The real problem is to know when and how the relation of authority ought to yield progressively to a relation of critical collaboration, and above all, what is the role of authority in relations among adults.

Extension of Paternal Authority

Let us note that, in the political or religious domain, appeal is very often made to the image of the father to express the respect due a charismatic leader. The father of a country is a political leader whose action had been, and sometimes continues to be, creative and protective. The "Founding Fathers," the founding fathers of the United States of America, are the ancestors who have established the American Constitution, and contribute to the respect which surrounds it. Ancestor worship is very well known in many countries of Asia and Africa. The Judeo-Christian tradition is remarkable in this respect for to who God the respect and love owes Him, one calls Him by "our father, our king"; and, in Christianity, the daily prayer begins with the well known words, "our father who art in heaven." The majesterium of the church is simultaneously the authority of the father and the authority of the master, knowing salutary truths and watching over the welfare of the faithful.

In the Hebraic tradition, God is the holder of political power and all royal power can only result from a delegation : the Lord's anointed is the vicar of God, all political power emanates from God and is answerable to God.

It is again this image of the father which served to establish in the Middle Ages the relations of the lord to his tenants and, later, to confer good conscience on colonizers with regard to colored peoples, those "big children." The paternalism which expresses this attitude is entirely discredited today.

Authority and Scientific Method

The philosophical tradition of the West, from Socrates to our day, has always been opposed to the argument from authority : and has taken this attitude in the name of truth. One of the reasons for the condemnation of Socrates was that he was in opposition to paternal authority in the name of truth. Later, Bacon opposed the authority of his senses and experience and Descartes opposed the authority of reason to the traditional authorities. In the conflict between the church and Galileo, the latter opposed observation and the experimental method to the authority of the Bible and Aristotle. The *philosophes* of the Enlightenment regarded as prejudices all affirmations offered in the name of religious or secular authorities.

And in fact, every time methods based on experience exist, enabling one to test the soundness of an affirmation and to check its truth, no authority can set himself in opposition to such methods; *a fact is more respectable than a Lord Mayor.* Everyone validly using experience or calculation arrives at the same result and without miscalculation, will arrive at the same result. In this case recourse to an authority is not only useless but bizarre. In order to admit that two plus two make four, I have need of no authority: when methods exist, which everybody can apply, and which lead to the same result, everyone is equal and invoking authority is quite frankly ridiculous.

Negative Authority of Reason in the Domain of Action

For centuries the classical tradition, resting on religious, as philosophical considerations has been able to claim that a true answer exists to all clearly posed human problems. This answer, that God knows from all eternity, is the one which all reasonable people must endeavor to rediscover.

But is it true that to any question that men can reasonably ask themselves there is a single answer that will be true? Can one admit this truth, that there exist some methods which permit the testing of any hypothesis which one would be able to formulate?

It is undeniable that in a great number of areas, when it is a matter of knowledge, the ideal of truth ought to prevail over any other consideration. But when it is a matter of acting, of knowing what is just or injust, good or bad, what to encourage or proscribe – do there exist verifiable objective criteria? Can one speak of objective truth in matters of decision or choice, when it is a matter of indicating preferable conduct?

If this were not the case, is reason able to guide us in action? Is the idea of practical reason, as Hume held, a contradiction in terms?

Personally, I hold that there is a role for practical reason, but that it is purely negative : it allows us to discard unreasonable solutions. But, in practical matters, nothing guarantees us the existence of only one reasonable solution. This being the case, if there is not some unique solution in practical matters, like that which a correct answer in theoretical matters supplies us, the choice of a solution rests more on will than on reason.

Authority of laws

It is in this perspective that the laws, the obligatory rules in a State, have been presented as the will of the sovereign, who according to a good number of theoreticians, from Thrasymachus, whom Plato made known to us, to Marx, would impose on everyone all the laws most propitious to his own interest.

If, contrary to natural law theorists, according to whom some valid objective rules exist which the legislator ought to discover and promulgate, obligatory rules are the expression of the will of the legislator, it is natural that those upon whom they are imposed demand to participate in their formulation, to grant their consent, directly or through their representatives. Thus, in this way that, since the Magna Charta of 1215 – which promised the nobles and the bourgeoisie that no tax would be imposed upon them without their consent – we have seen democratic ideology progressively develop, according to which powers do not emanate from God or his representatives on earth, but from the Nation and its elected officials.

Democratic ideology is opposed to the existence of objectively valid rules in matters of conduct, because what the majority decides is not what is true or false. Those who, like Godwin, the anarchist disciple of Bentham, have believed that in matters of conduct there is a way of objectively determining that which is "the greatest good for the greatest number," are opposed to the idea that a legislator is indispensable to formulate our rules of conduct. And, in effect, in scientific matters, there is no question of a legislator imposing his authority. If everyone possessed in his heart and conscience the objective criteria of justice and injustice, the idea of recourse to any legislator whatever would not only appear to be odious, but quite simply ridiculous. But if, for us, anarchy signifies not only the absence of government, but also disorder, this is because when decisions are to be made, rules developed, or persons chosen to discharge certain functions, after having averted unreasonable solutions, it is indispensable to confer on a selected individual or a constituted body, the power of making a decision that will be recognized as authoritative. Only the legislative power can formulate the obligatory rules in a given territory. And as these rules can very often be the object of diverse interpretations, it is indispensable to confer to a judicial authority the right to interpret the law.

Authority, Legitimacy, and Rationalization

The constituted powers charged to direct a politically organized community would be ineffective if they had to count on force alone to be obeyed. It is essential for the exercise of power that its legitimacy be recognized, that it be possessed of an authority that carries the general consent of those who are subject to it. That is why ideologies are indispensable, whether religious, philosophical, or traditional. They aim beyond truth at the legitimization of power. Its legitimacy often results from its legality, that is to say from the fact that it was designated by legal procedures; but this presupposes that these same procedures are not contested, that they accord with a recognized ideology, explicit or implicit.

Indeed, scientific procedures, aspiring to establish the true or the false or at least the probable or improbable, never enable us to justify our decisions, nor furnish us with reasons for acting, choosing, or preferring; scientific methods allow the establishing of facts, but not the consideration of reasons for acting.

For certain positivist or naturalist philosophies, the sole motives of our actions consist in the pleasure they procure or the pain they avoid, in the satisfaction they can give us in allowing us to gratify our instincts, our needs, our interests of any sort. All judgment of value would be a disguise for an interest, a rationalization of a desire. Any ideology would only be the delusive mask of an enterprise for serving the strongest. This is exactly the thesis which is revealed in the works of a Marx or a Nietzsche.

Ideologies, Revolution, and Evolutionary Change

Philosophical criticism of the dominant ideology, when it bares the fallacies and sophisms which legitimatize a power in establishing its authority, is the precursor of revolutionary action. When power is considered as the simple expression of an arsenal of force, one will not hesitate to oppose it with a revolutionary force in the service of antagonistic interests. But the partisan of revolution cannot be content to counter with a revolutionary force the force which protects the established order; he ought, besides, to be the apologist for the new order, which will be more just, more humane, which will rescue man from his diverse alienations while restoring to him his lost liberty. In the end, another ideology must be elaborated to show the superiority of the new order over the old, of the revolutionary order over the established order.

As scientific methods are able, at most, only to test the facts on which an ideology is based, but cannot criticize the reasons which serve to justify preferences, so it is in terms of another ideology, of another ideal of man and society, that the dominant ideology can be criticized. But this new ideology itself will not for long be able to escape criticism; the philosophical debate thus appears as a permanent struggle between ideologies which endeavor to impose themselves on all in the name of truth. Accordingly, these critiques with which one group opposes the others, are the occasion for both sides to experience spiritual progress, because each, to the extent to which it takes into account objections of the other, modifies his position when it seems vulnerable. After a prolonged debate – sometimes a century long – the competing positions will be very different from what they were at the beginning.

Ideologies and Violence

But today we very frequently witness not a struggle between ideologies, but an uprising which, doing away with all theoretical structures, borrowing slogans from anywhere which though they be inconsistent, or directly contradictory, yet are always insulting, and unwilling to recognize any authority in the established order, is content to resist the established order with violence.

This attitude can find its justification among those to whom the establishment refuses to listen, whose representatives are denied an opportunity to state their grievances, and who are obliged to resort to violence to make themselves heard. But such a reaction merits respect only if it avails itself of an ideology which demands, for example, respect for the dignity of the person, or the establishment of a more democratic society. In the case of disorders in the universities, only an ideology justifies revolt against calling in the police, for without it, why be shocked that the defenders of the established order resist force by force?

Indeed, if it is traditional in the universities not to resort to outside force in order to maintain discipline, it is because, traditionally, the universities distrust governmental power, considering it as a menace to academic liberty. It is in the name of respect for the ideal of academic liberty that universities do not like to appeal to the police power which could endanger the free expression of opinions. It is because the universities are considered in the West as the traditional sanctuary of liberty of thought and expression, of free pursuit of the true and the just, that they ought to be protected against the use of violence, from any source whatever. And it is only in the name of ideology that recourse to force can be prohibited. But if one rejects all ideologies, as being unsound rationalizations, if political life is presented as a preponderance of force, then not only is the most stringent law always the best, but the very idea of law disappears to produce universal violence.

Conflict of Ideologies

In conclusion, in order to prevent social and political life from being merely a pitting of force against force, we must recognize the existence of a legitimate power, whose authority is based on an acknowledged ideology. Criticism of this ideology can only be made in the name of another ideology, and it is this conflict of ideologies, whatever they may be, which is at the root of the spiritual life of modern times. To oppose competition between ideologies is to reestablish dogmatism and orthodoxy; it is to subordinate the life of thought to political power. To deny the worth of ideologies is to reduce political life to an armed struggle for power, from which the victor, incontestably the military chief, will emerge victorious.

To enable universities to operate under the safeguard of academic freedom is to recognize the existence of values other than force; it is to admit that none among them is immune to criticism, that no ideology need count on brute force to assure its survival.

NOTES

1. Translated by J. E. Hansen, Brock University, and William Gerber, University of Maryland.

2. John Stuart Mill, *On Liberty*, New York, 1954, Everyman's Library, p. 65.

3. J. Butler, *Fifteen Sermons Upon Human Nature* (London, 1726), in A. I. Melden, ed., *Ethical Theories*, Englewood Cliffs, 1967, pp. 252-253.

4. *Le Pouvoir*, Paris, 1957 tome II, pp. 26-28.

5. Bertrand de Jouvenel, *De la Souveraineté*, Paris, 1955, p. 45.

REASON AND THE ART OF LIVING IN PLATO[1]

Wilfrid Sellars, University of Pittsburgh

I

IN BOOK VI of the *Republic,* Plato begins his exploration of the principles in accordance with which the city must be governed if it is to be an enduring and autonomous embodiment of the various forms of excellence of which men, individually and collectively, are (at least in approximation) capable. These principles have a two-fold status. In the first place, they must, if the city is to endure, be 'objective' in the sense that the distinction between truth and falsity is relevant to them and in the second place, they must be capable of being known, where 'knowledge' contrasts with that mere 'belief' or 'opinion' which, however true it may be, is, as lacking the support of rational insight, at the mercy of sophistical argument and the persuasive techniques of the orator.

The knowledge of these objective principles, must be present in the city as the possession of its rulers if the city is to endure. This knowledge must also be acquired by Socrates and his companions if the city they are constructing is to be more than a play of the imagination which expresses the happenstances of their political experience.

These points can be paralleled at the level of the individual, for it is a central theme in the *Public* that the city is the individual "writ large." Just as the excellent city must contain the knowledge of what makes for excellence in the individual.

The above paragraphs contain several expressions which can be expected to arouse the spirit of controversy in any one con- concerned with how life is to be lived. Indeed, I have woven into its fabric four words which, taken one, two, three, even four at a time, in various permutations, define the subject-matter of this essay: 'principle,' 'objectivity,' 'knowledge,' and 'excellence.' Now 'subject-matter' is, in Aristotelian terms, a special case of matter for form: and to indicate the form I am striving to realize in this subject matter, it will suffice to remind the reader that according to Plato, beyond the excellences of individual and community, beyond the knowledge of these excellences, indeed (Plato tells us in a tantalizingly obscure passage[2]) beyond all knowledge and beyond all being is the Form of the Good. It is this which I propose to discuss, and everything I say will be directed to this end. The fact that, as I hope to show, these two ways of describing the subject matter of this essay ('Plato's conception of the objectivity and knowability of the principles of excellence' and 'the key role in Plato's philosophy of the Form of the Good') ultimately coincide, both illuminates Plato's thought and makes possible an appreciation of the profound truth it contains.

II

If one asks a metaphysician to say which sweeping classification of the things (in the broadest possible sense of the term) which confront our minds and bodies he finds most illuminating one gets such answers as 'atoms and the void,' 'matter and form' 'substance and power,' 'appearance and reality,' 'the mental and the physical' – not to mention more recent answers of great subtlty and sophistication. It is notoriously difficult to see what these answers have in common, or, even, in what sense they are answers to the same question. But, then, the most difficult task of philosophy has always been to define itself in meaningful ways. Fortunately my initial aim in this essay is historical rather than systematic, and it is with a sense of relief that I turn from the impossible to the improbable, from the evaluation of philosophical categories to the task of exhibiting, as closely as possible in his own terms, the fundamental structure of Plato's metaphysical thought.

What, then, are Plato's basic metaphysical categories? A formula trips readily off the tongue. The mature Plato distinguishes between

1. the unchanging realm of Ideas or Forms – the proper objects of mind or intelligence;

2. the changeable realm of physical things – the objects of the senses in perception;
3. the mediating realm of souls or minds, which animate bodies and, distinct from both Forms and physical things (though more akin to the former), have the task of shaping and controlling changeable things in the light of their degree of insight into the Forms.[3]

These three categories of 'what there is' are mutually irreducible, yet so related that each 'makes sense' only in relation to the other. Thus, the Forms are essentially *intelligibles,* which means that one cannot understand what it is to be a Form without grasping it as something which is capable of being understood by an intelligent being or mind. Again, a mind is, at heart, something which is capable of grasping, more or less adequately, intelligible connections – connections which are independent of its fancies, and are such that thinking does *not* make them so.

The role of mind or soul as the mediator between the intelligible realm of Forms and the visible world of the physical is rooted in the fact that thinking is, in its own way, a process, an activity which has its goals, its means and ends, its standards and principles. Others (e.g. Aristotle) may conceive of thinking at its best as an act of contemplation, an actuality which endures without change, as does the continued hearing of a single musical note, and is an unchanging vision of unchanging Forms. Those who share this conception are tempted to think that a universe which consisted of unchanging intelligibles and unchanging intellects would be a coherent one; indeed, that such a universe would be not only coherent, but ideal. Plato, himself, may have flirted (e.g. in the *Phaedo* and the *Phaedrus)* with the idea that an unchanging contemplation of truth could exist in abstraction from the internal dialogue of question and answer which is thinking to some purpose. But I think it reasonable to say that to the mature Plato, the Plato, for example, of the *Sophist,* the concept of contemplation makes sense only in relation to that of the discursive thinking of which it is the culmination, and the concept of a mind which is capable of nothing but contemplation is incoherent.

If there is mind, then, there must be becoming, change, goal directed activity. But why *physical* becoming? Why could not the Universe consist of disembodied spirits exploring intelligible connections between eternal Forms? It it were conceptually necessary that minds be embodied, or if it were conceptually necessary that the realm of Forms include Forms pertaining to physical becoming, then it would be an intelligible fact that the changeable world includes bodies as well as minds, physical becoming as well as thought. Yet the existence of such conceptual necessities has not yet been demonstrated to the general satisfaction of the philosophical public. There may be answers to the above questions but Plato does not face them directly, and we seem to be left with the brute fact that there is physical becoming, and Form pertaining to physical becoming. On the other hand, perhaps Plato's implicit answer is that among the pre-eminent Forms are those of Courage, Temperance and Justice, and that these would not 'make sense' unless there were bodily hurts, and scarce as men of satisfying bodily hungers.

III

As Plato's thought developed, he became more and more concerned with the overall structure of the realm of Forms, and came to conceive of philosophy as an exploration of this structure in a continuing and disciplined dialogue in which, as Hegel reminds us, the 'evident' continually generates the 'absurd' and only reasserts itself, chastened and modified, when the dialogue reaches out to new horizons. In that stretch of the dialogue which took place within his soul, Plato came to see that Forms are related to each other in many ways none of which can be ignored without distorting the other. Some of these ways are of particular interest to formal logicians, and to those metaphysicians whose concerns make abstraction from the distinctive features of ethical and political Ideas. But this abstraction, legitimate as a moment in the larger dialogue, is fatal if it becomes settled policy. It might, indeed, seem that ethical and political Forms are simply that subset of the total domain which is important to us, confronted, as we are, with the problem of how to live our lives; but that they have no pre-eminent role in the intelligibility which, as we have seen, pertains to the very essence of the Forms. Yet it is clear that, at the time of composing the *Republic,* Plato was convinced that the very *intelligibility* of the Forms involves the *distinctive* traits of ethical and political Forms. The form of the Good is the Form of Forms, and to grasp it clearly is the culmination of the philosophical enterprise. There are many who believe that this elusive conception was a vision which Plato was never able to reproduce in concrete, or even meaningful, terms, an unsupported conviction that values are not incidental to the Universe, but somehow the ground of both its existence and its intelligibility.

In recent years, philosophers, particularly in the Anglo-American tradition, have been prone to take as their paradigm of intelligibility, the intelligibilities of logic and mathematics or, to the extent that they find these 'empty,' the intelligibilities of the results and methods of the natural sciences. The latter indeed, have advanced so rapidly in recent years as to make moral and political thinking appear static, if not retrograde, and to deal with intelligibilities neither in method nor in results.

The dimensions of intelligibility on which recent Anglo-American philosophy has focused its attention are, in the traditional sense of the term, 'theoretical.' They contrast with 'practical' intelligibility, i. e., that intelligibility which pertains to ends and means, to instruments and their uses, and to rules, conventions and principles of conduct. Usually the contrast between these two modes of intelligibility is no sooner drawn than dismissed as sound but insignificant. It is argued that the intelligible connections involved in 'practice' (in that broad sense in which all purposive behavior is practice) are simply the intelligible connections of logic, mathematics and science, used as a framework which, given our circumstances, can connect our desires and appetites, into a compatible, i. e. jointly realizable, system. That some practical intelligibilities are, in this way, derivative is non-controversial. Whether *all* the intelligibilities of practice are, in this way, derivative is, perhaps, *the* key issue in the philosophy of practice, thus, in ethical theory. Plato's thesis in the *Republic* to the effect that the Form of the Good is the Form of Forms, the ground of all the Forms and of the intelligibility which is essential to them, would seem, however, to be an outright rejection of the idea that all intelligibility pertaining to practice is theoretical intelligibility (causal and logical) at the service of appetites and desires, in other words, as Hume put it, the slave of the passions.

service of appetites and desires, in other words, as Hume put it, the slave of the passions.

IV

To interpret Plato correctly on this point we must begin, as he does, with familiar examples of practical intelligibility. Only after small scale distinctions have been drawn, can we hope to understand the Form of the Good as the supreme principle of the realm of Forms.

As might be expected, the distinction which provides us with our initial insight into the characteristic features of practical intelligibility is the familiar means-end relationship between actions and outcomes. Perhaps the most obvious point – the importance of which, however, is often overlooked – is that reference to actions is correlative with reference to the circumstances in which they are done. A circumstance is roughly a standing[4] condition in which a given action may or may not be done.

In the simplest case, causal truths of the form

Bringing about E imples doing A, if the circumstances are C

appear in practical guise in the form

If one wants E, then if one is in C, one 'must do (or 'ought' to do) A

This is the simple means-end intelligibility which Kant (misleadingly) baptized with the phrase 'hypothetical imperative.' The words 'ought' and 'must' express practical concepts which carve up and transpose into the 'practical mode' the causal connections which exist between doing A, being in C and bringing about E. In the case we have considered, E is an event or happening, the bringing about of which, if one is in C, requires and is fulfilled by doing A. Typically, the same outcome (or what counts as the same outcome) will eventuate, even if the circumstances are different, if one compensates by doing a correspondingly different action. This generates the more complex schema.

If one wants E, then if in C_i, one ought to do A_j where 'C_i' indicates a range of circumstances and 'A_j' the corresponding range of action which would eventuate in E.

The preceding remarks do little more than rehearse familiar distinctions. It is now time to introduce a related family of concepts, central to Plato's thought, which pertains to that kind of practice which is *making* something (a product, e.g., a shoe), as contrasted with bringing about an event (e.g., an explosion). One might try to assimilate the two cases by referring to the making of the shoe as the bringing about of the event of a shoe's coming into existence. But the assimilation is superficial and obscures important distinctions.

The product of a craft (or art – the Greek term is *techne*) is, typically, an instrumentality which is used (or, to extend a familiar term, 'consumed') in a certain way. Thus, to consider two out of many possible examples, the product may serve as part of the raw material for the product of another craft – as a nail is ingredient in shoes – or, to take an example from the other end of the spectrum, it may serve to provide enjoyable experiences.

In considering the structure of a craft as a form of practice, we are led to distinguish the following categories : (baking a cake provides a particularly useful example)

- Ingredients :
  - Materials : flour, cups of; butter, tablespoons of; etc.
  - Objects : eggs (these might be compared to products of another craft – the producing of eggs by hens)
- Recipe :
  - Number and proportion of ingredients combined
  - Program of action :
    - (If one wants) to bake a cake : if ingredients are in state C_i, one ought to do A_j.

The concept of 'making' can be extended to include (a) contributing to making (as where a number of craftsmen must cooperate); and, in another direction, to cover (b) maintaining (and repairing) products to keep them in something like their optimum state.

If we simplify our schema of the practice of a craft to read

(If one wants) to make an O, then : in C_i one ought to do A_j

we can characterize the family of statements of the form

In C_i one ought to do A_j

as the action-principles of the craft. It can hardly be stressed too much that such principles may be extremely complex and numerous. Anyone who has done such a 'simple' thing as successfully bake a cake will recognize this fact. It will be important to bear this in mind as more interesting cases are considered. For our present purposes, however, the important point is that statements which purport to formulate the action-principle of a craft are subject to rational debate and that the distinction between truth and falsity applies to them. They are matters of 'objective fact' and belong to the rational order. Furthermore, there is an important sense in which they exist 'by nature,' if the latter term is so used as to contrast with 'convention.' But this remark is but the opening shot in a long campaign.

We distinguished above between an artifact and its use or 'consumption.' If we call the use or consumption for which is an artifact is designed its *external* purpose, we can say that whether or not an artifact serves this external purpose is, in general, also a matter for rational discussion, and that the distinction between truth and falsity is relevant. On the other hand, whether the *ultimate* ends served by artifacts are themselves subject to rational discussion and to the distinction between the true and the false (or, to put it differently, whether these ultimate ends are in any interesting sense 'objective'), has at least the appearance of being a question of quite a different kind. That the crafting of instrumentalities belongs, as practice, to the intelligible order, is not surprising. On the other hand, if one could show that the *ultimate* ends served by instrumentalities have in their own way a practical intelligibility akin to that of the crafting of instrumentalities, one would be well on the way to illuminating the *objectivity* of ultimate ends.

V

The above account of the structure of craftsmanship, schematic though it may be, gives us a powerful tool for analyzing the contrast between 'nature' (*physis*) and 'convention' (*nomos*) the validity of which is the central issue between Plato and the Sophists. The word 'nature' should not mislead, for that which exists 'by nature' and is contrasted with convention is as it is, regardless of what we think it to be. It is characterized by objectivity, and is discoverable, if at all, by rational methods. Conventions, on the other hand, exist as *ways of thinking,* in that broad sense of 'thinking' which includes attitudes. That a certain mode of practice is a convention, is itself, of course, an objective fact. Yet this objective fact is a fact about the existence, in the community, of a certain way of thinking which might well have been otherwise. Philosophers, almost from the beginning, have given the term, 'convention' and its approximate equivalents in other languages – e.g., the Greek *'nomos'* – technical senses which so extended and modify their original meaning, that it is a philological task of the first magnitude to trace the family trees of the uses to which they have been put. For our purposes, it will be helpful to construe conventions as general imperatives which have come to be accepted and enforced in a community, either by deliberate initiative on the part of specific individuals, or by the slow process which is the coming to be of tradition.

The conventions in which we are interested are those which correspond, in ways to be defined, to the principles of a craft. For, as I hope to show, an understanding of how this distinction works in simple cases provides the essential clue to the contrast between positive law and political principle which Plato seeks to defend against the attacks of the Sophists.

The first point to be made is that statements which purport to formulate *principles* are not, as such, in the imperative mood. In this respect they are like any matter-of-factual statement, e.g., "The sky is blue." But although statements of principles are not general imperatives, to each statement of principle there corresponds, in a straightforward sense, a sentence in the imperative mood. Statements of principle are either true or false; imperatives, as such, are neither. Imperatives are used to tell people to do something, and are capable of being enforced, i.e., accomplished by the threat (or promise) of sanctions.

The distinction I have in mind can be illustrated in simple terms by the contrast between

If it is raining, John ought to use an umbrella

which we may suppose to be a true proposition resting on the tacit premise that John wants to keep dry, and the corresponding imperative

If it is raining, John, use an umbrella!

Notice that although a person who uses the imperative sentence to tell John to use an umbrella, if it rains, might offer as *his* reason for doing so "because you, John want to keep dry and using an umbrella is the way to do it," he may neither *have* this reason, nor *offer* it. He may *have* quite another reason, and yet *offer* the above reason; or, perhaps, have no reason at all. Yet whatever his reason, if he has any, by using this sentence he has genuinely told John to carry an umbrella, if it rains; and may undertake to treat John in friendly or unfriendly ways depending on whether or not he does as he is told.

On the other hand, the statement.

If it is raining, John *ought* to use an umbrella is no mere 'say so' independent of reasons. There is no difficulty in supposing it to be an objectively true statement which is grounded in the fact that John wants to keep dry, along with familiar scientific facts about umbrellas and rain.

That we often use 'ought-' statements in such a way that they enable us to achieve results which we could obtain by using imperative sentences, must not blind us to the difference between 'ought' statements and imperatives. After all, I can use the non-imperative.

There is a spider on your head.

to get someone to slap his head, where the imperative

Slap your head!

might be met by a hostile stare.

Let us apply these distinctions to the case of the builder's craft. In the interest of simplicity, let us suppose that the purpose of a house is to provide shelter, and that there is only one type of house which satisfactorily serves this purpose. Consider the family of practical statements.

If one wants to build a house, then if the circumstances (including the state of the raw materials) are C_i, one ought to do A_j

or, equivalently,

The principles of house building are:

If in C_i, one ought to do A_j.

It is readily seen that the statements making up this family are either true or false and, if true, are true by virtue of (a) the 'nature' of the materials and (b) the design of a satisfactory house.

Let us now suppose that our builders form a guild. Some of its members are experienced builders; others mere apprentices. Even experienced builders will differ in their skills and in the extent of their insight into the principles of the craft. They may even have different beliefs concerning these principles. Let us, therefore, suppose that, formally or informally, the guild adopts a 'builders' code,' a system of enforced imperatives, thus

In building a house :

If in C_i , do A_j !

We can conceive that, if pressed for reasons for this 'legislation,' they might offer something like the following :

... because these are the things it is necessary to do to build a house, and by enforcing this legislation we will insure that this is what builders do.

In other words, the builders' establishment might believe that in the absence of this code, many builders would follow false principles even though their sincere purpose was to build satisfactory houses. Or the builders' establishment might believe that many builders are not so much ignorant as corrupt, and that in the absence of the code they might deliberately build defective houses to line their pockets. We might call both types of reason for adopting and enforcing a code,*craft-oriented reasons.*

There is always the possibility, of course, that the builder's establishment has as its reason for adopting and enforcing a certain code, not that it embodies what they believe to be the true principle of the craft, but rather (though they would be understandably reluctant to publicize the fact) that action in accordance with the code would be to their advantage, in that, for example, the establishment has privileged access to certain kinds of material. This type of reason for adopting and enforcing a code might be called an *external reason.*

Now it is clear that individual builders will tend to regard the code as a guide to what a builder ought to do, *qua* builder, only to the extent that they believe the collective wisdom of the establishment to be a more reliable guide to the objective principles of the craft than is their own unaided judgment. They would regard it as silly to say that something is a principle of the craft simply by virtue of being promulgated and enforced imperative, i.e., a convention.

Of course, since the code is enforced by fines and other

sanctions, each builder *qua* person will have a reason for conforming to the code. But this reason, in its turn, can be called an external reason. Thus, supposing a builder to be convinced that one of the principles of the craft is

In C_i one ought to do A_k !

whereas the enforced code says

In C_i, do A_k !

He will regard this latter enforced imperative as throwing no light on what he ought to do *qua* builder, but as by no means irrelevant to what ought to do *qua* having hungry mouths to feed.

VI

Now it is familiar fact that Plato's moral and critical philosophy makes use of structures of ideas fundamentally akin to those involved in the analysis of the builder's craft. The early dialogues make constant use of analogies with features of craftsmanship to throw light on specific philosophical puzzles. The pattern recurs in the more systematic philosophy of the later dialogues. The most obvious case is the *Timaeus* where Plato makes use of the concept of a Divine Craftsman who builds the world, as a device for explicating the general categories in terms of which the world is to be understood. Even where the use of analogies with craftsmanship is not explicit, it is often present to the discerning eye, and provides essential clues to the understanding of his thought.

Plato regards the study of humble crafts as philosophically illuminating, because he sees them as the lesser members of a hierarchy which culminates in two crafts of intrinsic concern to the philosopher : (a) the craft of the statesman or, as I shall put it, of the citizen; (b) the craft of shaping one's life as an individual.

Our primary conception of craftsmanship is the production of instrumentalities. We are therefore not surprised to find Plato speaking of statesmanship as a craft, for we are fully prepared to think of the well-ordered city as an instrumentality for the general welfare, and, therefore, to find the analogy between statesmanship and familiar crafts as illuminating. (It would be tempting to turn our attention to other crafts, e.g., medicine, in order to highlight other analogies, but the fundamental points can be made with reference to the builder's art as I have described it.)

The product, then, of the stateman's craft is a city ordered to the well-being of its citizens, and its proximate raw material involves, in addition to physical instrumentalities, persons with diverse characters and talents. Now, in the case of some crafts (e.g., cooking and building) it seems reasonable to say that consumers 'know' how the products are to be used and can transmit their 'knowledge' to the craftsman. It is less plausible to suppose that 'consumers' of cities 'know' how they are to be used, i.e., in what the well-being of the community consists. Compare the case of the physician's art. Plato, however, thinks that 'tradition' embodies substantial insights into these matters; it is, to use his metaphor, an 'image' or 'likeness' of the truth. But he also thinks that in the Athens of his day, the insights of tradition are at the mercy of sophistry and the rhetorical skills of ignorant men.

If we postpone questions concerning the specific character of well-being or 'happiness,' and make what philosophers call a purely 'formal' or 'placeholding' use of the term 'general welfare' we can continue our exploration of the craft of the citizen along the following lines. We have already referred to the 'eternal' aim of the craft (the general welfare), and to its proximate raw materials. It remains to explore the political counterpart of the principles or programs of action in accordance with which a craftsman shapes his materials to make the finished product. Analogy suggests the following general schema

If a citizen wants to contribute to making and/or maintaining a city ordered to the general welfare, then

If a citizen is in C_i, he ought to do A_j.

(It must be borne in mind that the simplicity of this schema conceals the number and complexity of the principles it represents.) As in the case of the builder's art, these statements of principle will be 'objective' in the sense that the distinction between truth and falsity is relevant to them. They express belief about the impact of various kinds of action in various kinds of circumstance on the life of a community. It is clear that the question whether they are true or false presupposes a specific conception of the welfare which is to result from the use of the instrumentality which is the so-ordered city. But given such a specific concept, that a specific plan of action is required to order a city to welfare, thus conceived, is an objective matter for rational determination.

If we continue to draw on analogies between statesmanship and the builder's art, we arrive at the following account of the distinction between *nomos* (convention) and *physis* (nature : in other words principle and truth) in the political context. The principles of the craft of the citizen are, no more than those of the builder's art, to be confused with enforced imperatives, whether the latter exist as traditions informally enforced or as positive law enforced by specific agencies, themselves created by law. The conceptual distinction between *principles* and *conventions* is as sharp as it was in the case of the builder's craft, and the relations between principles and conventions in politics are at bottom, the same as those which were sketched in our parable of the builder's guild.

We contrasted builders engaging in their craft, without being organized in a guild which adopts and enforces general imperatives pertaining to building-type activity, upon builders so organized. We can similarly draw a contrast, in principle, between a number of citizens engaging in the citizen's craft, without being subject to enforced general imperatives pertaining to citizen-like activity, with citizens so organized as to exist in an ambience of enforced conventions.

If we assume that our citizens are organized into a guild (i.e., city) and subject to positive law, and refer to those who have the power to adopt and enforce general imperatives as the 'establishment' of the city, we can transpose our parable of the builder's guild into the political context along the following lines. Assuming that the establishment has reasonably true opinions or opinions as to what constitutes the general welfare of the city, and assuming that the legislative and administrative activity of the establishment is, as we put it, craft-oriented in its motivation, we would expect the resulting conventions to correspond in rough approximation to the principles which specify the program of action by which individual citizens can make their contribution to ordering the city as an effective instrument for the general welfare.

As in the case of the builder's guild, a citizen who has the well-ordered city as his end-in-view will not, unless confused, regard the fact that a course of action is prescribed by an enforced imperative as making that course of action what he ought to do *qua* citizen. Principles specify what he *ought* to do, conventions tell him to do certain things under certain penalties. Even if these conventions are *formulated* in terms of 'ought' they do not *as conventions,* bring it about that, as citizen, he *ought* to act in the manner prescribed. As in the case of the builder's guild, a citizen may regard the fact that a course of action is prescribed by enforced legislation as a good, though not conclusive reason, for supposing that the course of action *does* correspond to a principle.

Again, as in the case of the builder's guild, a person who views himself on a particular occasion, not as citizen but, say, as one who has his own interests at heart, may find the penalty attached to the law to constitute a compelling reason for conforming to the law, whether or not, as citizen, he concedes that the law tells him to do what in fact he ought to do.

So far the parallel works out smoothly. It is now time to note a complication which can generate confusion. The raw materials relevant to making a shoe are, for example, rubber, nails, etc., and the program of action of the shoemaker concerns the shaping and arranging of such raw materials. In the case of the art of the citizen, however, the materials with which he is concerned include, in addition to what we have already mentioned, such things as

(a) current beliefs about the principles of the citizen's craft as well as beliefs about the specific nature of the general welfare to which the city is to be ordered as an instrument.

(b) currently enforced general imperatives.

The second special feature of the circumstances in which the citizen must act involves an interpenetration of principles and conventions which, misinterpreted, can lead to a confusion of the two categories, a failure to find the distinction between principles and conventions, in the political context, meaningful.

Suppose that one of the principles of the art of the citizen is

In C_i one ougnt to do A_j

and suppose that there is *no* enforced imperative to a contrary effect, for example

In C_i, do A_k !

On these assumptions, what one ought to do *qua* citizen, if one is in C_i is A_j. But suppose, now, that the latter imperative comes to be promulgated and enforced. Then, although an adequate account of the implications of this fact would require a more sophisticated apparatus, the following gives the gist of the matter. There now cease to be circumstances of the kind originally referred to as C_i – for these were defined in terms of the *absence* of this legislation. The closest counterpart of such situations now become those which are like C_i but involve the additional element of the existence of the enforced imperative

In C_i do A_k! ($L_{i,k}$) where 'L' stands for 'law'

Let us represent such situations by

C_i [+ $L_{i,k}$]

We now note that it could very well be the case that the promotion of the general welfare requires that in *such* situations a citizen does A_k ; that it be a *matter of principles* that

In C_i [+ $L_{i,k}$], one ought to do A_k

It is along these lines that a convention

In C_i, do A_k!

could, *in a sense,* generate a principle

In C_i [+ $L_{i,k}$], one ought to do A_i

which one might be tempted to represent as

In C_i, one ought to do A_k

and confuse with the corresponding convention.

On reflection, however, it is clear that although this provides a sense in which convention (enforced imperatives) determines what a person exercising the craft of the citizen ought to do, it nevertheless determines it *not qua convention,* but *qua* just another factor in the circumstances in which a citizen must act. Like other circumstance-factors it contributes to determine, along with the nature of the instrumentality to be produced or maintained, the manifold principles of the craft. And, as in the case of any craft, these principles, however complicated, have an objective status which distinguishes them from conventions, even though they take account of and even refer to convention.

To sum up, Plato – and I have simply been representing the structure of his thought – argues that what one ought to do *qua* exercising the art of the citizen is *never,* except in the above derivative sense, a matter of convention.

Before proceeding to the next state of the argument, some terminological points will be helpful. The principles of the art of the citizen, or, to put it in superficially different terms, the principles of the stateman's craft, are what we would be tempted to call 'principles of political obligation.' It must, however, be borne in mind that the line between the ethical and the political is difficult to draw, and it will be conducive to clarity to conceive of the principles in question as simply those principles which relate to our obligations to others in so far as the relevant instrumentality is the well-ordered city as a whole, as contrasted, for example, with those principles pertaining to the family as an instrumentality for the well-being of a more limited community. The relationship of the citizen's craft to the craft of the houshold is a subtle one, for like all crafts, that of the household has its own relative autonomy and generates its own 'oughts' or principles. Yet, since families are among the ingredients to be shaped into the well-ordered city, which is the proximate instrumentality for the *general* welfare, the principles of the craft of the household are subject to overriding principles pertaining to the craft of the citizen.

But what does 'overriding' mean in this context? Here we must remember that although the principles of a craft are *objective,* they are relative to two ends : (a) one immanent to the craft, the end of making and/or maintaining a certain instrumentality (i.e., an automobile); (b) the external end which is defined by the characteristic use to which the instrumentality produced by the craft is put. To say that a person is acting, during a certain period, *qua* practitioner of a certain craft, is to say that whatever the larger framework of purpose he has in mind, he has committed himself, during this period to the immanent end of the craft, i.e., to seeking to contribute to the making and/or maintaining of the relevant instrumentality. If, then, a person, during a certain period, has making this contribution as his proximate end or purpose, then the principles of the craft *objectively* specify what he ought to do, given his circumstances (the raw material, so to speak, which he must shape) to make this contribution. Thus, although the principles are *objective,* they are, in a familiar sense hypothetical. They tell him what he ought to do in given circumstances if he proposes to make his contribution to the existence of the product. Thus the principles of the shoemaker's craft specify the steps a person must take if he is to make good shoes out of available raw material. If he has no interest in making shoes, he will, so to speak, simply look the *objectivity* of the principles in the eye and move on. Again, one who has only the interests of his family at heart and is consequently engaged in the craft of the household, may acknowledge the objectivity of the overriding principles of the craft of the citizen yet, unless he is committed of the overriding end of the latter craft, will look the objectivity of these principles in the eye, but limit himself to the practice of the family craft.

This conception of the subordination, coordination and relative autonomy of the various crafts is the key to Plato's thought. It is now time to show how he puts this concept to use in defending the objectivity of 'justice' – in the sense of our obligations *qua* citizen to our fellow man – against the attacks of the Sophists.

The first point to emphasize is that it is not too difficult for Plato (in the person of Socrates) to get his opponents to admit that abstractly considered there are many crafts, ranging from shoemaking to the crafting of a city ordered to the well-being of its citizens. There is, of course, much controversy about such philosophical issues as 'what is objectivity'' 'how is it to be determined which principles are objectively true? ' – in short the omnipresent issues embodied in the skeptic's challenge. Yet the philosophical skeptic can be led to admit that in whatever sense there is a craft of shoemaking with objective principles, there are other crafts which pertain more closely to living, and perhaps, even, a craft of so ordering a city as to promote the happiness of its citizens. Needless to say, any such formal admission leaves room for argument concerning what constitutes happiness or, to introduce a familiar phrase, 'the good for man.'

Thus it is worth noting that among the Sophists Protagoras is closest to Socrates in his general outlook on how life is to be lived. Plato was convinced that the traditions of Athens embody confused but substantially true opinions about the principles of the art of the citizen. (In Platonic terms, confused but substantially true opinions about justice, i.e., the principles of just action.) To the extent, and it is a large one, that Protagoras is an effective representative of these traditions. Plato looks on him with a sympathetic and even admiring eye. What Plato attacks in Protagoras is his failure to appreciate the objectivity of principles, the relevance of rational argument to deciding what they are, and, above all, his failure, in the case of the political art, to appreciate the distinction between principles and conventions. Protagoras' failure, in these respects, combined with his talents as a persuader, prepare the way for the influence of persuaders less friendly to tradition and the images of truth it embodies.

How are we to construe the controversy between Socrates and Thrasymachus in the First Book of the *Republic?* Is it possible for the latter to grant that there is a craft of the citizen (or statesman) along the lines we have defined, and yet disagree with Socrates in an interesting way about its status? The answer is yes. Thrasymachus makes two central contentions :

> (1) What point is there in recognizing the existence of a craft of shaping the city to serve the general welfare, if no one in any genuine sense *engages* in this craft' He, Thrasymachus, can perhaps be led to admit that by 'justice' we mean the principles of such a craft, but if no one commits himself to the end in terms of which this craft is defined, these principles, however *objective,* are as irrelevant to life as the principles of the craft of building ladders to the clouds.
>
> (2) Thus, even if it is granted that our conception of justice involves the conception of a craft of a citizen along the lines we have defined, and that this concept is, in a sense, the core of its meanings, the hard fact of the matter is that as far as the *usage* of "the term 'justice' is concerned" ("what is called justice"), it is employed by the establishment to describe the political imperatives they promulgate and enforce. Furthermore, the purpose of the political establishment in enforcing this legislation is not the 'internal' purpose of embodying their beliefs about the true prin-

ciples of the craft of the citizen in effective conventions, but rather the external purpose of shaping conventions to serve their private interests.

With respect to the first point, it is as though no one who shaped pieces of leather did so with the settled purpose of making shoes, but only, for example, with immediate personal interests in view. In this case, it would be, so to speak, an accident that he ever finished a shoe.

With respect to the second point, it is as though (a possibility we have already glanced at) the builder's establishment called its enforced imperatives concerning the manipulation of housing materials 'principles of building,' even though it was moved to adopt and enforce these imperatives not to facilitate the making of houses well-ordered to the shelter of those who live in them, but rather to promote the economic interests of the builders themselves.

Clearly, to reply to these contentions, Plato must make some points like the following :

(1) He must convince us that people generally do, as a matter of fact, have a settled interest in the well-ordering of the city for the welfare of its citizens. We would expect him to add, however, that this settled interest largely rests, not on insight, but on tradition and upbringing, and is correspondingly vulnerable to sophistical arguments and the techniques of persuasion. Since it is clear that, according to Thrasymachus the only *settled* interest people have is in their own well-being, Plato must show not only that this is in point of fact false, but that a settled and at least relatively autonomous interest in the general welfare has a justifiable place in a well-conceived life.[5]

(2) Plato must show that, in point of fact, the establishment does not legislate solely with a view to its own interest, *as contrasted with* interests of citizens generally. More positively put, he must show that the imperatives enforced by the establishment are (to a greater or lesser extent) designed to embody its beliefs concerning how to shape the city for the common good. He will grant, as before, that the fact that the establishment is so disposed is rooted in tradition and upbringing, and is consequently vulnerable to temptations and sophistry. At a deeper level,

however, he must show that it is a part of a well-conceived life that those in a position to legislate seek to embody in their legislation their convictions concerning the principles of the craft of the citizen, the art of statesmanship.

I pointed out at the beginning of the section that Plato conceives of arts or crafts as constituting a hierarchy which culminates in two supreme crafts : (a) the craft of the statesman or citizen; (b) the craft of shaping one's life as an individual. It is to the latter that I now turn, for the conception of such a craft or art of living is, as I hope to show, the keystone of Plato's thought.

The first thing to notice is that references to an art or craft of living are at their most explicit in the controversies with Callicles in the Gorgias, and with Protagoras in the final stages of the dialogue of that name. The conception of such an art or craft becomes less explicit (though evident to the discerning eye) in his constructive account of how life is to be lived in the *Republic,* and, particularly, in the *Philebus.* The reason is not far to seek. Craftsmanship in the literal sense is concerned with instrumentalities. Even the craft of a statesman has as its immanent end the shaping of an instrumentality, a city ordered to the well-being of its citizens. On the other hand, the central issues pertaining to the life of the individual concern not instrumentalities, but that which gives all instrumentalities their ultimate *raison d'etre.*

Nevertheless, although the satisfactory life is not an instrumentality, the program of action by which it can be realized has, in all other respects, the structure of craftsmanship. In this case, however, the internal and external ends of the craft are so intimately related that they seem almost to coincide. Roughly speaking the instrumentality is a system of abilities ordered to form a character, while the 'use' or 'consumption' of the instrumentality is the actualization of this character in satisfying activity. The crafting is done by those who shape and maintain the character, not the least important of whom is the individual himself.

The word 'character' is perhaps too Aristotelian to use in the context of the *Philebus.* Aristotle, in discussing the satisfying life lays great stress on habits and dispositions. Plato lays equal stress in the *Republic* on habits of feeling, thought and action when discussing the happiness available to men of silver and bronze. In the *Philebus,* however, where he is discussing life at its best, the stress is less on habits and dispositions than on insight into the nature of soul and its relation to other dimensions of reality.

The instrumentality crafted by the art of living is knowledge of the nature of the satisfying life, and it is crafted by dialectic, i.e., well-ordered philosophical thought. Yet the true product of the art of living is not this instrumentality, nor is this knowledge itself *merely* an instrumentality. The ingredients which are shaped to achieve the purpose of the craft are shaped not into an instrumentality, but into a pattern of enjoyed activities. These ingredients can be classified under two headings : 'knowledges' and 'pleasures.'

> Socrates : Then here, we may say, we have at hand the ingredients, intelligence and pleasure, ready to be mixed, and the materials in which, or out of which, we, as builders, are to build our structure : that would not be a bad metaphor. (*Philebus,* 59DE)

The lists of ingredients must not be misunderstood. Early in the dialogue the life of pleasure unmixed with any form of knowledge *and* the life of "intelligence, thought, knowledge and complete memory of everything without any pleasure" are contrasted with a 'mixed' life which includes pleasure, on the one hand, and reason with intelligence on the other. We are told that neither of the unmixed lives "is sufficient and desirable for any human being or any living thing (21DE)." In 33B, the unmixed "life of reason and intelligence" with "no experiencing of pleasure, great or small," is reintroduced, and Socrates tells us that "perhaps it is not a wild surmise that this of all lives is the most godlike." To which Protarchus adds "it is not to be supposed that the gods feel either pleasure or its opposite."

> Socrates : No, of course it is not; it would be unseemly for either feeling to arise in them.

From this latter exchange it has often been concluded that the godlike life is devoid of pleasure, and that only the ideal life *for man* involves pleasure as well as knowledge. But this is surely a misunderstanding, as Socrates hints, when he adds to the sentence quoted above "but to that question we will give further consideration later on if it should be relevant." For implicit in the subsequent discussion is a distinction between those feelings of pleasure which arise out the satisfaction of needs, where the needs either may be painful (as in the case of thirst) or, as in the case of "the pleasures which attach to colors which we call beautiful, to figures, to most odors, to sounds," imperceptible and painless, but their fulfillment "perceptible and pleasant," (50E), and of those enjoyed activities which would not usually be called pleasures.

Thus when it is said that "it is not to be supposed that the gods feel. . . pleasure," this must not be taken to mean that a divine life is without enjoyment. For in 60BC we are told that

> A creature which possesses [the Good] permanently, completely and absolutely has never any need of anything else; its *satisfaction* is complete.

and in the account of the recipe of the satisfying life which concludes the dialogue, reference is made to "the pure pleasures of the soul itself, some of them attaching to knowledge, others to sensations." (66C)

VII

Before I began my exploration of the conceptual structure of craftsmanship, I was engaged in pointing out that Plato conceives of the realm of Forms as a realm of intelligibilities. I then pointed out that whereas recent British and American philosophy has tended to take as its paradigm of intelligibility the intelligibilities of logic, mathematics, and the natural sciences, there is *prima facie*, a domain of intelligibility, not unrelated to the former, which can be called the domain of practical intelligibilities.

In exploring the intelligibilities of craftsmanship, I pointed out that these intelligibilities involve such mathematical intelligibilities as numbers, ratios, and such other intelligibilities as pertain to the causal properties of the materials to be shaped by the craft. Yet these theoretical intelligibilities are, insofar as they contribute to the practical intelligibilities of the craft, subordinated to that organizing intelligibility which is the *recipe* of the product. We might put this by saying that the Form of the practical intelligibilities of a craft is the Form 'recipe for making something to some purpose.'

When Plato tells us that the Form of Forms is 'the Form of

the Good,' is he not telling us that although there are many varieties of structure which relate Forms to other Forms, the most illuminating way of conceiving of the realm of intelligibilities is a complex system of recipes for crafting a world which includes not only instrumentalities, but satisfying lives. The second book of the *Republic* begins with a classification of goods into :

(a) those which we desire for their own sake
(b) those which we desire both for their own sake and for their consequences
(c) those which we desire only for their consequences.

To say that the Form of the realm of Forms is the Form of a complex system of recipes is to imply that it contains not only recipes for instrumental goods (e.g., the Form Bed) but also for goods which are not instrumentalities, and that the latter Forms are the recipes for different levels of satisfying life, divine and human. We have seen that the practical intelligibilities involved in the instrumental crafts are hypothetical. They specify what must be done if one wants to make or maintain an instrument. Is there such a thing as a nonhypothetical practical intelligibility? A practical intelligibility which is not of the above form? Plato surely thinks that there is, for he tells us on a number of occasions that statements of the form

S wants to lead a satisfying life

or, as he puts it,

S wills the good

are final answers to the question 'why does S do what he does? ' Such answers are 'formal' in that S's specific beliefs about what kind of life would in point of fact be satisfying may well be mistaken. But that the question 'what kind of life would really satisfy me? ' is, *in principle,* capable of a reasoned answer, though it involves a self-knowledge which has passed through all the stages of disciplined reflection on the source of things, is Plato's abiding faith as a philospher.

It is surely along these lines that the supposedly mysterious passage in Book VI of the *Republic* in which Plato describes the 'place of honor' of the Good in the system of Forms is to be understood.

> Glaucon : you are giving it a position of extraordinary splendor, if it is the source of knowledge and truth and

> itself surpasses them in worth. You surely cannot mean that it is pleasure.
>
> Socrates : Heaven forbid, I exclaimed. But I want to follow up our analogies still further. You will agree that the sun not only makes the things we see visible, but also brings them into existence and gives them growth and nourishment; yet it is not the same thing as existence; and so with the objects of knowledge : these derive from the Good not only their power of being known, but their very being and reality; and goodness is not the same thing as being, but even beyond being, surpassing it in dignity and power.

If my account of Plato's thought is correct, this passage paints no picture of an abstract essence which has no intelligible connection with what we ordinarily mean by 'good,' but simply sums up in compendious, if dramatic, form the conception of the realm of Forms as constituting a complex of recipes for building an intelligible world, the intelligibility of which is *practical* intelligibility, the intelligibility of the satisfying life, whether human or divine.

NOTES

1. Presented in a conference of «Greece: The Critical Spirit, 450-350 B.C.» held at Ohio State University, April 5 and 6, 1968. A discussion of closely related issues is to be found in my essays "The Soul as Craftsman" in *Philosophical Perspectives* (Springfield, *Illinois*, 1967).

2. *Republic,* VI, 508.

3. He distinguishes a fourth level of being, Space (or Place), the receptacle and, as it were, the womb of physical becoming. But nothing I shall have to say hinges on its distinctive role.

4. Needless to say, a standing condition need not be static – the term 'standing' simply reinforces the contrast between the circumstance, and that which may or may not be done by an agent in that circumstance.

5. That, for Plato, the ultimate court of appeal of the life of reason is self-interest adequately conceived is a theme to be explored on a subsequent occasion.

IS ART A LANGUAGE?[1]

Wladyslaw Tatarkiewicz, University of Warsaw

An Investigation of Three Ambiguous Words

In vain would one search through old manuscripts and books for the idea that art is language. Of course, no one ever doubted that some arts, like poetry and rhetoric, are making use of language; however, only *some* of them do so, and *using* language is not the same as being a language. Perhaps Vico was the first to lean to the view that "Art is language." Kant divided arts into as many kinds as there are means of communication between man, thus dividing them like language; he stressed, nevertheless, that he only used "the analogy" between art and language, and analogy[2] is quite different from identity.

Nowadays, however, the problem whether art is language acquired great topicality. Many writers answer this question in the affirmative. The idea that *art is language* was proclaimed by Croce,[3] and Dewey,[4] and the English followers of Croce,[5] by the philosopher E. Cassirer,[6] and the logician Charles Morris,[7] the historian of art E. Gombrich[8] of the Warburg Institute, and many others.

In order to judge whether this view is correct, one has, first of all, to explain the meanings of the terms "art", "is" and "language." We may expect difficulties because all three terms are ambiguous.

1. Art

The term "art" is not simply ambiguous -- its vagueness is threefold.

THE FIRST AMBIGUITY OF "ART" is partly due to the fact that over the centuries the term acquired new meaning without losing the old one; both meanings exist side by side in contemporary speech. "Art", (more precisely, its earlier equivalents : the Greek "techne" and Latin "ars") covered in ambiguity a wide field : it stood for every kind of productive ability, based on principles and rules. In this sense Aristotle described art as a "disposition to any production founded on correct reasoning." [Et. N. 1140 a 9]. Art was contrasted with nature but also with man's actions which are not based on knowledge and skill, but ruled by chance; for the ancients the opposite of art was not only nature but also chance. Seneca wrote: "That which accidentally achieves its aim is not art." [Ad Luc. 29, 3]. On the other hand, everything that was neither a work of nature nor a product of chance, was considered as art. Therefore the classic concept of art covered more ground than it does today : together with such skills as painting or architecture it included others, like carpentry or cobbling.

For at least 2,000 years this broad concept of art has been the only one; no other concept of art was known and used. Though in the eighteenth century "fine" arts were already singled out, the word "art" [without adjective] continued to comprise also "mechanical" arts, i.e., crafts. Only in the second half of the nineteenth century did painting or architecture begin to be called simply "arts," with the adjective "fine" left out; it was only then that the concept was narrowed down and fine arts acquired a kind of exclusive right to the name of "arts."

Still the old classic concept of art coexisted alongside the new. The action of the nineteenth century to rehabilitate crafts brought it about that the division between fine arts and crafts was again questioned and that aesthetics in some degree returned to the classic concept of art. Nowadays two concepts are valid – the old and the new, the wider and the narrower – and the term "art" is ambiguous : it denotes either fine arts together with crafts or the fine arts only.

SECOND AMBIGUITY. According to the classic conception "art" meant the ability to produce something, e.g., making a sculpture or composing music; it meant the skill of mind and hands. Nowadays we also use it in this sense when we say, for example, "the art of playing bridge" – by art we mean here the skill. However, we apply the term art also [and foremost] to the actual *products* of the skill : to sculptures, musical compositions, poems. Thus the word "art" has two meanings : that of a skill and that of a product.

In our aesthetic speech we have two basic expressions – "art" and "work of art." When we say "art" we usually mean products, while "work of art" we understand as a work of skill; the word "art" when coupled with "work" signifies the skill and with the word "work" left out – signifies the product.

THIRD AMBIGUITY. Even if we disregard the old, broader concept of art and concentrate on fine arts only, we are still faced with various ways of understanding and defining them; while some definitions enlarge the concepts, others narrow them down. The Renaissance was aware of the difference between fine arts and crafts but lacked certainty as to what it consists in; various attempts were made on various grounds to arrive at a definition : alternately arts were described[9] as inventive [as G. Manetti suggested], musical [M. Ficino], noble [G.P. Capriano], memorial [because they serve to fix events in human memory, as L. Castelvetro wrote], picturesque [because they employ images and not abstractions], metaphorical [E. Tasauro], pleasant [G.B. Vico], elegant [J. Harris]. Only about the middle of the eighteenth century, mainly as result of Batteux's book in which he called them "fine," it was accepted that *beauty* is the characteristic feature of these arts distinguishing them from others.

This view became established and concord prevailed; this particular ambiguity was eliminated – for quite a long time, but not forever. In the twentieth century new doubts arose whether it is really beauty which distinguishes such arts as painting, music, poetry? Different descriptions were sought and more than one found. Today's theoreticians say : the distinctive features of those arts are, in fact, *the creativity,* originality, endeavor to produce things which did not exist before; the most beautiful object which is only imitating or copying something is not a work of art. Or else theoreticians say : the distinctive feature of these arts is *expression;* their essential quality is expressing human experiences. Or else : their basic characteristic is the strong *impact* they have upon man [not ex-pression but im-pression],[10] impact – not necessarily harmonious, or aimed at feeding the recipient with beauty, but rather a strong impact, a shock, a violent shaking of man.

These are different definitions of art, and depending on which one is accepted – whether art is defined as beauty, or as creativity, as expression, or as the shaking of people – it will, or will not, be language.

2. Language

The ambiguity of the word "language" is as manifold as that of the word "art."

FIRST AMBIGUITY OF LANGUAGE. Language – in the commonest, technical meaning of the word – is a multitude of coordinated conventional signs by means of which a group of people living together communicates. Polish or English are such languages; so was Latin first used for communication by the Romans and then by those who took it over from the Romans. The characteristic feature of those languages is that *signs* which make them up are *conventional;* that these signs constitute a *system,* and perform their functions as collectives; that they have their constant [although growing] vocabulary listed in dictionaries, and a set of rules recorded in their grammar. Prima facie these languages are vocal but may be translated into visual : speech and writings are their parallel forms; they may also appear in tactile form – for the blind. A language acquired in childhood becomes a natural tool for man who uses it as instinctively as he uses his hands or legs; he uses it constantly not only in order to communicate with others and to express outwardly his emotions but also in order to think. Such languages – English or Polish are referred to as *natural,* ethnic, colloquial, ordinary mother tongue.

Some linguists use the word "language" in such a way that it denotes only natural languages; others include in the meaning *artificial* languages as well. Hence the first ambiguity of the word. To natural languages belong also such as "the language of the deaf and dumb" : it is just a transposition of natural languages into signs made by hands, and accessible to those who cannot speak or hear; but its syntax and vocabulary remain the same. On the other hand, "the language of children," "of spies," "of lovers," while keeping to the syntax of a natural language add for their own purposes certain signs and modify the meanings of others: therefore they are to some extent artificial languages. They are "second languages" [as M. Mothersill calls them] [11] based on natural language which they, however, complement or change artificially.

Such languages as Esperanto or Ido are artificial to a greater extent : but they would like to become natural; their aim is to oust ethnic languages and to be used in the way ethnic languages are. Entirely artificial are "formal" languages of logic or mathematics (or formalized, symbolic, ideal, scientific, or whatever name we will give them); they consciously depart from the natural ones with the aim of achieving a greater precision, constancy, subtlety. [P. Edwards, *Encyclopedia of Philosophy,* 1967, I, 168.] They, however, come under the name of "languages" because they perform a similar task as natural languages, and are composed of conventional signs.

For our present purpose, however, another ambiguity is more important : indeed, the scope covered by the term "language" is sometimes expanded till further : it embraces even the language of gestures, musical notation, or painting. This enlargement brings about a radical change in the meaning of the word "language" because it ceases to be limited to *conventional* signs. Is this enlargement justified? Some linguists maintain that it is not because it breaks up the unity of the phenomenon of language; others do not fear such consequences.

Eventually, in contemporary speech and linguistic literature the word "language" is ambiguous : (1) The majority of the linguists use it in the narrower meaning of a system of conventional signs; if they sometimes use it in a broader sense [referring to gestures or painting] they do it metaphorically. (2) Others, however, use this word in a broader sense so that it denotes any system of signs. This is done, for example, by Charles Morris according to whom any "collection of interconnected signs" is language, or by the Soviet *Filosofskij Slovar,* 1963, which calls language "a system of signs of any physical shape, performing cognitive and communicative function in the process of human activity."

The ambiguity of "language" is particularly marked if we contrast language in the sense of "any collection of signs" with "natural" languages, which form the greater part among the languages *stricto sensu.* Art can be considered as a collection of signs, but certainly it is not a natural language.

A SECOND AMBIGUITY OF LANGUAGE rises from different views of its function. The first view assumes that the primary function of language was and is *expression.* It served first to express feelings and necessaries of life and *later* became a means of communication between human beings. Expression is primary, communication secondary; any expression is a language, even if it does not serve communication.

The other view assumes on the contrary that *communication* is the primary source of language. Any communication is a language, even if it does not serve expression. Both views have distinguished adherents.

A. The German philosopher W. Wundt,[12] when calling language "Gedankenäusserung durch artikulierte Bewegung" defined it as an *expression.* So did A. Marty,[13] a major authority on the turn of the century : language is "a sign of mental state," he said. In a similar way the *Wörterbuch der philosophischen Begriffe* by R. Eisler defines the speech as "Ausdruck von Erlebnissen," [1930, III 141]. The Italian *Enciclopedia filosofica* [1957, III 67] says : "Il linguagio è la facoltà degl' uomi di obbietivare in simboli fonici il moto dell conscienza." And the French *Dictionnaire de la langue philosophique* published by A. Foulquie [1960, 398] asserts that language is "proprement et absolument la faculté d'exprimer la pensée au moyen des sons." The identity of language and expression has in particular been stressed by Croce, Dewey and their followers. Some of them considered even blushing as a language because it expresses feelings.

B. On the other hand some writers define language as a *communication.* J.M. Baldwin's *Dictionary of Philosophy and Psychology* [1918, I 618] says, "Language is the communication of thoughts through speechsounds." It adds that language cannot be defined by expression alone because it is determined "quite as much by the consideration of intelligibility as by that of expression." Chambers' *Encyclopedia* VII 347 shares this point of view: interjections have not very much importance in the language, it says. For G. Révész[14] and for many linguists he is quoting the essence of language is "mutual understanding."

C. The third view on language can be already found in the works of Leibniz.[15] According to him the essential function of language is to be a means of *thinking.* Without it thinking would be impossible; communication and expression are its secondary functions. Leibniz' view was shared by Condillac and by some philosophers of the XIXth century, like B. Erdmann "Language is a kind of thinking," he said .

These three views – that language is a means of expression, of communication, of thinking – do not exclude each other. By some scholars they are considered as being of equal importance. For instance, the *Encyclopedia Britannica* 11 ed., XVI 191 says that language is the whole body of words and combinations of words as used "for the purpose of expressing *or* communicating" thoughts. H. Reichenbach[16] considers even the expressive and the communicative functions as *one* function of the language, which he calls "cognitive." Probably all linguists would agree that language has several functions; [17] but they disagree *which* function is the *primary* function and has to define language.

A THIRD AMBIGUITY. F. de Saussure[18] distinguished two significations of "language" : on one hand it denotes the totality of signs common to a human group, and on the other it means the individual way in which the members of the group are using this totality. He called these two meanings "langage" and "parole" respectively. The corresponding English terms are "language" and "speech"; they can be found, e.g., in the book of A. H. Gardner.[19]

De Saussure's concepts correspond to the essential concepts of semiotics : "sign" and "use of sign." Now the use of signs implies a skill. And art can be considered as a skill. This would be a common feature of art and language.

3. The Connective "IS"

The sentence "art is language" contains still another word, namely, the connective "is." The ambiguity of this word is also manifold.

FIRST AMBIGUITY OF "IS." This ambiguity comes to light when one compares, e.g., the following two sentences : "man is a rational animal" and "man is a vertebrate animal." In the first one "is" denotes the identity of object and predicate; in the second one – not the identity but the relation of a subclass to the class. In the first one not only every S is P but also every P is S; and in the second one every S is P but only some P-s are S.

In which of the two meanings is the connective "is" used in the sentence "art is language"? Certainly it does not denote here the identity [of art and language], but at most the relation of a subclass to the class.

SECOND AMBIGUITY. It appears in another set of sentences : "man is a vertebrate animal" and "man is a thinking reed" [as Pascal used to say]. In the first sentence we understand "is" literally, while in the second one – metaphorically; in the second sentence "is" indicates that the subject possesses one or several characteristics of the predicate [in this case frailty], but not all of them.

In which of the two meanings is the connective "is" used in the sentence "art is language"? Are we to understand it literally or metaphorically?

4. Art and Language

At one time there existed schools of rhetoric where students were taught to defend contradictory theses : first they argued that something possesses certain qualities, and then that it does not. Nowadays such schools do not exist; but in the humanities there are problems which could furnish such schools with appropriate topics. Problems, even when considered with a reasonable accuracy, may equally well produce answers in the affirmative as in the negative. This is caused by the ambiguity of terms which are used in the formulation of these problems : if we take those terms in one meaning – the answer will be in the affirmative, if in another – in the negative. This is precisely the case with the problem : is art a language?

I. Let us first establish in which sense *art* is language and in which it is not.

A. According to the *broad* [classic] sense or to *the narrower* one [arts = fine arts]? It is certain that art in the broader sense includes arts (such as carpentry or tailoring) which are not languages because they produce things and not signs. Those who maintain that "art is language" think only of art in the later, narrower meaning, that of the *fine arts* only.

B. If art is language, is it in the sense of *product* or of *skill?* Important differences exist between the products of art and those of language : one of them is that art constantly produces new objects while language relies mainly on its inherited stock. Then : each individual work of art performs its task on its own, without support from other works of art, while words fulfill their aim only in conjunction with other words. On the other hand, an analogy does exist between art as *skill* and language as skill.

C. If we understand art as production of beauty, the analogy with language becomes problematic. The essential values of language are its intelligibility, clarity, economy; beauty is in language of a marginal importance. The analogy is problematic as well, when we define art as creativity. The same is the case when we see the essence of art in its strong effect upon men. And the same – if we find its distinctive feature to be production, the making of things. On the contrary, if we take art to be *expression* then it is like a language.

II. Which meaning of the word *"language"* may render true the statement that art is language?

A. Art is not in its entirety a language in the narrower meaning of the word language, because it is not a system of *conventional* signs. Some artists, like portrait and landscape painters, use iconic and not conventional signs; and architects, as well as composers of music do not (on the whole) use any signs. Forcing those differences some theoreticians would say : language uses signs and (visual) art – likenesses.[20] Or else : language names things while art shows them.[21] Or else : language points to things while art shapes them.[22] On the other hand, art may be a language in the *broader* sense of this word.

Second difference :natural languages [and all *strictiori sensu* languages] may appear in different forms, accessible either to hearing, or to sight and touch. Moreover, they are intertranslatable. On the contrary, strictly speaking, works of art are *not* translatable : tunes are not translatable into pictures nor pictures into tunes. The inscriptions on medieval paintings or on modern engravings, regarded by some writers as translations, are very imprecise translations.

Three : natural languages are characterized by continuity and traditionalism while art achieves more by breaking with traditions and continuity, by creating new forms.

Four: in art there are no such criteria of correctness as in a language.

Five : basically speaking, languages are man's tools for achieving his aims, while art is one of these aims which is only secondarily used as a means. Hanslick wrote that sounds in a language are only means and in music – the end. It is similar with other arts.

What appears to be most certain is that art is not a natural, an ethnic language and that it is not like any (ethnic) language studied by the linguists.

B. Communication between men does not seem to constitute a feature common to art and language. For language is *the tool* of communication, and art – its *subject*: one of the things which men communicate to one another. Men communicate indeed to one another their artistic works; but they communicate everything they do. And this is a secondary function of the artist: as a rule he does not create works of art in order to communicate them, but he communicates them because he had created them.

On the contrary, *expression does* bring together language and art; but does expression exhaust the function of language and art?

C. The proposition that art is language is not true if – according to de Saussure's differentiation – art is understood as "langage." This is so because the latter consists of a, more or less, permanent, hereditary vocabulary, idioms, and rules, while every new work of art transforms the heritage of the past. On the other hand, art comes close to *"parole,"* the speech which, while based on the inherited stock, uses it individually and transforms it in various ways.

III. How should we understand the *connective "is"* so as to render true the sentence "art is language"?

A. If "is" is supposed to denote the relation of identity then art certainly is *not* language. At most art is (or may be) language if "is" denotes the *relation* of a subclass to a class.

B. There is no reason why the sentence "art is language" should not be true if we understand the connective "is" *metaphorically*. The crux of the problem is, however, would this sentence be true if "is" be understood literally?

IV. Let us state clearly the thesis of this argument. It is not that art is not language. Nor the opposite. The thesis is here that art is, and is not, language depending on how we understand the words "art," "is," "language."

The additional thesis is that the linguists, as well as all of us in colloquial speech, use these three words more frequently in such a way that art is not language.

The point of greatest likeness between art and language is

their expressive function. Art is expression and language is expression. But let us note the syllogism :

EVERY ART IS EXPRESSION
EVERY LANGUAGE IS EXPRESSION

As anyone knows, it does *not* follow from these premises that art is language.

It is different in the case of the following premises :

EVERY ART IS EXPRESSION
EVERY EXPRESSION IS LANGUAGE

These premises *do* lead to the conclusion that every art is language. But it is only this very broad understanding of the word "language" that renders true the premise that art is language.

V. Let us add a few marginal remarks : (a) If we are to regard art as language because it is expression then we must agree that some arts are languages to a greater, and some to a smaller, extent. Indeed, lyrics is more expressive than epics. (b) In the case of a certain understanding of art, namely in its broader classic understanding, it is true not that art is language but the opposite : language is art. (c) If art is not language it may, nevertheless, supplement it. This is the way R. Jakobson sees it when he writes that art makes permanent the perishable linguistic formations. (d) Even if art is not a language, anyone is allowed to call it metaphorically a language : this is a convenient and harmless idiom.

Let us add a historical parallel. Recent discussions on the relation between art and language recall in some way the Renaissance discussions as to which art is most perfect. These old-time discussions were concerned with a different matter but were just as frequent and animated as our discussions. They attained their summit in Venice 1546 when the connoisseur of the arts, Benedetto Varchi, conducted a poll, which art, painting or sculpture, is to be given priority. Illustrious artists were polled : the painter Pontormo, the sculptor Cellini, and Michelangelo himself. Some preferred painting, some other preferred sculpture. Michelangelo's opinion was different;[23] it is advisable, he said, to give up discussions which take more time than they are worth. He suggested *"lasciar tante dispute."*

NOTES

1. Translated by H. Carroll Najder.
2. I. Kant, *Kritik der Urteilskraft,* 1790, 51.
3. B. Croče, *Estetica,* 1902.
4. J. Dewey, *Art and Experience,* 1934.
5. R. G. Collingwood, *The Principles of Art,* 1938.
6. E. Cassirer, *The Philosophy of Symbolical Forms,* I, 1953.
7. Charles Morris, *Signs, Language and Behaviour,* 1946, VII 3 : "Are Arts Languages? "
8. E. Gombrich, *Art and Illusion,* 1960.
9. W. Tatarkiewicz, "L'idée de l'art," in : Homo V, *Annales de l'Université de Toulouse,* N. S. II, 2, 1966.
10. H. Bergson, *Essai sur les données immédiates de la conscience,* 1889, p. 12 : "L'art vise à imprimer en nous des sentiments plus qu'à les exprimer."
11. M. Mothersill, "Is Art a Language? " in *Journal of Philosophy,* LXII no. 20, 1955.
12. W. Wundt, *Essays,* 1885, p. 259.
13. A. Marty, *Untersuchungen zur Grundlegung der allgemeinen Grammatik und Sprachphilosophie,* I, 1908.
14. G. Révész, *Ursprung und Vorgeschichte der Sprache,* 1946, p. 147.
15. I. Dąmbska, *O narzędziach i przedmiotach poznania,* 1967, p. 166, 176.
16. H. Reichenbach, *Elements of Symbolic Logic,* 1948 – J. Pelc, *Logika i jezyk,* 1967.
17. On three functions of the language : K. Bühler, *Sprachtheorie,* 1934. On six functions : R. Jakobson, "Poetyka w świetle jezykoznawstwa," in : *Pamietnik Literacki,* 1960.
18. F. de Saussure, *Cours de linguistique général* 1949.
19. A. H. Gardner, *The Theory of Speech and Language,* 1957.
20. M. Rieser, "Théorie linguistique des arts plastiques," in : *Revue de L'Esthétique,* XIV 2, 1961.
21. M. Dufrenne, "L'art est-il un language? " in : *Revue d'Esthétique,* XIX, 1966, and in : *Rivista di Estetica,* XIII 2, 1968.
22. E. Souriau, "L'art est-il un language? " in : *Rivista di Estetica,* XIII 1, 1968.
23. Michelangelo's letter to Varchi in : P. Barocchi, *Trattati d'arte,* I, 1960. and in : W. Tatarkiewicz, *History of Aesthetics,* Vol. III, in print.

CONCLUSION

THE work of Marvin Farber, his colleagues, and his students, indicates the values and limitations of phenomenology and naturalism. One might have hoped for more analysis of the naturalistic philosophy, but this critique is just now making its appearance on the American scene along with the attacks on the inadequacies of positivism and linguistic philosophy. The next ten years should see a mounting dissatisfaction with these positions.

Phenomenology is above everything else a methodological attempt to find the pure nuclei of processes of subjective experience. In doing this it has gained the support of numerous idealists and the aversion of naturalists, materialists, and realists of various types. Phenomenology has been avoided rather than attacked for its strong subjectivity, that is to say, before Farber directed criticism to this problem. The collection of essays published in Part II of this volume represents the most sustained criticism yet made of the inadequacies of phenomenology by the realists and objectivists. We need not repeat the specific charges for they have been adequately mentioned in the introductory chapter.

If it is true that a thing cannot be understood without insight into its field and its opposition, then the accounts of naturalism in Part III of this volume are incomplete. A major reason for this is that naturalism has gradually become the tacit orthodoxy of American academic philosophy, where once the norm was idealism tinged with Christianity. Marvin Farber's view of naturalism is more historically and socially oriented than that of most of his colleagues and students here represented. He has stepped beyond the mechanical materialism of the nineteenth century and has moved in the direction of organic, evolutionary and dialectical modifications of materialism. This naturalism or materialism emphasizes the social and historical instead of the physical and mechanical. Where he parts company with "orthodox" American naturalists is in his concern for a unitary doctrine that includes the social and historical dimension along with the physical and logical. He cannot be satisfied, therefore, with the dualisms and bifurcation inherent in logical or "scientific" positivism or in the American naturalism that runs parallel to it and is intertwined with it.

On the other hand, his impatience with all forms of idealism is widely known. Yet amazingly, it has seldom influenced the rigorous balance he has achieved in his journal. Underneath his suspicion of subjectivism is a strong belief that it is a cover for fideism, an attempt to smuggle feudalism into modern philosophy under various guises. He has just the kind of hardboiled attitude that has given materialists the last word in every scientific and historical argument.

Farber sympathizes with some aspects of the rationalistic and scientific programs of both positivism and naturalism, but differs from them with regard to their conception of philosophy and its methods, problems, and sociohistorical conditions, as well as with regard to their social program, or better, their absence of a social program. Indeed, upon examination, such a program appears to evaporate into cautionary shibboleths. The naturalists and positivists generally refuse the dictum of Aristotle that the arts of man should be directed towards the solution of the political problem. Farber is more Aristotelian than he is Wittgensteinian or Schlickian. He prefers the insights and perspectives of Marx, Engels, Morgan, and Lenin to those of Mach, Carnap, Lewis, or Dewey. Although his name has been so conspicuously associated with phenomenology and Husserl, he owed at least as much to Ernst Zermelo, A.N. Whitehead, Ralph Barton Perry, and H.M. Sheffer, as well as to extensive studies in the natural and social sciences. This had an important bearing upon his formulation of a new phenomenology and an independent naturalistic philosophy.

VITAE OF CONTRIBUTORS

John P. Anton, Fuller E. Callaway Professor of Philosophy, Emory University. Author of *Aristotle's Theory of Contrariety, Naturalism and Historical Understanding, Philosophical Essays.*

Arnold Berleant, Professor of Philosophy, C.W. Post College of Long Island Univeristy. Author of *The Fugue in the Orchestral Works of Bartok, The Aesthetic Field.*

Edward S. Casey, Associate Professor of Philosophy, Yale University. Author of "Meaning in Art" in *New Essays in Phenomenology,* "Expression and Communication in Art," "Imagination: Imagining and the Image," and "Philosophy, Man, and Truth.

Kah Kyung Cho, formerly Professor of Philosophy, Seoul National University, now at State University of New York at Buffalo. Author of *Einheit von Natur und Geist, Philosophy of Existence.*

Tad S. Clements, Professor of Philosophy, State University of New York College at Brockport. Author of *Science and Man, the Philosophy of Scientific Humanism.*

Curt J. Ducasse, Late Professor of Philosophy, Brown University. Author of *A Critical Examination of the Belief in a Life After Death, A Philosophical Scrutiny of Religion, The Philosophy of Art, Nature, Mind, and Death.*

Mikel Dufrenne, Professor of Philosophy, University of Paris at Nanterre. Author of *La Phénoménologie de l'expérience Esthétique, La personalité de base, La notion d'apriori, Pour l'homme, Le Poétique.*

Lorraine Farber, formerly Instructor in Mathematics, University of Buffalo and Bryn Mawr College.

William Gerber, Professor of Philosophy, University of Maryland. Author of *The Domain of Reality, The Mind of India,* "Philosophical Dictionaries and Encyclopedias," "Technology and Work."

Rollo Handy, Provost of Educational Studies, State University of New York at Buffalo. Author of *Methodology of the Behavioral Science, A Current Appraisal of the Behavioral Science, Measurement of Values, Value Theory and Behavioral Science.*

James Edwin Hansen, Assistant Professor of Philosophy, Brock University. Author of "An Historical Critique of Empiricism," "A Dialectrical Critique of Empiricism," "Hook, Liberalism, and the Ideology of Naturalism," "Subjectivism and Political Action."

Roman Ingarden, Late Professor of Philosophy, University of Lwów. Author of *Intuition und Intellekt bei H. Bergson, Essentiale Fragen, Das literarische Kunstwerk, Untersuchungen zur Ontologie der Kunst, Time and Modes of Being.*

Paul Kurtz, Professor of Philosophy, State University of New York at Buffalo. Editor of *The Humanist,* Author of *A Current Appraisal of the Behavioral Sciences, Decision and the Condition of Man, International Directory of Philosophy and Philosophers, Tolerance and Revolution.*

Leon Livingston, Professor of Spanish and Italian, State University of New York at Buffalo. Author of "The Novel as Self Creation," "Ortega y Gasset's Philosophy of Art," "Interior Duplication and the Problem of Form in the Modern Spanish Novel," *Tema y Froma en las novelas de Azorín.*

Victor Lenzen, Professor of Physics, University of California at Berkeley. Author of *The Nature of Physical Theory, Procedures of Empirical Science, Causality in Natural Science.*

Franco Lombardi, Dean of the Faculty of Letters and Philosophy, University of Rome. Director of *De Homine,* Author of *La posizione dell'uomo nell'universo, Aforismi inattuali sull'arte, Il senso della storia ed altri saggi, Problemi della libertà, Kant vivo, Dodici canzoni napoletane.*

V.J. McGill, Professor of Philosophy, San Francisco State College. Author of *August Strindberg, Schopenhauer, Emotions and Reason, The Idea of Happiness.*

Edward H. Madden, Professor of Philosophy, State University of New York at Buffalo. Author of *The Philosophical Writings of Chauncy Wright, Civil Disobedience and Moral Law in Nineteenth Century American Philosophy, The Structure of Scientific Thought, Chauncey Wright and the Foundations of Pragmatism.*

D.C. Mathur, Reader in Philosophy, University of Rajasthan. Professor of Philosophy, State University of New York College at Brockport. Author of *Natural Philosophies of Experience.*

Norman Melchert, Professor of Philosophy, Lehigh University. Author of *Outline and Bibliography for a Course in Syntax, Realism, Materialism, and the Mind.*

Shia Moser, Professor of Philosophy, State University of New York at Buffalo. Author of *Absolutism and Relativism in Ethics.*

Enrico Musacchio, Professor of Romance Languages, University of Alberta. Author of *B. Russell, Gramsci and Dante, Utilitarismo, Edonismo e Egoismo, Goldoni e Pirandello, Rinuccini e Striggio.*

Enzo Paci, Professor of Philosophy, University of Milan. Author of *Tempo e relazione. La Filosofia contemporanea, Relazioni e signicati, Funzione delle science e significato dell'uomo.*

E.P. Papanoutsos, Vice-President of the Athens Technological Institute. Author of *Aesthetics, Ethics, Philosophy and Paideia, Das religiose Erleben bei Platon, La catharsis aristotélicienne, Poetry and Language, Moral Conflicts.*

William T. Parry, Professor of Philosophy, State University of New York at Buffalo. Author of "The Logic of C.I. Lewis," "War and Politics," "The Unity of Opposites," "Ideographic Computation," "Constructed vs. Artificial Languages."

Chaim Perelman, Ordinary Professor of Law, University of Brussels. Editor of *Logique et Analyse.* Vice-President of the International Federation of Philosophical Societies. Author of *The Idea of Justice and the Problem of Argument, Justice, The New Rhetoric, Justice et raison.*

Augusto Pescador (Sarget), Professor of Philosophy, University of Concepción. Author of *Logica, Ontología, Sobre lo que no sirve, Problemas Filosóficos en Nicolai Hartmann, La Filosofia y la Estetica de Leonardo.*

Paul Piccone, Assistant Professor of Sociology, Washington University. Editor of *Telos,* Author of "Dialectical Logic Today," Dalla Cultura dei Giovani alle Prassi Politica," "Functionalism, Teleology, and Objectivity."

Dale Riepe, Professor of Philosophy, State University of New York at Buffalo. Author of *The Naturalistic Tradition in Indian Thought, Radical Currents in Contemporary Philosophy, Reflections on Revolution.*

Nathan Rotenstreich, Professor of Philosophy, Hebrew University. Author of *Between Past and Present, An Essay on History, Spirit and Man – An Essay on Being and Value, Basic Problems of Marx's Philosophy, Studies in the Phenomenology of Ethics and Politics.*

Roy Wood Sellars, late *Emeritus* Professor of Philosophy, University of Michigan. Author of *Essays in Critical Realism, Evolutionary Naturalism. The Philosophy of Physical Realism, Philosophy for the Future, Reflections on American Philosophy from Within.*

Wilfrid Sellars, University Professor of Philosophy, University of Pittsburgh. Author of *Science, Perception and Reality, Philosophical Perspectives.*

Wladyslaw Tatarkiewicz, Professor of Philosophy, University of Warsaw. Editor of *Philosophical Review,* Author of *A History of Philosophy, Theories of Happiness, A History of Aesthetics, Collected Papers on Aesthetics, Collected Papers on the History of Architecture and Sculpture.*

INDEX